THE BOOK OF
TIVERTON

THE BOOK OF TIVERTON

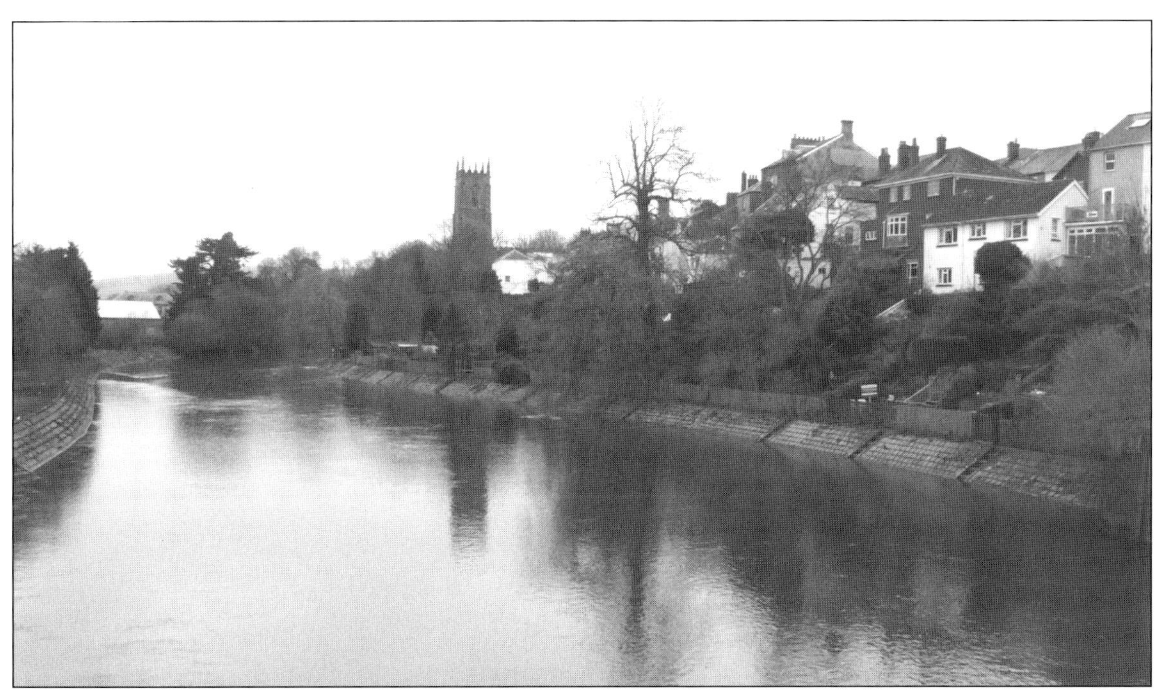

At the Heart of Devon

CHARLES NOON

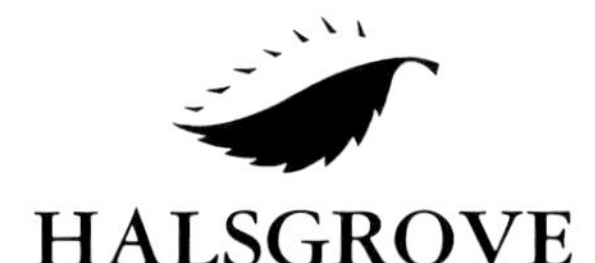

HALSGROVE

Title page: *View from the Exe Bridge that joins Westexe with the town centre, looking towards St Peter's Church.*

British Library Cataloguing-in-Publication Data.
A CIP record for this title is available from the British Library.

ISBN 978 1 84114 626 3

HALSGROVE

Halsgrove
Halsgrove House
Ryelands Industrial Estate
Bagley Road
Wellington
Somerset TA21 9PZ

T: 01823 653777
F: 01823 216796

e: sales@halsgrove.com
www.halsgrove.com

Printed in Great Britain by CPI Antony Rowe, Wiltshire

Preface

There are two reasons for writing any preface: to explain why the book has been written and to thank those who have helped in its production. There is, in this case, a third reason, which is to explain that all the author's profits will go half to Tiverton Museum and half to a fund to provide encouragement to the pupils of Tiverton High School. This is in no way generosity on my part, merely that I have got to the age when the saying that 'you can't take it with you' is increasingly relevant. It is also a sly trick to get folk of goodwill to buy *The Book of Tiverton*.

The Book of Tiverton has been written because Halsgrove asked me to do so and I had no good reason to refuse. It may be said that there have already been four histories of Tiverton, and naturally I have relied on them and appreciated what they have had to say. The first Tiverton historian, Martin Dunsford, wrote his *Historical Memoirs* in 1790, and the second, Lt-Col Harding, his *History of Tiverton* in 1840. Both of these books are immense labours of serious scholarship, but they are now essentially works of reference, especially as works of reference for people investigating whether charities and trusts are being properly administered. They both conceived their work as part of a campaign for rectifying errors. Dunsford was collecting ammunition against the plentiful political corruption of the times, (see Chapter 5), and much of Harding's work was directed towards achieving the proper administration of charities. (In my researches for this book I came across many modern charities and trusts that seemed to be being administered excellently, but I also found grey areas and I think that the town needs a modern Harding to produce a work taking the history of Tiverton's many trusts from 1840 to 2008.) The third of our historians was Frederick Snell, who published *The Chronicles of Twyford* in 1892. It is a jolly and amusing romp of a book, but essentially bedtime reading, as it is an unplanned, unfocussed collection of amusing tit-bits, from which one emerges with a fund of good stories, but no clear ideas about why Tiverton had its ups and downs or why its inhabitants quarrelled with one another and often so viciously.

None of these three 'historians' had never trained as a historian. Only Snell could have done so because 'History' has only been an 'academic' subject since the 1850s and our historical awareness is a surprisingly modern development. One has only to remember that even the well educated had no trouble accepting all the Old Testament as literally historical fact until the later nineteenth century. Only Tiverton's fourth historian, Mike Sampson writing in 2004, has produced a very scholarly *History of Tiverton*. I think it will come to be regarded as a definitive reference. He will realise where I have relied on his work and my gratitude. But there is not a book that offers the general reader an accessible story of Tiverton.

So I offer *The Book of Tiverton* to the general reader who wants a zippy story. I am sorry if that reader then finds a lack of 'zip' – that will be due to my inadequacies as a writer. But a 'story' is there, and without the 'story' history has always seemed to me a dull affair. That a story must have heroes and villains may lead to accusations of bias, because often one man's hero is another man's villain. But a story without heroes or villains is grey and insubstantial pap, neither hot nor cold. I used to try to explain to pupils what 'history' is by allusion to an artist painting a landscape. First, the problem of reducing square miles to square inches means that it is impossible to avoid 'over-emphasis' and 'down grading', thus it is a matter of knowledge and judgement as to what is emphasised or not. In attempting *The Book of Tiverton* some tough decisions about omissions had to be made. This problem became more difficult when, in modern times, information became so very much more plentiful. I have focused this story on the town itself, but even then there is a need for a whole number of monographs on topics such as private and public schools in Tiverton, the administration of the Poor Law, Tiverton market and religion and politics in Tiverton. The list is almost endless and local historians can never be unemployed.

Secondly, the problem of perspective. Stand here on Canal Hill and the Town Hall is to the left of St Peter's; stand there in Palmerston Park and the Town Hall is to the right of St Peter's. My heroes are the merchants who built the wealth and who were generous, the Parliamentarians who stood for their beliefs against Charles I, those who attacked the corruption of a rotten borough, those who made Tiverton free of cholera, those stroppy, bigoted local politicians such as Mayor Mudford, as well as Councillors Youknowhim and Whatshername who have fought for what they have thought right, those who rose to the challenges of 1940–45 and those who keep the town ticking today.

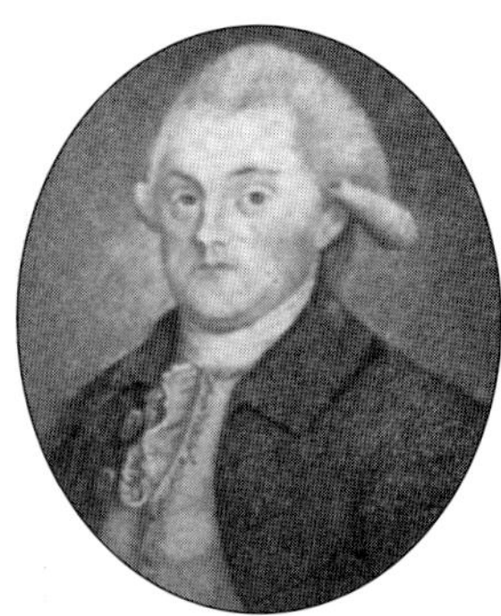

Left: *Martin Dunsford, the author's historiographical hero. Convinced of the venality of the Corporation, he set out to prove that the corrupt present had perverted past benefactions.*

Right: *Mike Sampson. His book is a marvel of research and will be a book of reference for years to come.*

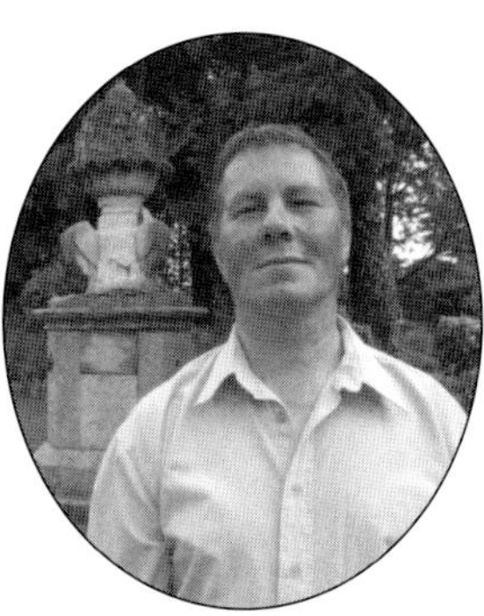

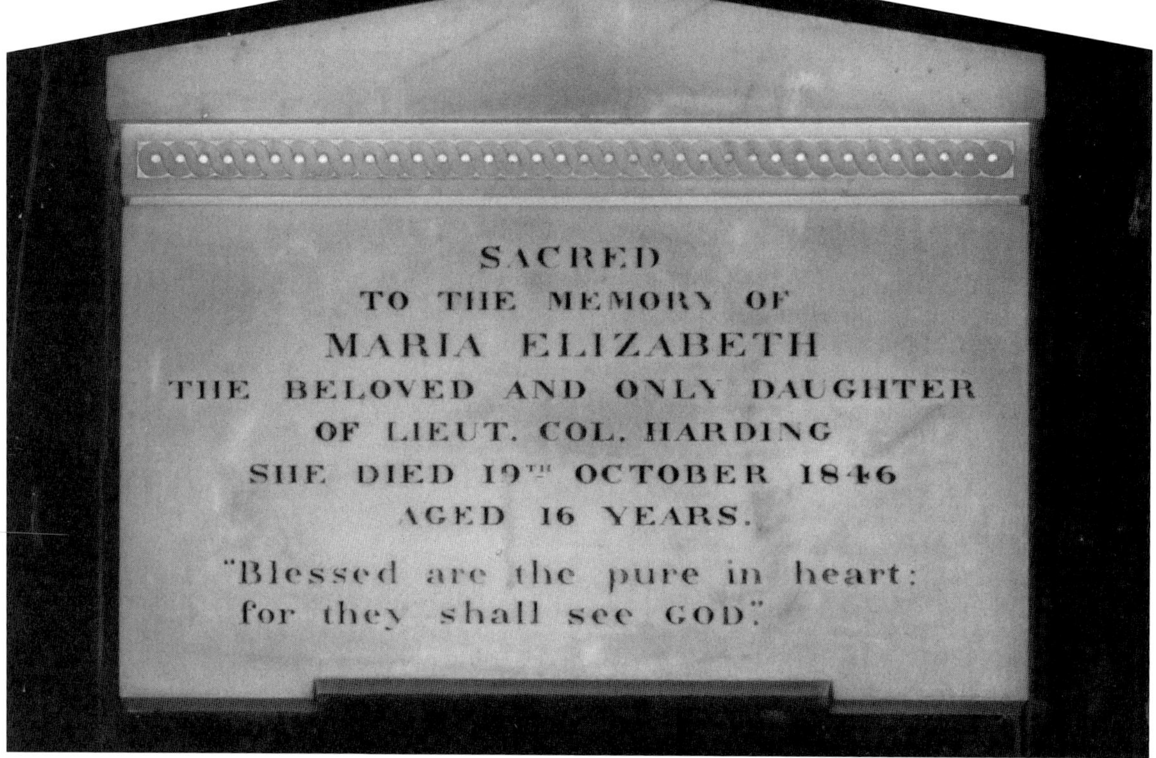

Above: *The memorial to Elizabeth Harding, Colonel Harding's daughter, on the north wall of St Peter's. Colonel Harding's history, published in 1847, espoused the Tory point of view.*

COLIN WHITE

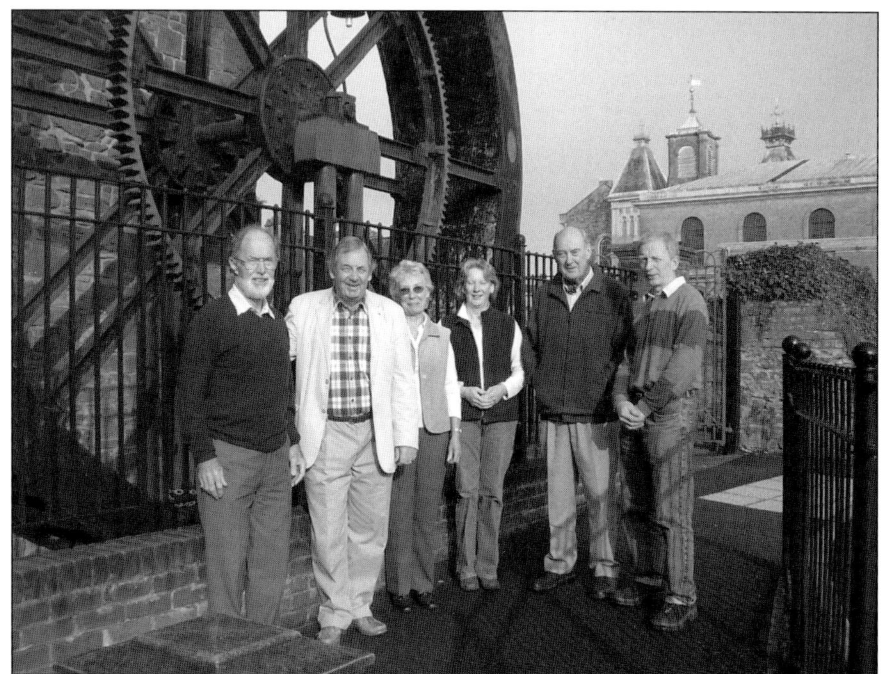

Left: *The indispensable guardians of our past, Tiverton Museum Trustees: Michael Herlihy, chairman Roger Lambert, Gill Bridson, curator Judith Elsdon, Patrick Brooke and Amyas Crump. Without a grip on our past, as a society, we will suffer 'Cultural Alzheimer's'.*

Contents

Acknowledgements

Now my thanks. Thank you to the IT department of Blundell's School, especially Nick Markell, without whom this could not have been written in a form acceptable to any publisher. Thank you to the Art department, who lent me a camera and showed me, repeatedly, how to use it.

Thank you to my son Adrian and my son-in-law, Colin White, for help collecting photographs. Thanks also to the many Tivertonians, who allowed me to ask them impertinent questions and who lent photographs.

Thanks to the staff of Tiverton Library, the West Country Studies Library and the County Record Office for their help and their courteous pretence of being pleased to see me again.

Above all my deepest thanks to Judith Elsdon, the curator of Tiverton Museum, and to Patrick Brooke, the keeper of the photos, for the enormous gift of their time and knowledge. Many other museum volunteers also deserve my thanks.

I must also acknowledge that various photographs that appear in this book and that were supplied by Tiverton Museum were taken by Lee Flaws. Many of the best of the modern photographs were taken by him.

Eagle eyed readers may find mistakes, but I hope they will not be serious mistakes. So many folk, who have given the Museum photographs, have not put either names or dates to their gifts, and this makes for difficulties. Many individuals and organisations have been extremely helpful and guided me to useful nuggets of illustration and interpretation. Naturally these have had fuller coverage than those who have been less forthcoming!

I hope some of those reading this book will enjoy it as much as I have enjoyed writing it.

Charles Noon 2008.

Chapter 1

The View From Cranmore Castle

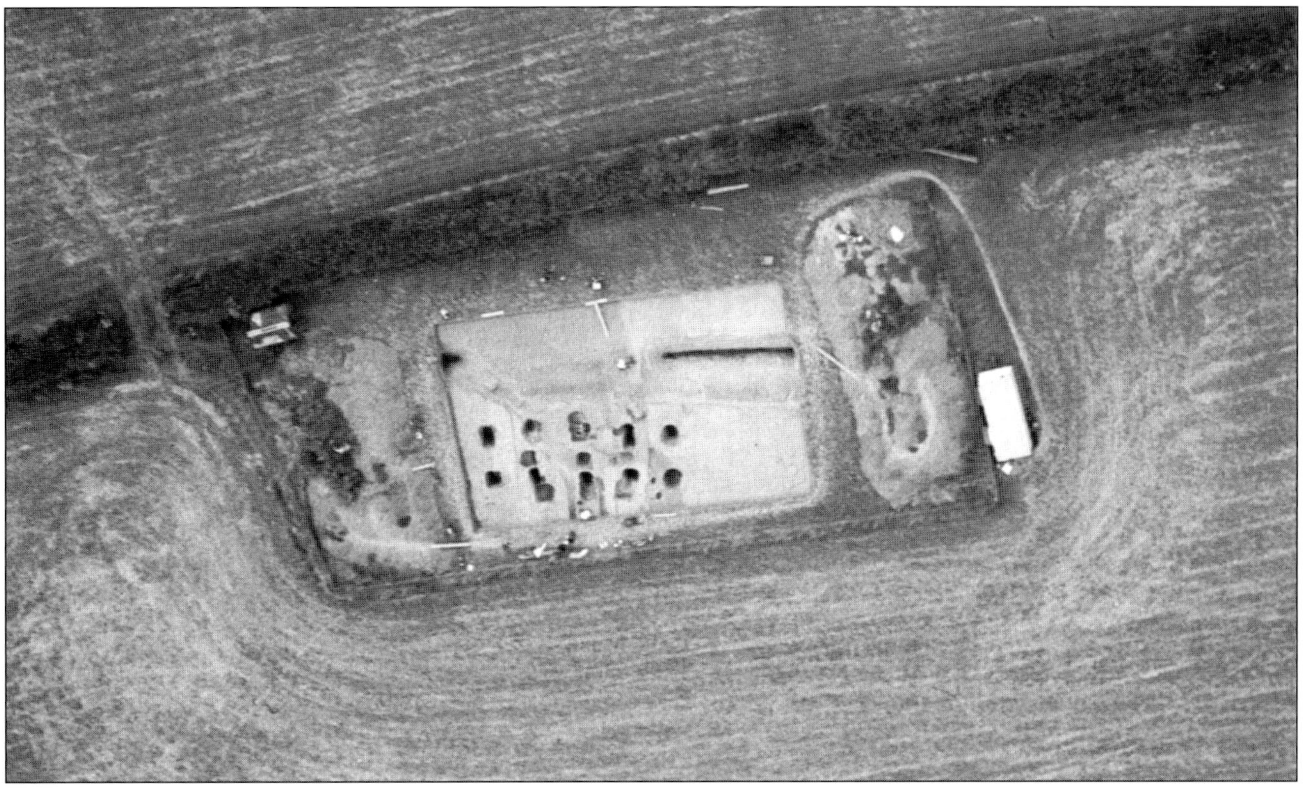

Aerial view of the excavations of the Roman camp at Rix Farm, beside the Link Road. MUSEUM COLLECTION

The historian should do more than collect the 'facts'; he must also try to tell a coherent story so that a wider public, that 'fair field full of folk', who may have studied no history since leaving school, can have a working explanation of the shape of things around them. A coherent story should have a beginning, middle and end. So the problem is three-fold. Unless you are a creationist, there is no beginning and, unless you believe that the end is very nigh, there is no true end. Writing the middle depends not only on collecting the facts, which is difficult enough, but also on interpreting their significance, which is even more difficult.

Imagine yourself standing on Cranmore Castle, seeing Tiverton laid out before you. The old town, a triangle, bounded by Old Blundell's, the castle and the bottom of St Andrew Street. The slightly less old industrial suburb of Westexe, dominated by the factory, a rectangular slab across the river, and the new suburbs of Pinnex Moor, Cowleymoor, Elmore, Tidcombe and Wilcombe spread out to the north and east. Further out, the posher suburb of Post Hill. Climbing up the hills to the west are Palmerston Park and Cotteylands. Around the town stretch large tracts of countryside, up the Exe valley as far as Cove, and, invisible to the south, as far as Bickleigh Bridge, and from Withleigh in the west to the golf course in the east, all have been from time immemorial parts of the parish of Tiverton.

In many of the areas under our gaze traces of human activities have been found, which suggest a more or less continuous habitation since the Stone Age. Cranmore Castle itself has been described as an Iron Age fort, its ramparts probably thrown up in the century before the Roman invasion. Its purpose remains a puzzle, as does its neighbour, Cadbury Castle. Both Cadbury and Cranmore are easily approachable from the south and they lack any obvious sources of water. Enormous effort went into the construction of these hill-forts, yet it is difficult to see them as effectively defensive. Perhaps they had ceremonial significance, or, like the pyramids and the Millennium Dome they were a folly of government or religion, a sacred enclosure or a prestige statement. Their story can only be told by archaeology.

Tiverton's history hardly begins with the Romans, who in their conquest set up a camp on the spur between Rix Farm and Knightshayes that was only

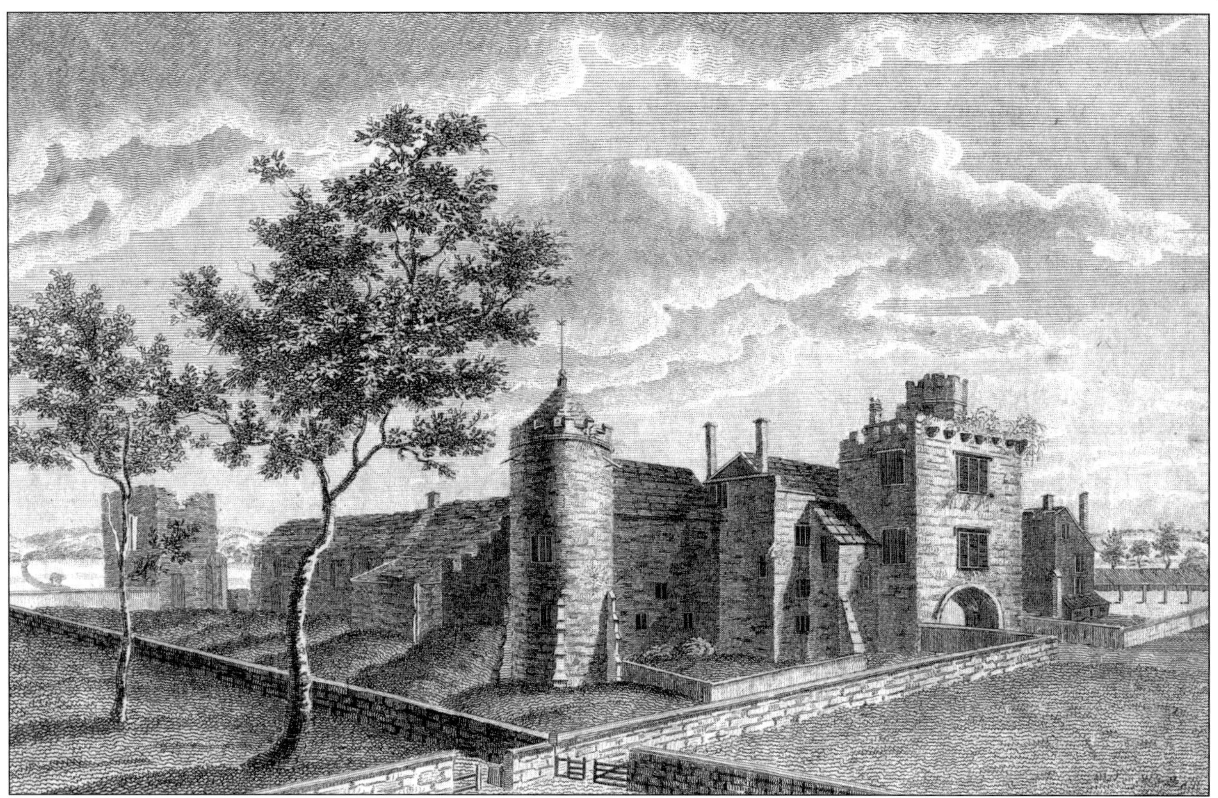

Tiverton Castle. No illustrations have been found to show it in its late-medieval pomp. Its ramparts stretched to somewhere between Park Road and Frog Street. The road to Bolham is modern. MUSEUM COLLECTION

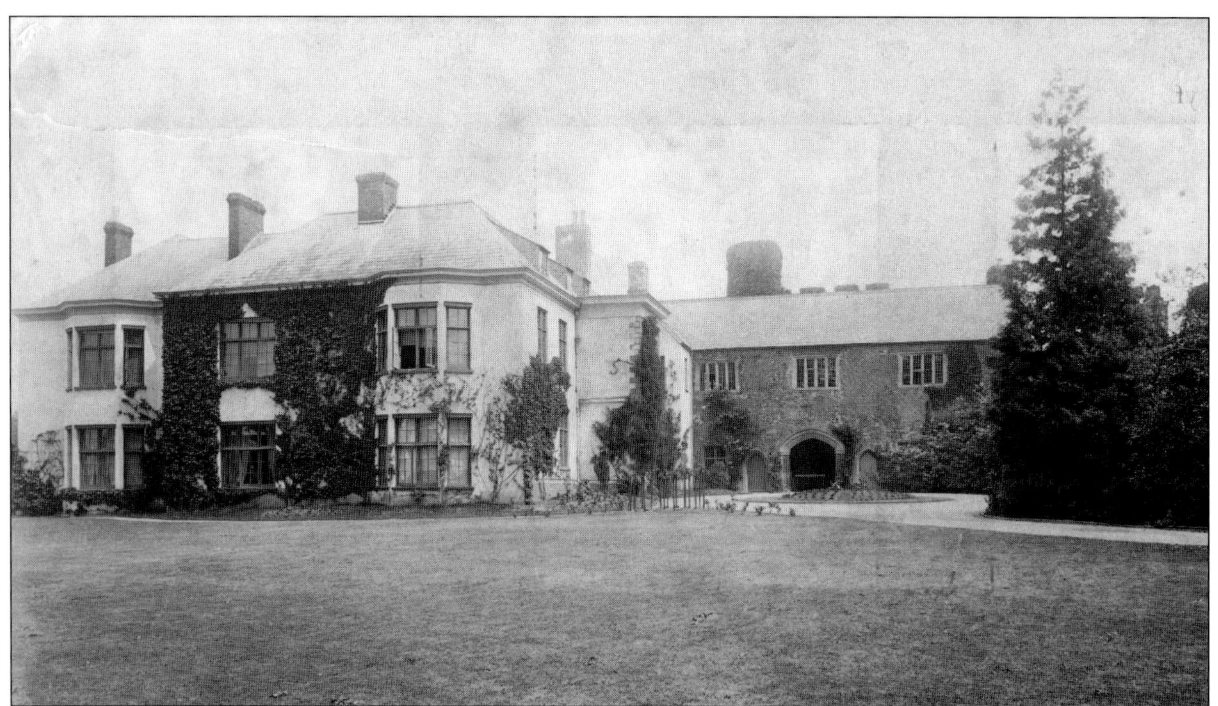

Tiverton Castle as a romantic home. MUSEUM COLLECTION

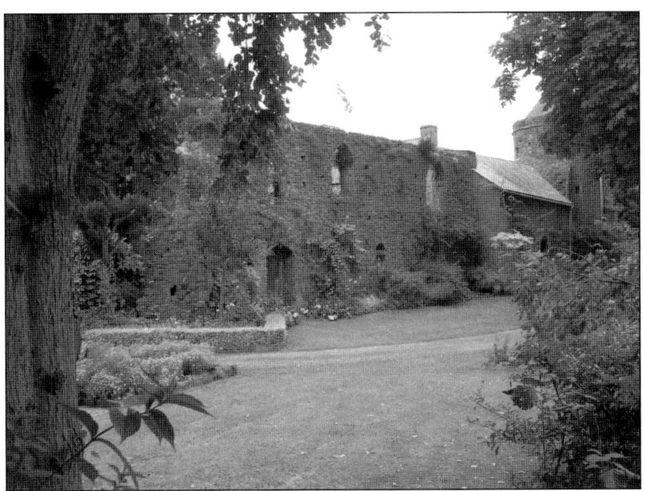

The castle ruins seen from St Peter's Church. COLIN WHITE

used until about 90AD. A model, based on recent archaeology, can be seen in Tiverton Museum, but surprisingly little evidence of settlement in the Roman centuries has been found, considering the number of well-watered, south-facing sites there are in the parish.

Tiverton really begins with the Saxons, who named it and made it the centre of one of their administrative subdivisions of the shire, the Hundred. The creation of Tiverton Hundred cannot be dated, but it probably took place in the tenth century, and its origins may be cross-threaded with the origins of Halberton Hundred, as it is unusual to find two Hundred centres so close together. Hoskin suggests 'about 650AD' as the date of Saxon settlement and that Tiverton was owned by the royal family of Wessex. It has been claimed that Tiverton is the 'Twyfiride' mentioned as a royal settlement in Alfred's will, written sometime before his death in 899, but this could have referred to Twyford in Hampshire, and there are Twyfords in Berkshire, Buckinghamshire, Herefordshire and Leicestershire as well. Although what we call 'parish boundaries' were not fully fixed until 1300, there can be no doubt that our Tiverton was well established as a number of settlements, or 'manors', when the Domesday Book was compiled in 1085–86. The main settlement was royal property, which had belonged to Gytha, the mother of Harold, before 1066, and to William the Conqueror after 1066. The compilers of Domesday called this settlement 'Tovretona', which, linguistically, seems a long way away from 'Twyfiride', the name that had been used 160 years earlier.

Indeed the evidence for associating 'Twyfiride' or 'Twyford' with Tiverton seems sparse. Traditionally 'Twyford' has been taken to mean 'Two Ford Town' and 'Tiverton' has always been a ford crossing-point of the Exe. But the other ford, over the Lowman, does not make much sense. The Lowman is so easy to cross for most days of any year. Indeed the governors of Blundell's School only thought it necessary to erect a plank footbridge over the Lowman in the 1690s, almost a century after the school's foundation. If there were 'two fords' they were probably both over the Exe, one in the town, the other by the Salmon Ponds, which would explain the siting of the Roman camp.

There is no evidence from Domesday to suggest where, within the parish boundaries, the royal manor of Tovretona was situated. It was worth £18 a year to the King, and it had 35 villeins (Halberton was worth £27 and had 43 villeins). A rough rule of thumb would have a 'villein' as a family-farmer of about 30 acres. Its centre of gravity may have been Knightshayes, which has been taken to mean the

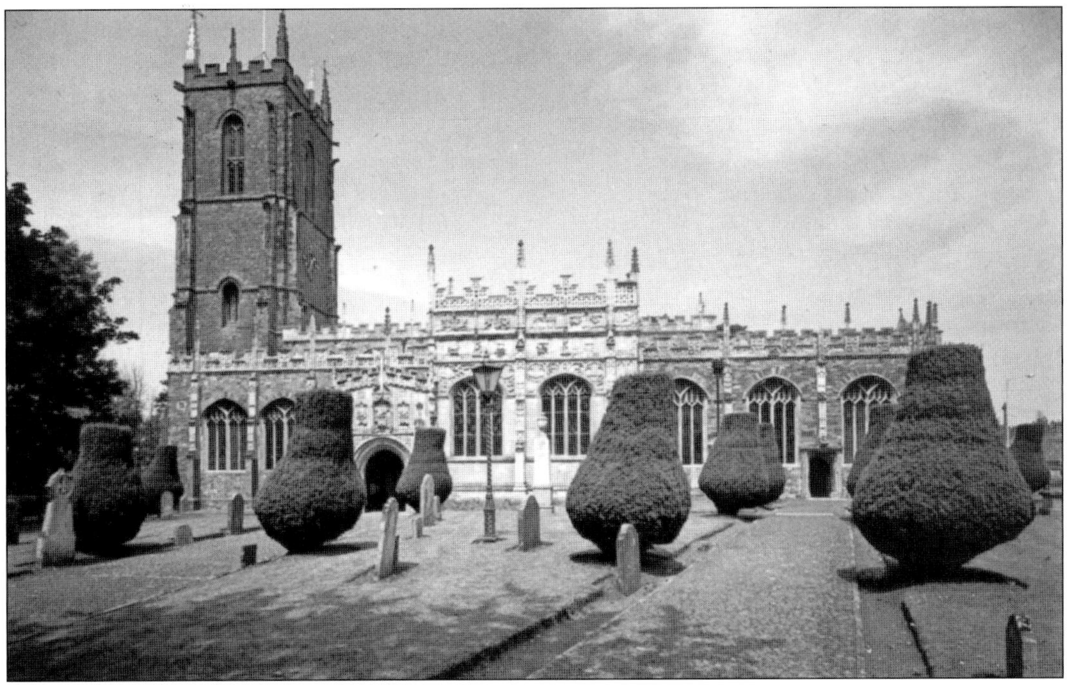

St Peter's Church. Tradition has it that the stone church dates from 1073. MUSEUM COLLECTION

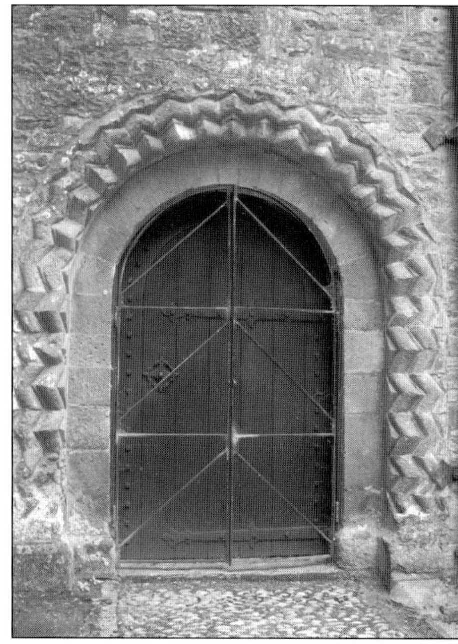

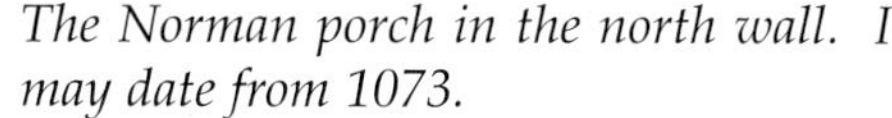

The Norman porch in the north wall. It may date from 1073.

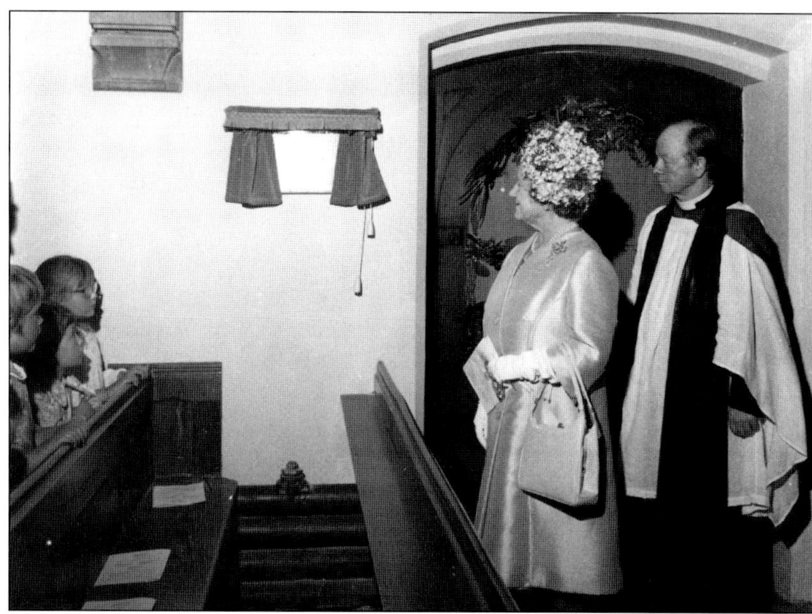

The Queen Mother and Rector Charles Nye at the 900th anniversary celebrations in 1973. The plaque is inside by the Norman porch.

MUSEUM COLLECTION

'enclosure' (*gehaeg*) 'of the bailiff' (*geneat*).

Domesday gives evidence of other parts of the parish. The Bishop of Exeter owned two Bradleys and Peadhill, and Harmeria de Archa owned another Bradley. Baldwin the Sheriff owned East Chevithorne and Chettiscombe with nine villeins. Ralph de Pomeria had West Chevithorne with four villeins, Walter de Claville owned Widhayes and parts of 'Uplowman in Tiverton', and Goscelin had Manley. Others owned Yearlstone, Pool Anthony and Northcott, so most of our farms were in some sort of existence in 1085. Ralph Pagan or Pagenel owned another 'Tovretona', which may have been Little Silver or Westexe and William the Usher had Bolham with 14 villeins. There were three mills, one at Bolham and two belonging to the King. In all, Domesday mentions about 85 villeins in Tovretona, a number of bordars, who were probably labourers with a few acres and some serfs, who were landless labourers. None of the larger landowners lived in the parish.

What gave Tiverton a nucleus, which would later become a borough, was the donation of the royal manor to Richard de Redvers by Henry I as reward for Redvers' support in a civil war. In the civil wars of Stephen's reign Richard de Redvers' son, Baldwin, strongly supported Matilda, the daughter of Henry I, and she granted him the title Earl of Devon. As Stephen had destroyed Baldwin's castle at Plympton in 1136, at some time, probably after 1136, Baldwin built a castle at Tiverton and made it one of his main residences.

During the same period, St Peter's Church comes into clearer focus. It is apparent that St Peter's was a portioners' church, in other words, a church whose revenues and duties were shared among a number of priests. Often churches so organised had been centres of missionary activity in the early years of Christianisation. Other similar churches locally were South Molton, Chulmleigh, Crediton and Ottery St Mary. Domesday mentions four 'presbyteri' at South Molton and other sources suggest between five and seven priests at Chumleigh. Crediton had as many as 18, reduced to 12 in the twelfth century. Ottery was as large as Crediton. Of the five churches, the establishments of St Peter's and South Molton were probably the two smallest.

There is adequate documentary evidence to show that St Peter's was served by four portioners in the twelfth century when a dispute with St James' Priory in Exeter meandered through the Church Courts right up to the Papal Curia. However, we cannot know when St Peter's began, though it probably started as a wooden church in the Saxon period. Tradition, unsupported by any strong evidence, suggests that the stone church dates from 1073. At some later date the four portions attracted the names Pitt, Prior's, Tidcombe and Clare. 'Prior's' because as a result of the aforementioned case, in the 1150s, a portion of the revenues of St Peter's would go to the support of the Priory of St James in Exeter, which had been founded by Baldwin de Redvers, who had in a cavalier fashion granted the Priory all the revenues of St Peter's. The Priory was the daughter house of a French Order and a burst of xenophobia early in the fifteenth century diverted the Prior's portion towards the building of King's College, Cambridge, who thereby obtained the right to nominate one of the four Tiverton clergy. 'Clare' seems to have taken its name from Bogo de Clare, a relation of Amicia, who was the widow of another Baldwin de Redvers, who died in 1245. This Amicia was the

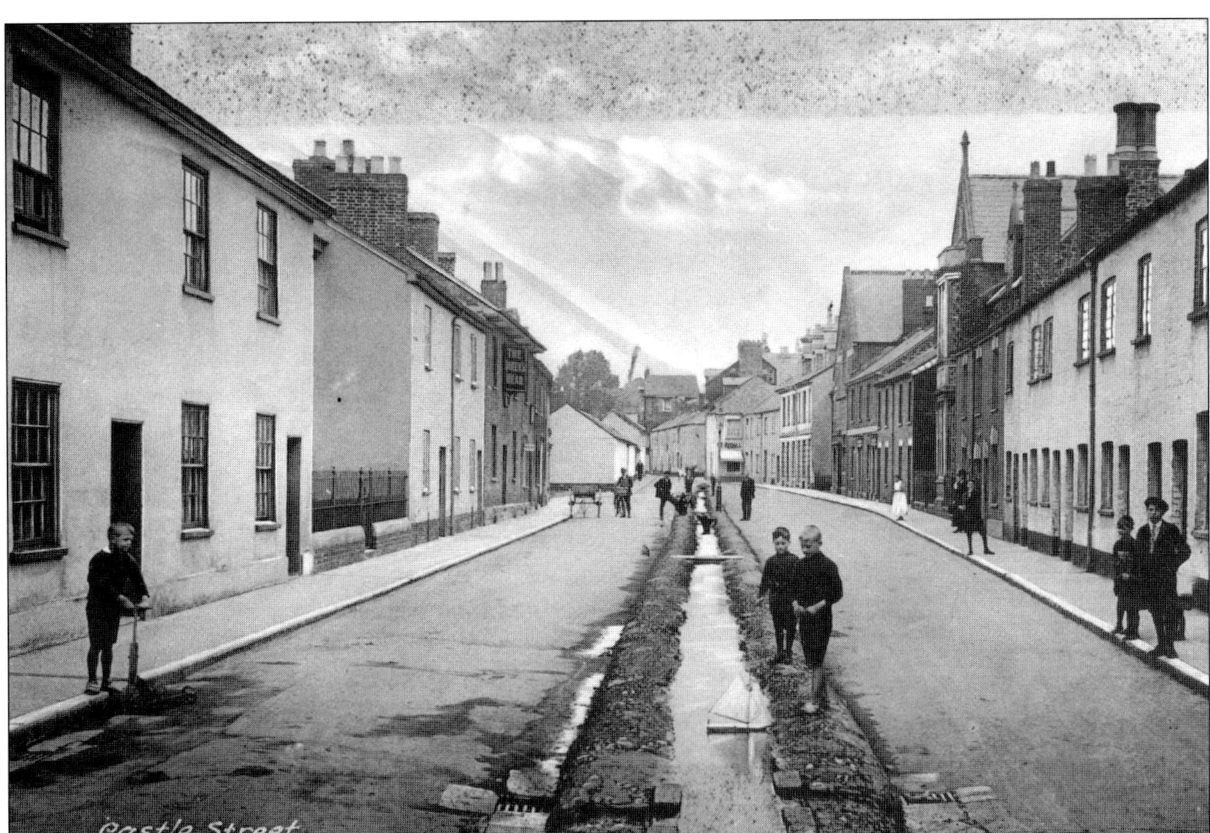

Above: *The water-supply granted to the town in about 1250, a necessity if Tiverton was to grow. Castle Street used to be called Frog Street and until the Civil War much of the area was within the castle defences.*

MUSEUM COLLECTION

Below: *Perambulating the leat in 1912. It was necessary to ensure that the leat was not blocked or diverted, so the custom of a septennial perambulation developed. 'Withy Boys' and latterly 'Withy Girls' were traditional. The shorter figure in the middle, leading the cheers, is Mayor Alfred Gregory, who was also Editor of the* Tiverton Gazette.

MUSEUM COLLECTION

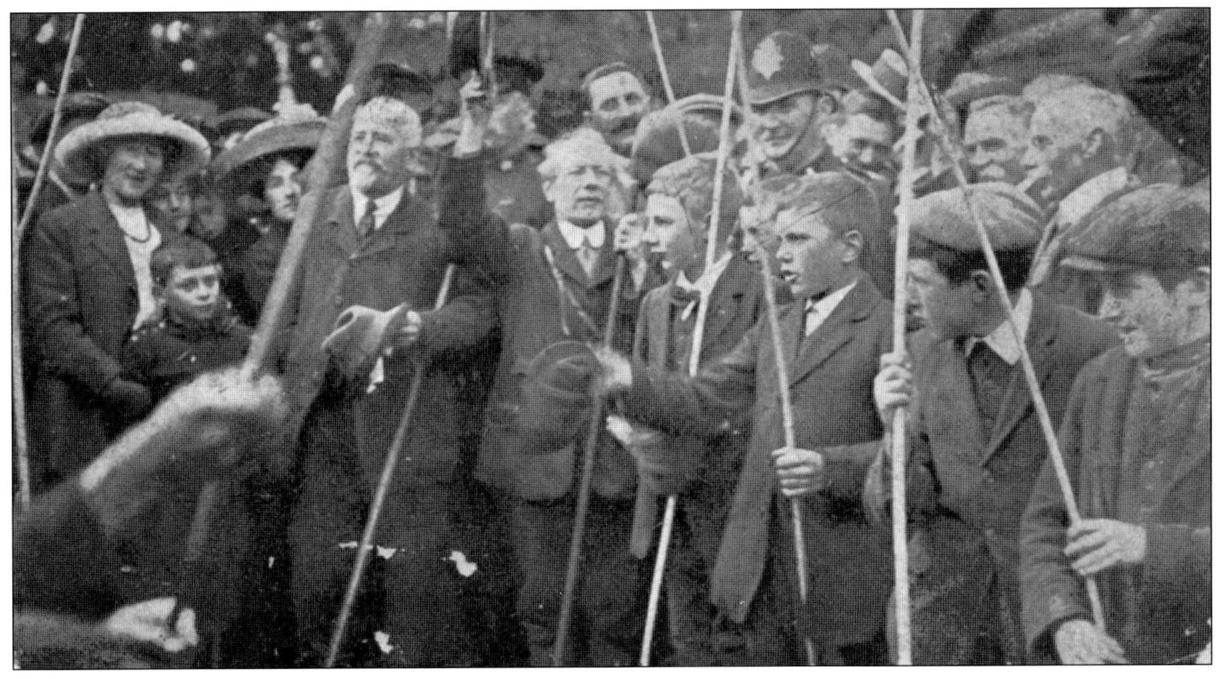

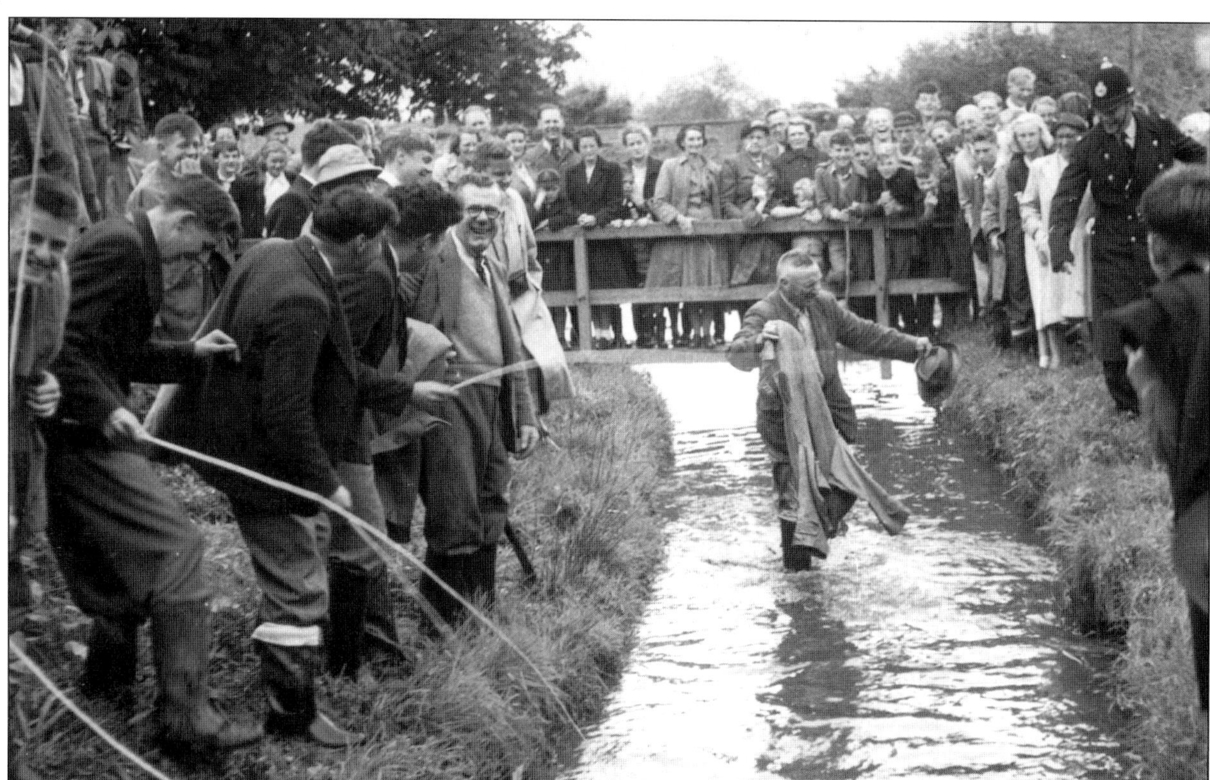

High jinks in 1961, during one of the regular 'perambulations of the leat' to confirm the town's right to its historic water-supply. Councillor Joe Chown gets pushed in at Chettiscombe. Councillor Skinner (left, wearing glasses) *is amused.* MUSEUM COLLECTION

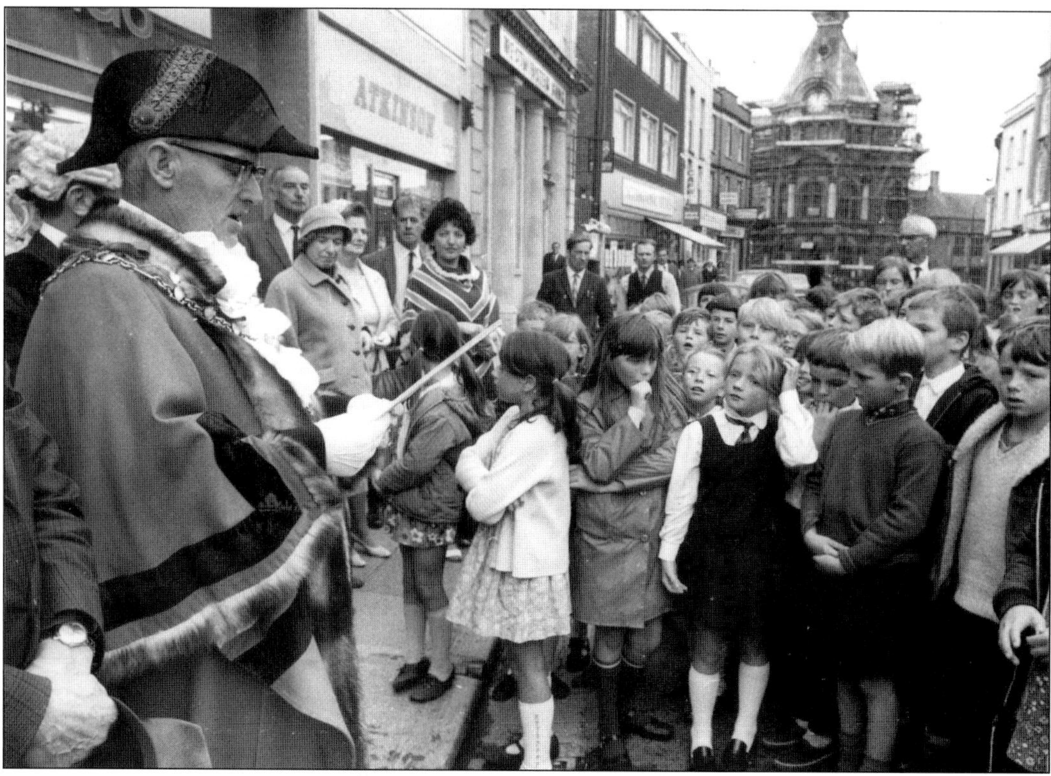

Mayor William Trickey proclaiming the Fair in 1970, standing at Coggan's Well, at the end of the leat in Fore Street. He was assisted by Councillors Peggy Allen, Eileen Trickey and Mary Turner. Later the children will scrabble for pennies. The teacher hovering behind the children is Mr Marsh of Heathcoat's School. MUSEUM COLLECTION

daughter of a Clare Earl of Gloucester. 'Pitt' and 'Tidcombe' are geographical.

The combination of an important church and a castle, the main residence of an important family, provided the nucleus around which a settlement grew. One of the ways that a landowner could try to increase the revenue from his estates was to grant 'borough status' to a settlement. This was done for Tiverton in about 1200, enabling the establishment of weekly Monday markets and four annual fairs at the festivals of St Thomas (6–8 July), St James (24–26 July), St Giles (31 August to 2 September) and St Andrew (29 November to 1 December). There is evidence of a street pattern and, by 1295, of a bridge over the Exe. A key event in the town's progress was the granting of a supply of fresh water by Alice de Ros in the 1240s.

The Redvers' male line died out in the mid-thirteenth century. Two heiresses, Amicia and Isabella de Redvers, held Tiverton until 1294 and a third, Avelina, died childless. The inheritance of the Manor of Tiverton then passed to Hugh de Courtenay, who already held Chettiscombe and part of Chevithorne. All three Redvers women had had very close links with the Plantagenets, which included Avelina's marriage in 1269 to the Earl of Leicester, a son of Henry III. It is likely that the presence of these grand ladies and their royal connections helped the small borough to grow.

Although Tiverton possessed all the necessary ingredients for growth – being the administrative centre of a Hundred, having a military presence and the purchasing power of a great household in the castle and having become an ecclesiastical centre as a rural deanery in the later twelfth century – it is clear that, as late as 1400, Tiverton's economic footprint was very small. A series of tax assessments around 1330 show Tiverton lying 16th in value out of 19 Devon boroughs. As late as 1428 the accounts of the Courtenays show that 'manorial Tiverton' provided £78 and Tiverton borough only £28. Yet a century later a tax assessment in 1520 shows Tiverton fourth among the Devon boroughs and 52nd nationally.

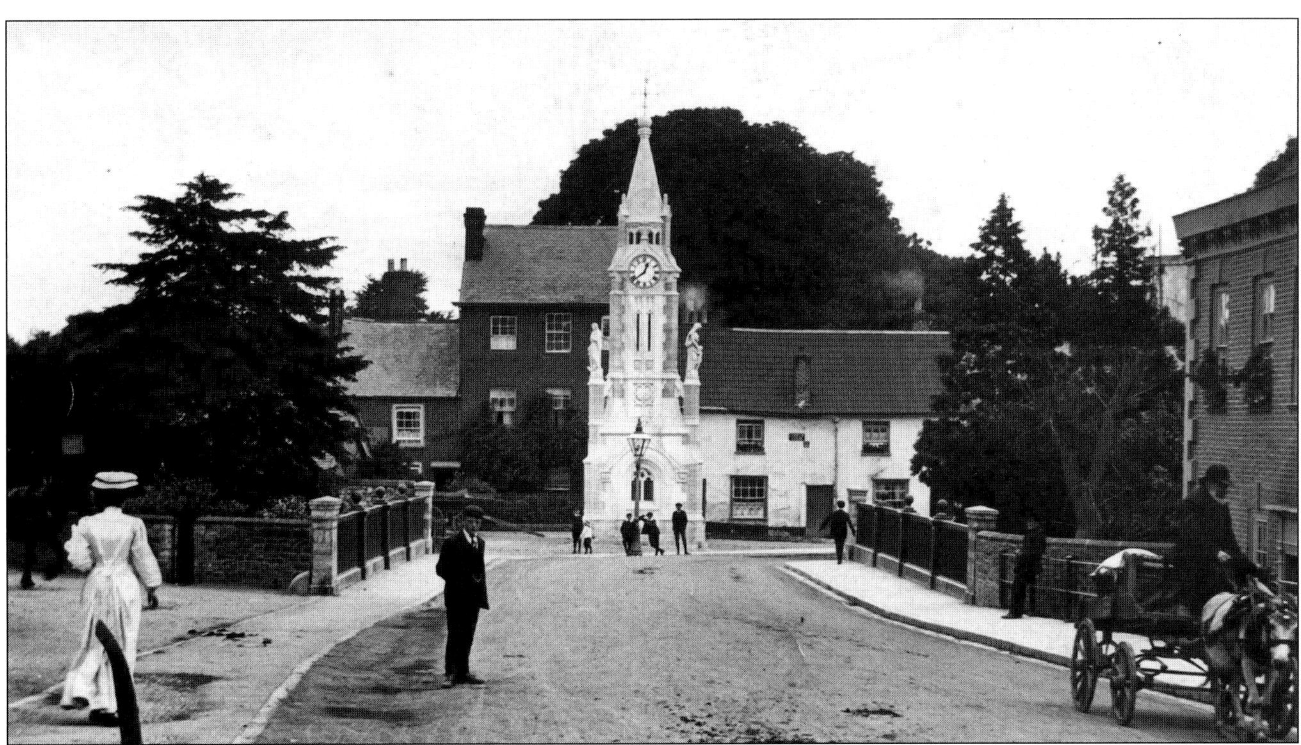

Above: *The eastern edge of the town, looking down Gold Street to the bridge over the Lowman. Greenway built his almshouses on what was then a greenfield site.*
MUSEUM COLLECTION

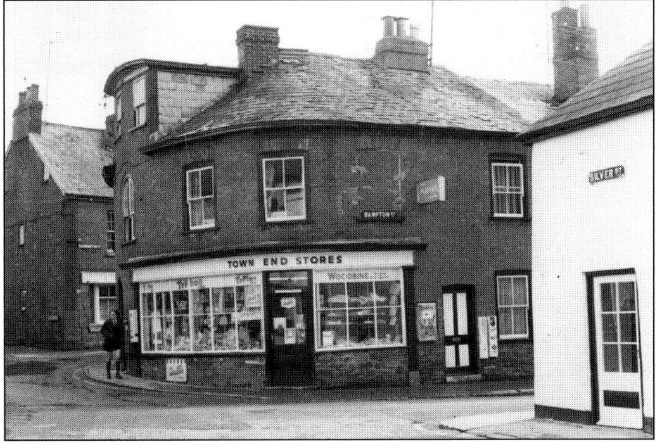

Right: *'Townend' the northern edge of old Tiverton. The road follows the gravel ridge to Chettiscombe, and over the hills to Bampton. The shop pictured here was called Town End Stores and the white building to the right was a pub, named the Morning Sun.*
MUSEUM COLLECTION

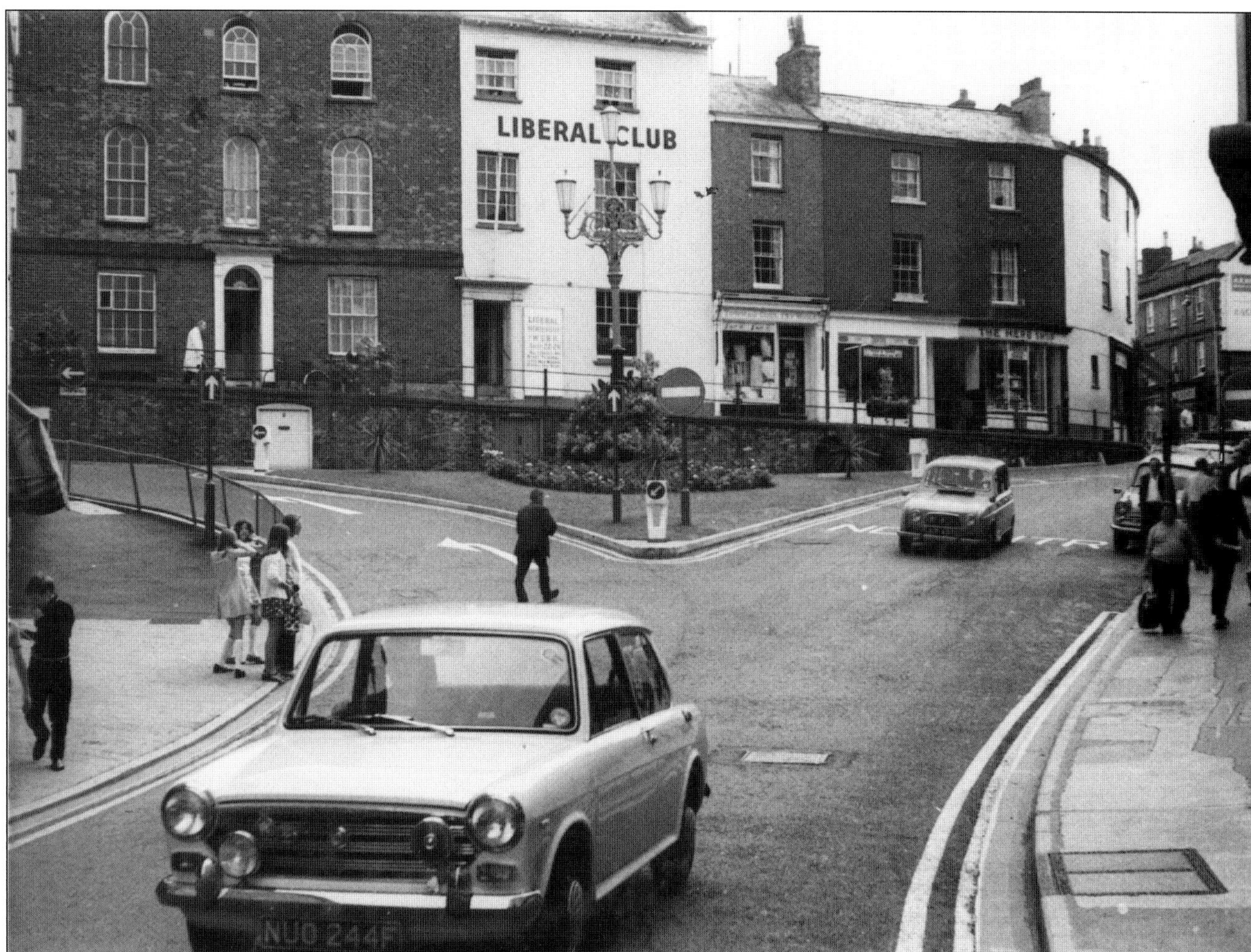

The western edge of the town. Now called Angel Hill after the hostelry that once stood on the site of the War Memorial building. It used to be called Oat Hill as the oat market was held there. The street gradient has been much changed, being once so steep that it was stepped, and the Congregational Church was once known as the 'Steps Meeting House'.

MUSEUM COLLECTION

So something happened to Tiverton's fortunes in the later fifteenth century. Astride the Exe and the Lowman, the town had had water-mills at the time of Domesday, almost certainly for milling corn. Until the reign of Edward III England was a wool exporting land, but in 1336 Parliament enacted that no wool produced in England should be exported, but that it should be made into cloth in England. The Act went on to encourage the immigration of skilled foreign clothworkers and fullers by giving them 'set-up' grants and tax exemptions. In the early-fourteenth century there is no evidence of local cloth making. The trades mentioned in a 1332 subsidy list are all connected with the castle and agriculture. A problem with charting the growth of industry in late-medieval Tiverton is that most of the documentary evidence concerns customs revenue, that is what merchants brought into the country, not what they took out. In the later fifteenth century these documents record the names of Tiverton merchants John Greenway father and son, Roper, Taylor, Glovier and Skinner. They are importing things such as tar, wine, raisins, sugar and as well as alum, teasels and madder, necessary in the manufacture of cloth. But we can only suppose that their main export was Tiverton cloth.

The Courtenays held Tiverton for over 250 years, from 1294 to 1556. Their careers were often chequered, particularly during the Wars of the Roses, when Thomas Courtenay strongly supported the Yorkists and took strenuous action against the local Lancastrians: the Bonvilles and the Powderham Courtenays. His son, also Thomas, inherited in 1457 and chose the wrong moment to switch to Lancaster, as Edward of York became King in 1460. Both Thomas and his brother Henry were executed, and Henry's son, John, was killed fighting for Henry VI. During Edward IV's reign Tiverton was granted to a number of Yorkists, including 'poor, perjured, fleeting Clarence', the King's brother. After the Battle of Bosworth the Courtenays recovered their estates and Edward Courtenay became Earl of Devon and his son William married Katherine, a daughter of Edward IV and sister of both Henry VII's wife and of the Princes who had been murdered in the Tower. These royal connections were both a glory and a danger. William Courtenay was arrested on a charge of treason in 1502 and remained in the Tower until released in 1509 by his nephew, Henry VIII. He died almost immediately and his widow, Katherine, decided to live out the rest of her life in Tiverton Castle.

Katherine died on 15 November 1527 and was given an immense funeral. Her corpse was embalmed and her coffin covered with a pall of cloth of gold, embroidered with a silver cross and six escutcheons of her arms. It lay in the Courtenay Chapel at the north side of St Peter's until 2 December, when with great ceremony it was carried into the main aisle. The funeral service was conducted by the Abbot of Montacute, assisted by the Abbots of Ford and Torbay. Many other clergy and over 100 gentlemen attended. Overnight the body remained in the church and on the following day masses were sung, the Requiem Mass and the Masses of Our Lady and of the Trinity. Only then was the coffin interred in a vault in the Courtenay Chapel. Then followed a splendid dinner in the castle with provisions for 500 people. Two pence each was distributed to 8,000 poor people to pray for her soul. Her son, Henry, erected a tomb topped by her recumbent effigy.

This Henry, although his wife had stood godmother for the infant Princess Elizabeth and to Prince Edward, was executed for treason in 1538 and his 12-year-old son Edward imprisoned. In Mary Tudor's reign Edward was suggested as a possible royal consort and he recovered Tiverton, but fled into exile when she married Philip of Spain and he died in Italy in 1556. The Courtenay estates were then divided among four heirs and the Courtenay connection with Tiverton ended. The Courtenay Chapel had already been destroyed during the reign of his mother's godson, Edward VI.

For the next 250 years Tiverton would bubble along without a dominant local family.

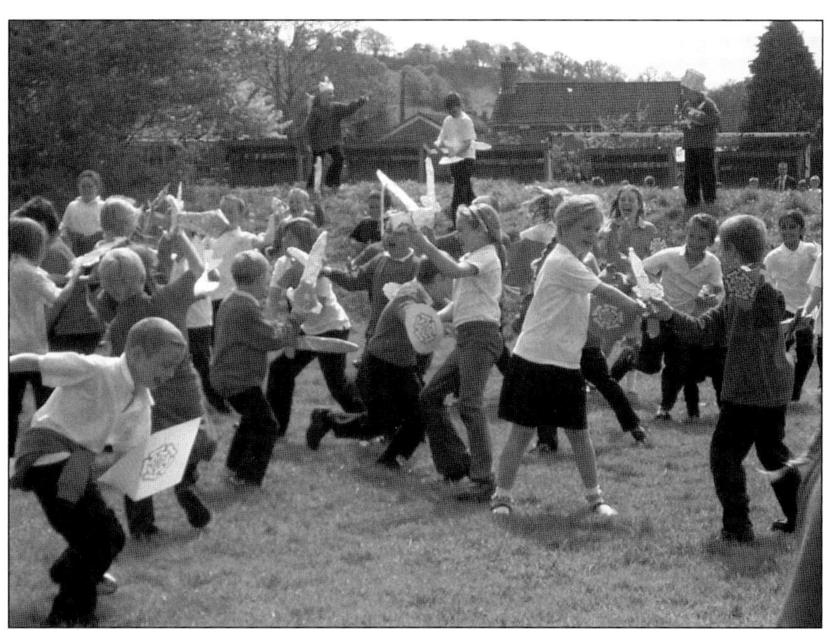

The Wars of the Roses, like the Hundred Years War, are historians' shorthand for complicated events. 'Roses' were not a contemporary emblem of either side. The children of Two Moors School re-enact the Battle of Bosworth with partly-historical gusto.

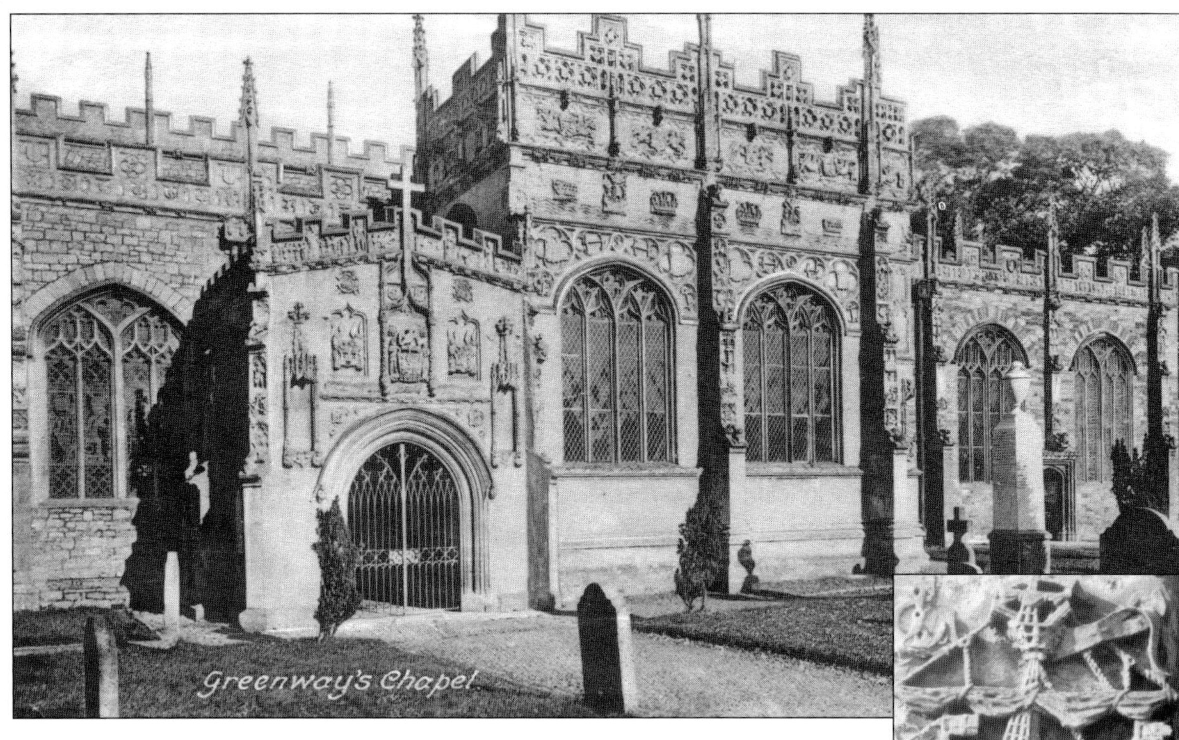

Above: *Greenway's Chapel, a symbol of merchant wealth.* MUSEUM COLLECTION

Right: *A carving of one of Greenway's merchantmen. Was Greenway a merchant or pirate or, like Chaucer's merchant, both?* MUSEUM COLLECTION

Below: *More carvings from Greenway's Chapel. Note the Tudor Rose and the JG sign.* MUSEUM COLLECTION

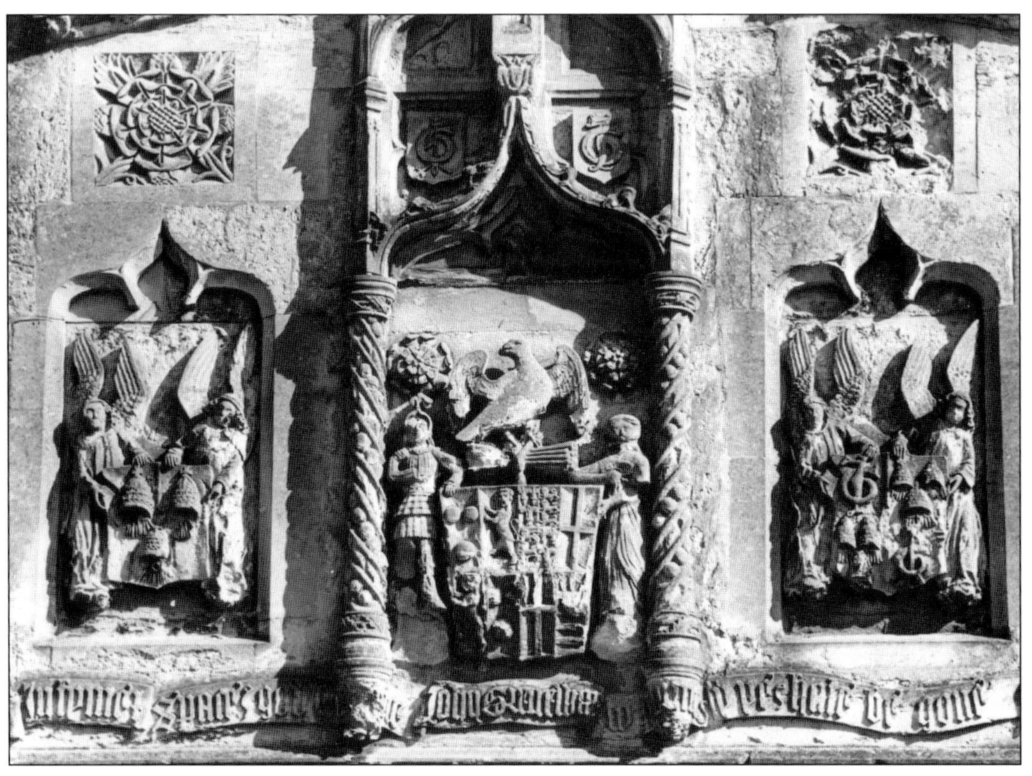

Chapter 2

Reformation

'The three great elements of modern civilisation, Gunpowder, Printing and the Protestant Religion' come to Tiverton!

Quotation adapted from Carlyle.

'Stately Tiverton, that brave Market of the West.'

Pamphlet, 1612.

Catherine Courtenay's obsequies present a picture of the 'Old Religion' in its sunset glory: three abbots, innumerable masses and prayers for the dead, colour and rich ceremony. Dunsford reported that 'the whole church was hanged with black cloth, magnificently adorned with escutcheons on every side and illuminated with 600 lights.' The body of this daughter of Edward IV, sister-in-law to Henry VII, aunt of Henry VIII and godmother of the future Edward VI, was laid in a grand tomb in the Courtenay Chapel, which stood on the north side of the church. A century later, in 1630, Risdon reported that the chapel was gone and only slender ruins left, much of the refuse is said to have been used to raise the floor under the Mayor and Corporation's pews, which then stood in the north aisle, being moved to the south aisle in the nineteenth century. As our eighteenth century poet, Kiddell put it:

There Edward's daughter mingles with the dust;
Defac'd the marble, and destroy'd the bust!
How base the hands that could such ruin spread,
And wreck vain vengeance on the illustrious dead.

There is a double symbolism here. The destruction of this chapel is an example of the changes brought about in the years of the Reformation, when the country's official religion became Protestant. The use of the chapel rubble to elevate the Mayor and Corporation illustrates the change from rule by aristocratic lords of the manor to rule by merchant burgesses, whose tombs pock the ground under chancel and nave.

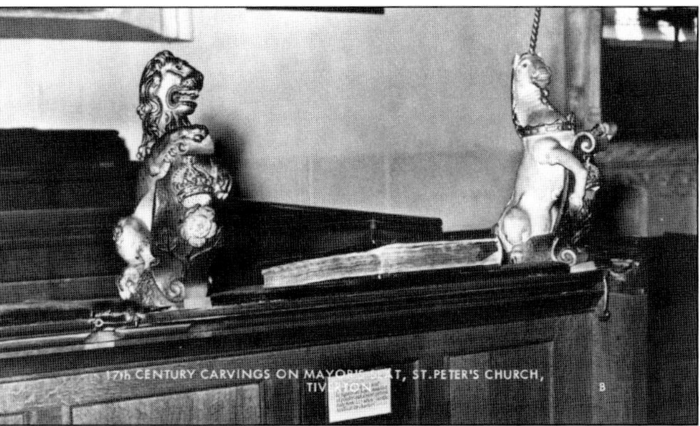

The Mayoral pews in St Peter's. The pew was originally in the north aisle and its raised platform was made from rubble from the Courtenay Chapel, a symbol of the transfer of power from castle to borough.

MUSEUM COLLECTION

Of course it is only with hindsight that we see the first quarter of the sixteenth century as the 'sunset' of the Old Religion. At the time it must have seemed in full vigour. The original stone church, traditionally built in 1073, was probably only the nave, but it had been added to during the following 400 years. The tower had been built in the 1300s; at almost the same time the north and south aisles and the Courtenay Chapel were added. Evidence from wills, where prayers for the deceased were endowed and to be said at specific altars, suggests that the interior held at least one altar per portion.

There is no evidence that the colourful religion centred on St Peter's was in any way unpopular. In the early-sixteenth century the church received some lavish investment. When John Greenway died in 1517 he gave it its most attractive ornament attached to the south aisle, Greenway's Chapel and the porch, all lavishly decorated. He also offered to enlarge the tower, but this was not taken up. Dunsford discovered another donation of roughly the same date, which left moneys for the maintenance of the parish church. Greenway also willed that:

... there may be some yearly obit kept in the said Church with five priests, to sing or say five masses, on the ninth day of February at Even, before Dirige, for the soul of me, my wife, our fathers and mothers, and all our friends [forever]. And also 5s yearly to find a lamp to be continually burning before the Sacrament at the High Altar, in the said Parish Church of Tiverton.

A few years later, in 1524, William Sellake died and his will made detailed arrangements for masses to be said for his soul and the souls of his father, mother, wife, children in particular and all Christian souls in general 'at Pytte awter' and 'with the orgones'. In addition he gave £36 to build a 'rood loft', presumably above the screen, which once divided the chancel from the nave.

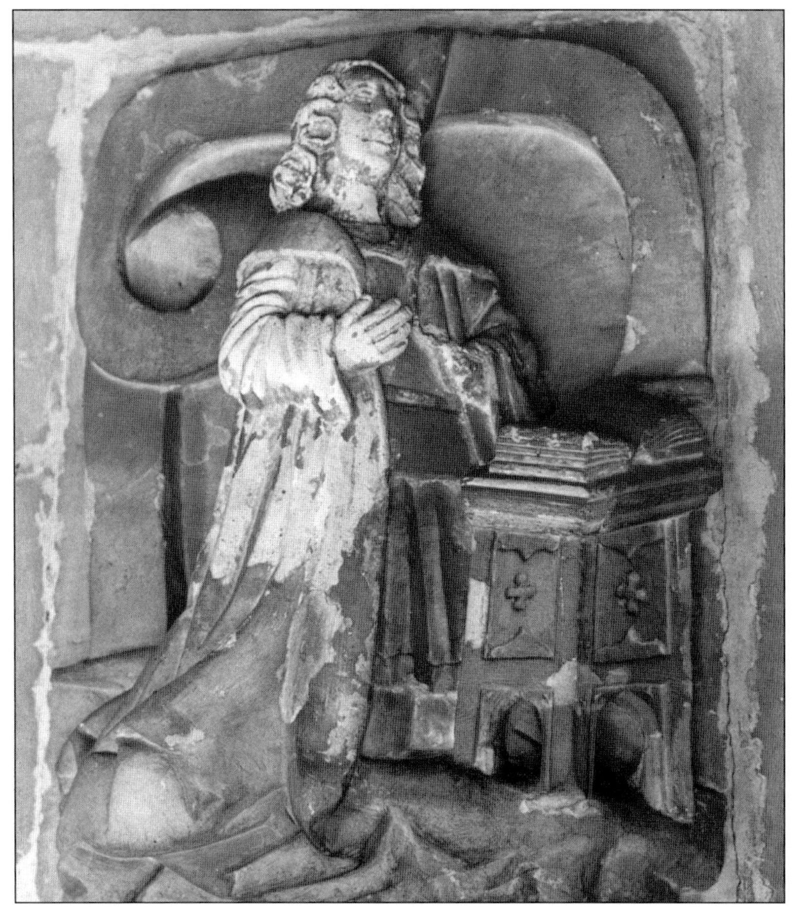

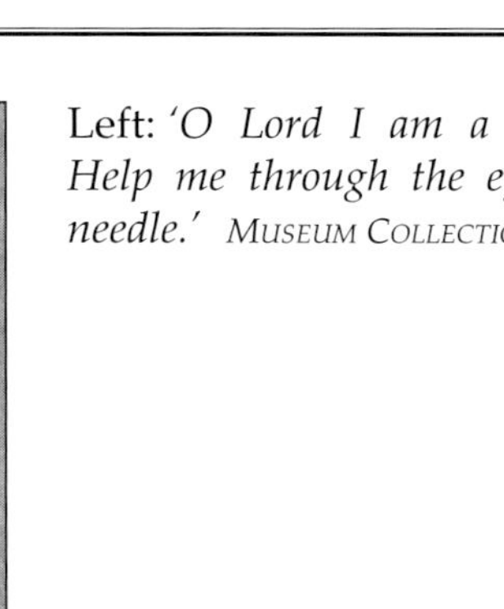

Left: *'O Lord I am a rich man. Help me through the eye of your needle.'* MUSEUM COLLECTION

Below: *The present trustees and administrators of the old merchant-pirate's wealth in the court at Greenway's almshouses. The almshouses were rebuilt after the 1731 fire, and the trustees now supervise Waldron's and Slee's bequests also.* From left to right: *Sue Coffin, Rachel Davis, Cathy Morgan, Linda Doherty, Peter Barton, Lisa Brooks, Alison Maunder, Sue Herniman, Michael Biggin, Brenda Starky, Janice Hutchinson, Brian Homer, Elizabeth Fathi, Dennis Knowles, Bryan Edwards.*
MARCUS THOMPSON, MID DEVON GAZETTE

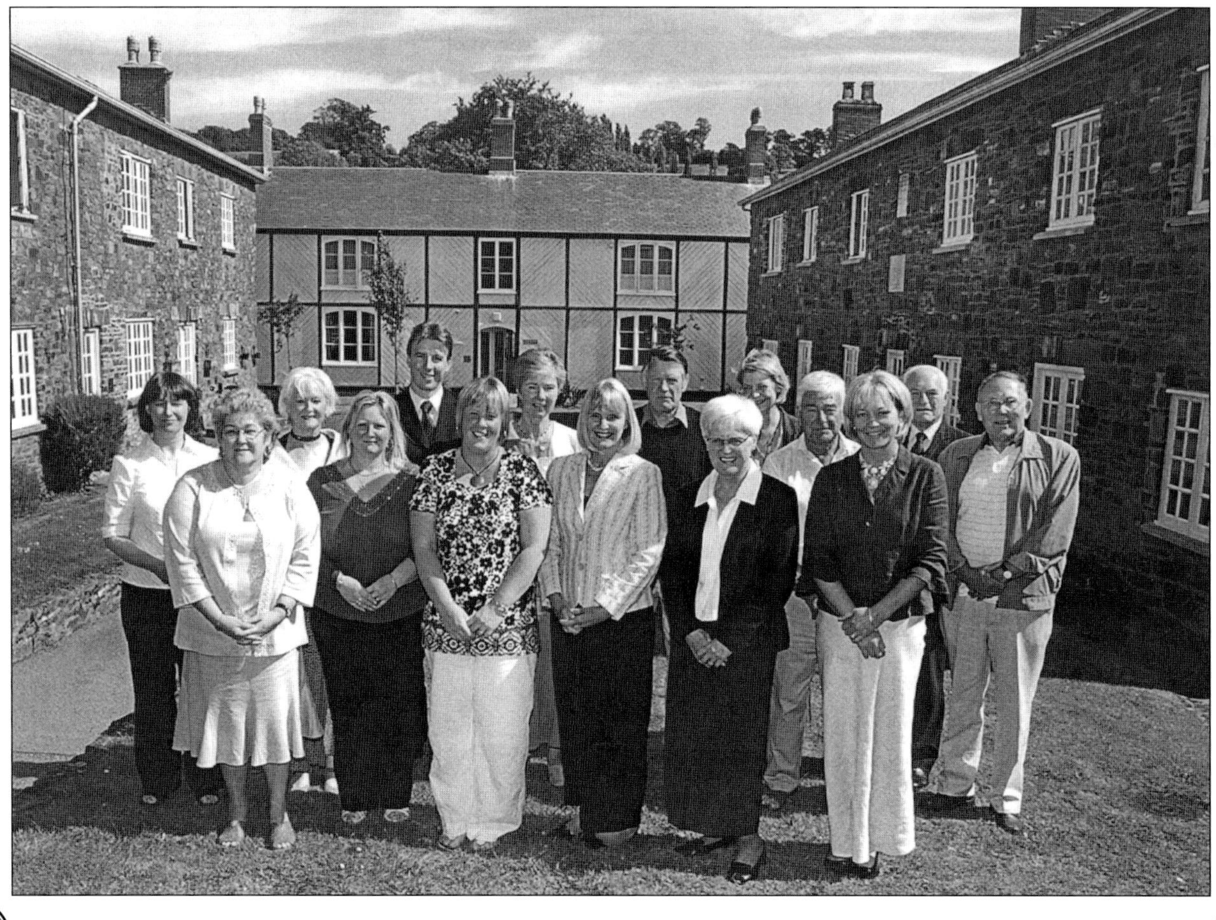

In town and parish the religion of St Peter's was multiplied by the presence of numerous chapels. Guarding the Exe bridge was St Mary's; on the site of the Town Hall was St Thomas'; St Peter's Chapel stood at the opposite end of St Peter Street to the parish church; St Andrew's Chapel gave its name to St Andrew Street and was probably on the site of the old gaol. In the parish at large St James was at Crazelowman, John the Baptist stood guard at Cove, St Lawrence and another saint whose name has been lost kept Tidcombe, St Bartholomew was at Bolham, St Mary at Chettiscombe, St John at Church Combe in Pitt, St James again at Seven Crosses, where suicides were sometimes buried, St Matthew at Palmers in Clare Portion. Other saints from their chapels watched over West Manley, Fairby and Tidcombe parsonage house. In total there were 17 chapels in town and parish, some public, others embedded in private houses.

This flourishing situation was not much affected by the Dissolution of the Monasteries in the 1530s. Tiverton's only important monastic connection, to St James' Priory in Exeter, had been ended with the suppression of the Priory a century earlier. But the wind of change was beginning to blow and Tiverton's clergy reacted as men do to the demon change: one opposed, one ran before and one kept his head down. Dr Thomas Raynolds, Rector of Pitt from 1541, was a traditionalist, promoted by Mary to be Bishop of Hereford, but put in prison by Elizabeth, where he died. George Carew, Rector of Tidcombe from 1539 was a 'reformer' and was deprived by Mary's government. Thomas Marshall, Rector of Clare from 1547–74, accommodated himself to all the changes and died still Rector of Clare.

After the accession of Edward VI in 1547, and despite the brief Catholic revival in Mary's reign, 1553–58, changes came thick and fast. Protestant Prayer Books were enforced by law in 1549, 1551 and 1560, that of 1549 causing widespread protests in Devon and Cornwall, some of the last embers of which were stamped out by royal forces on the slopes under Cranmore Castle. The Acts enforcing the Prayer Books of 1549 and 1551 were accompanied by Royal Injunctions. In 1547 they banned all traditional, but unscriptural, practices; in 1548 cults of the saints and religious fraternities were banned; in later years churches were whitewashed, statues and the contents of rood lofts carted off and burnt; stone altars were smashed and plain wooden tables placed in the body of the church and screens thrown down; 'orgones' were destroyed; priests began to wear ordinary black gowns and celebrate the Eucharist in both kinds in English. Simon Schama quotes a mid-century woman as saying to a friend:

> *What shall we do at church since all the godly sights we were wont to have are gone and we cannot hear the piping, singing, chanting and playing upon the organ that we could before.*

The sites and property of the last remaining chapels were handed over to laymen in 1567. It would be difficult to exaggerate the impact of the Edwardian Reformation, confirmed after 1558 by Elizabeth, on religiously conservative societies such as Tiverton.

Those of us able to remember the Cold War and the polarisation of life between 'Communists' and 'Non-Communists' can perhaps better understand the febrile mentality of Elizabethan England, particularly after the outbreak of the war with Spain. Protestants were desperately anxious about the succession to the throne as the unmarried Elizabeth's heir was the Catholic Mary, Queen of Scots. They were also anxious about the successes of the Counter Reformation abroad and anxious too about the massacre of the Huguenot leaders on St Bartholomew's Day in Paris in 1571 and about the apparently imminent suppression of the Protestant Dutch Revolt. Since her excommunication in 1570, Elizabeth had faced the fact that all Catholics were under an obligation to encompass her destruction, by assassination if necessary. A series of plots and rebellions, culminating in the Guy Fawkes' Plot in 1605, confirmed Protestant fears that the Church and State were in mortal danger and that everything Catholic was a sort of trafficking with the enemy. These fears were given a fresh and even stronger lease of life after 1620 with the outbreak of the Thirty Years War in 1618 and the Stuart royal family being seen as 'soft on Catholicism'.

It is in this context that various bequests should be appreciated. In 1621 Robert Reade of Tiverton, a clothier, gave St Peter's a 'fair velvet pulpit cloth and cushion'. Preaching was the weapon of choice for Protestants. In 1623 John Berry of Tiverton, clothier, made a bequest, realising £60 to go towards setting up a lecture in Divinity at Tiverton and in 1628 Richard Capron left the church his copy of Foxe's *Book of Martyrs* to be:

> *chained and kept in some convenient place, and always there to continue, for the benefit of those who are well disposed [Protestants] and desire to reap comfort thereby.*

Many of these bequests can be seen recorded on boards on the stairs in Tiverton Museum.

The greatest anti-Catholic bequest came from Peter Blundell, when he set up and endowed his school for 150 scholars in 1601. The high aim of the school was to produce a stream of 'good and godly preachers of the gospell' and the man asked by Blundell to supervise the establishment of the school, Sir John Popham, was described by a Spanish ambassador as a 'terrible Puritan'. When set up it was by far the largest educational establishment in the South West

Left: *Known as a portrait of Peter Blundell. However this is not accurate as the clothes and lace reflect a fashion current many years after his death in 1601.*

Below: *Old Blundell's, described by Defoe as 'the greatest glory of the town'. The buildings narrowly escaped demolition after the school was moved in 1882.*

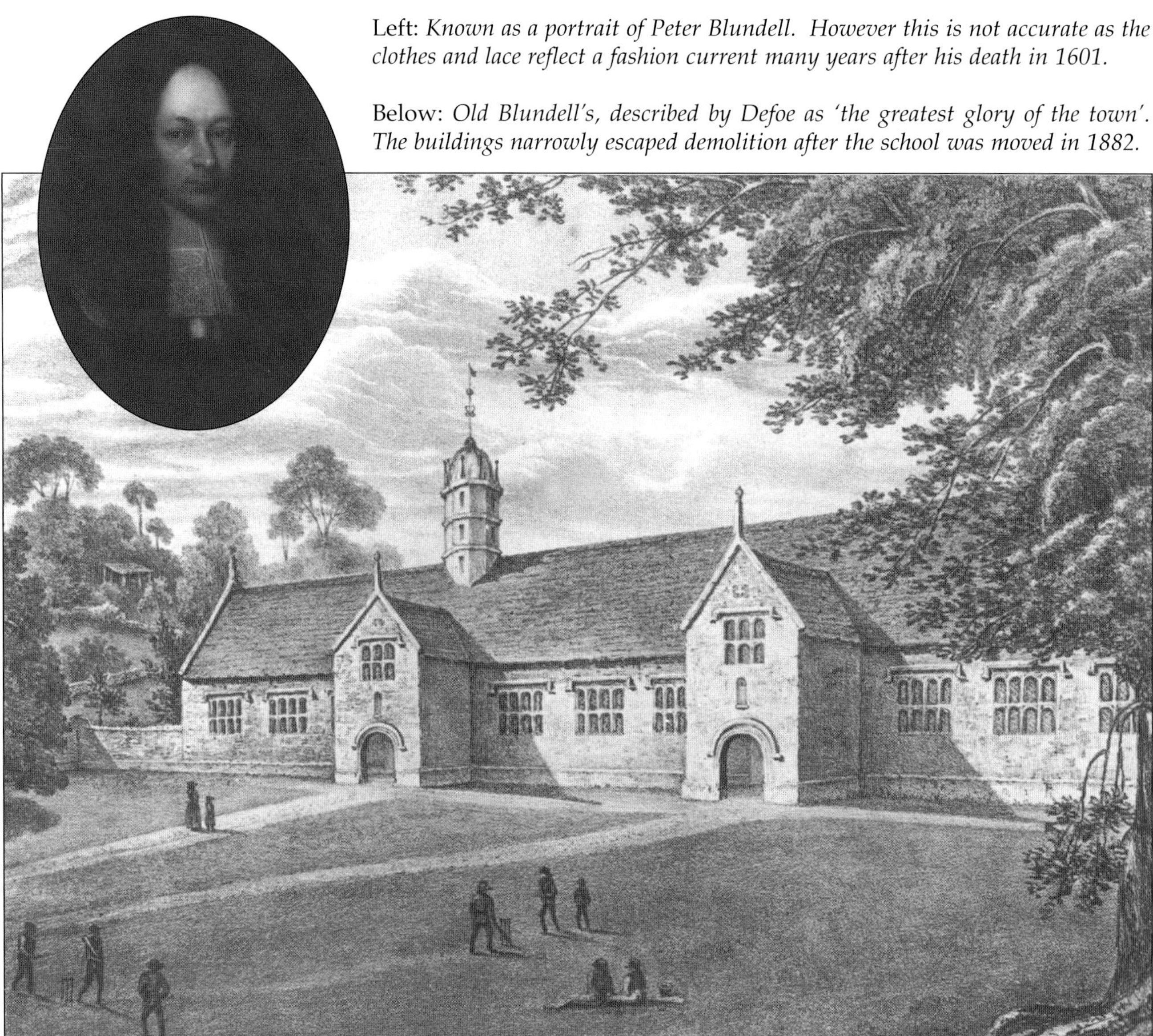

and was intended to make the West Country safe from Catholicism.

Other educational provision was made by Peter Blundell's nephew Robert Chilcott in 1611. Whereas Uncle Peter had set up a grammar school, teaching Latin and Greek to prepare pupils for university, ordination and preaching, nephew Robert's establishment was to be an 'English' school teaching the 3Rs in order to prepare them for entrance to the grammar school, or at the least to enable them to read their Protestant bibles.

One further aspect of Tiverton's religious history at this period was the growth of religious tension in the town. Increasingly the right of nomination to the four portions of St Peter's was being acquired by people out of tune with the increasingly Protestant, even Puritan, tone of the leading clothiers of the town. After the extinction of the Courtenay influence the advowsons had become fragmented and from 1570 the Crown seems to have made appointments. Certainly in the years before the outbreak of the Civil War in 1642 there were signs of a growing number of Protestant Tivertonians being dissatisfied with the ministry of the Established Church. In 1618 Bishop Cotton of Exeter opined that there were few Catholics in his diocese but an 'infinity of sectaries'. In 1624, JPs bailed Richard Berry (any relation of John Berry, who endowed the lectureship?) on condition that he refrained from making 'any conventicle at home or elsewhere' (a conventicle being a small gathering of laymen that met to discuss religious matters). Other documentary evidence testifies to the existence of an organised Anabaptist group in Tiverton in the 1620s and the Baptist Church in Newport Street is almost certainly built on the site where a conventicle met in a private house. This disillusionment with the religion of St Peter's was deepened after Laud became Archbishop of Canterbury in 1630. His policy of increasing respect for the Church and of reintroducing sacramentalism further alienated those who saw the devilments of Catholicism in every railed-off altar or clerical vestment. These are the beginnings of Tiverton's rich Dissenting history.

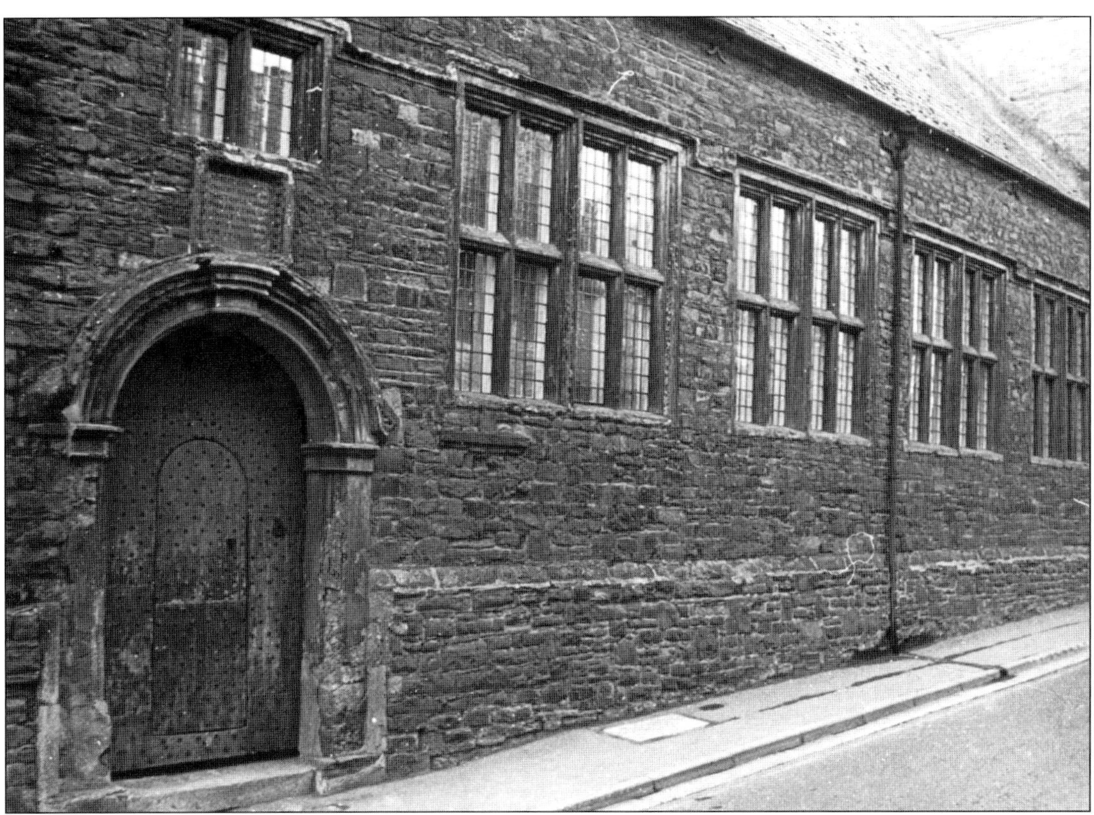

Above and below: *The Chilcott School, St Peter Street, founded in 1611 by Blundell's nephew.*

MUSEUM COLLECTION

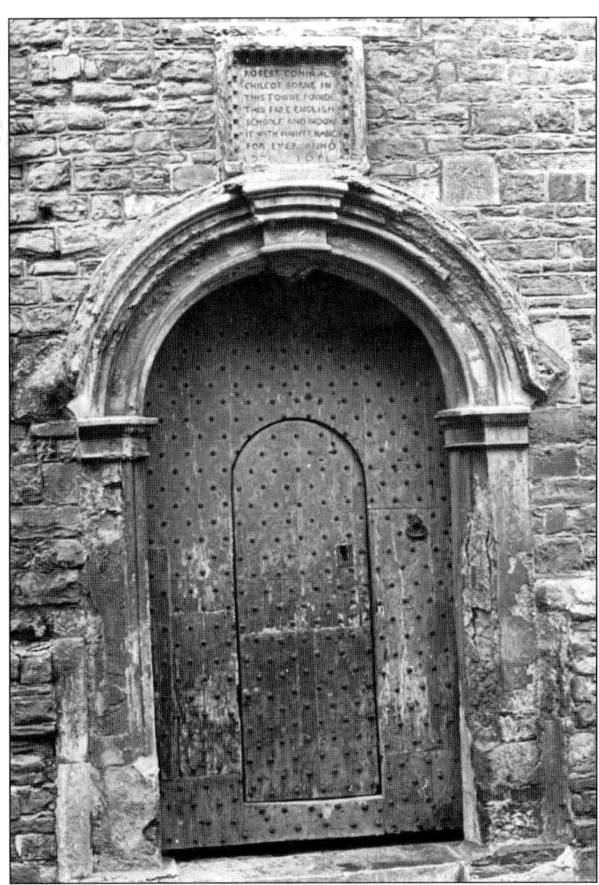

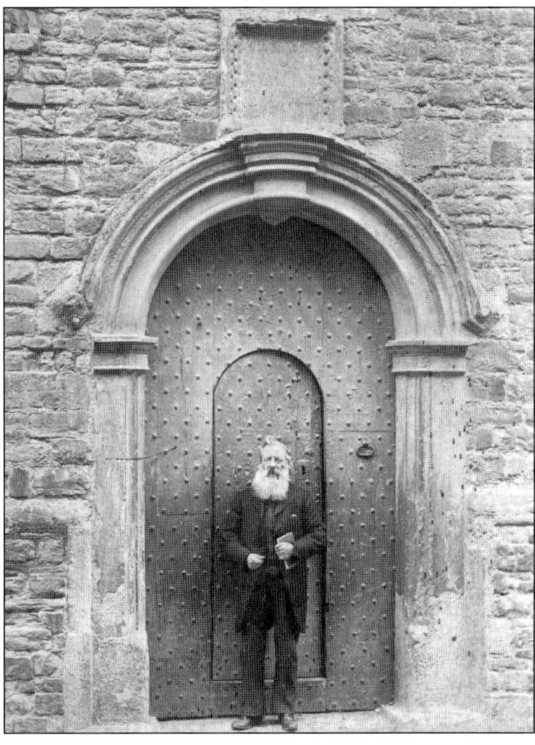

The Chilcott School with its last headmaster, A.R. Perkins, 1840–85. He taught English, Geography, Book-keeping, Mensuration, Land Surveying, Natural Philosophy, Navigation, Scripture, Latin, Greek and Algebra. He was 'mentioned with bated breath. Certain grave and dignified inhabitants' have 'still tingling recollections of his less delicate attentions'.

MUSEUM COLLECTION

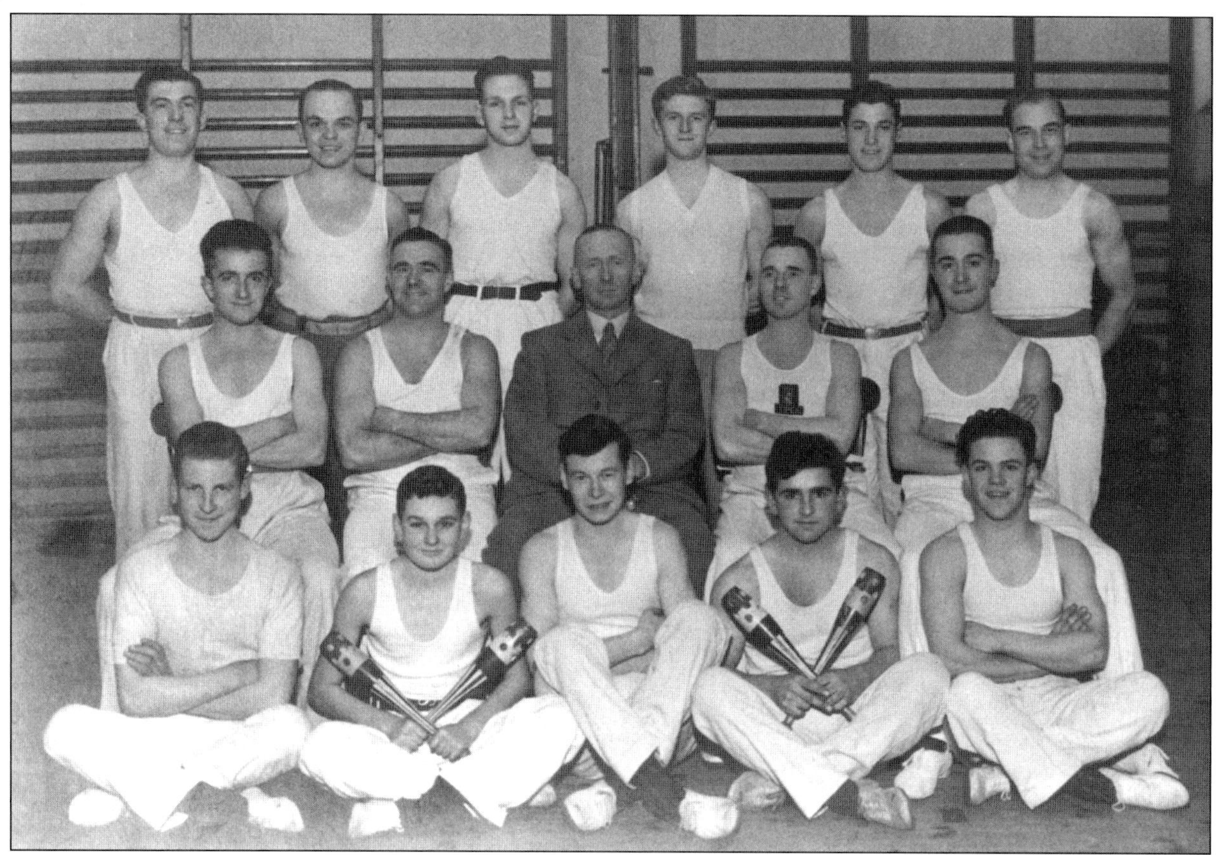

Above and below: *Chilcott's was closed when the new Middle Schools opened and became a gymnasium and function room, later Council offices, then auctioneers' premises.* MUSEUM COLLECTION

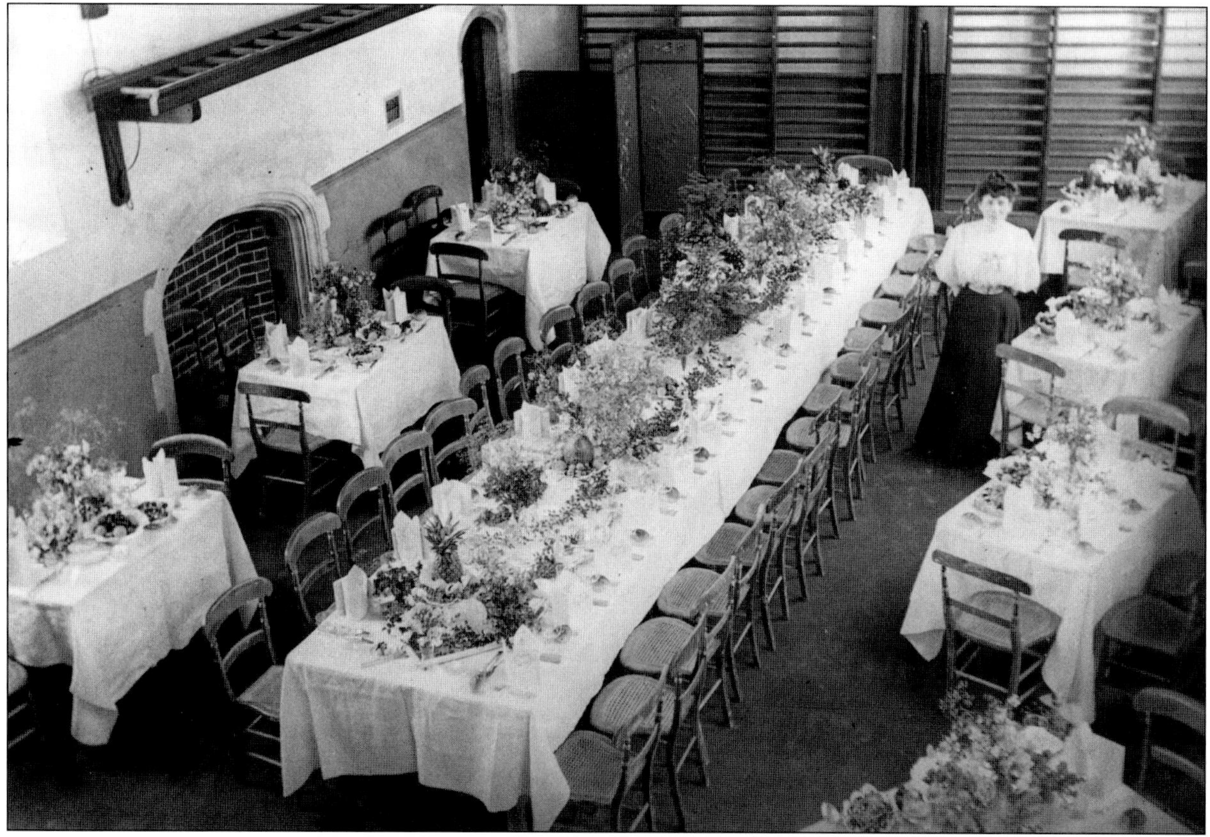

Chilcott Scool in use as a function room. MUSEUM COLLECTION

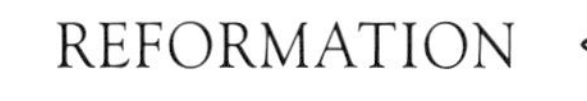

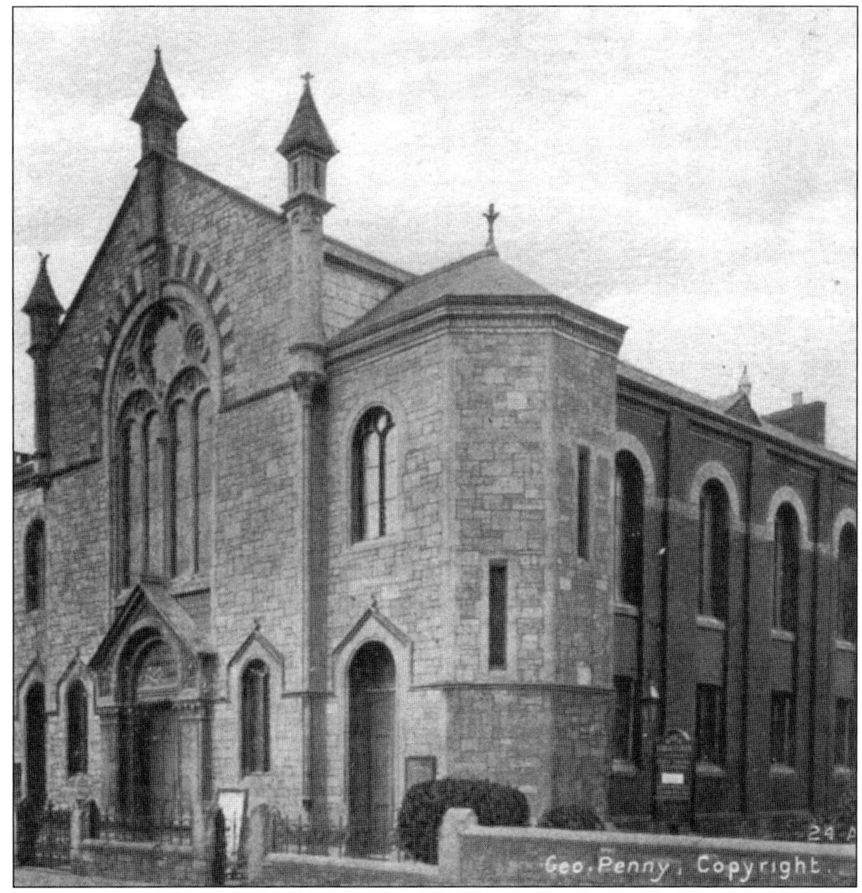

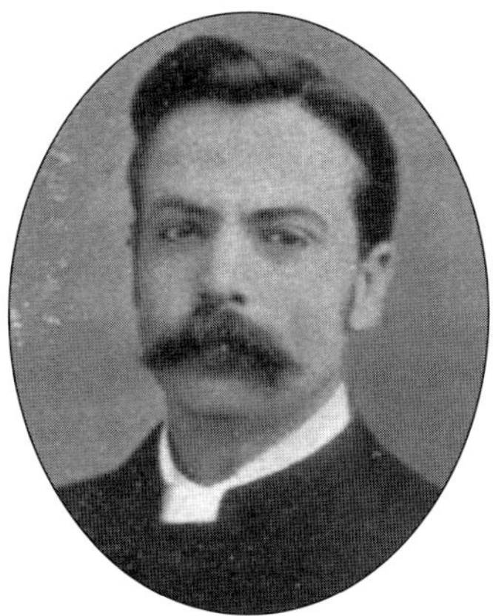

Above: *The Revd H.B. Case, Tiverton's Baptist Minister 1904–18..* MUSEUM COLLECTION

Left: *The Baptist Church in Newport Street. Those who worshipped here were the proud heirs of the Anabaptists of the early-seventeenth century. The congregation believes it began as a house church in 1607.* MUSEUM COLLECTION

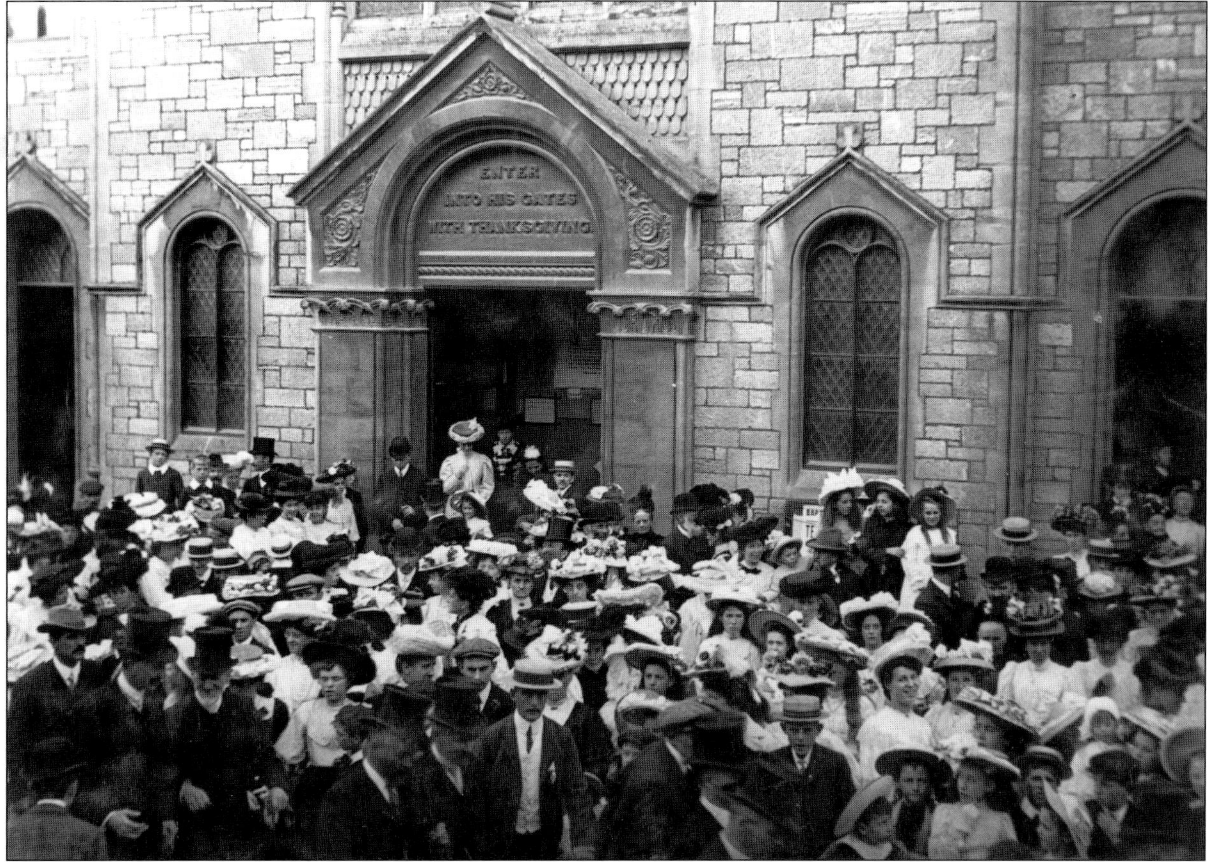

Celebrating the 300th anniversary of the Baptist Church, 1907. MUSEUM COLLECTION

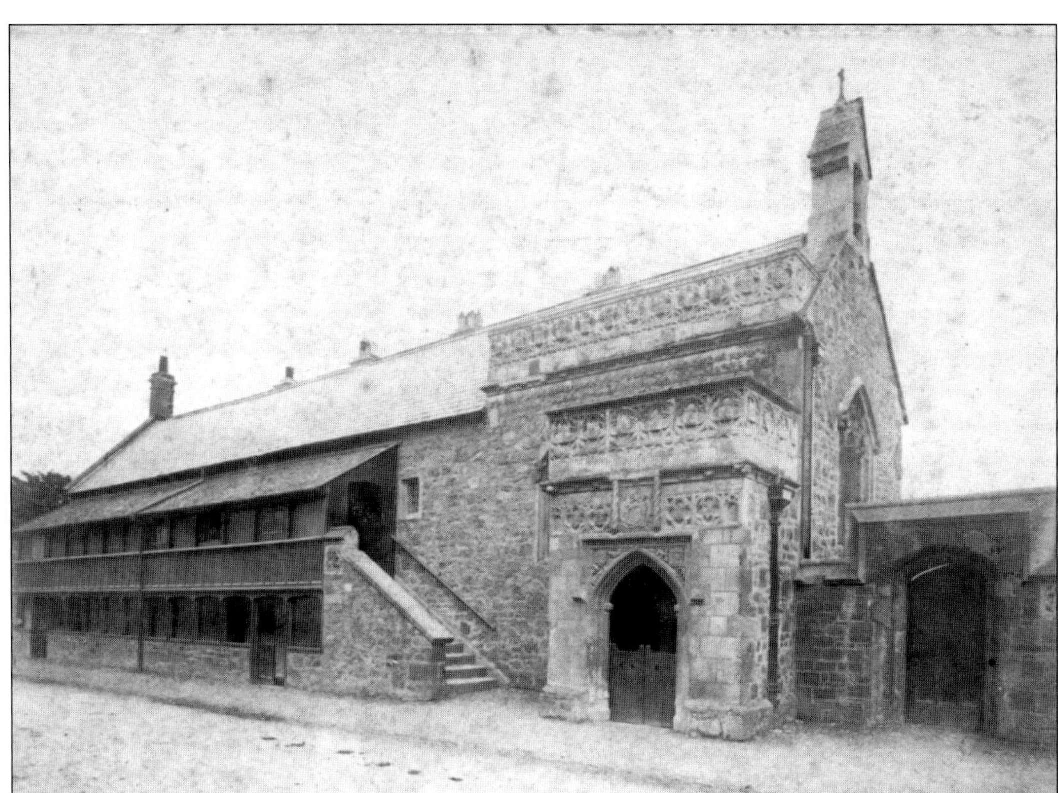

Above, below and opposite page: *Waldron's almshouses founded about 1580. These days it is too cluttered by cars to be fully appreciated.* MUSEUM COLLECTION

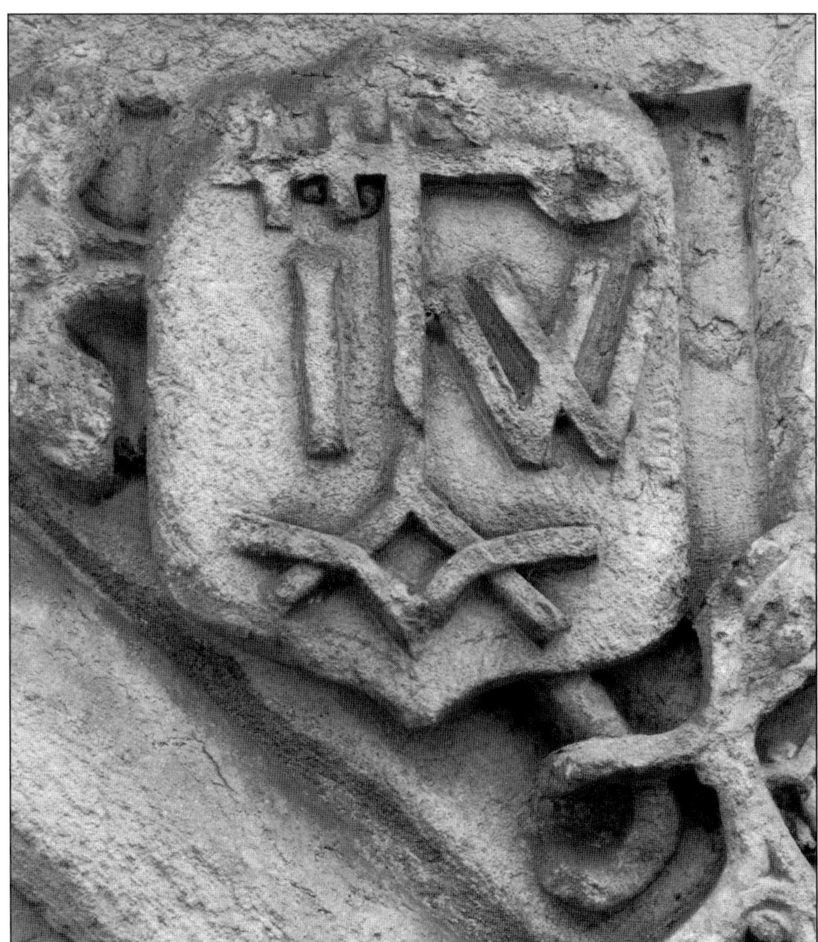

Waldron's wool mark. MUSEUM COLLECTION

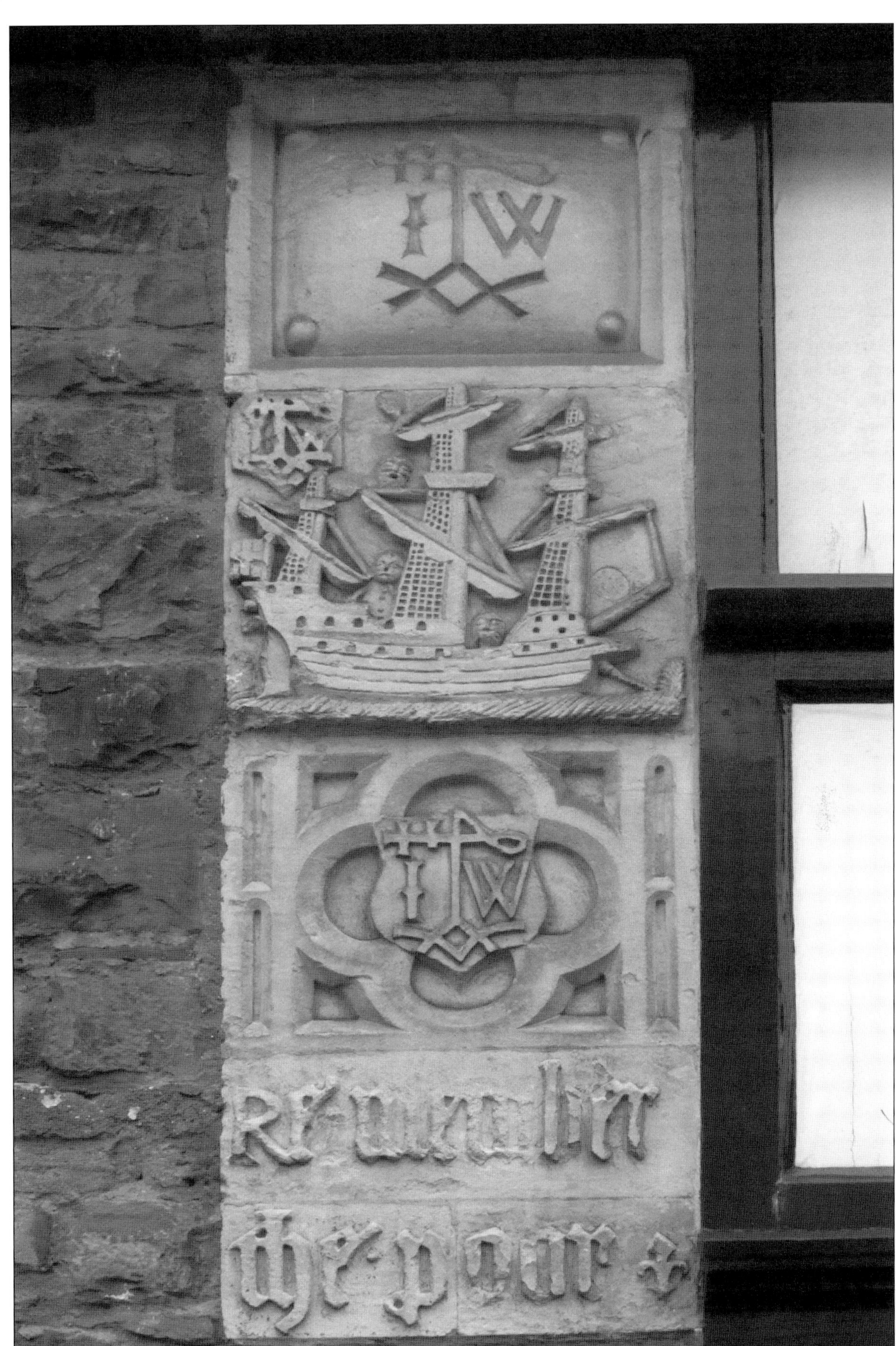

Waldron's wool mark and merchant ship. Part of the carvings on his almshouses. COLIN WHITE

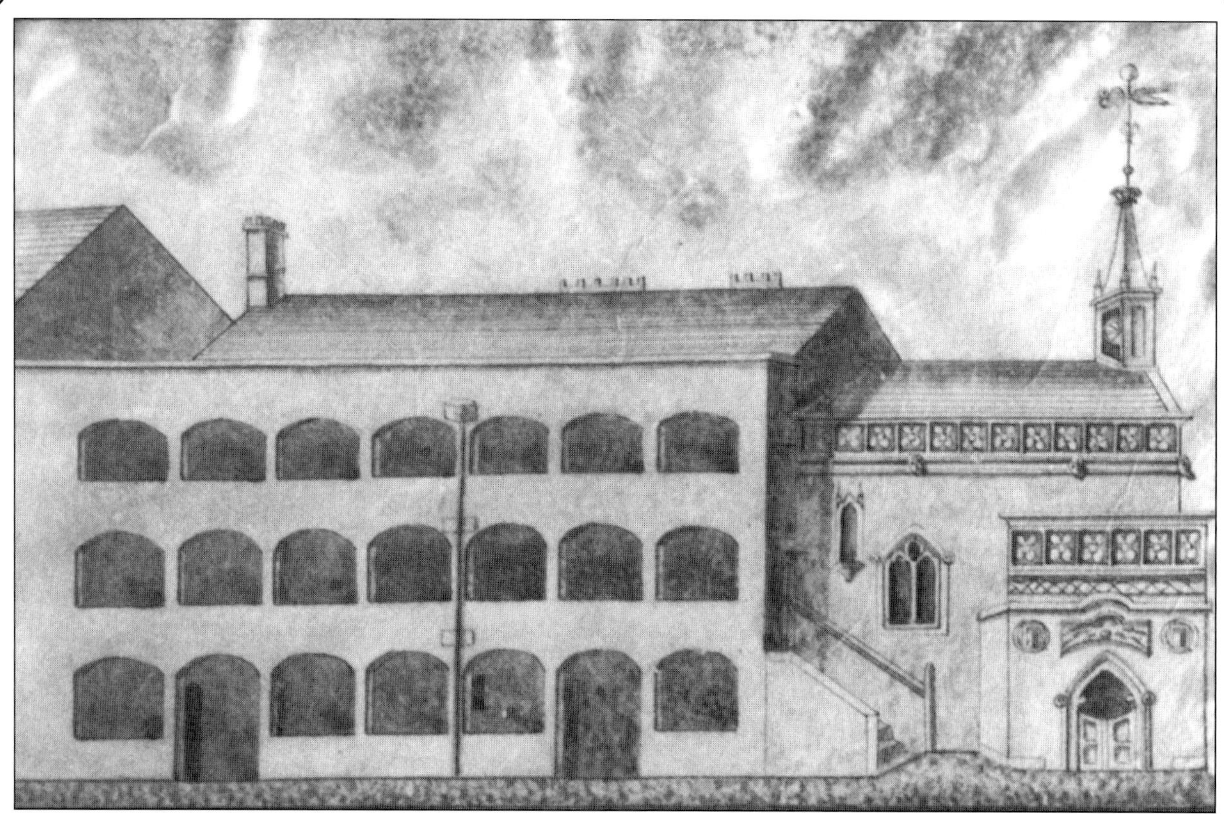

Greenway's almshouses from an eighteenth-century drawing. The galleried front was one that Waldron and Slee copied. Of necessity it was later removed to widen the roadway. MUSEUM COLLECTION/COLIN WHITE

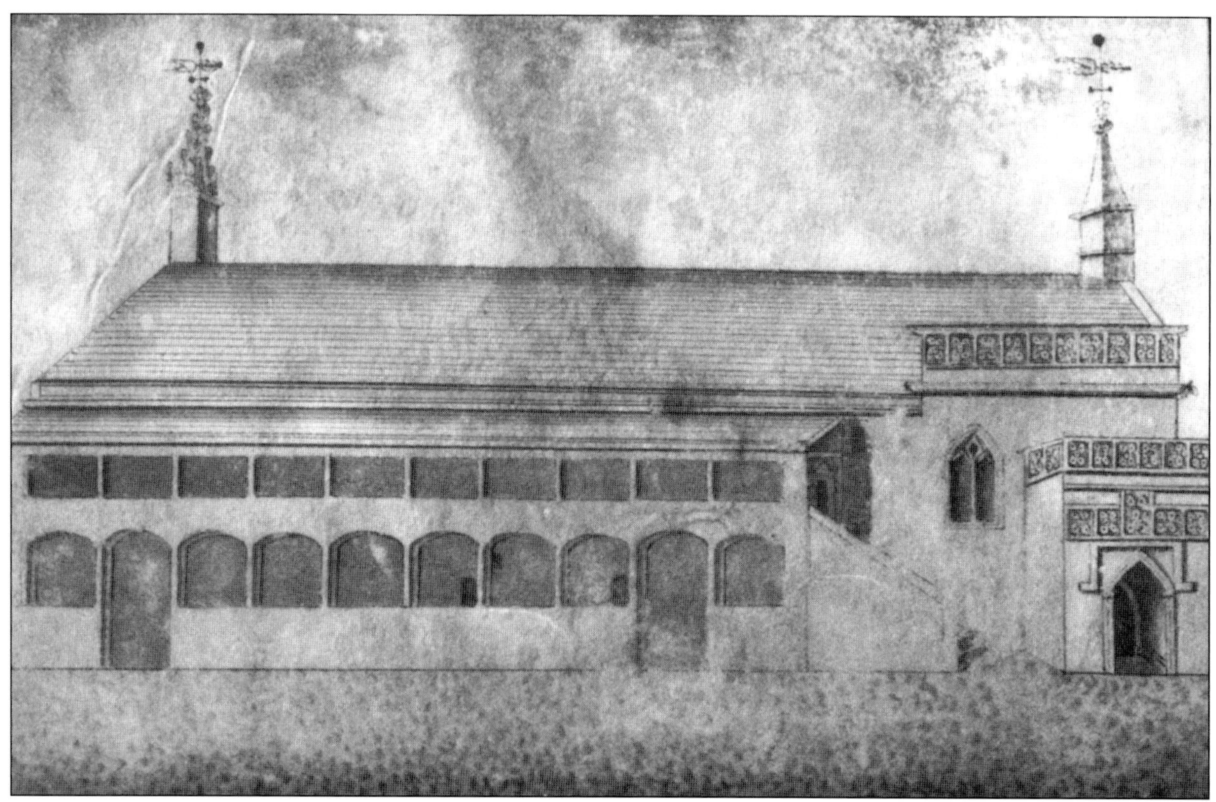

Drawing from an eighteenth-century map of Waldron's almshouses. MUSEUM COLLECTION/COLIN WHITE

It is generally accepted that advanced views in religion were usually associated with commercial activity and urban development, and in the period from 1530 to 1640 Tiverton had both. The clothiers best known to us are those who have left their mark on the town. John Greenway is remembered for his chapel and for the almshouses and chapel he had built off Gold Street. These were put up in the later 1520s, presumably on a greenfield site, which is some indication of how small the town still was and which explains how they avoided destruction in the fires of 1598 and 1612. Dunsford called them the 'Eastern Almshouses' and relates that their Gold Street front was much damaged by fire in 1731. Originally Greenway willed that houses should be built for five poor men who were to have 8d. a week subsistence money. The charity was well endowed and surpluses enabled the trustees to increase the number of poor men's houses from five to nine in Dunsford's time. The 'Western Almshouses' or Waldron's almshouses were built about 1570, the time of John Waldron's death, and housed eight poor men, who also received a shilling a week. In 1613 George Slee endowed the 'Widows' Almshouses' at the south end of St Peter Street for six poor widows or maidens. While the establishments of Waldron and Greenway contained chapels for the inmates, that of Slee had no chapel. A curiosity of the endowments provided for the maintenance of these charities is that the Greenway bequest's largest single source of income came from Dipford, while that of Waldron's came from Daccombe, Slee's from Coldridge and Blundell's from Prawle. Of the four only Chilcott financed his school from the income of Tiverton property. (For further information on this topic, see the Appendix at the end of this chapter.)

Perhaps this suggests the wide-flung nature of the enterprises run by the Tiverton clothiers and merchants and the growing wealth of the town. Although Chilcott and Blundell almost certainly gained their fortunes in London, the wills of Waldron and Slee show that excellent money could be made in the Tiverton cloth trade, but just how is not easy to illustrate. Tiverton's births, marriages and deaths registers begin in 1560 and a guesstimate of the town's population in the 1560s is only 2,500, which, if based on the registers would include the rural areas of the parish too. This was a pre-industrial age, when nothing like a factory existed. Merchants bought wool and distributed it for carding and spinning to 'spinsters', collected the yarn and passed it on to weavers, collected the cloth and passed it on to fullers and dyers. The town was probably more a marketing and finishing centre than a centre of manufacture. The finished, or semi-finished product, usually at this time kerseys or serges, was then sold on. Most of the spinners, carders, weavers and dyers probably lived in the

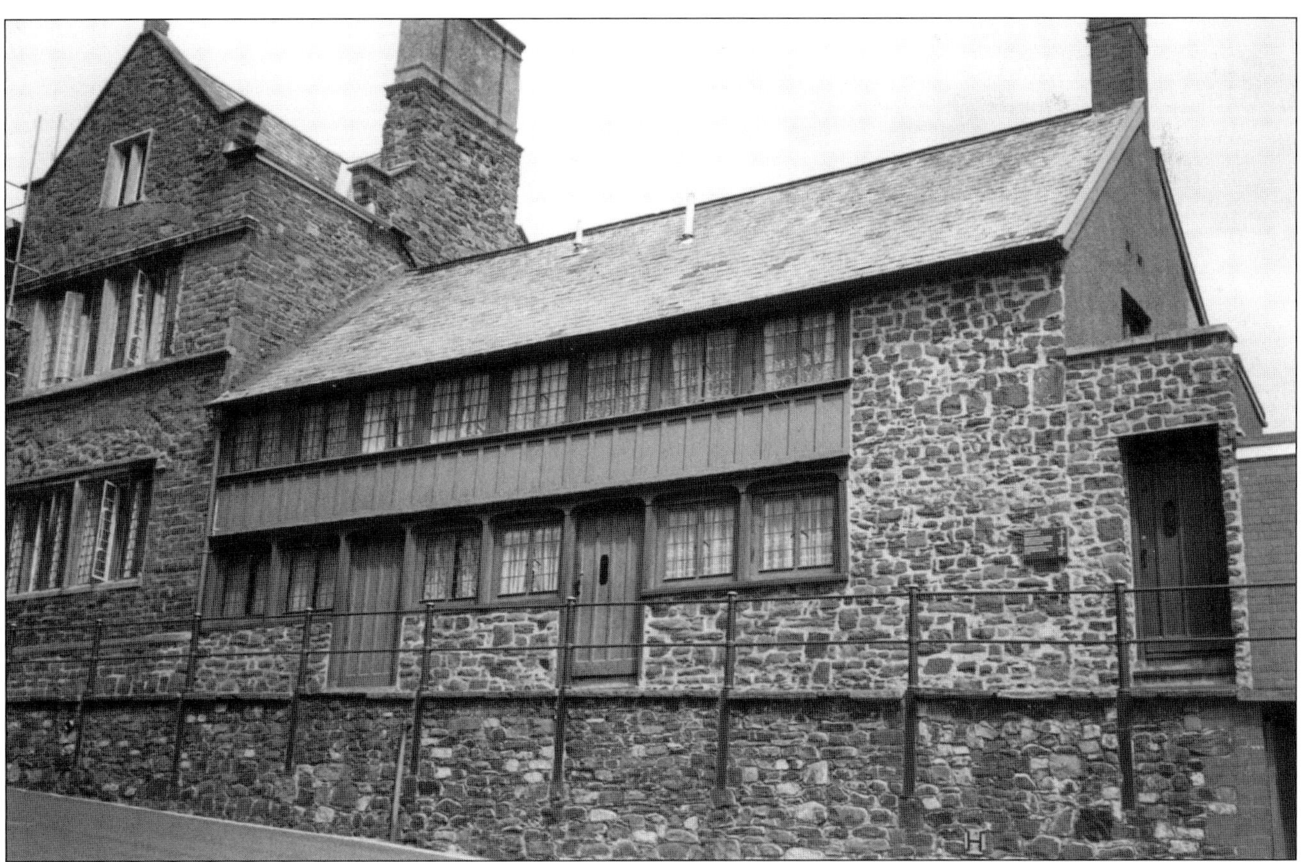

Slee's almshouses and the Great House, George Slee's property. Slee died in 1613, just before his Great House and the almshouses were completed in 1614. MUSEUM COLLECTION

surrounding countryside, but fullers, dependent on the town mills were probably urban.

Some clues about Tiverton's rising place in the world can be gleaned from the accounts written to describe the devastating fires of 1598 and 1612. As the purpose of these accounts seems to have been to highlight morals and to stimulate charity there may have been a bit of hype. But the 1598 account calls Tiverton 'the chief market of cloth in the west part of England', and the 1612 account asserts that 8,000 cloth makers were put out of work by that fire, which, if true, confirms the idea that the majority of cloth makers lived in the surrounding countryside.

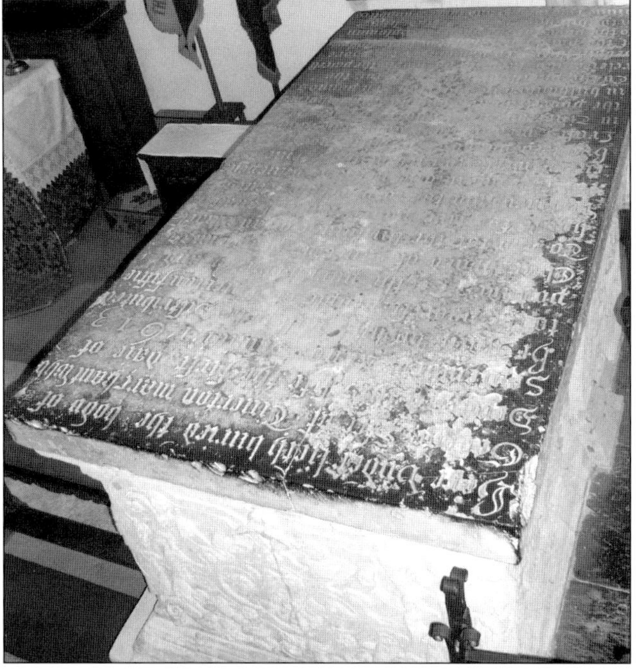

Slee's tomb (above) *in the chancel of St Peter's Church, across the aisle from Waldron's tomb* (below), *dated 1579. Waldron's wool marks are visible on the tomb.* Colin White

The 1598 fire began in April, on a Monday market-day, when two Westexe women tried to cook a mid-day pancake, using straw as fuel. The thatch was ignited and fire spread to a hay barn. Blazing hay was whisked over the river by a westerly gale and thus the roofs in the main town were ignited.

> *In less than half an hour the whole town was set on fire and after burnt; except the Church and Court house, which sometime belonged to the Earl of Devonshire... The fire increased so fast and was so vehement ... that there were about 400 houses on fire at once.*

Only 20 houses survived, 'the dwellings of poore and sillie men'. The writer suggested £300,000 or £400,000 as the value destroyed by the fire, but the writer of the life of the contemporary Archbishop of Canterbury put the loss at £150,000, a sum which must be multiplied by a thousand to give any contemporary value.

The account of the 1612 fire shows that Tiverton's recovery and rebuilding had been rapid. This fire was on a Wednesday in August 1612, at the end of a parching summer and was again seen as God's punishment for sins. It started in a dyer's shop on Angel Hill, where a boy had been left in charge of boiling up the dye. He overfed the furnace and the house caught fire.

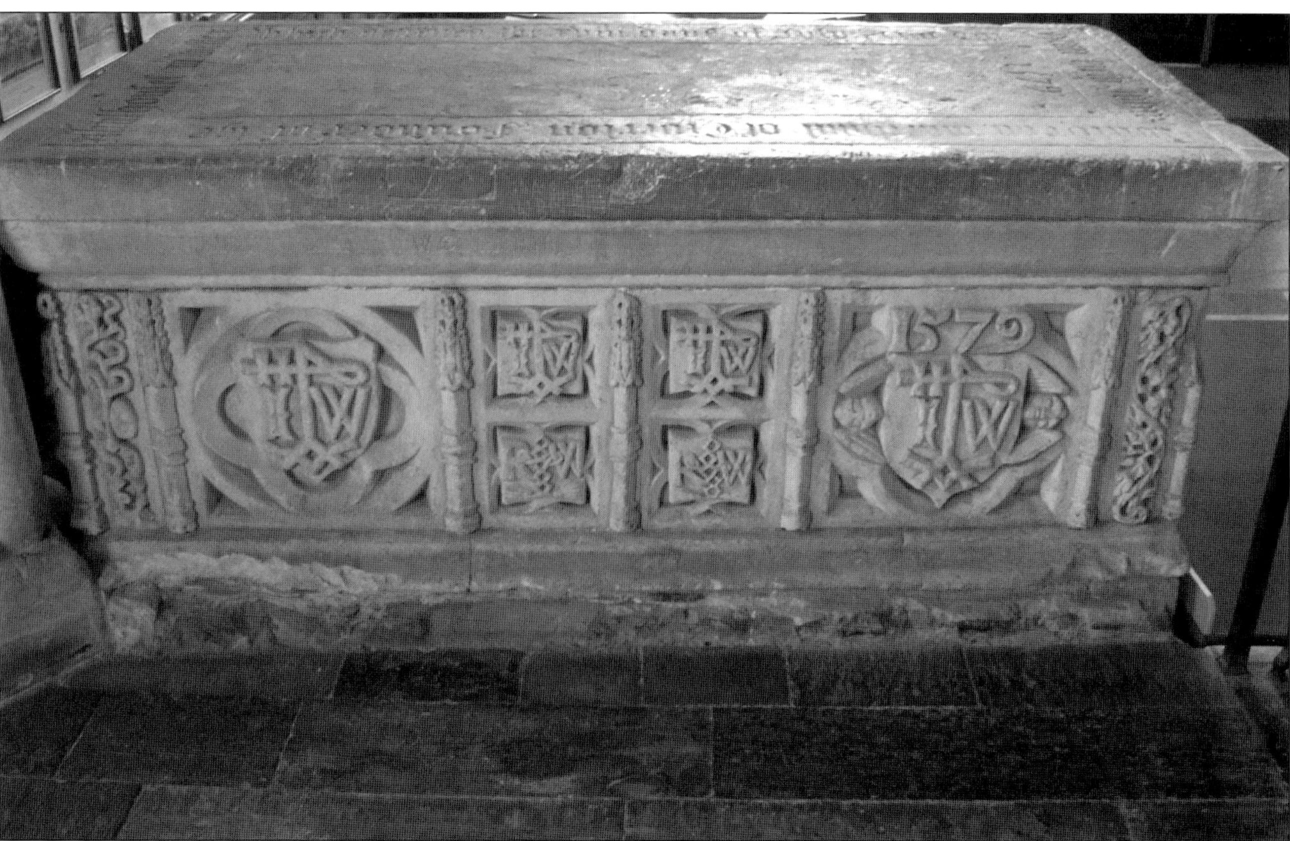

The fire, like a commanding tyrant passed along the High Street of the town [Fore Street] and there with his red flaming fury wasted both houses and goods to the utter undoing of many merchants and tradesmen, their wives and children... The fire unresistedly foraged other streets, being the seats and dwellings of many wealthy householders, as St Peter Street, beautified with many costly and comely buildings, Bampton Street, Barrington Street, St Andrew Street, with divers other lanes and back-places, the capital graces of this now decayed town. Here at one time burned they all; all in one fire gave light to the whole country.

There is a reminder too of the rural nature of the still small town when the writer mentions the roasting alive of pigeons, ducks, geese, hens. Again nothing was left standing but the two schools and the same 20 or 30 houses, probably in Chapel Street protected by the 'cliff'. The 1612 account estimated the town's population at 'very near two thousand', but went on to describe the town as 'stately Tiverton, that brave Market of the West, and wealthy and rich town.' Dunsford states that about 600 houses were destroyed, but that would only give three persons to a house, which is far too 'modern' a figure – one wonders what they were counting when they gave the population of the town as nearly 2000. Bearing in mind that the age profile of Tiverton's 1612 population would have been the same as that of a third world country today and therefore over half the population would have been under 20, it may well have been that the 'nearly 2000' were adults. In modern terms this would be translated as those on the voters roll, thus in terms of numbers this would have made Tiverton about the size of Uffculme today, but with hundreds more children and an average life expectancy of about 30. In 1642 Parliament demanded signatures of loyalty from all adult men and 1,767 signed as Tivertonians; Exeter had 3,262 signatures and Plymouth 1,440. Double the number of adult men to include adult women and one reaches 3,500 adults and double again to include children and, tentatively one has a gross population of 7,000.

There is another thing to be learnt from the fires of 1598 and 1612. As Lady Bracknell might have put it, 'To have one fire is a misfortune, to suffer two looks like carelessness.' The danger of fire in those days of thatch and wood construction had long been recognised. Regulations of 1284 decreed that a constable and six assistants should roam the streets at night to keep the peace and watch for fires. Yet both fires started in broad daylight when the town was thronged with people. The 1598 fire, fanned by a great wind and spreading so fast that it killed 33 people, may have been unstoppable, but the 1612 fire is described as raging for 'nineteen or twenty hours space', killing nobody. Indeed the author described the activities of thieves who took advantage of the chaos to ransack buildings. It seems that the fire-fighting organisation had been totally neglected and public order had broken down, which is not surprising since the town was in a constitutional no man's land: the authority of the lords of the manor and his portreeve had collapsed and nothing had been set up to replace it.

The double disaster explains why in 1615 the town petitioned for and obtained a Charter. The preamble to the Letter Patent clearly shows the connection with the fires:

Whereas the said town hath been twice consumed by fire, but not without great negligence of the inhabitants of the said town, who, not being compared by the care and diligence of magistrates, nor sufficiently fortified by the bonds of good laws as was meet for so great a town, and people do easily omit their duties in that behalf... that for the better government of the same town we would vouchsafe to make the same inhabitants into one body corporate...

The full document is quoted by Dunsford and in sum created a Mayor, 12 Capital Burgesses and 12 Assistant Burgesses 'to be chosen of the discretest and honestest inhabitants of the Town and Parish, to be called the Common Council.' Whenever a vacancy should occur in the Council the surviving Burgesses were to fill that vacancy by choosing a successor. They had powers to make by-laws and impose punishments and were charged with setting up a prison. It named the first Mayor, Richard Hill, who had a second surname 'Spurway'. The first Recorder was Humphrey Were and the first Town Clerk, Henry Newte the elder. It also nominated Henry Newte the younger to succeed his father. The Mayor and Recorder were JPs within the town and held a court of record every Tuesday. The Mayor and Burgesses, who were also named in the document, had the power to elect two Members of Parliament. They also had the power to control the participation of strangers in Tiverton markets. The town's right to hold two fairs, one on the Tuesday before Trinity Sunday and the other on Michaelmas Day, was also confirmed. As enforcers, the Mayor had two Sergeants at Mace.

The first Mayor was Richard Hill who, having bought the Spurway estate in Oakford, changed his name to Spurway. Presumably he was the leader of the group of merchants, who had petitioned for the Charter. He was connected to the closely related group of rich families who then dominated the town, having married a daughter of John Chilcott, who herself was a niece of Peter Blundell. Spurway, his son, grandson and great-grandson were feoffees of Blundell's School. Other families who were inter-related with the Blundells, Chilcotts and Wests were the Slees (who had just completed the building of the Great House) the Hams and Skinners. Certainly of the 25 named members of the first Council, only

George Giffard living in the castle, designated as 'Esq' and John Deyman, designated 'Gent' by Dunsford, were not merchants or clothiers. The days of a town dominated by an aristocratic lord of the manor were well and truly gone!

The Charter also ordered the creation of a seal, the building of a prison and necessitated building a working base for the new Council. The town seal has been pleasing enough to last almost 400 years; it would be nice to know who created it. There appear to have been two prisons. In 1630 Richard (Spurway) Hill's will gave a property in St Andrew Street to the town for conversion to a 'house of correction' on the cautious condition that, if it were not so converted, it would return to his family's ownership. As the property, almost certainly on the same site as the present Bridewell flats, was unconditionally transferred to the Corporation in 1650 by the first Mayor's son, it can be assumed that the property had been converted. However, a house of correction was probably not a 'prison' in the meaning of the Charter. The Corporation, through the JP status of the Mayor and Recorder, was empowered to 'correct and punish offenders and breakers of the peace'. This could only be done through fines if the culprit could pay (and fines went to the Corporation), or whippings or imprisonment with some sort of hard labour. The Charter expressly reserved felonies, treason and crimes involving injuries for the County Assizes, and those charged with such offences were to be sent to await the Assizes. It is in this context that the Charter mentions the need for a prison, that is to hold those arrested for felonies, and this prison seems to have been provided in the basement of the new Town Hall, which was built on the site of the former St Thomas' Chapel at the junction of St Andrew Street and Fore Street. No doubt the building was altered and enhanced between its building and its demolition in the 1860s. Surprisingly no illustration can be found.

Probably the new Council produced by-laws almost immediately, but the first ones we know of date from 1627. Snell quotes them in full. Arthur Culme, one of the Assistant Burgesses of 1615, was by this time Mayor. The first two deal with infringements of 'the Lord's day', decreeing a penalty of 2s.4d. for selling goods then and 5s. for slaughtering cattle then. Presumably they did not want to provoke the Lord to burn the town again. A number of by-laws deal with the Council's administration, for example, fines for being absent on Mayor-Choosing Day, or from Council meetings and Court Sessions, or for wearing unsuitable clothing or interrupting debate. Others concerned the procedures and fees for granting the younger sons of freemen, former apprentices and non-townsmen the right to trade in the town. A surprisingly modern touch is a by-law that laid down swingeing penalties for unauthorised building. Unsurprisingly, there were regulations to control industrial processes involving fire: no storage of fuel by 'Dyers, Clothiers, Colour Makers, Bakers or Brewers' in the same room as furnaces; no outdoor fires for drying cloth within 80 feet of a thatched building. No brewing was allowed between eight o'clock in the evening and three in the morning. It was decreed that all householders should 'clean, sweep and cleanse' the street in front of their houses every Tuesday morning and every Saturday afternoon and should repair the roadway in front of their houses. There were also fines declared for polluting the leat or diverting it. A further reminder of the rural nature of a seventeenth-century town is the by-law fining inhabitants 3d. for each pig they allowed to roam loose in the town or churchyard.

The reasons behind all these are comprehensible, but other by-laws need some explanation. For example, a long and precise by-law forbade any householder, on pain of a fine of 10s. a month, from taking in any stranger or foreigner without the consent of the Mayor and Capital Burgesses. The next by-law was the prohibition of unlicensed building and it was followed by a fierce injunction forbidding any townsperson from taking in any 'Bastard or Bastard's childe or children or children not born within the town and parish which shall be likely in the judgment of the Mayor to be chargeable to the town' unless good security was given that the children would not become a charge on the town. The fine for taking in children without permission was 40s. a month per child, a sum only exceeded by the fine of £5 for putting up a new house without permission and £1 a month for allowing it to remain standing. This was an age that was defined by poverty and the fears of those with property that they would be swamped by hordes of idle vagrants. Hiram Coram (1668–1751) was so appalled by the numbers of abandoned infants in London that he set up his 'Foundling Hospital' in the 1730s. The situation in the 1620s was much harsher even than the world Hardy created when he described the fate of Fanny and her bastard child in the 1870s in *Far from the Madding Crowd*.

Moreover the 1627 by-laws were written in a time of great stress in Devonshire. England was badly governed. James I seemed under the spell of his handsome catamite (the name given to the younger partner in a pederastic relationship between two males), the Duke of Buckingham, and was negotiating unsuccessfully for a Spanish Catholic marriage for his son Charles, then, successfully, for a French Catholic marriage. The Duke's clumsy diplomacy led to wars against sometimes France, sometimes Spain and incredibly sometimes against both. Meanwhile the Protestant cause in Germany, once led by James' daughter, Elizabeth, and her husband, the Elector of the Palatinate, was going to rack and ruin, and all this at a time when Laud appeared to be reintroducing Catholic abominations into the Church of

England. Unpaid, unfed and diseased soldiers and sailors, the detritus from unsuccessful attacks on France and Spain, were wandering and looting throughout the South West, the government was trying to extract illegal taxation and subjecting whole swathes of the country to martial law. A West Country MP, Sir John Eliot, whose three sons attended Blundell's School, led the charge that in 1628 forced the King to accept the Petition of Right, outlawing billeting, martial law, arbitrary taxation and arbitrary imprisonment. In March 1629 Eliot led the Commons to pass the Three Resolutions, thus labelling as public enemies any who introduced innovations in religion that tended to Popery or who proposed illegal taxation or who voluntarily paid illegal taxation.

Eliot was imprisoned and died in the Tower in 1632. His young sons he left in the guardianship of John Hampden, famous for his stand against the extension of the Ship Money Tax. After 1629 Charles I decided to rule without Parliament. His personal government, associated with Laudian High Church changes in the Church and such 'illegal' taxes as ship-money, was deeply unpopular in Tiverton. In fact, in 1637 Tivertonians owed more unpaid ship-money than any town in Devon.

Civil War appeared to be difficult to avoid and when it came, Tiverton would be decidedly against Charles I.

Appendix: Tiverton Trusts

In the 100 years after 1517 wealthy Tivertonians left property in trust for the benefit of the town and six of them were peculiarly long lasting. Firstly there were three almshouse trusts: Greenway's beginning in the 1520s, Waldron's in the 1570s and Slee's in the 1610s. Greenway's was the most opulent, producing a regular surplus that enabled the number of almshouses to be increased from the original five to sixteen in the nineteenth century. This property consisted of two farms in Diptford, Little Holwell farm in Tiverton, some fields in Westexe in the Broad Lane area, some houses at Brickhouse, property to the south of Belmont Road, property in Fore Street, where HSBC now trades, two sites in St Peter Street and property at the east end of the bridge.

Waldron's and Slee's were pinched for cash and had difficulty finding the weekly pension for the former's eight poor men and the latter's six 'poor aged women'. There was a fourth almshouse trust, set up in 1690 by John Alstone with the Mayor as sole trustee, but it fell for lack of endowment or casual dishonesty.

A peculiarity of all three trusts was that the two churchwardens of St Peter's were trustees – solely in the case of Waldron's and Slee's, but with a number of other trustees in the case of Greenway's. In 1939 the Charity Commissioners authorised the amalgamation of the three trusts, now known as Tiverton Almshouse Trust. Taking advantage of modern legislation designed to increase the role of any provider of housing, as long as it is not part of local government, Tiverton Almshouse Trust has increased its units of housing to 90.

The two educational trusts are still with us, but as shells of their former selves. For the history of Peter Blundell's see *The Book of Blundell's*. As a result of nineteenth-century changes it became a public school with some Tiverton connections, but these links have progressively been weakened and it is now connected with Chulmleigh School and not with any Tiverton school. Chilcott's School, financed from lands in Yorkshire, survived to the end of the nineteenth century, providing education for up to 100 boys in the 3Rs. A visit to its small, but dignified premises will explain why it ceased to be a school when national legislation established a national system.

The other trust was the Bridge Trust set up by Walter Tyrell in 1568 for the building and maintenance of the Exe Bridge, again with the churchwardens as trustees, but with a number of others as well. Their income derived from a line of cottages, backing on to the river in Westexe South, which the trust only sold very recently. The repair of the bridge was essential to the weekly Monday market and in progressive and complicated stages the Bridge Trust bought up the rights to the profits of the market, originally owned by the 'Castle Courtenays' and after 1570 divided among their heirs. In the process they acquired all the property from the site of the old Palmerston to the corn market along the west side of Bampton Street. The trust had built the first corn market in the 1690s, but it burnt down and the present building appeared in the 1730s.

The Bridge Trust's income was not adequate to maintain the bridge against the stresses of modern transport. A major early-nineteenth century rebuilding had to be subsidised from the rates and in 1953 it was given to the county. The Bridge Trust continued as it still ran the market, which was moved from the streets to the new Pannier Market in the early-nineteenth century. When this was handed over to the Borough Council the trust had no *raison d'etre* except to continue with monitoring the expenditure of charitable donations which had been specified by those owners of the market when they sold out to the Bridge Trust. In 1989 the Charity Commissioners completely amalgamated the elements of the Bridge and Market Trusts and placed the duty of nominating the six trustees with the trustees of Tiverton Almshouse Trust, so that in practice they are administered as one.

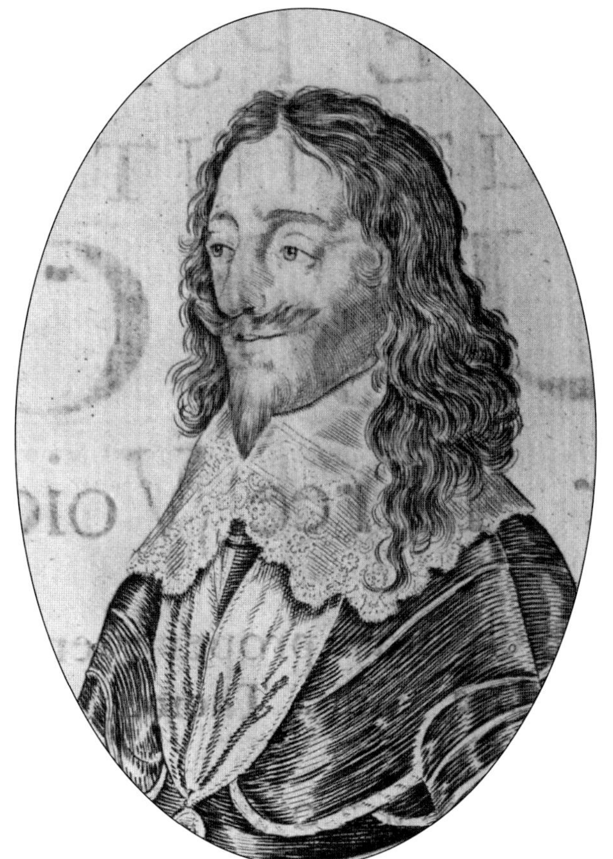

Left: *An idealised portrait of Charles I, part of the process that turned a mendacious incompetent into a royal saint. Taken from a pamphlet in the Newte Library.* COLIN WHITE

Below: *Oliver Cromwell, taken from the Market Charter of 1655, which moved the market from Mondays to Tuesdays.* COLIN WHITE

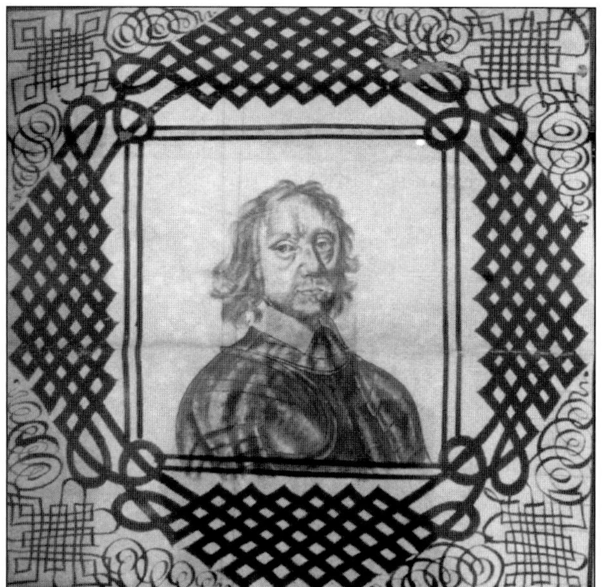

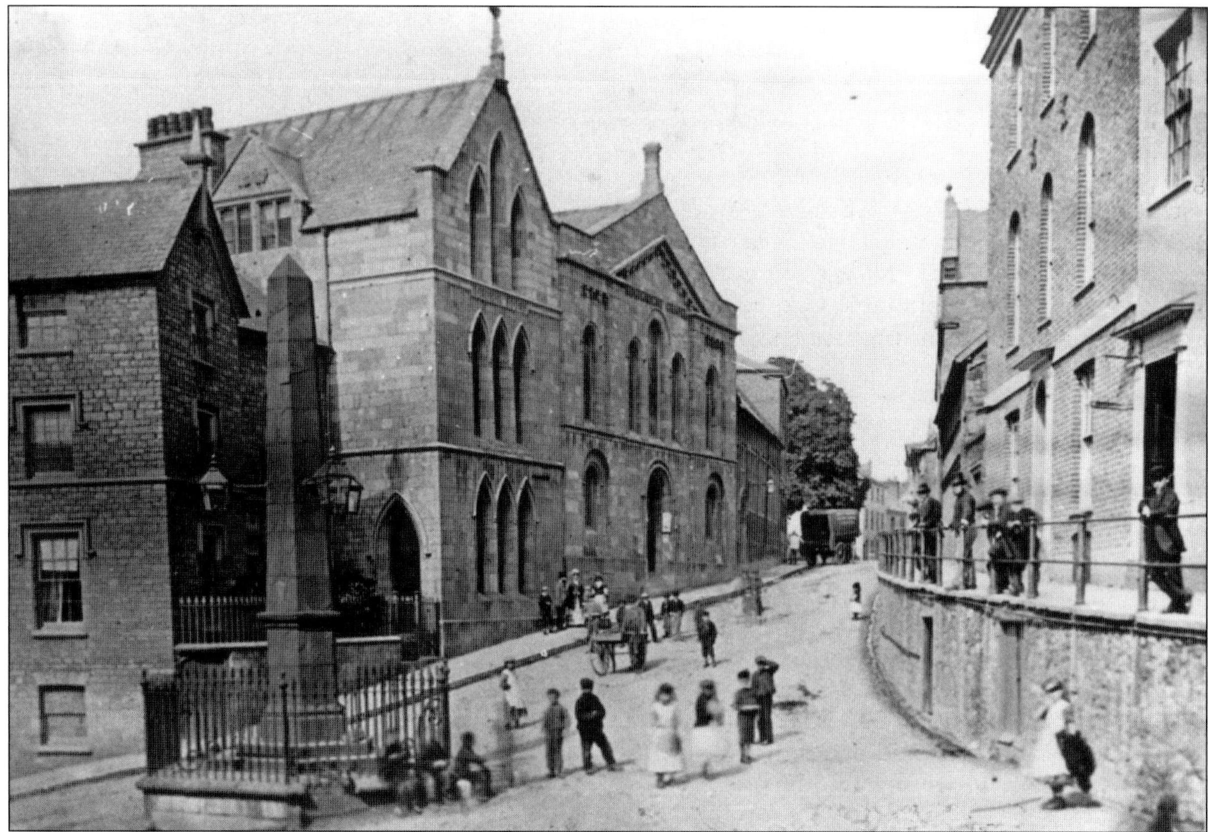

The Congregational Church on Angel Hill. The heirs of Cromwell's Ironsides. This is a nineteenth-century reconstruction (completed in 1837) and a development of the old Steps Meeting House, which John Wesley described as a 'dreary meeting house'. The obelisk was erected in 1840 and removed in 1868. MUSEUM COLLECTION

Chapter 3

Religious Strife and War, 1640–1715

The weaving and largely Nonconformist town of Tiverton.

From a letter from the Deputy Lord Lieutenant to the Duke of Albemarle 1684

By 1640 the government of Charles I was in deep trouble and deeply unpopular. His attempt to rule without Parliament had necessitated the collection of illegal revenue and the policies of Archbishop Laud, combined with the King's marriage to a French Roman Catholic Queen, seemed to be tending towards the revival of the Roman Catholic Church in England. An attempt to enforce the Prayer Book, as interpreted by Laud, on the Presbyterian Scots led to military and financial disaster. The formidable royal servant, the Earl of Strafford, persuaded the Irish Parliament to vote to provide the funds for an army to join in crushing the Scots, a largely Catholic Irish Army, and he misguidedly supposed he might similarly persuade an English Parliament. However, when Parliament met in 1640 it harped on grievances and was dissolved in three weeks. This so-called 'Short Parliament' left the King and Strafford determined to raise an army to defeat the Scots, which they signally failed to do and the Scots advanced into the northern counties, refusing to leave until they had been paid an indemnity and expenses. This forced Charles to call Parliament, as the country was in no mood to tolerate further illegal taxation or forced loans and this, the 'Long Parliament', met in October 1640 and sat, purged of its Cavaliers, until 1653.

A small echo of this quarrel can be seen in the composition of the clergy appointed to St Peter's in the 1630s. In 1634 the Crown obtained the right of appointment to Pitt and appointed George Peirce (as a Fellow of King's College he probably held Prior's as well.) Later events show him to have been a strong Royalist and critic of Parliament, so he was dispossessed in 1646 and restored in 1660. In 1641 Richard Newte became Rector of Clare, on the presentation of his father, Henry Newte, the Town Clerk. He was also the Chaplain of a prominent Royalist, the Earl of Bristol. Newte spent most of the Civil War abroad. Returning in 1646, he was expelled in 1650 for supporting Charles II. However, the fiercest Royalist of them all was Thomas Jones, whom the King appointed to Tidcombe in 1638. He was arrested in 1640 for preaching an anti-Parliamentarian sermon in St Peter's and was imprisoned at Taunton. He was later arrested again for superstitious practices (in other words, what Puritans considered to be Catholic) and fled to Rotterdam.

So there was in Tiverton a Royalist group created by royal power, centred on St Peter's. Probably royal inducements won over some of the Corporation, such as the first two Town Clerks, Henry Newte senr and junr who successively held office from 1615–55. Since 1626 they had chosen as one of their MPs, Peter Ball, a lawyer attached to the Court, whom they re-elected to the Short Parliament alongside Peter Sainthill, later a prominent Devon Royalist. To the Long Parliament they re-elected Sainthill and George Hartnoll, a Tiverton clothier. Sainthill later fled to Italy to escape Parliamentary vengeance and Hartnoll was expelled from the House for unreliability.

However this Royalist group was out of step with the mood of the town. Tiverton had long been a centre of Puritanism. In 1622 tradesmen had been indicted for contempt of the Prayer Book; William Chilcott and Henry Hobbs for being schismatical and holding secret conventicles. In 1624 and 1628 Richard Berry, clothier, had been imprisoned for separatist tendencies, and there was certainly a flourishing Anabaptist group in the town. In the 1630s a burst of Puritan-inspired iconoclasm destroyed the Courtenay Chapel. Moreover Tiverton was one of the foremost non-payers of ship-money in the county. A list of corporate non-payers, drawn up in 1637, is headed by Tiverton, which owed £130, followed by Exeter £35 and Barnstaple £11. The town was bitter as the government still owed money for billeting in the 1620s.

So when Charles raised his standard at Nottingham in August 1642, it is not surprising that Tiverton opted for a very warm support for Parliament. In 1642 a troop under Colonel John Were held Tiverton for Parliament, but probably because of the treachery of the Mayor, or perhaps of the Town Clerk, Henry Newte junr, Royalist forces from Cornwall snatched the town in May 1643, before moving eastwards. After their important victory at Marston Moor in July 1644, a Parliamentary force under Essex marched through Tiverton towards Cornwall and both Royalist and Parliamentary sources comment that the Parliamentarians were well received. Essex reported support for Parliament from Cullompton and Halberton as well. After Essex's defeat at Lostwithiel, Royalist forces only reoccupied the town with difficulty after skirmishing their way up Gold Street and the presence of a Royalist garrison in the castle can only have been because it was necessary to keep in check the town's tendency to support Parliament. Yet, in the autumn of 1645 local clubmen actually recaptured the castle for a time.

The most exciting part of Tiverton's war came in October 1645. After the Battle of Naseby, Parliamentary forces under Sir Thomas Fairfax moved west to capture Exeter, relieve the siege of Plymouth and defeat the Cornish Royalists. Fairfax might have moved through Cullompton to Exeter and left the Royalists in Tiverton Castle to wither on the vine, but this was judged an unnecessary risk, exposing the army's communications to raids from the Royalist Lord Goring's horse. So it was decided first to capture Tiverton and its bridge in order to keep Goring beyond the Exe.

On 17 October a vanguard under General Massey marched over the hill to Tiverton and set up his headquarters in Blundell's School. Forces were placed in Bradninch and Silverton to deter the Royalists in Exeter from any sortie. Saturday 18 October was spent preparing for the siege of the castle, which in those days had outworks that covered most of the northern parts of the churchyard and stretched to Newport Street and Castle Street. These outworks were defended by a moat, fed from the leat. Entrance to the castle over the moat was by a drawbridge.

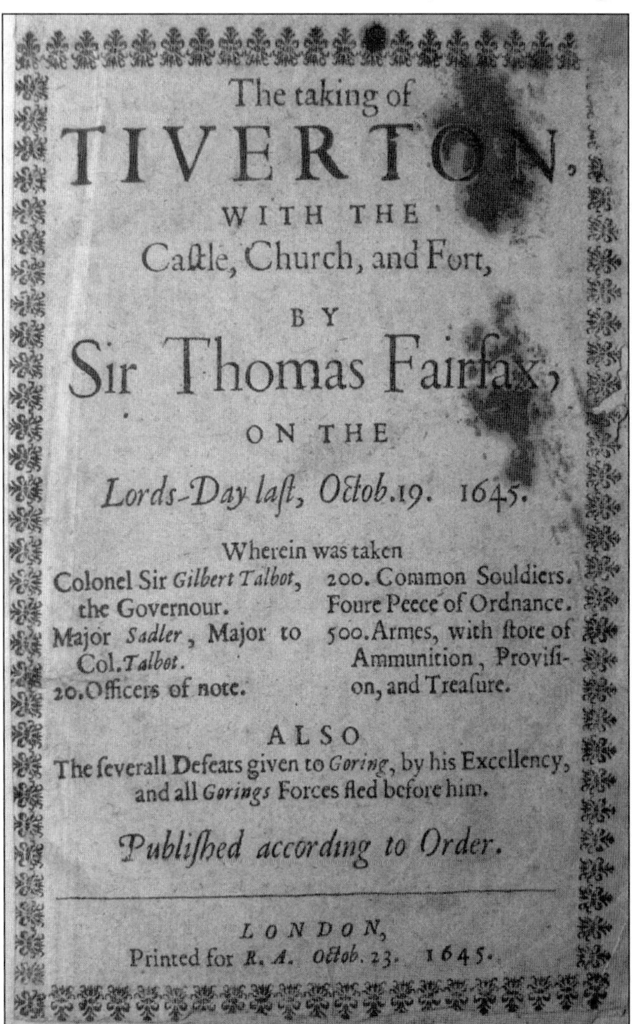

The taking of

TIVERTON,

WITH THE

Caſtle, Church, and Fort,

BY

Sir Thomas Fairfax,

ON THE

*Lords-Day laſt, Octob.*19. 1645.

Wherein was taken

Colonel Sir *Gilbert Talbot*, the Governour.

Major *Sadler*, Major to Col. *Talbot*.

20. Officers of note.

200. Common Souldiers.

Foure Peece of Ordnance.

500. Armes, with ſtore of Ammunition, Proviſion, and Treaſure.

ALSO

The ſeverall Defeats given to *Goring*, by his Excellency, and all *Gorings* Forces fled before him.

Publiſhed according to Order.

LONDON,

Printed for *R. A. Octob.* 23. 1645.

The frontispiece from a pamphlet in the Newte Library, part of the heritage of St Peter's Church donated by Revd John Newte. COLIN WHITE

It seems that, Puritans or not, the gunners began a cannonade on the morning of Sunday 19 October. The castle walls were not expected to stand for long as the attack was planned for the same afternoon, when a lucky shot is said to have burst the drawbridge chains and the bridge crashed down. Without waiting for orders, the godly soldiery rushed the castle and captured the churchyard, dividing the Royalist garrison into two, one part in the church, the other retreating into the castle. Some of the Parliamentarians pursued them into the castle, while some climbed through the windows into the church 'and attacked the Royalists with great fury in both places' (Dunsford). The surrender of the garrison and its commander, Sir Gilbert Talbot, soon followed: a total of 24 officers, 200 soldiers, four cannon, powder and provisions.

A letter was promptly dispatched to London with the glad news and the House of Commons:

> *... ordered that on the next Lord's day thanks be given unto God for the many successes it hath pleased God to give the Parliament's forces, this great blessing of God's delivering into the hands of Parliament Tiverton and the castle may be remembered, and thanks given unto God for this blessing also, the manner of taking thereof being very remarkable.*

It was now too late in the year to attack Exeter so Fairfax's army spent Christmas at Tiverton before destroying the last Royalist field army at Torrington in February 1646. The siege of Plymouth was lifted, Exeter captured in April and Charles I surrendered to the Scots in May. The first Civil War was over.

It cannot have been pleasant to have lived in Tiverton between 1642 and 1646. Civil War is always nasty and the years of Royalist success must have been alarming for the great majority. Plague hit the town in 1644 and 1646. Curiously previous accounts blame the plague's arrival on the arrival of Parliamentary forces, yet in both years there were Royalist forces in the town as well and plague was a visitant at times when there were no wars. But then Snell, Harding and Sampson were all pro-Royalist!

Certainly there had been very few Royalists in Tiverton. In 1655–56 Major-General Desborough, in charge of the South West, drew up a list of all the disaffected Devonians known to him, 963 in all. Taking Tiverton's male population in 1642 from the Protestation returns as between 1,700 and 1,800, the Tiverton names on Desborough's list work out at approximately half a percent, whereas for Exeter the figure was six percent of the adult male population. This small core of Tiverton's Royalists could expect hostility. The Royalist clergy, regarded by their neighbours as crypto-Catholics, would have to be ejected – after all the war had been as much against Laud's policies as anything else. Peirce was expelled from Pitt immediately and Royalist accounts harp on

Right: *Sir Thomas Fairfax, 1612–71, who took the castle and chased the hated Royalists out of town. A moderate Parliamentarian he resigned his posts in 1649, refusing to take part in Charles' trial. He and Samuel Foote probably had much in common.*

NATIONAL PORTRAIT GALLERY

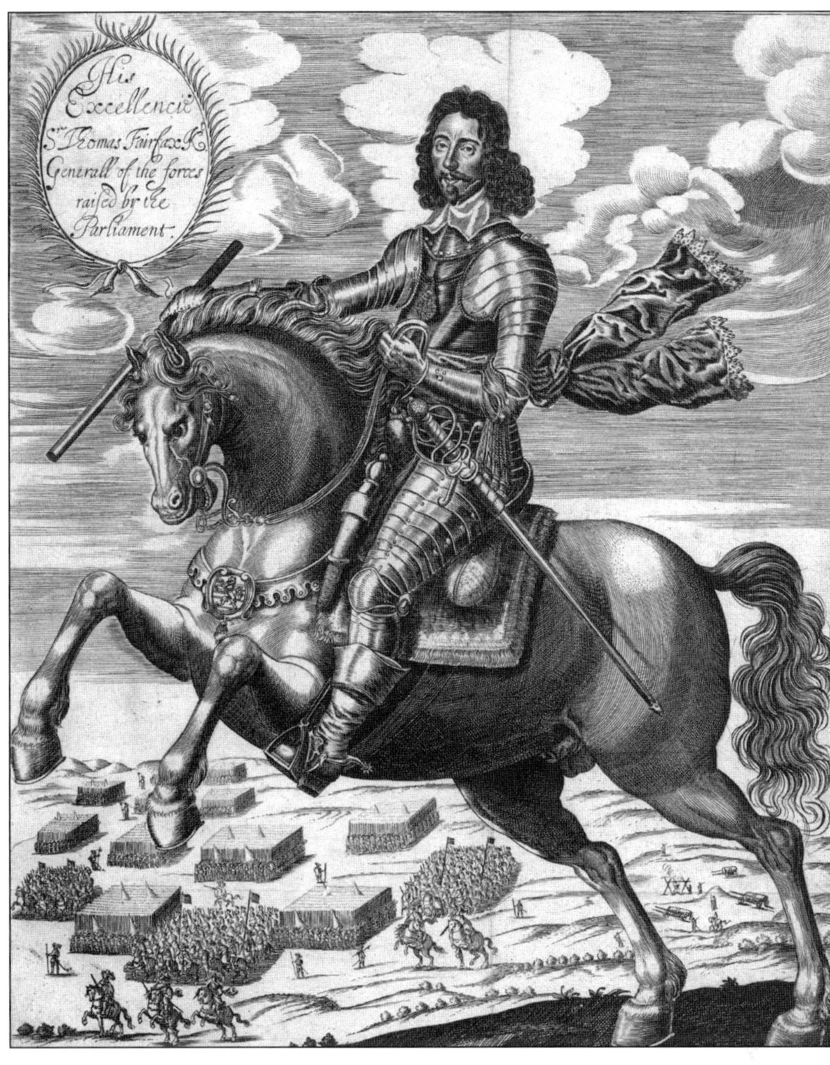

Below and below right: *Tiverton Castle, which Cromwell, or rather Fairfax, knocked about a bit in 1645.*

MUSEUM COLLECTION

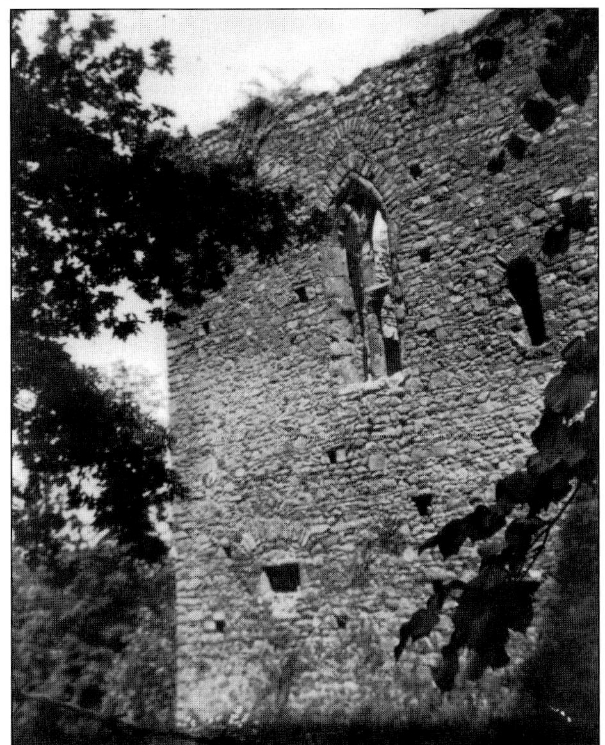

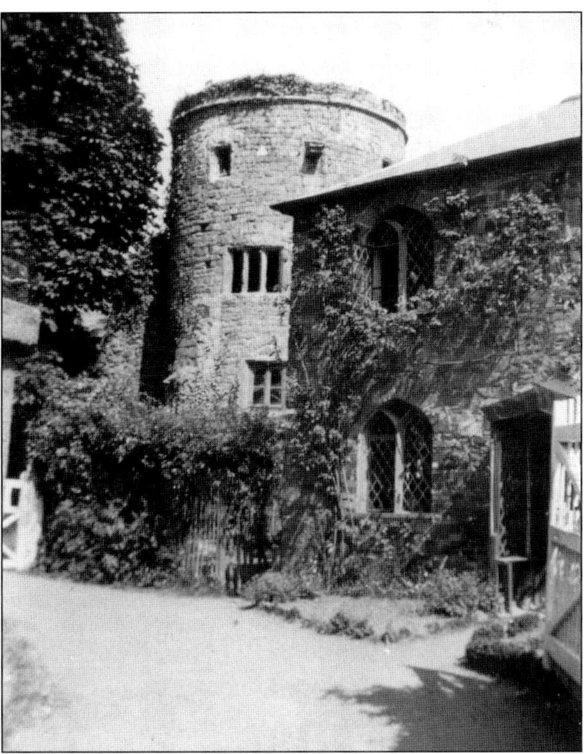

his sufferings, but he obtained livings in Kent, Hertfordshire and Bedfordshire, where in 1660 he had a stipend of £80 a year, so his was quite a comfortable suffering. Newte was examined by Parliamentary 'Triers and Ejectors', found to be unacceptable to the new regime and ejected, but he found a new berth at Heanton. Peirce and Newte were replaced by Chisul and Polwhele, Independents both. The Cromwellian 'system' divided church endowments between Presbyterians, Independents and Baptists and, as long as ministers were Protestant and did not use the hated Laudian Prayer Book, there was freedom of worship. Although the use of the Prayer Book and the open practice of Roman Catholicism were prohibited, the private exercise of their faiths was allowed to Anglicans. Even Jews were allowed back into England. This wide and humane religious toleration explains the genuine power and popularity of the Commonwealth in towns such as Tiverton. Later, competitive propaganda accounts made much of the sufferings of the ejected Cavalier clergy of 1646–50 and of the ejected Puritan clergy of 1660–62 and these accounts nurtured bitterness for 200 years.

The total military defeat of the Royalists did not end political controversy. Two big issues remained to be decided. What was to be the new Church settlement? And what form would the government of the country take? During the war, as the price of a Scottish alliance, Parliament had promised to introduce a Presbyterian Settlement: a Church without bishops and ruled by elders, an order of service conforming with Calvinist theology and a system of moral discipline imposed by the state, which could be compared with Sharia Law. Most of the MPs who supported Parliament were Presbyterian, and probably George Hartnoll was one of them. However, Cromwell and the Army wanted Independency, meaning freedom for individual (Protestant only) consciences and independence for each self-governing congregation. Extrapolating from the pre-war evidence I suggest that the wealthier merchants, such as Hartnoll were Presbyterian, while the majority of the artisans and tradesmen were Independent. Further victories by the Army ensured victory for Independency.

The form of government was also finally decided on the battlefield. The Presbyterian Scots and the Presbyterians in Parliament tried to do a deal with the King, tried to persecute Independent congregations and tried to avoid settling the soldiers back pay. A trinity of miscalculations. The Army was bubbling with ideas of freedom of conscience and rank democracy. As Colonel Rainsborough put it, 'The poorest he in England hath a life to live as the greatest he.' The laws of both God and Nature proved every man ought to have 'the choice of those who are to make the laws for him to live under.' The defeat of the Presbyterian Scots at Preston led to Colonel Thomas Pride's Purge of the Presbyterian MPs, the execution of King Charles I in January 1649 and the abolition of the House of Lords in February 1649. It has been said that the Tiverton Corporation changed their red gowns to black in mourning for Charles I, executed in 1649. Equally likely, the change was a typically Puritan rejection of colour in favour of sobriety, a lay equivalent to the whitewashing away of colour in the churches. The next few years were spent establishing the Army's control of Ireland and Scotland, with the ultimate defeat of Charles II, the Royalists, the Roman Catholics and the Presbyterians at Worcester in 1651.

In 1653 Cromwell tried to rule in partnership with a Parliament nominated from the Independent congregations, named after one of its prominent members (Praise-God Barebones) the 'Barebones Parliament.' This unusual body anticipated the future by proposing to abolish tithe and establishing civil marriage before a JP, the first Tiverton example of which, between Joshua Fursley and Margaret Hollbiam, took place before the Mayor in October 1653. A total of 559 marriages are recorded in the registers between 1653 and 1660, almost double the usual rate for the period between 1600 and 1800. In fact St Peter's may have been used by more Tivertonians between 1653 and 1660 than at any time since the end of the Old Religion in the 1540s.

The new system of government introduced in 1654 allowed a House of Commons elected by all who possessed property worth £200, a not dissimilar qualification to the £10 householder franchise of 1832. So Tiverton saw its first proper election in 1654, when Robert Shapcott was re-elected. Shapcott was first elected in 1646 and served continuously to the end of the Convention Parliament of 1660. He was swept away in 1661. Changes were also made in the Corporation after some Royalist disturbances in 1655, disturbances that Tivertonians had been involved in suppressing. As a result of the unrest, Cromwell temporarily divided England into regions under the control of Major-Generals. Desborough, in charge of Devon and Cornwall, ordered the removal of Skinner, Deyman, Waldron, Prowse and Hartnoll from the Corporation, all names associated with the wealthy merchant families of the Tiverton establishment, and their replacement by Bere, Berry, Fitzwilliam, Foote and Wood, some of whose names are 'strange', but those like Berry which are familiar had been associated with the pre-war Anabaptists. Some of the 'Desborough men' would have long local careers and were probably not in fact strangers. Foote survived the Restoration and became an MP, 'elected' by the Corporation from about 1670 to the 1690s, a Thomas Bere was elected in the 1690 and lasted until 1710. Fitzwilliam was Town Clerk from 1655–86. At points of high Tory revival, such as the 1680s, they tended to lose their places, to recover them after 1688.

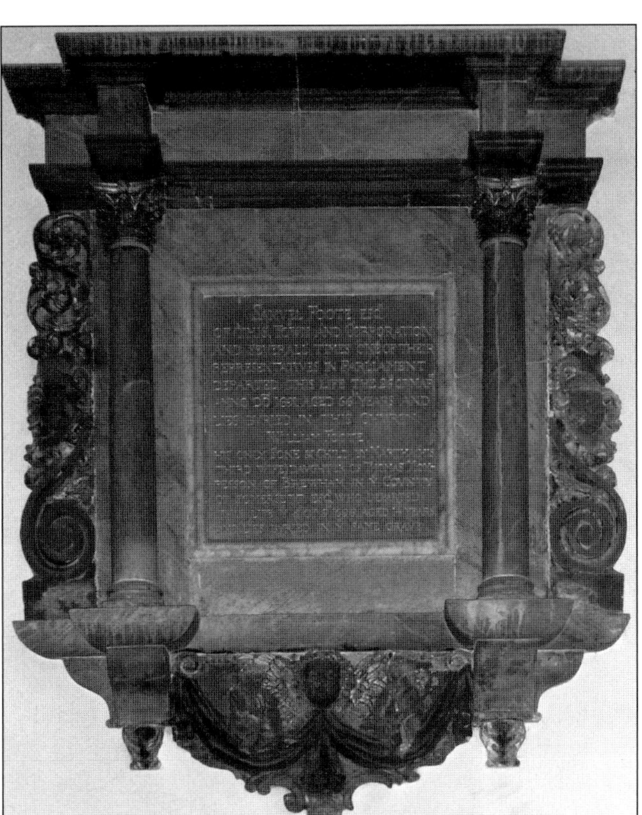

The memorial to Samuel Foote, 1625–91, on the south wall of St Peter's Church. In the 1650s he was one of the pillars of the Parliamentary establishment in Tiverton. However, he was a 'survivor'; come the Restoration he became a Churchman, member of the Corporation and Mayor and 'the furious persecutor of those he had formerly owned as Saints'. Despite all this, he never became a Royalist of the Newte sort and was a supporter of William of Orange in 1688. COLIN WHITE

A permanent result of the changes of 1655 was the removal of the market from Mondays to Tuesdays, a good Puritan measure as it avoided folks working to prepare for market on the Sabbath, thereby avoiding divine punishment by fire.

Religious toleration, a wider franchise, civil marriages and a triumphant foreign policy probably led to the Protectorate being more popular in Tiverton than any government before 1832. As Dunsford wrote, 'during the Protectorate the trade of Tiverton was in a prosperous state and population rapidly increased.' However, all of this depended on the life of Cromwell and after his death in 1658, only the Restoration of a carefully circumscribed monarchy, dependent on Parliament, seemed to guarantee the rule of law. Charles II's return in 1660 was greeted by a temporary hysteria of joy, similar to that which greeted New Labour in 1997, and equally prone to evaporate. In May 1660 the Restoration was a product of the temporary unity of Presbyterians and Catholics as well as the temporarily displaced ruling classes of peers and squires – of all who feared the Army, Independency and the germs of democ-

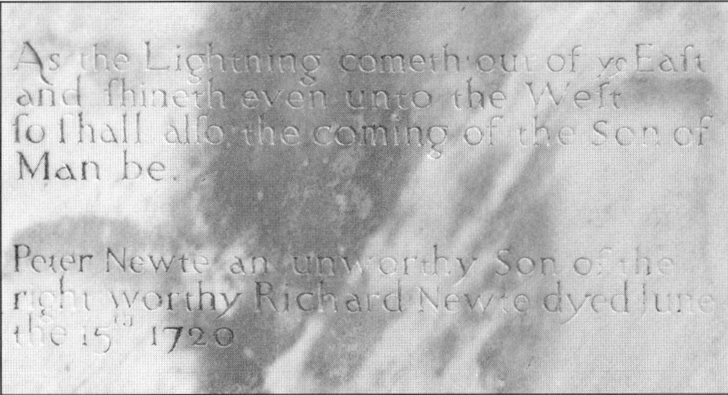

A Newte memorial. COLIN WHITE

racy that had accompanied both. The initial split was in the Church, with a later split taking place in Parliament. Both had an impact on Tiverton.

The years 1661–63 saw a large, if not larger, ejection of clergy from the Church of England, than that which had taken place in 1646. It has been estimated that 2,000 clergy were ejected for refusing to make the required declaration under the 1662 Act of Uniformity that the Prayer Book contained nothing contrary to the word of God. Pastor Chisul was ejected from Pitt and George Peirce returned. Polwhele was ejected from Tidcombe and Clare and Richard Newte, the son of the first Town Clerk recovered his livings, and began the Newte dominance of St Peter's which lasted until 1792. This Richard was succeeded in Tidcombe by his son John in 1678, by his grandson Samuel in 1716, his great-grandson, also Samuel, in 1742, and his great-great grandson John in 1782, who died in 1792. Richard Newte also held Clare from 1660–78 and was succeeded by his son-in-law from 1678–21. John Newte held Pitt as well as Tidcombe from 1680–1716 and Samuel Newte II held it from 1734–81. They built Tidcombe Rectory and the hill behind is named after them.

The Newtes were obviously wealthy and important and during the years of their prominence St Peter's received many good things. The most famous of these was the organ, and the most elegant the candelabra which dates from Queen Anne's reign.

However, they were party men, devoted to the Church of England, particularly in the years 1660–1715 when that Church vigorously persecuted Dissenters. As Dunsford wrote:

> *Mr Newte [John] was much attached to the interest of the Church of England and assiduous in promoting its principles in the minds of the rising generation... He had imbibed the political principles of passive obedience and non-resistance.*

Dunsford did not intend these words to be ones of praise and must be seen in the light his judgement of the reign of Charles II:

> *The dissipated, corrupting and despotic principles of that impolitic government revived with augmented*

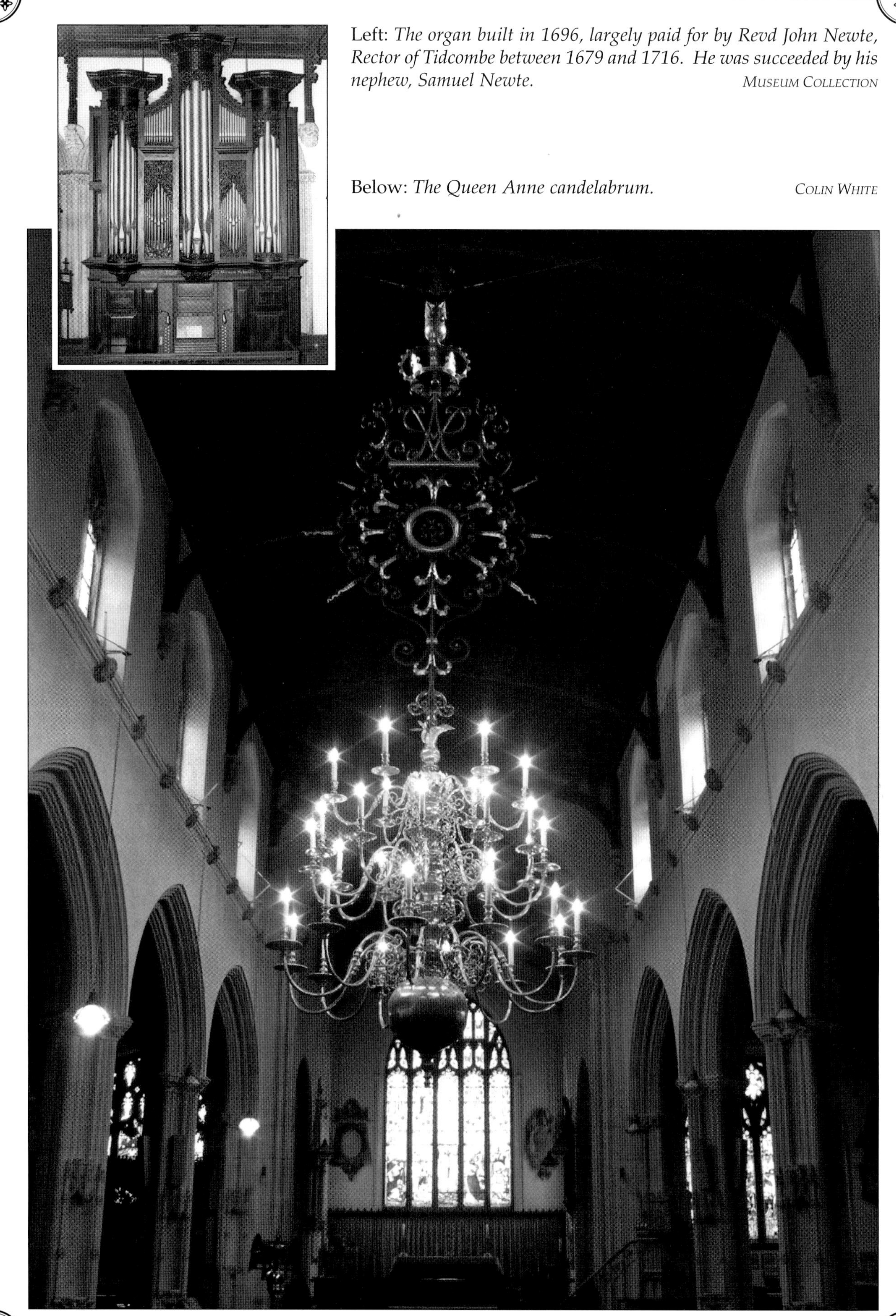

Left: *The organ built in 1696, largely paid for by Revd John Newte, Rector of Tidcombe between 1679 and 1716. He was succeeded by his nephew, Samuel Newte.* MUSEUM COLLECTION

Below: *The Queen Anne candelabrum.* COLIN WHITE

bitterness the feuds... that had occasioned the late Civil Wars... the persecuting spirit of the times established unfriendly distinctions between citizens... reputable traders, manufacturers and labourers were harassed, imprisoned and impoverished for their non-conformity to the religious opinions and public services of the Church of England.

Local persecution there certainly was. The Clarendon Code was strictly enforced. This was a series of statutes passed in the early 1660s that denied non-Anglicans membership of town Corporations, forbade attendance at non-Anglican religious meetings and forbade any non-Anglican educational activity within five miles of a town. Both Richard Saunders and Polwhele were persecuted for holding conventicles in Tiverton. In 1672, not to help Dissenters, but as a plan to win their support in his project to turn England Catholic, Charles issued a Declaration of Indulgence which allowed freedom of worship. There were immediate applications from Tiverton dissenters; Polwhele's flock asked that a licence be given to hold services at the house of Peter Bere, the Steps Meeting House, and Saunders requested permission to use first Blundell's School then William Wood's house. William Facey asked to use a house in St Peter Street. Facey was a Baptist, Polwhele a Congregationalist and Saunders perhaps Presbyterian. A survey of religious opinion in 1676 gave the number of active Nonconformists in Tiverton as 500, second only in Devon to Plymouth.

If St Peter's was in the hands of the High Anglican Newtes, probably the Town Council and the Blundell's feoffees were not so inclined. No Newte was ever Mayor or Blundell's feoffee and, when in 1715 John Newte left lands in Bampton to endow a scholarship at Balliol College, Oxford, for a pupil of Blundell's School, he willed that the pupil be chosen by the Rectors of St Peter's and not by the Blundell's Feoffees. As stated, Richard Saunders had asked to use the school as the venue for Dissenting meetings and in 1684 the feoffees appointed his son John to the Blundell's mastership, in spite of the fact that his father had been sent to jail as recently as 1681 for illegal preaching. It is clear that there were deep divisions in Tiverton in the 1680s, which corresponded to the national divisions that would be called Whigs and Tories.

National politics in the 1680s were dominated by fears of Roman Catholicism in the royal family. Charles II's mother was a Roman Catholic, his favourite sister and his brother and heir, James, were dedicated Catholics and there were well-founded fears that the nominal head of the Church of England, Charles II himself, was a secret Roman Catholic. A series of Parliaments espoused 'Exclusion' – to exclude James from the succession and to put the Protestant Duke of Monmouth, an illegitimate son of Charles II, on the throne after Charles. In these Exclusion Parliaments one of Tiverton's MPs was Samuel Foote, who had risen in Tiverton's life after his appointment to the Corporation by Desborough in 1655 and who was surely a keen Exclusionist, particularly as state papers suggest he was importing arms for the Civil War that might have broken out.

When the Exclusion campaign ran out of steam and Charles felt able to dissolve Parliament, he set about reshaping Town Charters so that the MPs elected by towns such as Tiverton would be well disposed to the Stuarts. In 1683 the new Charter appointed Henry Blagdon as Mayor and the Duke of Albemarle as Recorder and some obvious outsiders, Sir Hugh Acland and Sir Peter Prideaux, on to the Corporation. One point of these changes was that the party that possessed the Recordership possessed the ability to use the law to persecute the other party. Such a grandee as the Duke, key courtier and Chancellor of Cambridge University, would not have done the job himself, but would have appointed a deputy. He was also made Recorder of Colchester, and probably of other towns too, all as part of a Royalist Anglican attempt to produce a more pliant Parliament. James II's first Parliament sat in 1685 and the remodelled Corporation elected Sir Henry Acland and William Coleman. Foote was returned again in 1688 after the Glorious Rebellion had placed William of Orange on the throne. His memorial is on the south wall of St Peter's; he was obviously a politician of skill.

Sharp politics became sharper with the Monmouth Rebellion in 1685. Many Tiverton men joined this Protestant enterprise, but after its defeat at Sedgemoor, the bells of St Peter's were rung in celebration of the victory of the Catholic King James II. While the Tories rejoiced, other Tivertonians were whipped, fined, transported and beheaded in the peculiarly brutal form of 'hanging, drawing and quartering'. Some of the butchered limbs, preserved with tar and salt, were erected for deterrent display at the roads on the edges of the town and the head of a Dissenting minister was put on a pole in Fore Street.

James took heart from Monmouth's defeat and tried to persuade Parliament to repeal the Test Act and allow Catholics legally to hold office. Even this most Tory of Parliaments refused, so James again began a comprehensive policy of remodelling Chartered Corporations to insert Catholics into positions of power. To do so he issued a Declaration of Indulgence to try to win the Dissenters to his side. In the winter of 1687–88, 15 members of the Council and Albemarle, the Recorder, were all dismissed. Tiverton's Charter was again called in and reissued in 1688. The nominated Mayor was Roger Pomeroy, two Catholics Cary and Southcott became Burgesses and the Catholic Earl of Castlemaine, Recorder.

However no MPs were chosen by this body as national events led to the abdication of James II and the reign of William and Mary. The political monopoly

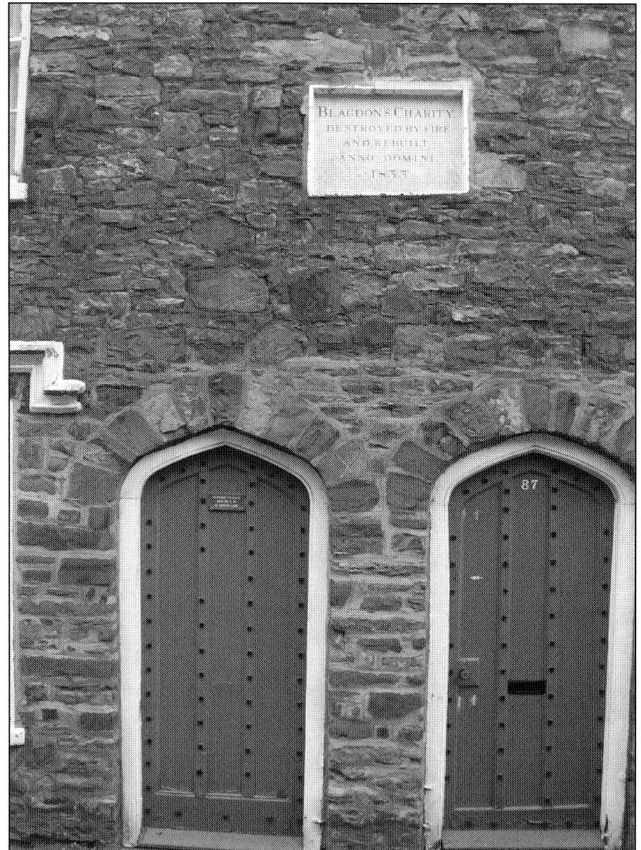

Above: *Blagdon's Charity in Barrington Street. Henry Blagdon died in 1715, and was one of those who planned the building of St George's Church as a place of refuge within the Anglican tent for Presbyterians who might have otherwise been discriminated against if Queen Anne had lived longer.*

of the Church of England was re-established, but it was accompanied by religious toleration. This allowed the previously intermittent dissenting congregations to emerge into the full light of day. Polwhele's Congregationalists now had a continuous history at the Steps Meeting House; the Presbyterians, under Richard Saunders were at Back Lane, Westexe; the Baptists in Newport Street. The law made tacit allowances for Dissenters who 'occasionally' attended Church of England services, thus qualifying for office.

The settlement of 1688–89 did not end the conflict between Anglicans and Dissenters in Tiverton, but it took some of the sting out of it. When the Tories came to power in 1710 they attempted to get at their enemies through the Occasional Conformity Act to prevent Dissenters qualifying for office by 'occasionally' attending Anglican services, and through the Schism Act to destroy Dissenters' schools as a prelude to further persecution. As part of Anglicanism's triumph, a beginning was made to a new church at the top of St Andrew Street, its foundation stone laid in 1714. One of the main subscribers was Henry Blagdon, probably a Nonconformist and a wealthy merchant, whose name is on a property in Barrington Street.

Perhaps the Tories were planning to bring back the Catholic son of James II, but Queen Anne died in 1714 before their plans were ready, and the perceived need for a new church for conforming Dissenters evaporated. With the accession of George I, in spite of rebellions in Scotland, the age of religious civil conflict, as opposed to bitchiness and mob violence, ended in Tiverton. St George's use as a church only started in the 1730s.

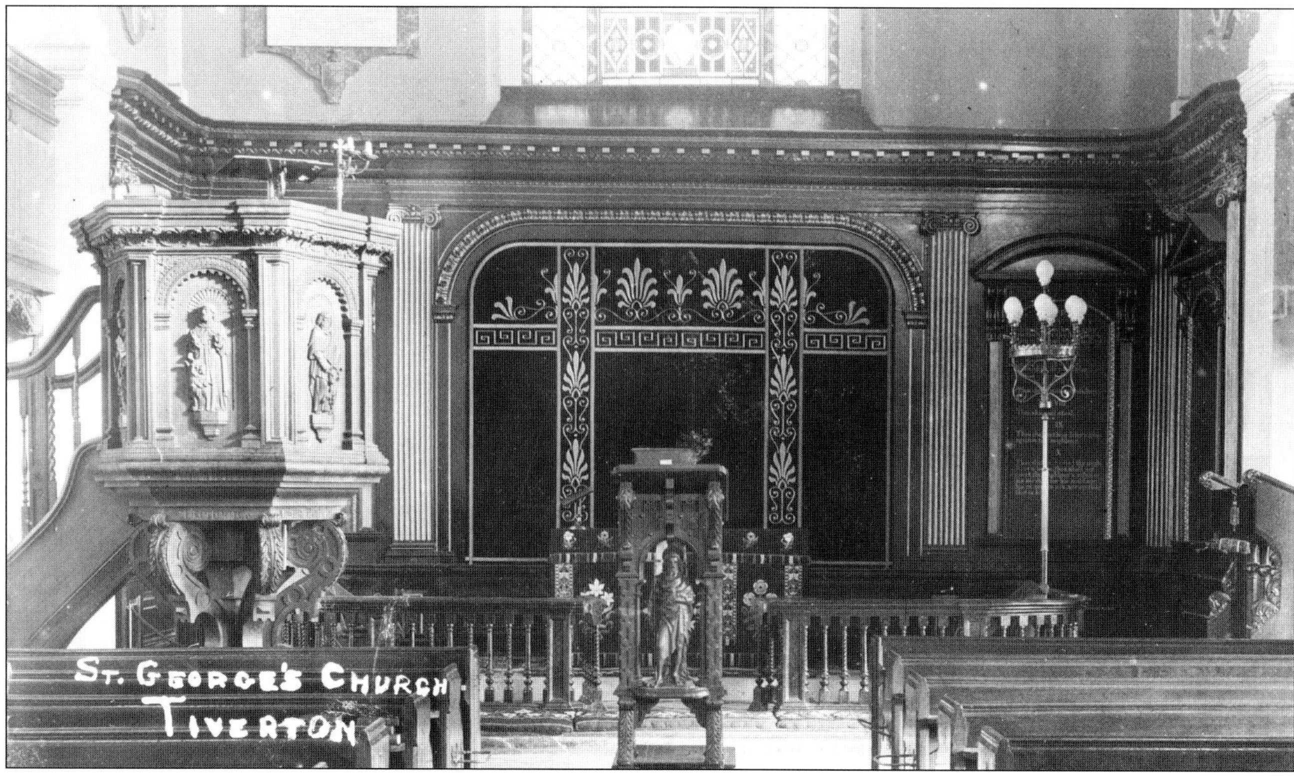

Below: *St George's interior.* MUSEUM COLLECTION

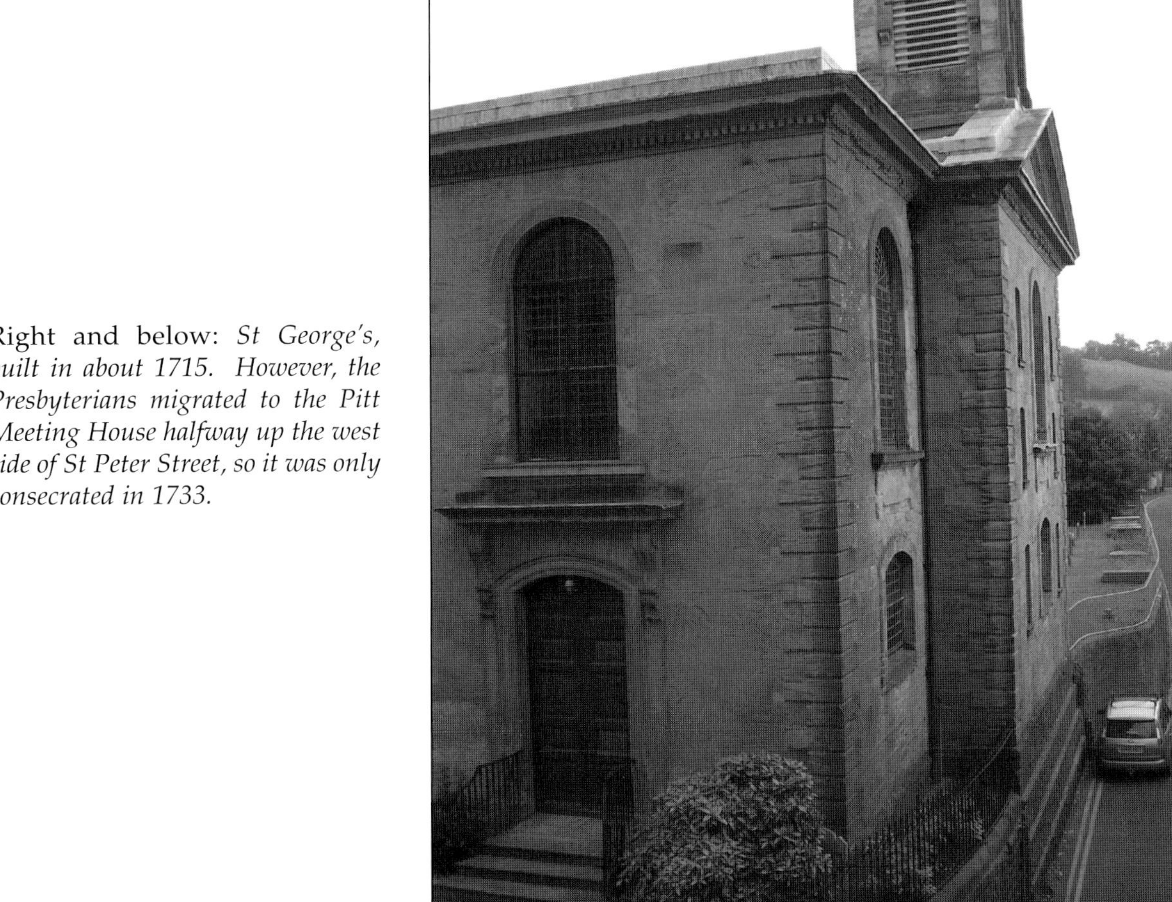

Right and below: *St George's, built in about 1715. However, the Presbyterians migrated to the Pitt Meeting House halfway up the west side of St Peter Street, so it was only consecrated in 1733.*

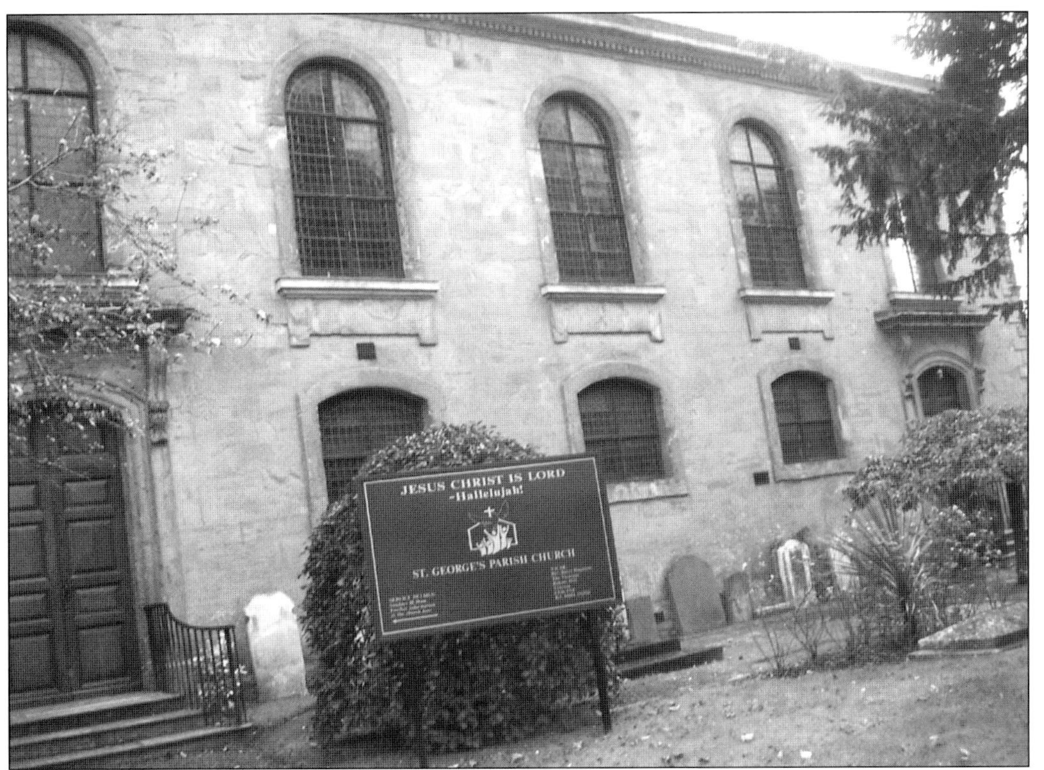

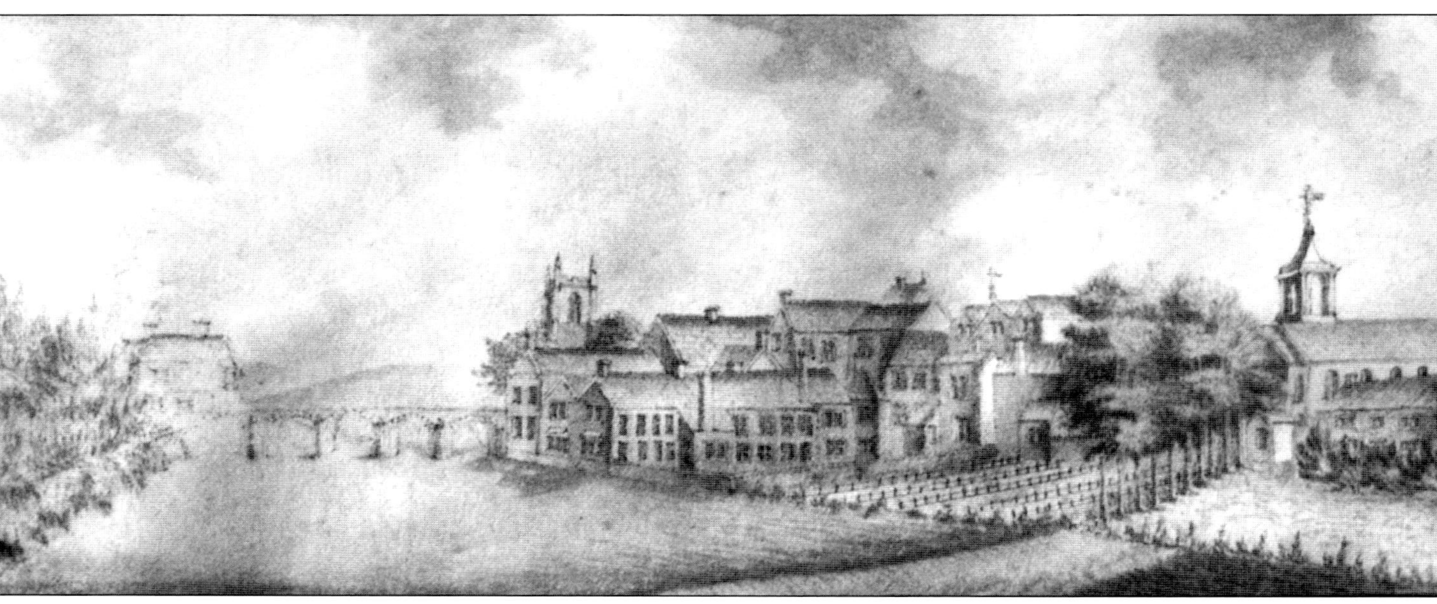

Right: *This eighteenth-century drawing shows the newly completed St George's as well as the old tennis-court area heavily built upon and the rear view of the old Angel. Note the rows of cloth-drying racks, probably for drying cloth that had been dyed. The fire of 1612 was started by the furnace of a dyer's shop on Angel Hill. The arched bridge lasted until the 1960s.*

COLIN WHITE

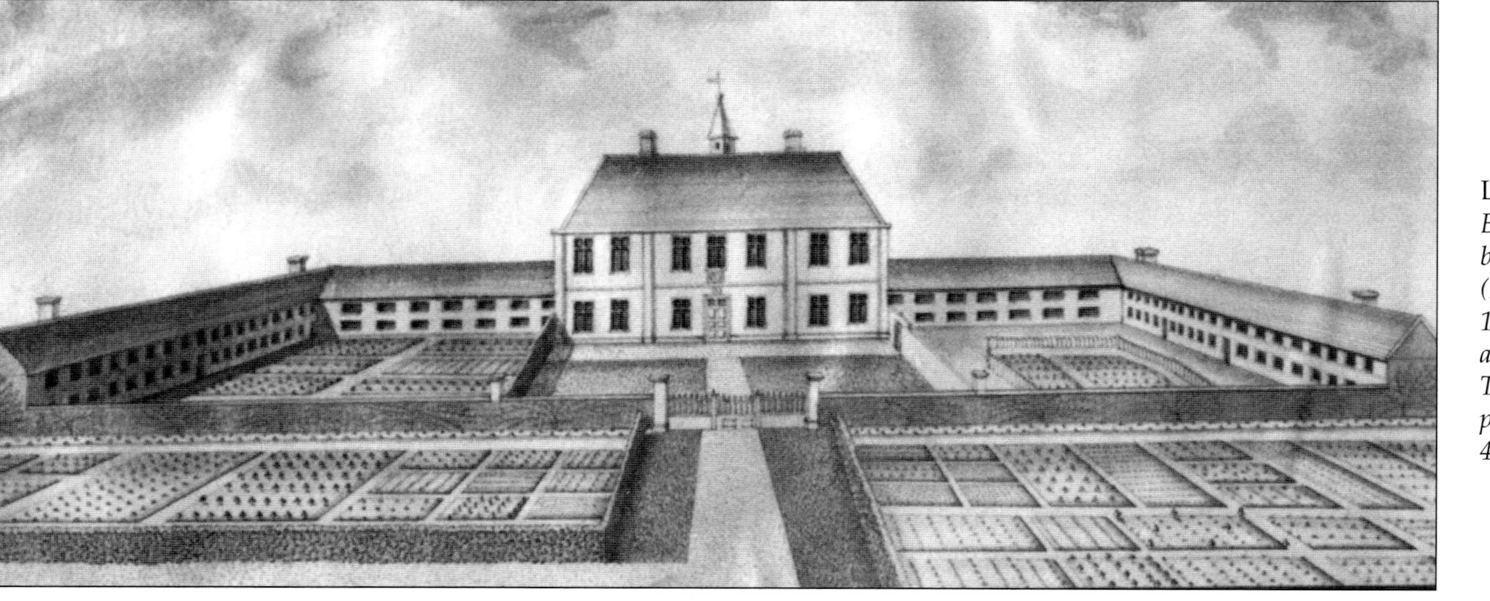

Left: *Tiverton Hospital. Built in 1699 and replaced by the Union Workhouse (Belmont Hospital) in the 1830s, this was a civilised attempt at a solution to Tiverton's 'third world' poverty. See map on page 46 for its location.*

COLIN WHITE

Chapter 4

Georgian Tiverton: Elegance, Riot and Decay

Next to Exeter Tiverton is the greatest manufacturing town in the county and, of all the inland towns, is next to it in wealth and numbers of people.

Defoe, 1724

They have a small manufacture here of serges and druggets, which with the thorough fare is the chief support of the town.

Richard Pococke, Travels through England,1750

In the sixteenth century, Tiverton had been one of the great cloth towns of England and most of that prosperity lingered to the end of the seventeenth century and into the early eighteenth. Attempts at arriving at accurate population figures for any period before the first census in 1801 are very difficult. Dunsford surveyed the parish in 1790 and produced some interesting results. His gross population for the parish was 7,096, of which the 'town within the turnpike gates' share was 5,343. Children accounted for 2,933 out of that 7,096, or 41 percent. Unfortunately he does not say what he meant by children. Did he mean, at one arithmetical extreme, those incapable of work – the 'under eights' – or, at the other extreme, those under 21? Working from the parish records Dunsford found that the number of burials over the six years prior to 1790 worked out at one burial to just over 43 inhabitants. Using that ratio he estimated Tiverton's population as having been 2,545 in 1565, rising to 8,228 in 1645 (surely an overestimate as the death rate in that time of dislocation was probably higher than one in 43), and becoming 6,742 in 1665. The maximum was reached between 1700 and 1730 when Dunsford thought the population was about 8,700. The first census in 1801 gave Tiverton only 6,505 inhabitants. Even if Dunsford was only half right we are still looking at a population decline of about 20 percent between 1730 and 1801.

Tiverton's population decline is even more serious when seen in the national context. In 1688 Gregory King came to the conclusion that the population of England and Wales was 5.5 million. The 1801 census showed the population of England and Wales to be 8.9 million, an increase of over 60 percent since King's estimate in 1688. In the 1730s Sheffield's population was less than 50 percent of Tiverton's town population, yet by 1760 its population was more than double Tiverton's. Furthermore, one finds that between 1801 and 1931 Tiverton's population rose 50 percent from 6,505 to 9,610, while the population of England and Wales rose 400 percent from just under 9 million to 35 million. Equally serious one also finds that whatever spells of industrial prosperity the town achieved after 1740 were achieved through the intervention of outsiders and were not home grown.

As to the prosperity of early-eighteenth century Tiverton one can do no better than to quote Dunsford:

The sensible and prudent administration of George I [Whiggish Walpole], elected by several Parliaments to preserve the civil and religious liberties of the people, extinguished the torch of persecution and the rage of opposition. Throughout the whole reign trade and commerce greatly flourished in Tiverton; population arrived at its highest state; and multitudes from all the surrounding parishes within a circuit of ten miles, and many manufacturers in Exeter were employed in the trade of Tiverton.

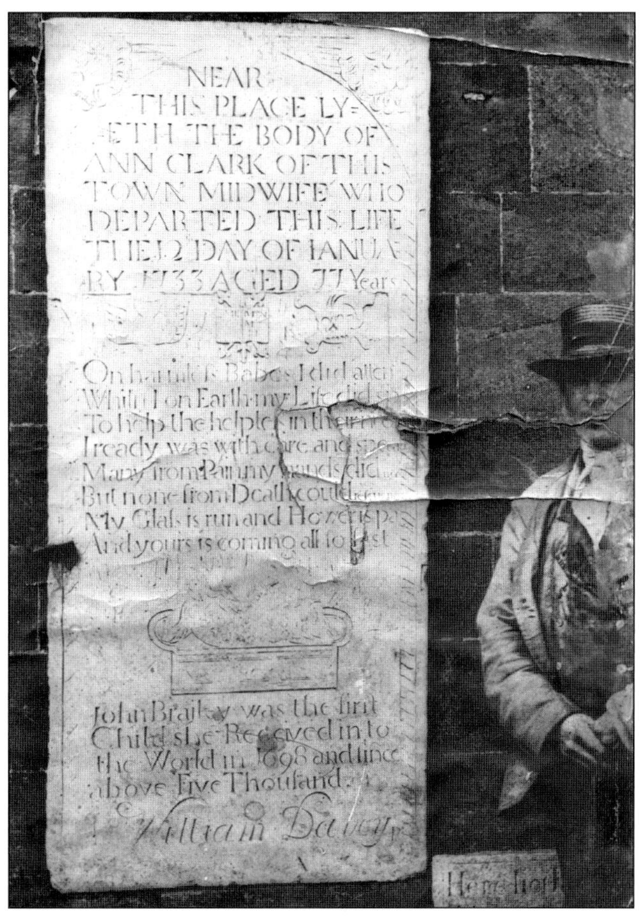

A famous tombstone in St George's churchyard, remembering Ann Clark, 1666–1733, midwife to Tiverton's growing population. The stone is graced by a charming verse – read it on your way to visit the museum! MUSEUM COLLECTION

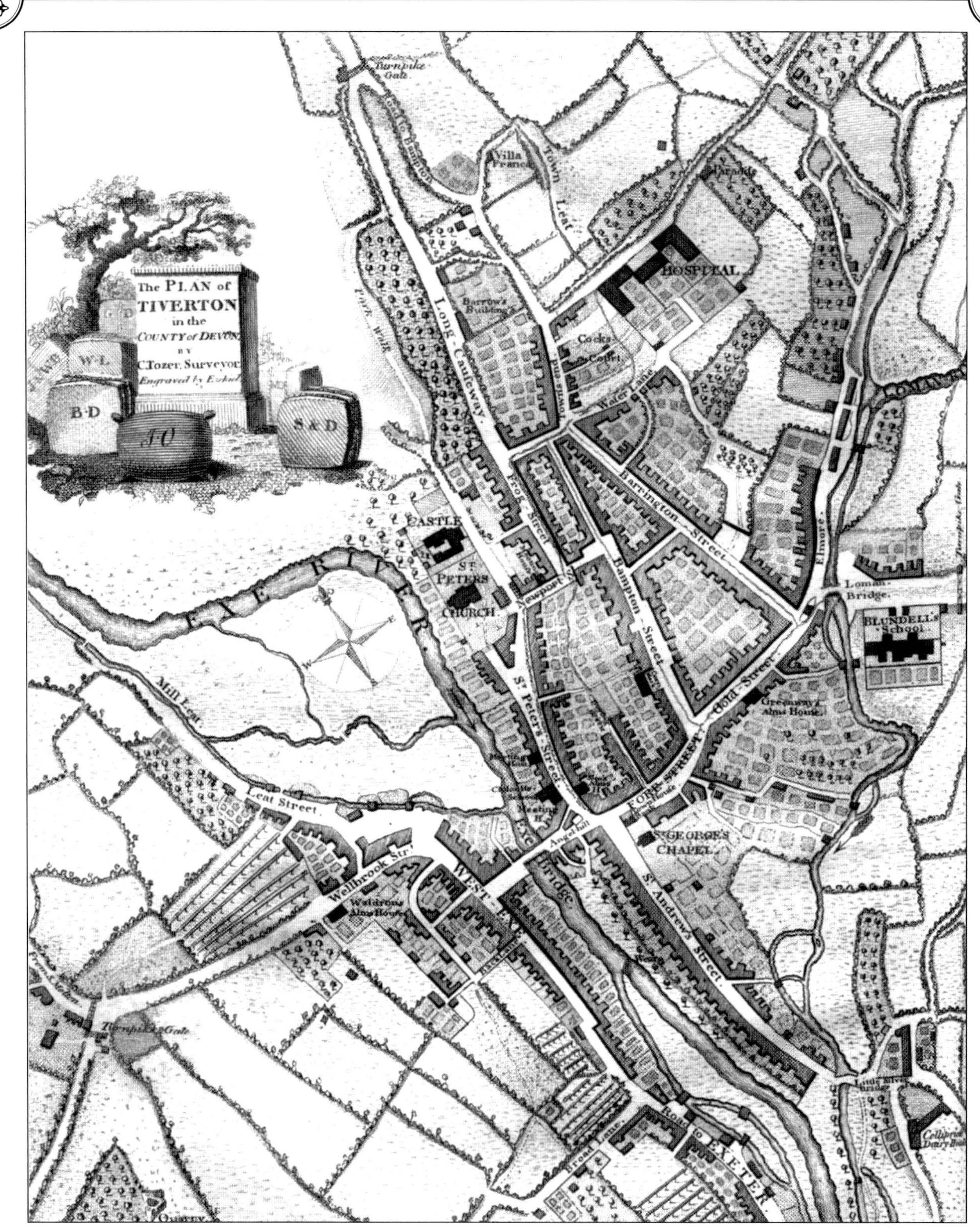

The map of eighteenth-century Tiverton from Dunsford. Note the drying racks to the west of Leat Street and in Westexe South. In mid century there were said to be over 50 mills in Tiverton and this explains the great number of leats on the rivers. The Town Leat can be seen and its tributaries can be seen flowing down all the main streets. Looking at the map will help understanding of the view of the factory on page 52. The Pitt Meeting House, later the Theatre, is half way up St Peter St on the left. At the exits from the town the Turnpike Gates can be seen.

He continues by listing the names of the leading merchants: Burridge, Thorne, Enchmarch, Upcott, Lewis, Carthew, Peard and Broad, many of whom he suggested exported 600 serges a week. He stated that perhaps 1,500 looms were in regular use in the parish, 700 wool combers employed and lists 56 fulling mills in regular operation.

This is still a picture of pre-factory industry. The merchants used their capital to oil the trade, buying wool from farmers, distributing it washed to the carders or combers, collecting it from them and distributing it to the spinsters (who, being women, do not take a great part in the story), collecting and distributing it to the weavers, who may have been full-timers, but who were often farmers who wove part-time. The unfinished cloth would then be collected and fulled, dyed, finished and marketed.

Occasional shadows of disquiet suggest all was not entirely rosy. In 1720 the merchants tried to import worsted yarn from Ireland, where labour costs were lower. It provoked the fierce resentment of the wool combers, who attacked the merchants' houses and destroyed the Irish goods. This led to the Battle of Oat Hill (now Angel Hill, but then so called as it was the site of the oat market), between the special constables enrolled by the magistrates and the wool combers, who had armed themselves with staves from a plundered load of wood. Public order was only restored with the aid of the military.

The decline, when it came, seems to have been rapid. There was some sort of bitter dissension in the Corporation, which may have reflected rivalries among the merchants, perhaps connected with this Irish yarn business. It certainly reflected the ambitions of those 'out of power' to have the good things that control of a 'rotten borough' could bring. On Mayor-Choosing Day in 1723, then August 27, the Mayor, Samuel Burridge, absented himself, so that it was impossible for the remainder of the Corporation legally to elect the Mayor for 1723–24 so the Charter immediately lapsed. The majority of the Corporators, led by John Upcott, a Westexe merchant, illegally elected John Tristram, and on Mayor-Choosing Day in 1724 Upcott's party, meeting in Wyatt's Coffee House, elected Roger Chamberlain. An A.W. Upcott had been Mayor in 1715, but John Upcott, Tristram and Chamberlain were never Mayors. It looks as if a group of 'lesser' Corporators were trying to displace the dominant Burridge-Thorne clique – between 1710 and 1740 a Burridge was Mayor six times and a Thorne seven times.

That Dunsford describes the Upcott party as 'more friendly to the liberties of the people' raises another question, that of the right to vote. Apparently Thorne and Burridge used all their influence to gain signatures on a petition begging for a new Charter 'insinuating' (Dunsford's word) that all freemen might have the right to vote in this new Charter. The Upcott party also petitioned for a Charter that would promise the vote. However, the richer and better connected Burridge-Thorne clique achieved their Charter, which nominated Nathaniel Thorne as Mayor, and this was followed by the election of Samuel Burridge in 1725.

The Thornes were interesting survivors. George Thorne had been Mayor in 1710, when the Whigs were turned out in favour of the Tories, and George gave the casting vote that tipped the evenly balanced Corporation towards the winning Tory MPs, who included the new Tory Attorney-General, Sir Edward Northey. George Thorne soon received the lucrative post of Receiver of Taxes, which allowed him to use the flow of government revenue as collateral capital to finance his business. By 1723 the family had obviously switched to a pro-Walpole line, as Nathaniel Thorne was also a Receiver of Taxes, and could be relied on to guide the Corporation into electing Walpole supporters.

The new Charter was received with joy by crowds of gullible townsfolk on Christmas Eve, 1724. They escorted the glossy document with music and alcohol from Gornhay to outside Old Blundell's, where it was handed over with ceremony to George Davey, the Town Clerk named within it. The foolishly happy people then cheered it up Gold Street to the Three Tuns, where there was a halt for further refreshment, toasted it with more alcohol at Nathaniel Thorne's house in Bampton Street, then down St Peter Street to Samuel Burridge's base at the Great House for yet more festive cheer. By now delirious, the crowd heard the document read to them in Latin, then as now, a language maintained by the educated to dupe the uneducated. Only at the next few elections did the people learn that the vote was not yet for them.

This keen quarrel is also an indication that the route to prosperity was increasingly through political manipulation and patronage rather than the cloth

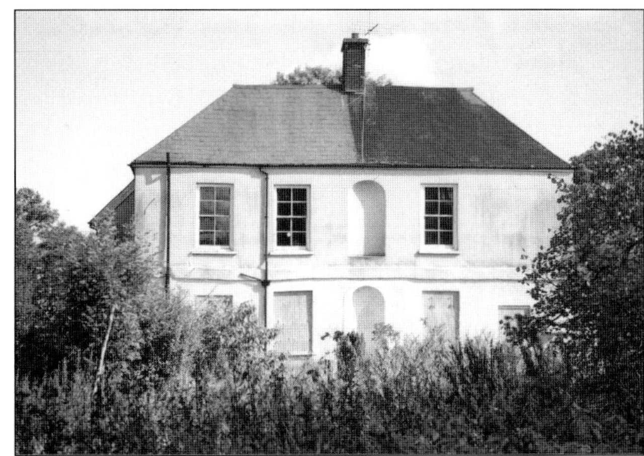

Great Gornhay Farm in a state of neglect. In 1724 the Tiverton mob came out here to greet the new Charter. The Charter itself was a nasty 'con' by Mayor Burridge and his faction. Later in the 'hungry' 1840s a mob attacked the farm, thinking a store of wheat was kept there.

MUSEUM COLLECTION

trade. From the death of Thomas Bere of Huntsham, one of the members for Tiverton from 1690 to 1722, the Corporation chose influential 'foreigners' as their MPs, notably members of the Ryder family, who sat in succession for Tiverton from 1735 to 1832. They were accompanied by such other members as Sir William Yonge of Honiton, Walpole's friend, Henry Pelham brother of the Duke of Newcastle and Spencer Perceval, the son of the Prime Minister murdered in 1812. From 1768 to 1830 the Ryders shared the borough with the Duntze family from Exeter. MPs of this calibre were elected because they could direct 'good things' to the Corporators and their kith and kin. Control of the Corporation was a route to wealth and a good thing to win, which explains the bitterness of the 1723 fight.

Dudley Ryder, Lord Sandon, MP for Tiverton, later 2nd Earl of Harrowby. His father, the first Earl, was violently anti-reform, but Lord Sandon supported the Reform Bill and was consequently 'de-selected' by the Corporation and replaced by his brother Granville in 1831.
NATIONAL PORTRAIT GALLERY

Another stage in decline was probably the fire of June 1731. It began in a bakery on the north side of Gold Street, where most houses were thatched. Dunsford describes the chaos of the fire-fighting, with the engines having trundled round from St Peter's, the crew having forgotten vital parts. The engines were themselves consumed by the blaze and the fire burnt unchecked until it was blocked by coming up against strongly built brick and tiled residences in Bampton Street and Fore Street. It then burnt itself out. A survey revealed 298 houses were destroyed, including Greenway's almshouses, and later computations stated that about £60,000 worth of private property had been lost while insurance only covered £1,135. The charitable response was swift. George II led the way with £1,000 and soon £10,000 had come in and was distributed with surprising equity. Most went to those who had lost all, but 29 of the richest households declined to take any of the charity, even though their combined losses totalled over £20,000. A useful result of this fire was an Act of Parliament in 1732, which ensured that any new houses were roofed with fire-proof materials. Nevertheless fires continued, presumably of the old unthatched dwellings; in 1738 and 1739, two fires in St Andrew Street destroyed 20 houses.

By mid-century unrest in the cloth industry seems to have become endemic. The country was at war from 1742–49, again from 1756–63, from 1776–83, and from 1793–1815, bringing dislocation to Tiverton's markets in northern Europe, where the serges had been sold. Improvements in transport, notably canals, left Tiverton at a disadvantage compared with towns on the canal system. Attempts to introduce varied, lighter and more colourful fabrics had moments of success, but ultimately failed. Riots in 1733, 1738, the spring of 1749, another in the autumn of the same year, in 1754 and one in 1765 show all was decidedly unwell. Some of these riots were so serious that the military had to be called upon. In the case of some, it is the old story of the combers objecting to the import of Irish yarn, whereas in others it was the weavers protesting against the sale of serge 'seconds' undercutting their goods. In 1754 there was a riot to claim the right to vote. In 1765 the death of the largest merchant, Oliver Peard, occasioned fears that the trade itself would close and the disturbances were most serious. The rioters wanted Baring, a prosperous Exeter cloth merchant, to be elected to fill one of three vacancies on the Corporation, as he had promised to save the trade, but the Mayor, John Webber, and the majority of the Corporation were opposed. Some of the rioters hounded the Mayor into the Angel Inn, pulled off his wig, twisted his nose and generally duffed him up and forced him to sign a paper promising to vote for Baring. Suspecting that Webber was trying to wriggle, the combers and weavers marched to his Bolham house and thoroughly wrecked it, and placed threatening letters around the town. When the election finally happened and the Tiverton merchants George Lewis and Thomas Enchmarch and John Duntze of Exeter were chosen, the mob threw stones at the Town Hall and roughed up the offending Corporators. Once the military had arrived, some of the ringleaders were arrested and taken to Exeter, but their escort found Silverton blocked to them so that they had to take their captives around that village through the fields. As a postscript Webber's Bolham mansion was burnt down in 1766.

However, no era is totally glum. Although Tiverton missed out on the early years of canal building, with

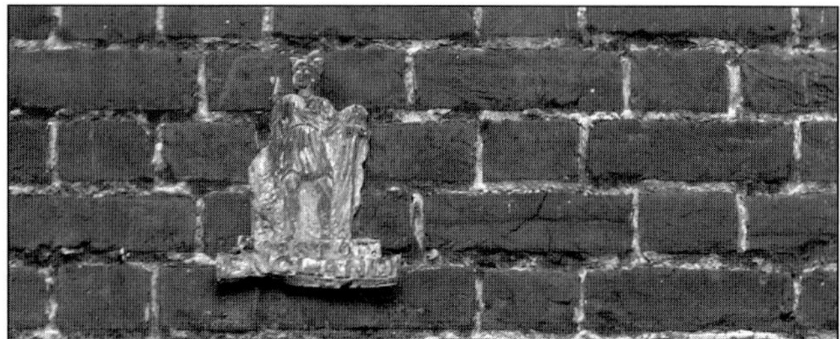

A fire insurance plaque in St Andrew Street. Fire was a terrible hazard before new building regulations in the 1730s insisted on brick and tile, rather than cob and thatch. It remained a serious hazard until the motorised fire-engine.

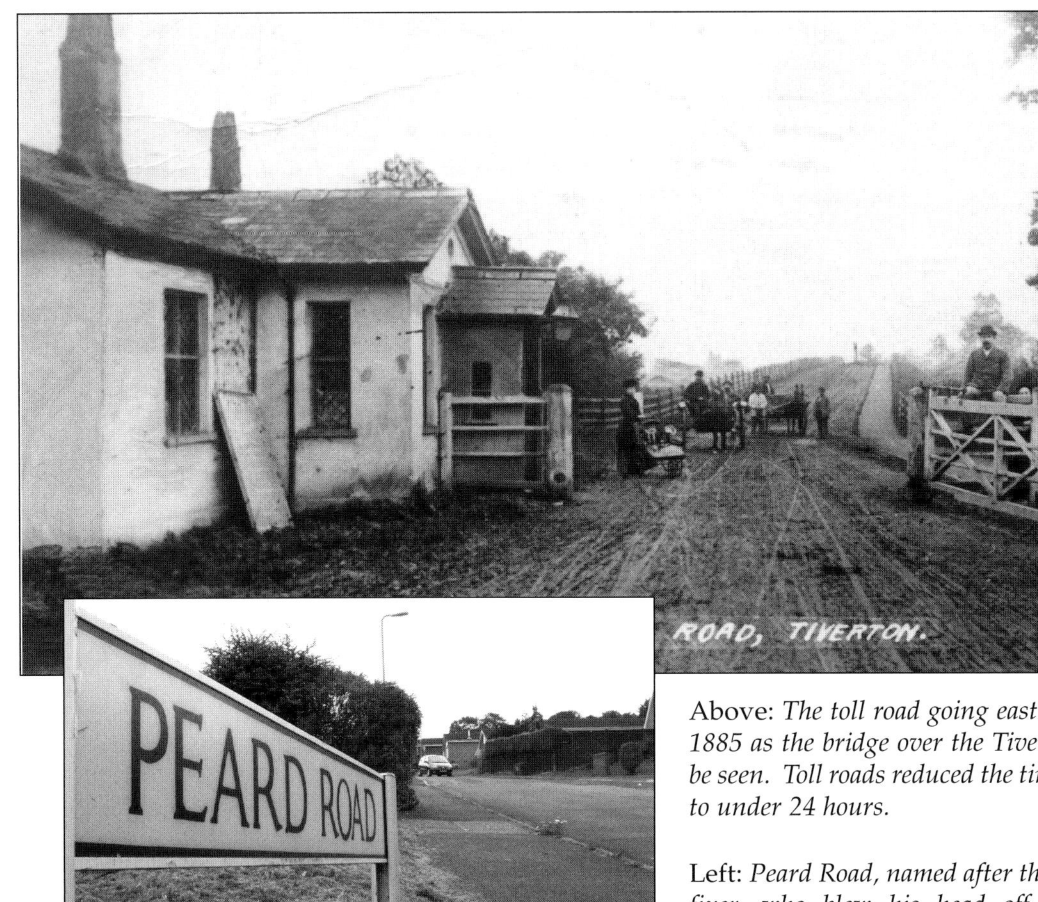

Above: *The toll road going east in a photograph of about 1885 as the bridge over the Tiverton to Bampton line can be seen. Toll roads reduced the time of a journey to London to under 24 hours.* MUSEUM COLLECTION

Left: *Peard Road, named after the mid-eighteenth-century fixer, who blew his head off with a blunderbuss in December 1764, having destroyed his only will a few days earlier. His sister Mary used some of his money to provide for the maintenance of St George's Church.* COLIN WHITE

ideas first aired in 1766 of building a Bridgwater–Exeter canal via Tiverton and the Exe valley coming to nothing, the town took part in the improvement in communication by road that had been brought about through the introduction of turnpikes and new methods of road construction. According to Dunsford the initial steps were taken in 1758, and the first 'post-chaise hire' business was begun in 1760. At first the turnpike trustees used their powers to improve the existing roads, but an early 'new' road was built from Westexe towards Bickleigh following the floor of the valley, and continued in 1767 from Bickleigh to Silverton along the eastern side of the Exe valley, replacing the old over-the-hills route via Butterleigh. After 1813 the old road to Bampton via Chettiscombe was supplemented by the valley road through Bolham and Cove. Other new roads came later. The Tiverton to Nomansland road up Long Drag was started in 1837, helped by a generous donation of cash and land from the Cruwys family. Sentimental Christmas cards remind us of the system of stagecoaches and coaching houses that the building of these toll roads produced. (They are somewhat anachronistic, as 'Christmas' as a festive season only began some time after the railways had minimised stagecoach use.) Snell gave details of their routes. A passenger to North Devon could start from the Angel and would go up the Rackenford to change horses at the 'Bell' or start from the Three Tuns in Bampton Street and have a first 'stage' at Nomansland. The first stop on the way to London was Wellington and the coach went on its 24 hour journey to London via Taunton and Bridgwater. These coaches carried letters. On 2 January 1788 the governors of Blundell's School wrote to the Bishop of Exeter in London and received his reply, dated 8 January, soon after, so the post worked well. A number of local services by carters carried people and goods around the area and, as 'Jan Strewer' relates, would continue to do so in the more rural parts into the 1930s.

An important legacy from this period of decline is St George's Church, consecrated in 1733, and the private houses of grace and distinction, which lie partly within the town and partly in the surrounding countryside. The dignity and serene self-confidence of these houses contrasts starkly with the message of John Wesley and is a reminder that the past is as varied and self-contradictory as the present.

The age produced Tiverton's only important home-grown literary figure: Hannah Cowley (née Parkhouse). Her father Philip Parkhouse, 1712–90, was a Fore Street bookseller and her mother a cousin of John Gay of Barnstaple, who wrote *The Beggars' Opera.*

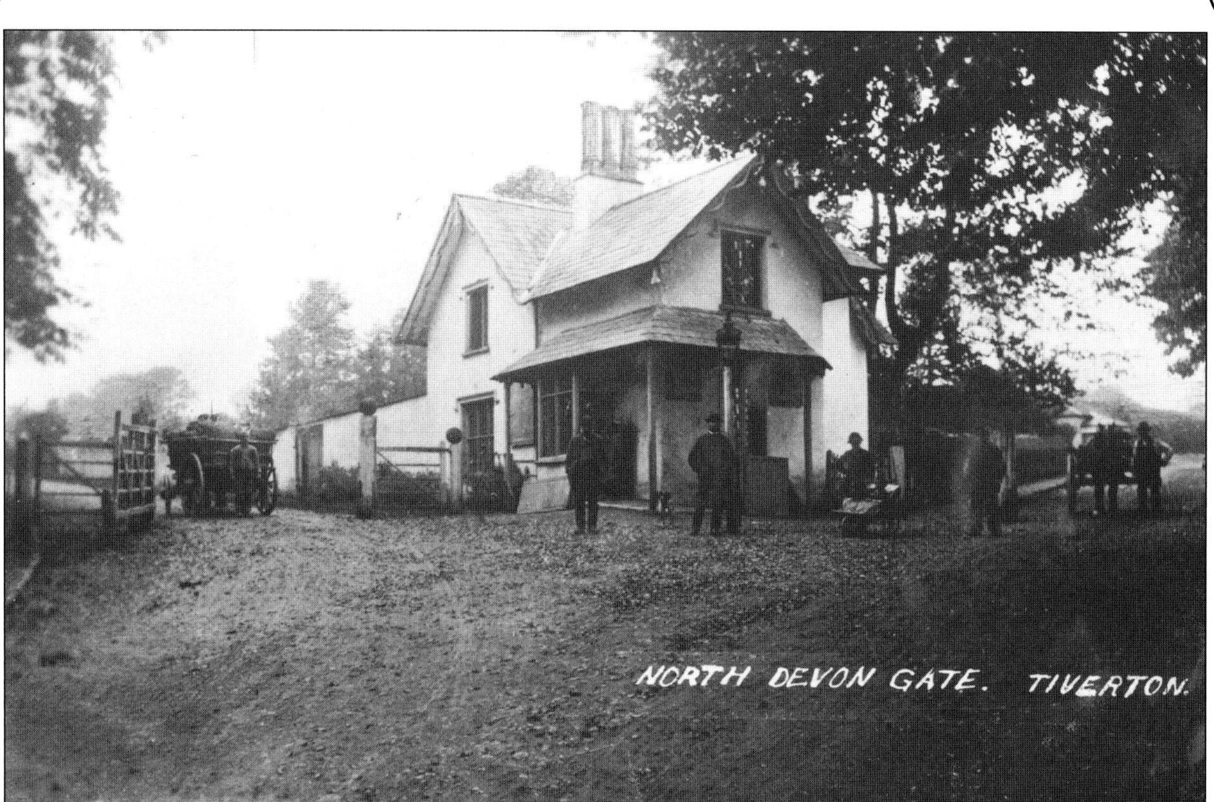

At the bottom of Long Drag, covering the new road to Witheridge and the improved road to Rackenford.

MUSEUM COLLECTION

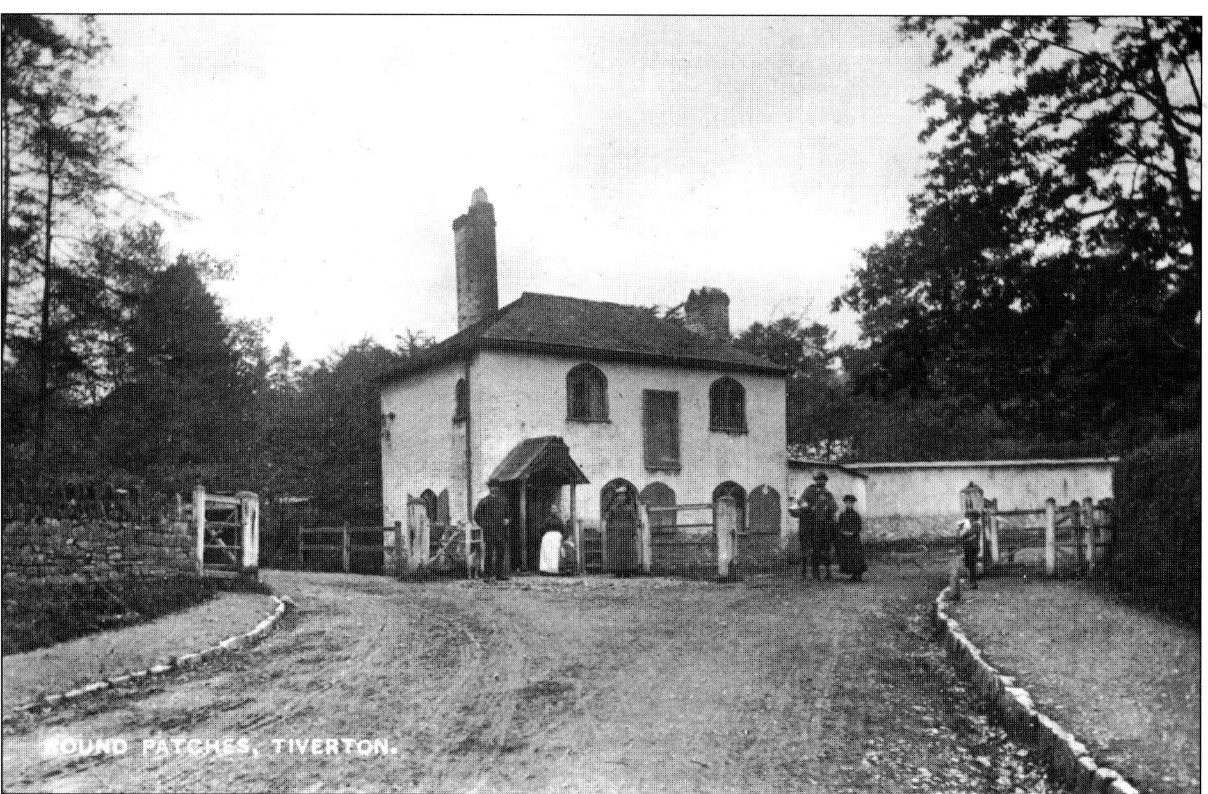

A tollroad and turnpike were established mainly to cover the improved road to Seven Crosses.

MUSEUM COLLECTION

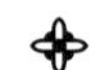

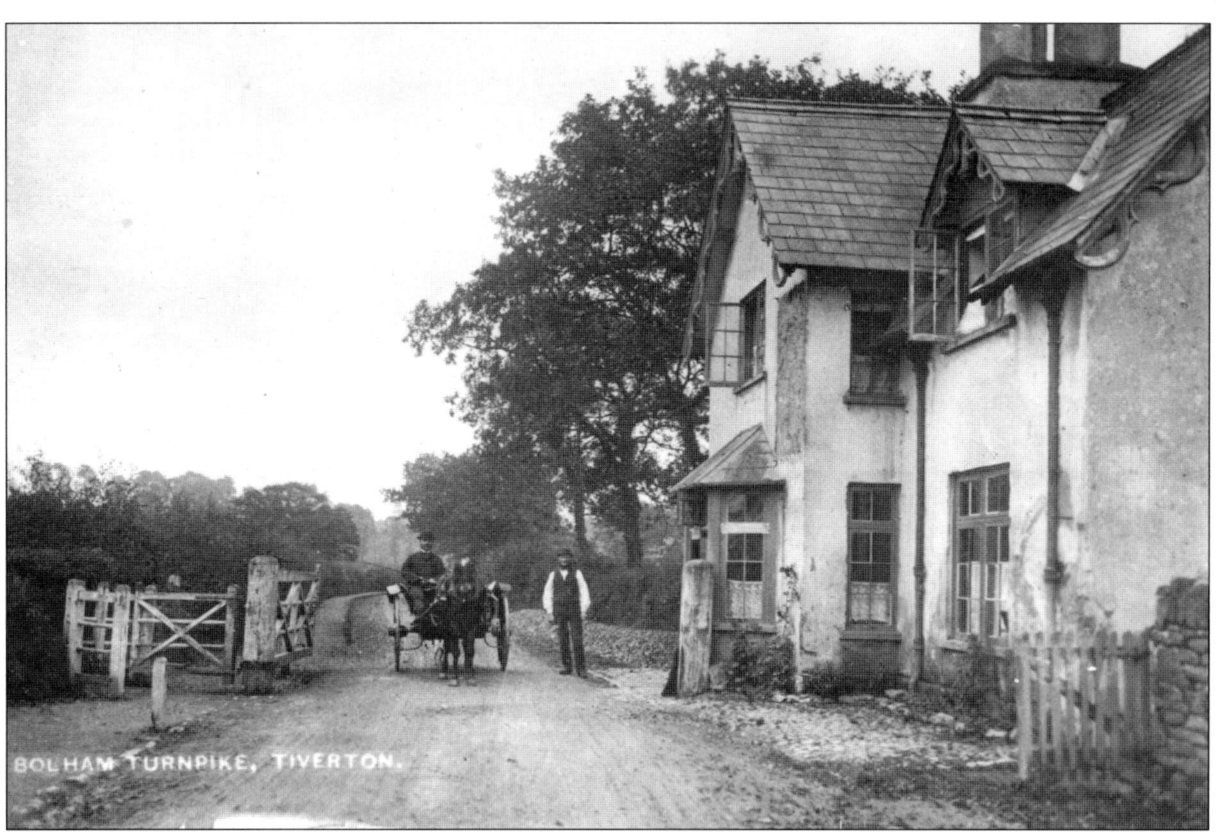

On the new road to Bampton, near the present East Devon College. MUSEUM COLLECTION

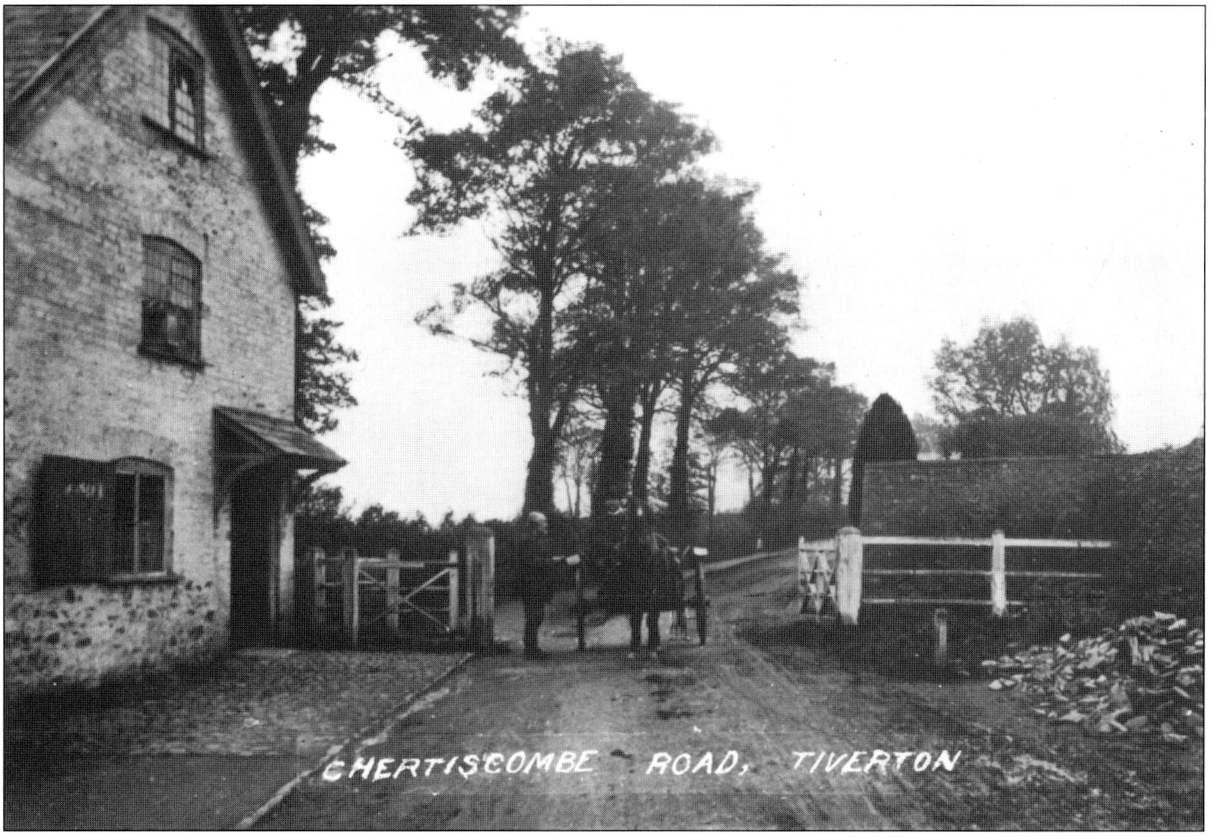

On the road to Chettiscombe and Bampton. MUSEUM COLLECTION

Parkhouse was an Assistant Burgess and a friend of the Ryders' local agent, Beavis Wood, the Town Clerk, who described him as a 'sound man among lame brothers'. Parkhouse, educated at Blundell's, is said to have educated his daughter, who married Thomas Cowley. Hannah Cowley's first play, *The Runaway*, was produced in London in 1776 and received a Royal Command Performance. Further plays followed at regular intervals until *The Town before You* appeared in 1794. Her career provides an illustration of how the pocket borough system worked. In London the Ryders pushed her works and found her husband a good post in the East India Company, while her father used his vote 'wisely' in Parliamentary elections in Tiverton. In London she was an important figure in Society. She returned to Tiverton and died in 1809. She was buried in St George's churchyard, where the authorities have seen fit to preserve the gravestone of the undeniably second rate literary figure, Samuel Wesley, but not hers.

Samuel Wesley, headmaster of Blundell's, 1734–40, and older brother of John Wesley. His gravestone, fulsomely inscribed, is on the exterior of the east wall of St George's Church, where it is rapidly becoming illegible.

By the time Hannah Cowley died, Tiverton's trade was dwindling. The closure of traditional markets during the Napoleonic Wars was the last straw. As a symbol of the end of these things Martin Dunsford, clothier and historian, became bankrupt in 1802. A brave attempt to stem the decline was the building of the factory in Westexe by a fluctuating consortium, which, starting in the 1780s, contained people such as the two William Smales, Nicholas Denys, Richard Lardner and Thomas Heathfield. They bought out the owners of the land between the leat and the Exe, and, an interesting forerunner of Heathcoat's, brought in machinery from Sheffield. (Smales and Denys were clients of the Barings so it may have been 'wheels within wheels'.) However, the partners were either unlucky or incompetent because it failed to make money and was advertised for sale in 1815 in the *Exeter Flying Post:*

> *[A] spinning and weaving factory, five storeys high, three under-rooms for combing, drawing... and spinning worsted, two upper storeys full of machines for spinning; large buildings containing spinning jennies; fulling mill driven by the same stream after it has passed the spinning mill.'*

This marked the end of any large-scale woollen manufacture in the town.

Let us end this gloomy saga with the words of Harding who, writing in 1845 on the subject of the year 1815, stated:

> *Few, if any towns in England have experienced greater vicissitudes than Tiverton. Fire has several times laid desolate the dwellings of the poor, and the habitations of the rich, and the reverses frequently experienced in trade, have fallen on the town with a heavy hand. Much injury has been occasioned by the disaffection of the labourers [Harding was a Tory and was prone to blaming the workers for all ills], and at this period of our history, the woollen manufacture, that had hitherto been the principal support of the town, ceased, almost entirely, to exist.*

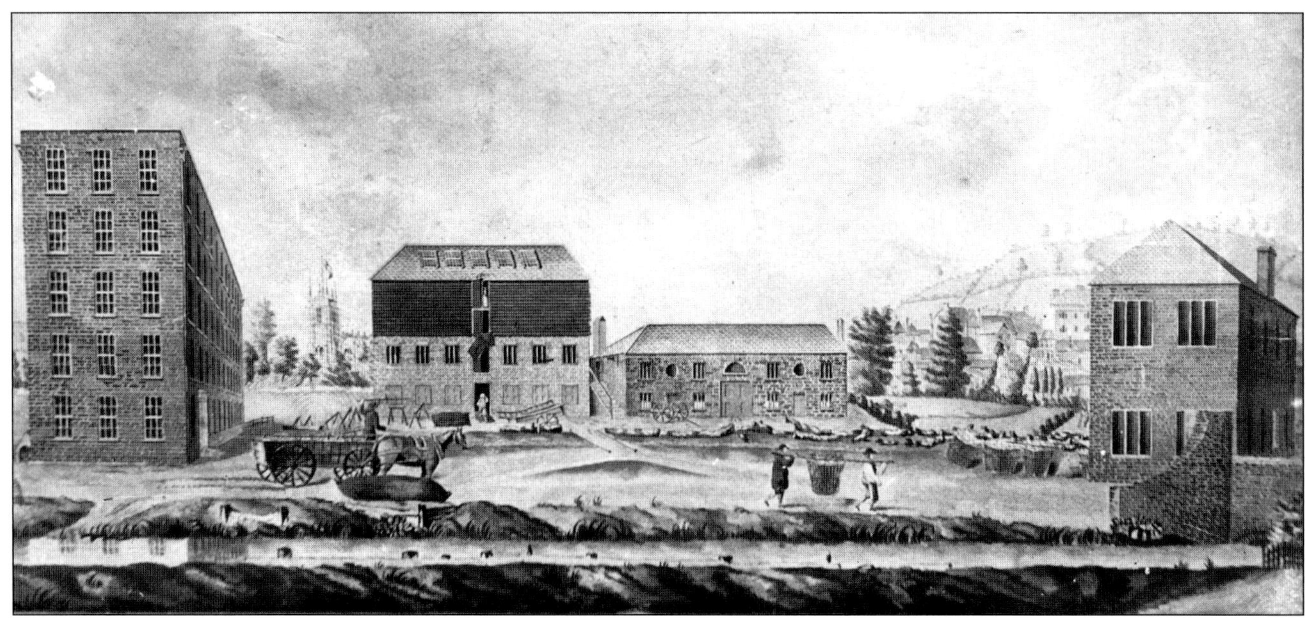

The newly built factory in 1770. The leat is in the foreground, St Peter's is left of centre and Cranmore Castle is in the background to the right. MUSEUM COLLECTION

Chapter 5

Corruption and Reform, 1790–1840

'The history of England is emphatically the history of progress.'
Macaulay

'I never saw so many shocking bad hats in my life.'
Duke of Wellington of the reformed House of Commons

At the outbreak of the French Revolution, Tiverton was a divided, declining, unhealthy and unhappy place. On the one hand there was the Corporation, linked firmly to the Ryders and Duntzes through the efforts of Beavis Wood, the Town Clerk and Ryder's agent, supported by the influence of the Dickinson family, who had inherited much of the wealth of the great Oliver Peard, and who would marry into the Walronds. The wheels of the Corporation were well greased with Crown patronage. Dickinson's brother and brother-in-law had government salaries, as did Beavis and William Wood, Bernard Besley and Philip Parkhouse. Two Burgesses were Duntze's employees and two others his relatives. After 1832 the Ryders claimed that they never bribed their 25-strong electorate. They were probably correct; they did not have to as they used the public purse by channelling appointments to public office towards those whose votes they required. An analysis of the Corporators in 1823 showed four of the Capital Burgesses ineligible for non-residence and three holding incompatible offices. Five of the dozen Assistant Burgesses were non-resident. There were six father and son or son-in law pairs, as well as other family links.

On the other hand there were the reformers, led first by Martin Dunsford, then by George Coles, later by John Heathcoat. In the years before the outbreak of revolution in France there was a strong movement for Parliamentary reform in England, which chimed in well with the perennial demands of Tivertonians for the right to vote for their two MPs. In 1782 Martin Dunsford chaired a public meeting, which drew up a petition that declared the present rights of the Corporation 'injurious' to the town and a 'national disgrace'. It is of interest that the petition was supported by Smale and Denys, the commercial rivals of the Dickinson faction, and was signed by almost every man in the town, who was not a Corporator. In retaliation the Corporation promised themselves never to elect any of the petitioners to their body. After the meeting the leading signatories dined in the Three Tuns, where, Dunsford relates, 'some country gentlemen, of considerable property, applied for leave to sign it.' The existing MPs made sure the petition was ignored.

Of course there was more to it than Reformers versus Reactionaries. There was the large majority of the poor and ignorant, who never enter the story unless rioting from fear or hunger or as actors, manipulated by others. In many ways the movement for reform was the search for a new coalition of the 'haves', that would keep the 'great unwashed' in their subordination.

Dunsford had the ear of his fellow townsfolk. For four years in succession, 1783–86, he was elected churchwarden by the annual Vestry meeting, where all male ratepayers had the vote, and churchwardens had considerable powers of oversight in the administration of parish charity and the maintenance of church fabric. In 1784 Dunsford called a meeting which raised the question of the inequitable assessments for the various rates that had to be paid. The meeting decided to make a fresh valuation of property based on an estimation by committees of local people. At the Vestry meeting in December 1784 a rate based on the new system was passed, but it proved impossible to collect because too many of the locally great and powerful fought it in the courts. From Beavis Wood's letters to the Ryders it is clear that the 'status quo-ites' regarded Dunsford as a dangerous radical, and in 1785 they determined to oppose his re-election. However they ultimately had to back down in the face of overwhelming public support for Dunsford.

In June 1785 Dunsford called another Vestry meeting to establish Sunday schools. By 1790 nine schools had been established with 240 pupils. At this stage the schools attracted cross-party support with the Church of England clergy working with Dissenters. The children received a few hours of instruction in reading so that they might read the sacred texts and were then marched round to whatever was their denominational place of worship. However this interdenominational co-operation was damaged by the refusal of Parliament to repeal the Test and Corporation Acts which prevented Dissenters from taking any public office. In 1787 the majority against repeal was over 70, in 1789 it fell to 20, but in 1790 it rose to over 150, as the MPs were so scared by events in France. It is difficult at this remove to appreciate the Establishment's fears, but in the early-nineteenth century an Anglican Bishop actually compared Dissenting Sunday school teachers to Jacobins, in the same way that, today, more excitable readers of the *Telegraph* see the BBC as a hotbed of Communism.

The war against France strengthened the hand of

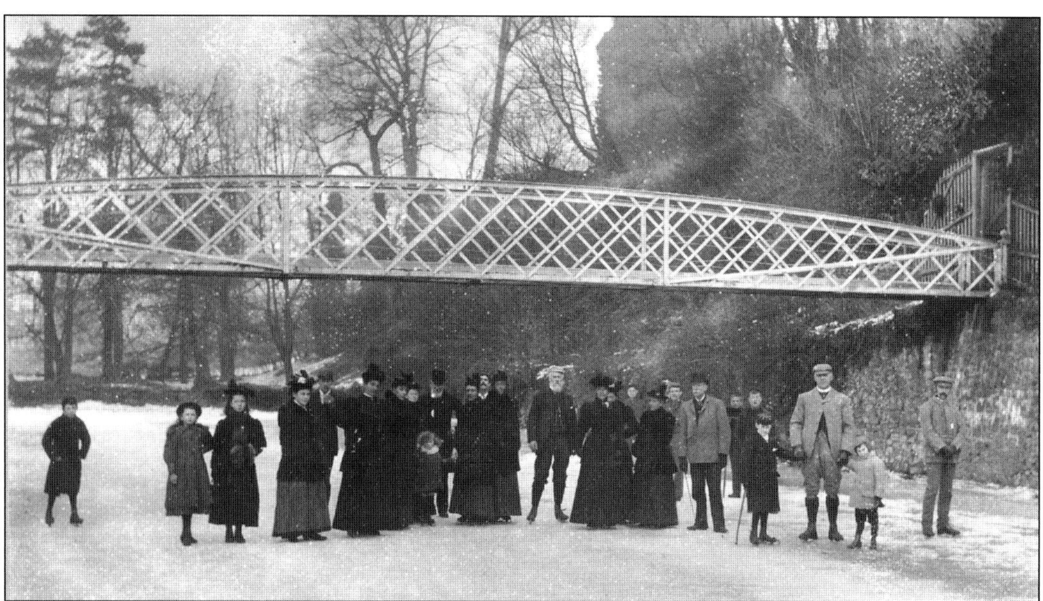

Skating on the Exe in the 1890s. Note the bridge, probably built to connect the factory with Heathcoat's St Peter Street house. Note also the romantic ruins of the castle. MUSEUM COLLECTION

the 'status quo-ites', and although much needed to be done, the only other piece of pre-war reform was the Paving Act of 1794. In February a petition had been sent to Parliament describing the streets as 'ill-paved, dangerous and greatly encumbered by various encroachments and buildings, and obstructed by spouts and gutters.' Being Tiverton, it was opposed by a counter petition claiming that the expense of remedy was not worth the potential improvement. Nevertheless the Act was achieved. The first job was to clear the streets of encroaching buildings. A glance at Dunsford's map will show Angel Hill, the top end of St Peter's Street, Newport Street, and Lowman Green so encumbered. Problems in Bridge Street and Westexe were solved dramatically by a fire in the same year, which broke out in a workshop and destroyed 120 buildings, almost all of Westexe and up Angel Hill as far as the bottom of St Peter's Street. The Act of 1794 set up the first body, the Paving Commissioners, to be responsible for paving and maintaining the fabric of the public thoroughfares in the town; before that the only provision, stated in the 1615 Charter, was for householders to remove rubbish from an area from the front of their houses to the mid-point of the highway. Difficult to imagine what a winter's stroll down Fore Street must have been like in 1790! In many areas 'paving' was just papering over the cracks of problems. As few houses had piped water or were connected to sewerage, filth still slopped around, over the paving or under it, seeping into wells. Cholera was an occasional visitor until the last outbreak in 1866.

The Napoleonic Wars, as wars do, brought their own alarums and excitements. There were two serious invasion scares: in 1797 when much of the Fleet mutinied, and in 1804 when Napoleon massed his Army at Boulogne, waiting for the Franco-Spanish Navies to outwit Nelson and transport his troops to England. Throughout the wars there was much military activity in Tiverton. In 1795 the York Militia, stationed in the town, helped fight the Westexe fire. Lord Rolle brought his regiment of South Devon Militia to Tiverton for their annual training, a popular source of extra income, particularly for publicans. In the scare of 1797 Mr Worth raised a troop of 'Tiverton Volunteer Cavalry' who had a fetching uniform of scarlet and gold, but no swords, only sticks. In the period from 1803 to the Battle of Trafalgar in October 1805, the invasion scare was much more serious. All Tivertonians were required by Act of Parliament to state what they could do in case of invasion, and all farmers were asked to declare what live and dead stock they possessed. Those who declared themselves able to fight were formed into a body under Sir John Duntze, calling themselves the Tiverton Fencibles. The Armada system of beacons was reinstated. However, the scare subsided and the Fencibles became civilians again.

Some Frenchmen did come to Tiverton, but as prisoners of war on parole, not as invaders. Among them were Admirals Dumanoir and Villeneuve, who had led their fleet at Trafalgar. All accounts repeat that the French were a popular addition to the life of the town, and at least one of them stayed on after the end of the wars in 1815. This was Alexandre de la Motte, who taught French at Blundell's.

The wars made for hard times for many, good times for a lucky few. The woollen manufacturers were going out of business, but farmers did well. In many war years Britain was entirely cut off from sources of corn imports and the population was rising fast. A great recipe for the producer; an awful one for the labourer. In the 1780s the average price for wheat had been 46s. a quarter, but in the early-nineteenth century it was rarely less than 80s. a quarter. While the price of the labourer's food went up, his wages often went down, and in 1815 a Parliament of landowners passed the Corn Laws to protect British agriculture from foreign competition. In this macro-climate poverty in Tiverton became a major issue. Poor rates had risen above £2,000 for the first time in 1772, and above £3,000 in 1786. Harding produced a table of Tiverton prices in 1794 and 1800: wheat rose from 7s. to 12s.6d. a bushel, cheese from 16s. to 35s.6d. a cwt, beef from 2d. to 4d. a lb. In 1801 wheat rose to 23s. a bushel, beef to 1s. a lb. and 'bread was so scarce that instances occurred where money was unable to procure it.' The misery of the poor was exacerbated by the bitterness of many of the winters. In January 1814 the diary of a Mr Mildon records that the temperature inside in a heated room was 10 degrees Fahrenheit (minus 12 degrees Celsius) and on 13 January the Exe froze so hard that skating and parties on it were possible. Harding recorded of 1816, 'the summer and winter proved unusually wet and corn was spoilt. The season was cold and in some parts of England snow fell in July.'

Knowledge of this state of affairs adds meaning to the local 'celebrations' of the coronation of George IV in July 1821. Tory Harding recalled that a celebratory 'cold collation' at 3s.6d. a head was 'partaken of by 300 respectable persons' at Old Blundell's. (This sum is equal to half an agricultural labourer's weekly wage in 1821.) 'The bells rang, but there was little rejoicing among the lower orders.' Snell rounds off the story of the day with evidence that suggests that, although many of the 'lower orders' may have gone to bed hungry, they may have been not altogether unhappy. Everyone leaving the cold collation would have had to go through the one gate, where the mob was waiting for them, and they were thoroughly duffed up. Snell ascribes political motivation to the event, but it was probably hunger.

There were some useful developments in these dark years. In 1814 the canal reached Tiverton. Sadly it was not really the Grand Western Canal planned to run from Bridgwater to Exmouth, with a spur to Tiverton, but a dead-end of a canal from Bridgwater to Tiverton, which although useful to Tiverton, could have no commercial viability. It did, however, bring coal prices down. The governors and masters of Blundell's, ever mindful of the health and comfort of the scholars, installed stoves in the hitherto unheated schoolrooms, but they did not get round to it until 1827. The stoves were fired by coal, bought from Goodlands, who then had premises at the Canal Basin, but the main business of the canal was bringing in stone to be burnt into lime in the many limekilns at the Basin. The coming of the railway 'killed' the canal, which had never been profitable and all commercial traffic ceased in 1924.

Some steps were taken to improve the squalor of the streets. The weekly Tuesday market was held in Fore Street, Bampton Street, and Newport Street, with the various traders having their own traditional pitches. Earthenware goods were displayed in Bampton Street between Stags (the old Boar's Head) and the former Council Housing Department, with cloth stalls on the opposite side of the street. Pigs were sold outside the Boar's Head, sheep on Park Hill beside the Baptist Chapel, and bullocks in Newport Street. The potato market was on the St Peter Street side of Angel Hill. Meat, poultry and butter were sold in Fore Street, where the officially certified scales were kept, so that weights could be tested. In 1825 an Act of Parliament was obtained, empowering trustees named in the Act to purchase land away from the streets and build a market house. In 1829 these powers were taken up and properties in the centre of town, including the old bowling-green, were bought and the market opened in stages in the following years. The old bowling-green became the cattle market, which survived in a declining way until the 1970s. The cost, which was just under £8,400, was met by the sale of £50 shares to be paid off by market tolls. However, the market never paid its way, partly because of the development of shops. Further expense was incurred in 1876 when the market had to be rebuilt and in 1888 it was facing bankruptcy with £7,800 of the original debt unpaid and £17,400 interest owing – the whole to be serviced out of an income of £350p.a. The market has continued to struggle on, a drain on the purse of the authority responsible for its upkeep. Other casualties of the development of shops were the two annual fairs traditionally held after Whitsun and Michaelmas. They faded away, leaving behind them the quaint march of the Town Council to Coggan's Well.

An undoubted improvement was the formation of a gas lighting company in 1831. John Heathcoat provided the gasworks and in 1832 the streets were lit. Shops and private houses soon followed.

Better toll roads enabled people from the surrounding area to come to Tiverton and patronise events in a way that was previously impossible. Between 1820 and 1844 Tiverton possessed a theatre in St Peter's Street in the shape of the converted Unitarian Meeting House. Sadly in 1844 it was pulled down and our thespians had from then on to camp out in the Athenaeum in Fore Street and later in the Drill Hall. One of the actors who played there, wrote a play, *Tiverton Castle*, based on the siege of 1645. It does not receive many performances.

The most important strands of Tiverton life in the 1820s were the growing clamour for political and religious reform, and the growing success of John Heathcoat and Company. As time went on the two were intertwined. What rankled reformers such as

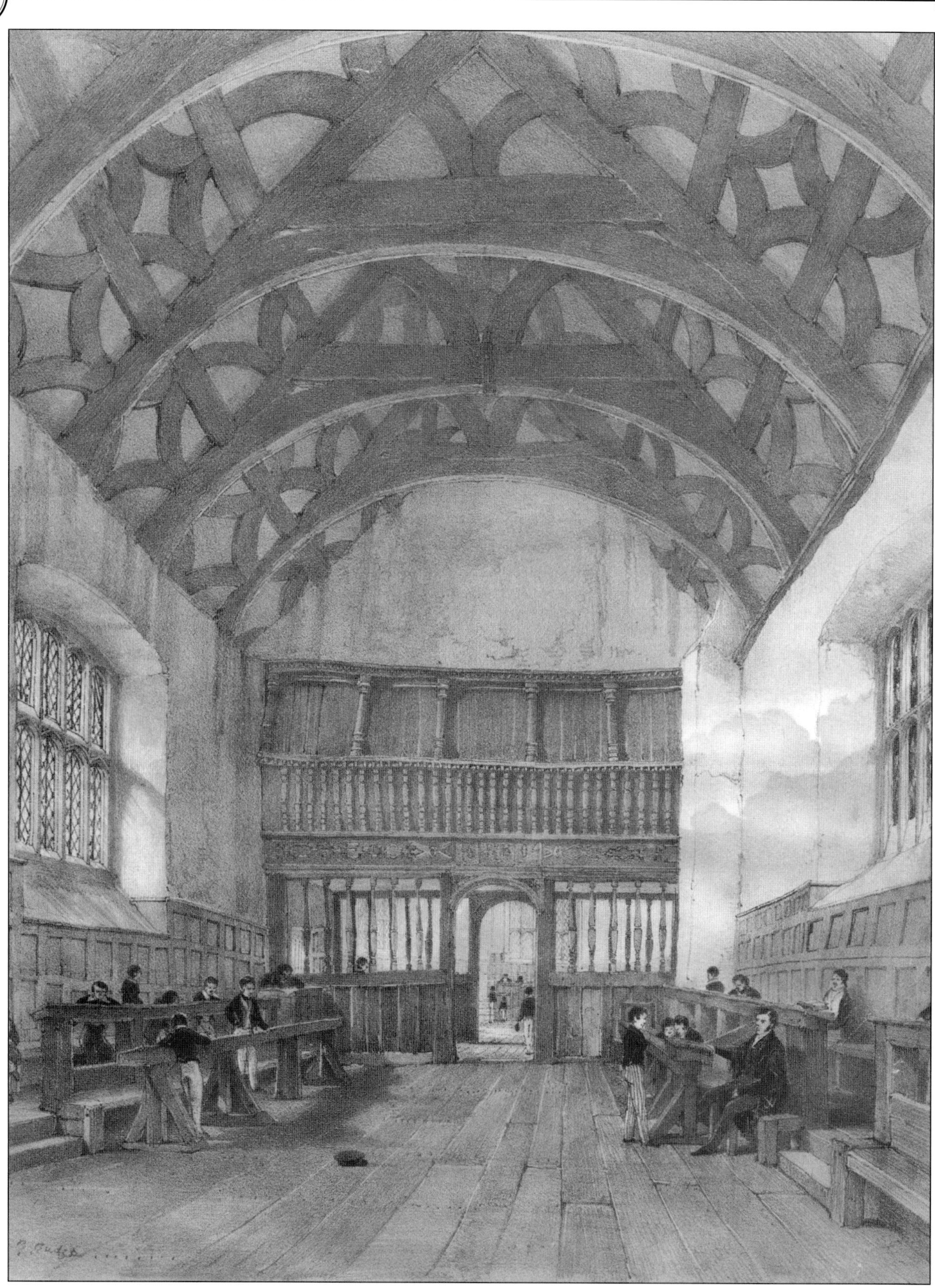

The interior of Old Blundell's. A stove was installed in the 1820s fuelled by coal brought to Tiverton by canal and purchased from Goodland's who then had its depot at the basin.

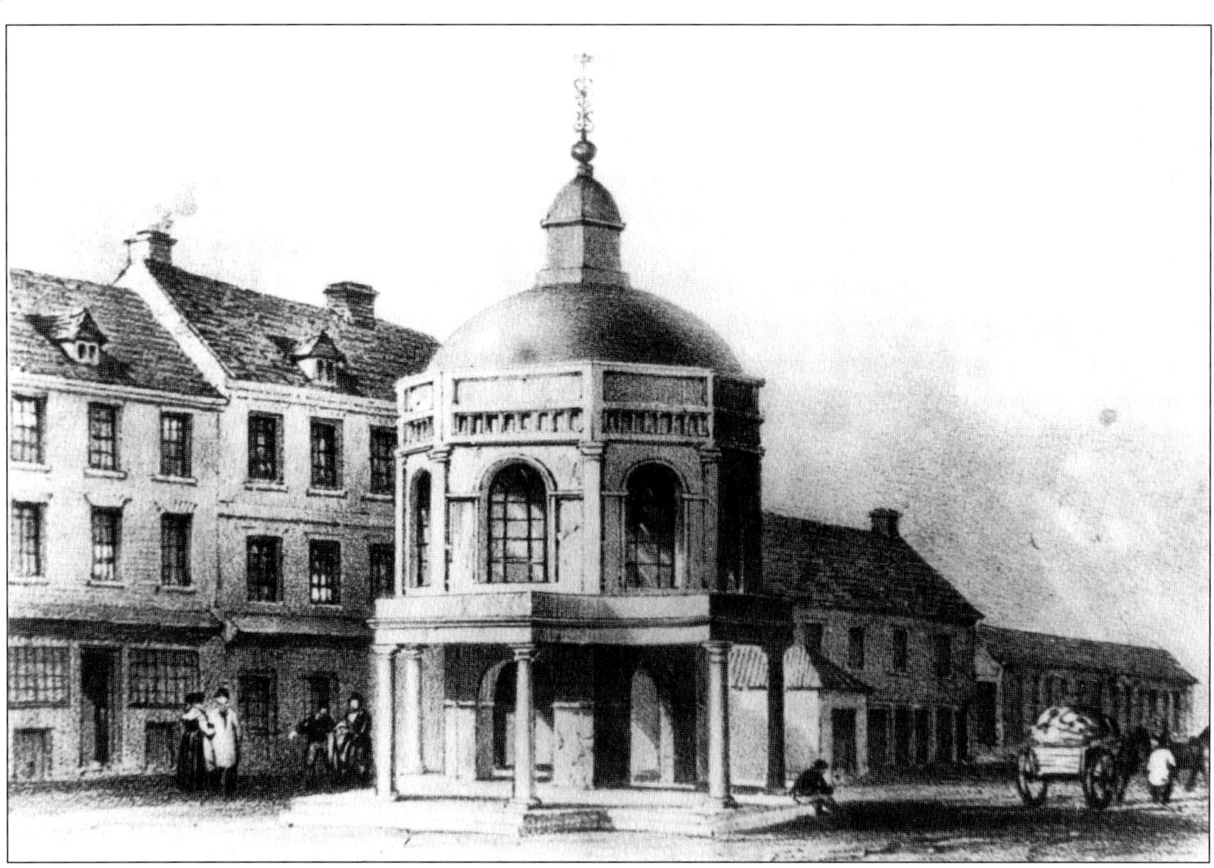

The Old Market Cross which from 1770 to 1830 decoratively blocked Fore Street, where the market took place.
MUSEUM COLLECTION

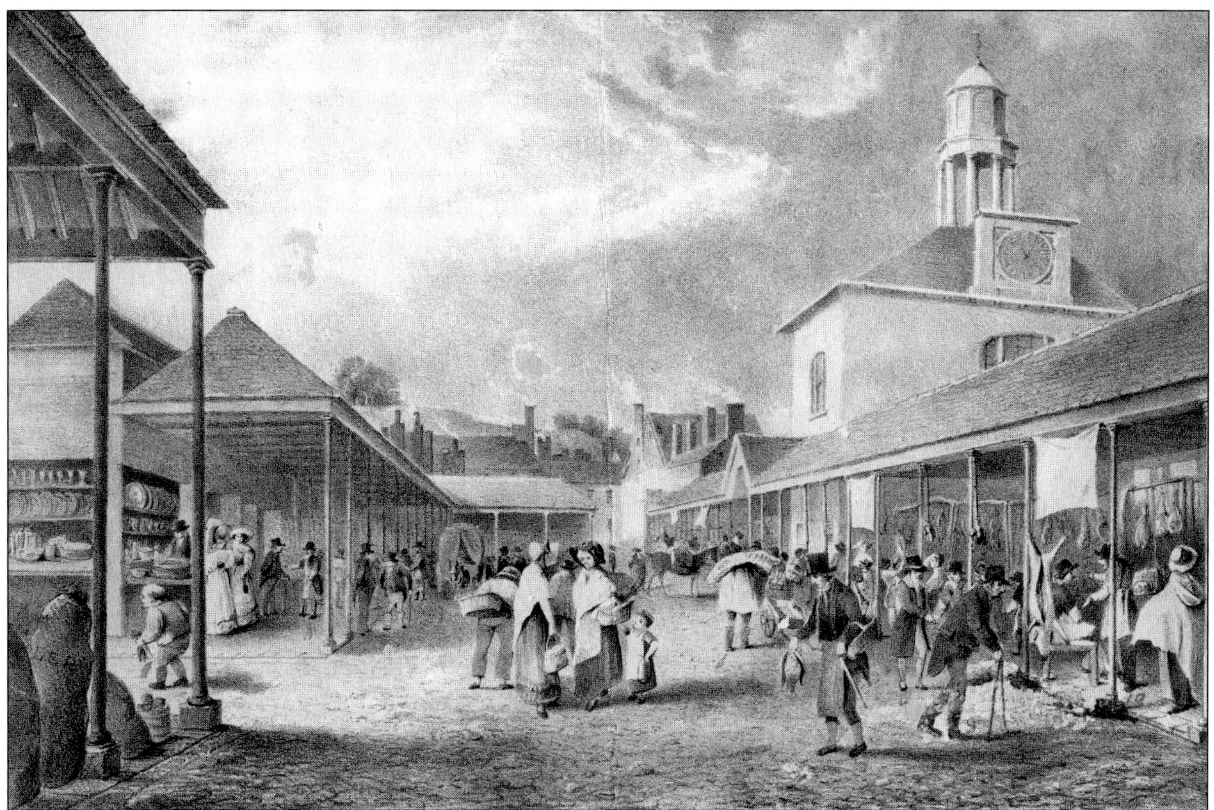

The new market in the town centre. It has not yet made money. Soon after it was built, modern shops were developed and weekly markets became peripheral.
MUSEUM COLLECTION

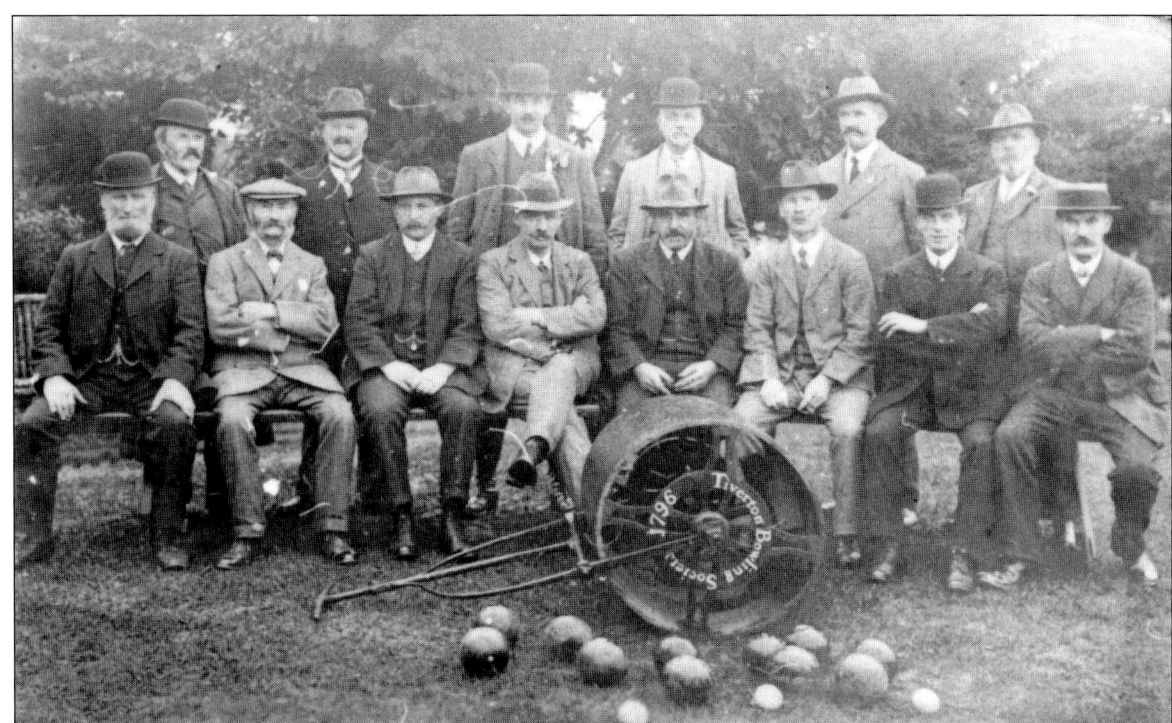

Above: *The new or Pannier Market and cattle market replaced the bowling-green shown on Dunsford's map. Only the roller survives; it is in the museum.* MUSEUM COLLECTION

Below: *Gas was another improvement of the 1830s. The first plant was on the factory site. This plant near the railway station was closed in the 1950s.* MUSEUM COLLECTION

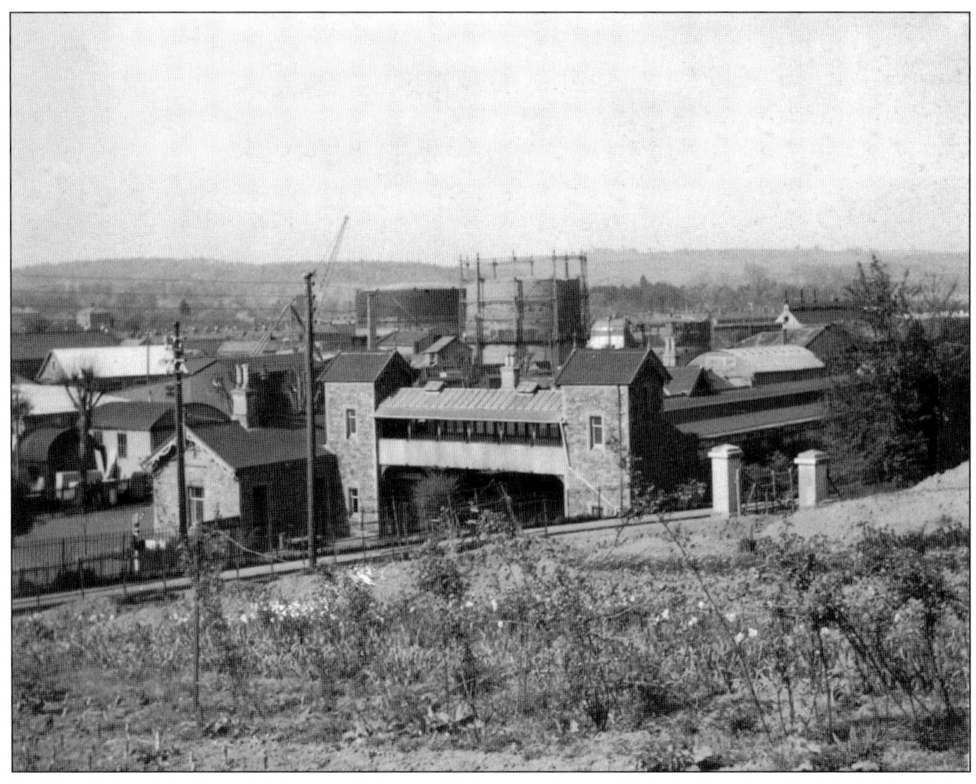

George Coles was that the town's assets had fallen into the hands of outsiders. Two publications, probably written by Coles, appeared in 1823 and 1824. In them the author pointed out the that half of the Corporators were technically ineligible for their office because they lived outside the parish or were office holders of the Corporation. It was also pointed out that the body did nothing for the prosperity of the town and that the denial of the suffrage to the people as a whole was a monstrous injustice. The author also attacked the masters and feoffees of Blundell's School for misdirecting the resources of the charity to the benefit of boarders and outsiders.

William Page Richards, 1797–1823, the headmaster who caused immense trouble by driving a coach and horses through the provisions of Peter Blundell's will. He resigned after a flogging scandal.

To the twenty-first century mind the criticisms were unanswerable, but the feoffees and Corporators could claim that they were obeying the letters of the law. Undoubtedly feoffees and Corporators were empowered to choose whomever they liked to fill vacancies. (Between 1799 and 1828 30 new feoffees were appointed, but only one, Benjamin Bowden Dickinson, was a Tivertonian, though another came from Washfield.) The world was moving beyond seeing virtue in obedience to the strict letter of early-seventeenth precedents and towards a time when law and tradition might be seen as the dead hand of time denying justice and restricting the energies of the present. If only Anthony Trollope had written *Barchester Towers* in a Tiverton setting, with the Corporation, feoffees and masters cast as the varied forces of unthinking reaction or thoughtful conservatism and Coles, Heathcoat and the reformers in the guise of admirable reformers such as John Bold or grisly hypocrites like Obediah Slope.

To the reformers Blundell's was a running sore. The timing of Coles' attack on Blundell's came at the same time as a nasty little court case, which may have been a contributory cause of Coles' campaign. In February, a pupil, Houston, the son of an apothecary, hit another boy, Henry Barne, the son of a wealthy Tiverton banker, connected with Benjamin Dickinson. Barne had snitched on Houston for truancy. On 10 February 1823, the Usher, Ley, flogged Houston. Witnesses for the prosecution said blood had been drawn in 59 places and that the victim was partially paralysed. Witnesses for the defence said the flogging was normal and the victim had subsequently been seen swimming and dancing. The case came up in August 1824; by then both Ley and Richards had resigned. Houston was awarded 6d. damages.

As a father of seven boys who had attended the school between 1816 and 1835, Coles knew all about the headmaster, William Richards, one of the keenest floggers in England. He had come to the school in 1797 and by 1814 had increased the numbers well above the 150 limit specified in Peter Blundell's will, most of them boarders. Blundell's will also specified that the teaching of classics should be free. In 1803 the feoffees regulated the scale of fees for 'foreigners' and boarders, but decreed 'No charge be made for schooling in future to any boys whose parents reside in Tiverton.' However, charges crept in for 'extras' such as writing, arithmetic and French. According to Coles, a Tiverton resident, Richards demanded a fee of £6. Coles sent it as a gratuity, on which terms Richards returned it. Hornsey Gamlen, scion of another important Tiverton family, whose father refused to pay fees, was told to go to the feoffees' clerk and be registered as a 'pauper'. William Quick, also the son of a Tivertonian, was demoted from the top to the bottom of his class, hit round the head by Richards, and told to get his father to send him money. Other testimony says that pupils who did not pay fees were discriminated against in competition for the ten or more very valuable Exhibitions to the universities available for Blundellians. George Coles later had experience of this discrimination. In 1837 one of his sons failed to gain a Blundell's Exhibition, which was awarded to a candidate, who proved to be so poor that Balliol refused to accept him until he reached the necessary standard.

A glance at the opening chapters of *Lorna Doone* will show how 'foreign' boarding Blundellians treated Tivertonian Blundellians in the 1820s and 1830s. 'Helots for whom no treatment was too bad', was how Blackmore described them.

The issues of Blundell's School and the wider reform of Parliament were definitely linked. The Town Clerk from 1806 was John Wood, the cousin of the reactionary Beavis Wood, who was also clerk to Blundell's feoffees from 1802–37, when he was succeeded by Frederick Patch, the Tory party's man of business in Tiverton. One of the main Tory propagandists in Tiverton was Anthony Boulton, the Blundell's usher from 1827 to 1844. The non-Tivertonian boarders, who won the coveted Exhibitions, largely became clergy of the Church of England and, for Tiverton Reformers who were often also Dissenters, Blundell's was definitely part of the devil's army.

The reforming wind started howling in the later 1820s. In the election of 1826 the Mayor and Corporation were surprised when two London barristers, Kennedy and Heath, declared themselves candidates to represent the Borough of Tiverton. Kennedy arrived and joined the Corporation and the two previous MPs, Viscount Sandon, the heir to the

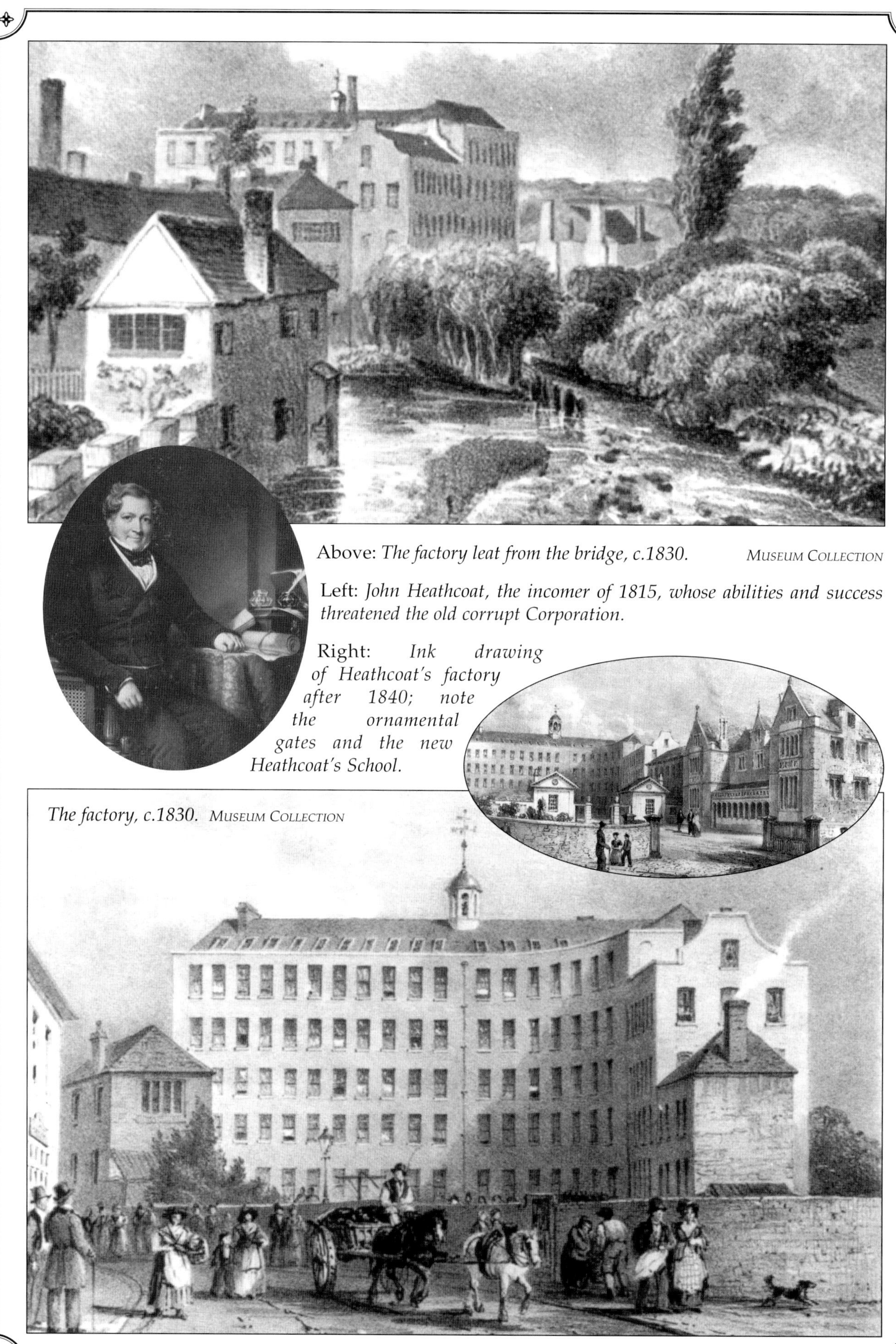

Above: *The factory leat from the bridge, c.1830.* MUSEUM COLLECTION

Left: *John Heathcoat, the incomer of 1815, whose abilities and success threatened the old corrupt Corporation.*

Right: *Ink drawing of Heathcoat's factory after 1840; note the ornamental gates and the new Heathcoat's School.*

The factory, c.1830. MUSEUM COLLECTION

Ryder Earldom of Harrowby, and his brother Granville Ryder. However Kennedy's attempts to participate were ruled out of order and the Burgesses 'elected' the Ryders. Kennedy addressed an excited crowd afterwards.

Serious breaches in the defences of the Anglican and Tory monopoly of Church and State occurred in 1827 and 1829. In 1827 the Test and Corporation Acts were repealed, allowing Dissenters to take full part in political life at both local and national level, to the great benefit of the nascent Liberal party. In 1829, under pressure from the threat of revolution in Ireland, the Catholic Relief Act was passed , allowing the same privilege to Catholics. Simultaneously in Tiverton both communities raised their profile. One of the candidates in elections in the 1830s was Colonel Chichester, a Catholic, and in 1836 a start was made in the building of the first Roman Catholic Church in the parish since 1558. The Congregational Church, led by its very influential minister William Heudebourck, decided on a massive rebuilding of the Steps Meeting House, which began in 1831. As part of the scheme the Steps from the bridge to St Peter Street were removed and the road widened. (See photo on page 34.)

Having lost the backing of the Ultra Tories as a result of his support for Catholic Relief, the Prime Minister, Wellington, lost the support of the moderates by making a speech attacking any sort of Parliamentary reform. The new King, William IV, invited Lord Grey to form a ministry pledged to reform. His first Bill was carried in the Commons by

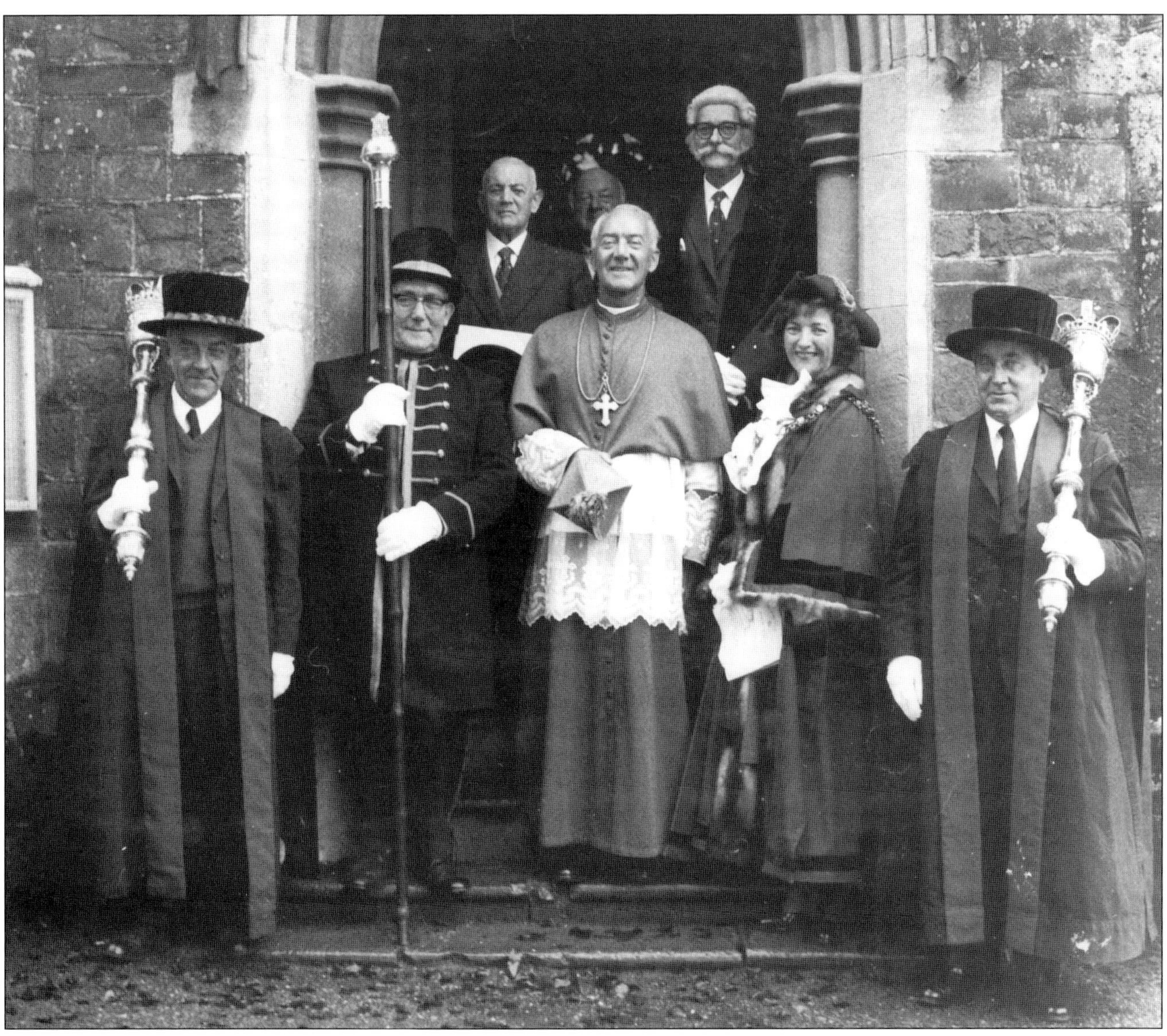

The Catholic Relief Act of 1829 allowed Catholics to emerge from the shadows. The Chichesters of Calverleigh largely financed St John's at the bottom of Long Drag. The church, its foundation-stone laid in 1836, eventually became too small for its congregation and has recently been sold. Included in the picture are: *Mary Turner, the Town's first Roman Catholic Mayor in 1976, with the Roman Catholic Bishop of Plymouth, Ron Butt (beadle), Syd Chowings and Clarence Burnett (mace bearers). Councillor Sydney Cox and Town Clerk Phillip Camfield are also present with a shadowy Councillor Bill Dunsford between them.* MUSEUM COLLECTION

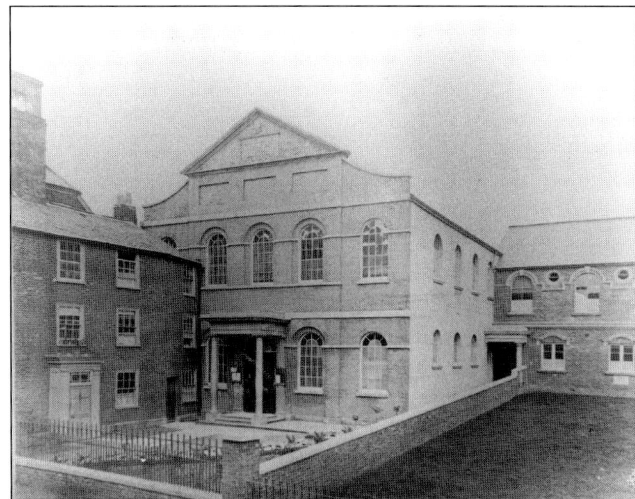

The new Methodist Chapel, built with great financial sacrifice. MUSEUM COLLECTION

one vote, but thrown out by the Lords and an election was called in the spring of 1831. Harding set the scene as follows:

> *The General Election that took place in April, was the last which occurred in Tiverton before the passing of the Reform Bill, and it was attended as might be expected, with more than usual excitement. On this occasion Mr Ryder and Mr Perceval were returned as representatives of the Borough, the corporation declining to re-elect Lord Sandon, on account of his having expressed opinions which they considered adverse to their interests. On the opening of the town-hall, the crowd rushed in, and the election was conducted amid considerable riot and disorder. The churchwardens refused to allow the bells to be rung, and in the evening the effigies of both members were paraded round the town, and afterwards burnt in Fore Street. The members did not give their election dinner as usual, but presented the proprietors of the Subscription Rooms with three beautiful chandeliers.*

There was more to it than that. Firstly the 'more than usual excitement' does not reflect the fact that the election was taking place against the background of serious rural unrest and arson, the Captain Swing riots, seen by some as the last Labourers' Revolt, which caused the authorities considerable concern. There had been a revolution in France, and revolts in Belgium, Spain and Italy. The young Gladstone, at that stage of his political odyssey a strong Tory, in a speech at the Oxford Union in May 1831, saw reform as breaking up social order not only in Britain but also in the whole civilised world. So did the Anglican Bishops who consistently voted against reform, the Bishop of Exeter being the most vociferous. Secondly, Viscount Sandon had broken with his father, a violent opponent of reform, and had decided to stand as a reform candidate in Liverpool. The Ryders had parachuted Spencer Perceval, the son of the assassinated Tory Prime Minister of the same name, into their borough. Spencer Perceval II was definitely unhinged. He had likened the clamour for reform to deadly sinfulness and had called on the nation to repent in a day of national fasting, so it was only appropriate that, when he tried to address the crowd from a window of the Three Tuns in Fore Street they pelted him with fish heads. The local papers reported that the fish was cod. Once representing Tiverton in the Commons he was a vigorous and eccentric opponent of reform. On one occasion, Bible in hand, for an hour and three quarters he denounced the nation and Parliament in the name of Jehovah, prophesying that the land would be desolate and that pestilence would be loosed upon it if reform were enacted. (He was right about the latter – there was a cholera epidemic soon after, though of course the epidemic has not accurately been attributed to Divine wrath.) Like any religious fundamentalist he contrasted the will of the people with the will of God and referred to the former as blasphemy. In January 1832 he filled seven columns of Hansard, the published transcripts of Parliamentary debates, and would have achieved much more if the exhausted scribes had not deserted their pens with such comments as 'the Hon Member read extracts from the Bible to the same effect', or 'the Hon Member then read the proceedings against Nineveh'. At one point he screeched at the House 'You are all infidels! You sit there like a race of infidels. If you reject me, you reject God, in whose name I appear.' His performance was a fitting *reductio ad absurdum* of Tiverton's years as a rotten borough.

The first 'reformed' elections took place in December 1832 and the hustings were at the top end of St Peter Street. (Presumably the Corporation was sulking and refusing to allow use of the Town Hall.) The electorate was now about 480, each with two votes, based on property qualifications, that could be challenged by opponents. (Further reform in 1867 raised this to over 1,000. In 1884 the town ceased to have its own MPs and was merged in a single member constituency with a large rural area.) John Heathcoat easily came top of the poll with 376 votes, while Kennedy won 265 votes. Benjamin Wood with 55 and the Catholic Charles Chichester of Calverleigh with 40 votes brought up the rear. The extensive victory celebrations and the fact that Heathcoat attracted the support of 80 percent of the electorate shows how isolated the Corporation, Blundell's and the Church of England had become in Tiverton.

One wonders what became of the 'beautiful chandeliers'. As Harding explains, the Subscription Rooms had come into being in 1831 as a result of an initiative taken 'by the principal gentlemen of Tiverton, to erect a public hall, reading and billiard rooms.' In March 1831 they acquired a building at the Fore Street entrance to the market. The whole cost £3,000 and John Heathcoat bought out the rest in

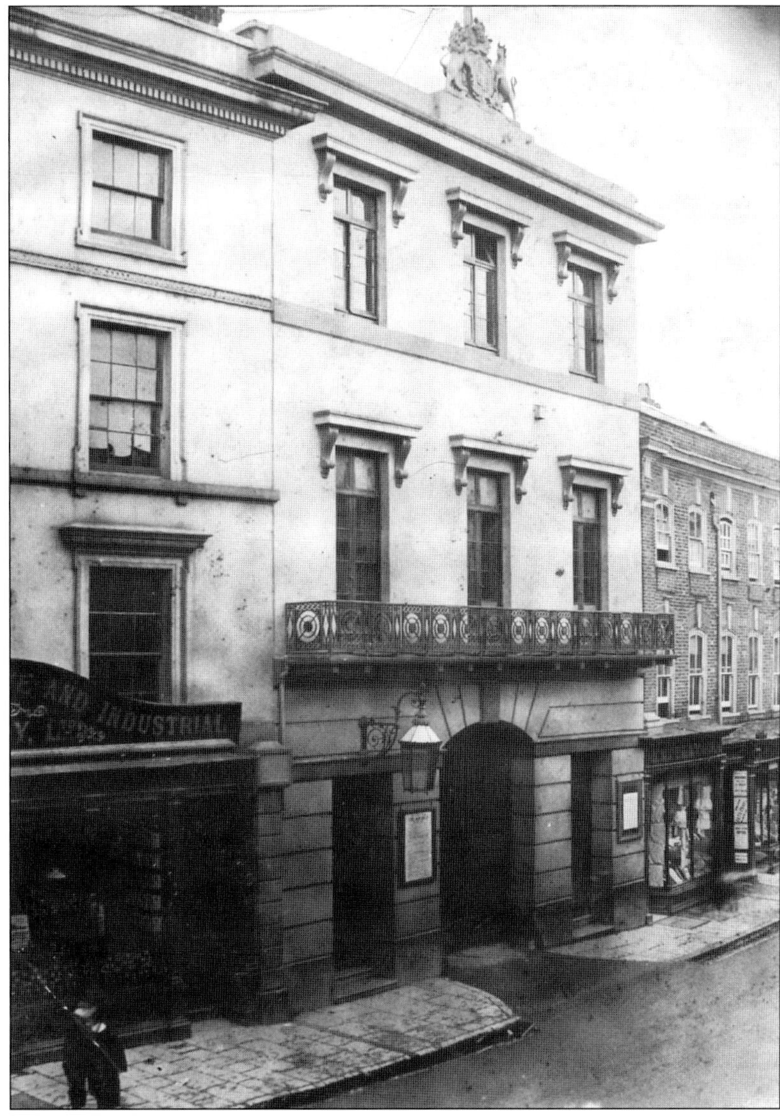

Right: *The Assembly Rooms in Fore Street that Heathcoat largely financed. They served the public under many names, including the Athenaeum and later the Technical Schools. Civic vandals demolished them in the 1960s and they were replaced by what now 'graces' the Fore Street entrance to the market.*

MUSEUM COLLECTION

Below: *The rooms within. Was this one of those 1831 chandeliers?*

MUSEUM COLLECTION

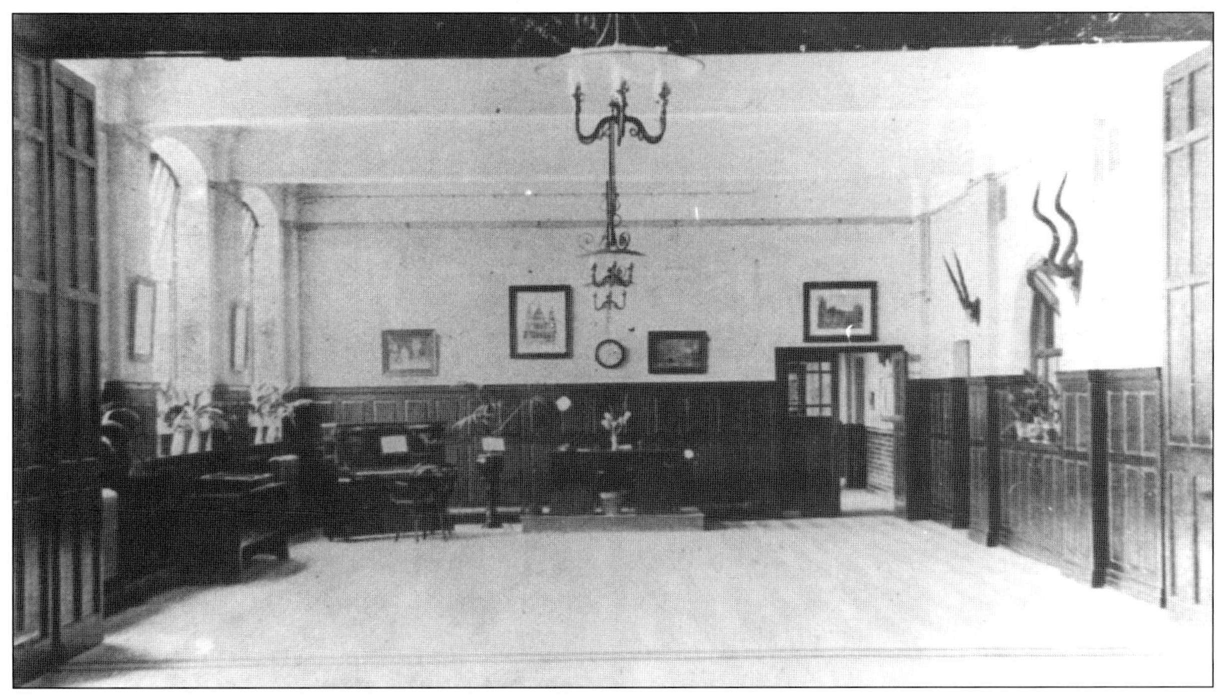

1843 and became the sole proprietor. The property seems to have languished, changing its name rather grandly to the Athenaeum, until in 1885 it was taken over by the Tiverton School Board. But the chandeliers?

After losing their right to nominate the town's MPs (the streets being run by the Paving Commissioners and the market in the hands of trustees), the Mayor, the self-perpetuating Burgesses and Assistant Burgesses of the Corporation had no further reason to exist, nor was there now any reason why anyone should want to be a Burgess. A Parliamentary Commission investigated the state of the nation's boroughs and were particularly damning in their report on Tiverton:

> *In no place we have visited do the pernicious effects arising from the connection between a Corporation having the right to return Members of Parliament and an influential nobleman as patron of the borough, appear to be more clearly displayed than in the borough of Tiverton. The management of the public affairs by the corporation has neither deserved nor obtained from them the confidence of the inhabitants.*

Few tears can have been shed when the Municipal Corporations Act of 1835 replaced the Corporation with a Borough Council elected by all male ratepayers, aged over 21 who had lived in the town for the previous three years. Elections would take place in three wards – Castle, Lowman and Westexe – where six Councillors would sit for three years. The elected Councillors could choose Aldermen who sat for six years. There was a duty to hire a Treasurer and Town Clerk and to create a police force. The new Town Council would last until 1974.

One last bastion of old Toryism remained to be stormed: the masters and feoffees of Peter Blundell's Free Grammar School. The foundation was awash with money. Its income from the lands in South Devon, bequeathed to the feoffees by Blundell, had risen considerably in value. Indeed, ever since its founding there had been a regular surplus which the feoffees had squirrelled away in government stock. In the 1750s the school's average income had been about £250 p.a. and in the 1830s income was over £1,000 p.a. The legal advice was that this surplus could only be spent on the upkeep of buildings and the funding of more scholarships, so that by 1840 there were more than ten scholarships to Oxford and Cambridge tenable by Blundellians who had been elected by masters and feoffees. By 1839 there was over £1,000 in hand in cash and over £6,000 in readily cashable investments and so the feoffees decided to modernise the living accommodation so that 'each boy should have his own bed' with the aim of producing accommodation for 140 boarders and to make it easier to admit non-Tiverton pupils. As a result of the wording of Peter Blundell's will, which seemed to forbid fee taking (thus clearly favouring Tivertonians over 'foreigners') and which limited size to 150 pupils, the feoffees had to proceed by making an application to Chancery. There were 14 feoffees at the meeting in 1839 who decided to petition Chancery. Not one of them lived in the parish of Tiverton. The town's patience snapped. Any sons they had sent to the school had been bullied unmercifully by the 'foreign' boarders and had probably been discriminated against in the award of scholarships. They wanted a 'free' school for Tivertonians with a broader education.

The Mayor called a public meeting on 26 December 1838 and decided to send a letter to the chairman of the feoffees, the Earl of Devon, protesting against their plans. The feoffees ignored the letter and pressed on with their petition to Chancery. A counter petition that the school should have more properly salaried teachers and a wider curriculum was dismissed with costs against the townsmen. On appeal this decision was reversed in 1841 and the Lord Chancellor decreed that there should be a full judicial investigation. The court almost begged both sides to come to a mutually acceptable conclusion, but blood was up – there had been too many insults traded in the press, pamphlets and verse.

The law's decision was disastrous all round and expensive. Five years later the Court decided that there would be no more boarders, all education was to be 'grammar' and free, only freely educated pupils could have scholarships, a scheme was to be drawn up for the payment of salaries, and all costs of the case (about £7,000) were to be paid by the Foundation. So the education to be provided was what the boarders wanted, but they could not go. The townsfolk's sons could attend, but could not be taught the subjects they wanted. Numbers fell to 31. The Tories no longer held any of the levers of power in the town, but in politics all victories are conditional, and many are Pyrrhic!

Chapter 6

Heathcoat and Palmerston, Railways and Sewerage

'As one who long in populous city pent,
Where houses thick and sewers annoy the air
Forth issuing on a summer's morn to breathe
Among the pleasant villages and farms....'

Milton, *Paradise Lost.*

'Upon the education of the people of this country the fate of this country depends.'

Disraeli, 1874.

Tiverton existed as a 'reformed' borough electing two MPs to Parliament from 1832 to 1884. From 1832–35 the town was represented by Heathcoat and Kennedy. Kennedy's attachment to reform was rewarded by some *douceur* and his place was taken by Lord Palmerston, who was the town's MP until his death in 1865. Heathcoat and Palmerston stayed in partnership until Heathcoat retired in 1859. In that 24 years the electorate of less than 500 only had to go to the polls once: in 1837 when the incumbent Liberals were challenged by the Tory, Benjamin B. Dickinson, who later assumed the surname Walrond when his father-in-law died (and who was the father of the later and successful Tory candidate). As a protest against the inequity of the 'reformed' system a Chartist candidate, demanding 'One Man, One Vote', stood in 1847, but retired before the poll. From 1859 to 1865 George Denman sat with Palmerston, losing his seat to Tory John Walrond. On Palmerston's death Denman recovered his seat. The Reform Bill of 1867 increased the electorate to over 1,100, and John Heathcoat Amory, the grandson of John Heathcoat, joined Denman and won an unopposed election, Walrond having decamped to a new county constituency. On Denman's appointment as Judge, he was replaced by another Liberal, Massey, and Walrond's challenges were beaten off in 1872, 1874 and 1880. A by-election in 1881 saw Lord Ebrington join Heathcoat Amory. Disraeli rewarded Walrond's services to the Tory cause with a baronetcy in 1882. Heathcoat Amory had become 'Sir John' in 1874 on Gladstone's recommendation.

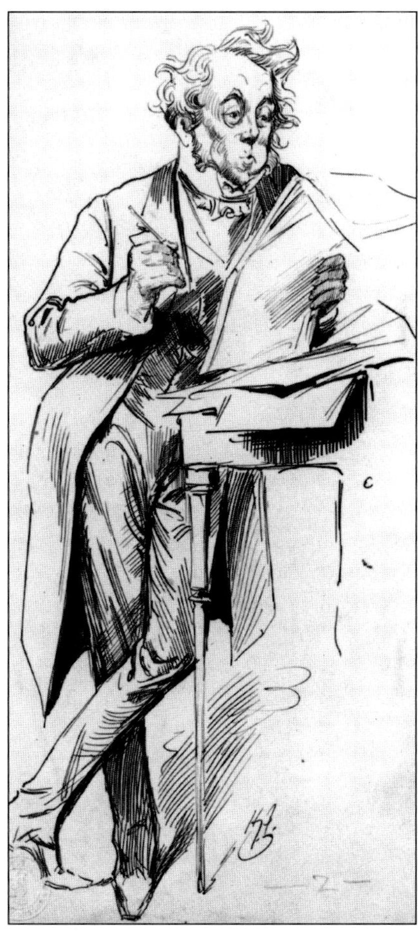

Lord Palmerston, MP for Tiverton 1835–65. He bought the seat for £2,000 and was Home Secretary, Foreign Secretary and Prime Minister almost continuously from 1855–65. He shamelessly manipulated the press, opposed any extension of the franchise and would take lessons from no man about gunboat diplomacy. A more flattering portrait can be seen in the Town Hall. NATIONAL PORTRAIT GALLERY

Palmerston was an unlikely MP to have to rely on the votes of small-town Liberal Nonconformity. His main interest was foreign policy and he had the Whig aristocrat's disdain for absolute monarchy, so his attacks on the Habsburgs and Romanovs, as well as his support for Liberals in Italy and Spain would have been popular, but his dress, his ton, his support for the Tiverton Races and his distance from the Temperance Movement made him an unlikely recipient of votes from members of the Baptist, Methodist and Independent congregations. His political career relied heavily on the Heathcoat local influence. His presence brought Tiverton into the world spotlight at election times, and the main hotel, The Three Tuns, where W.H. Smith's is now located, was renamed The Palmerston in his honour.

In 1884 Tiverton's electoral importance was extinguished and the Heathcoat Amorys lost their pocket borough. The 1884 Reform Bill drowned the town in

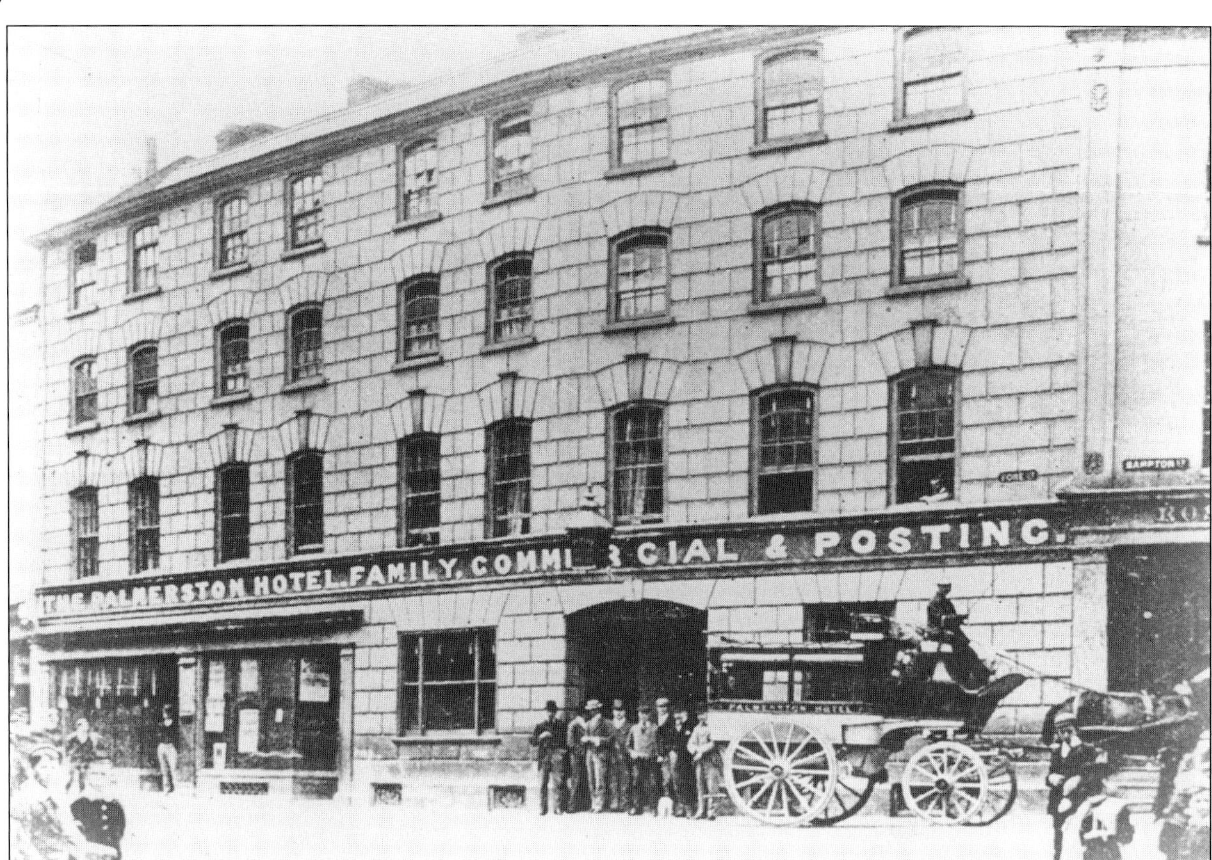

The Palmerston Hotel, formerly the Three Tuns, renamed in honour of Lord Palmerston, one of Tiverton's MPs from 1835, and Foreign Secretary and Prime Minister almost continuously from 1855–65. His election speeches were usually made from a balcony window. The hotel was replaced by a concrete mess in the 1960s.

MUSEUM COLLECTION

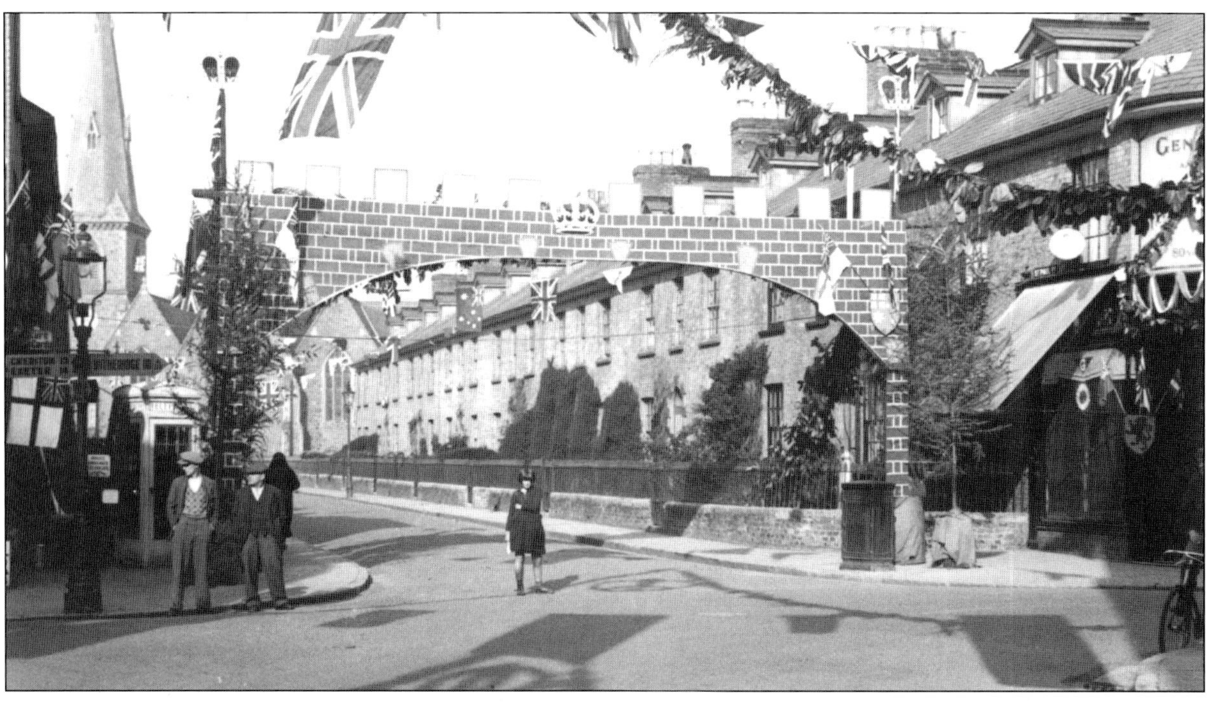

St Paul's and Church Street, an excellent piece of town planning. The archway reappears in later celebrations. Note the gas street lighting. The church was endowed by Caroline and Ambrose Brewin, Heathcoat's daughter and son-in-law. Heathcoat himself and his other son-in-law, Samuel Amory, may have favoured Dissent.

MUSEUM COLLECTION

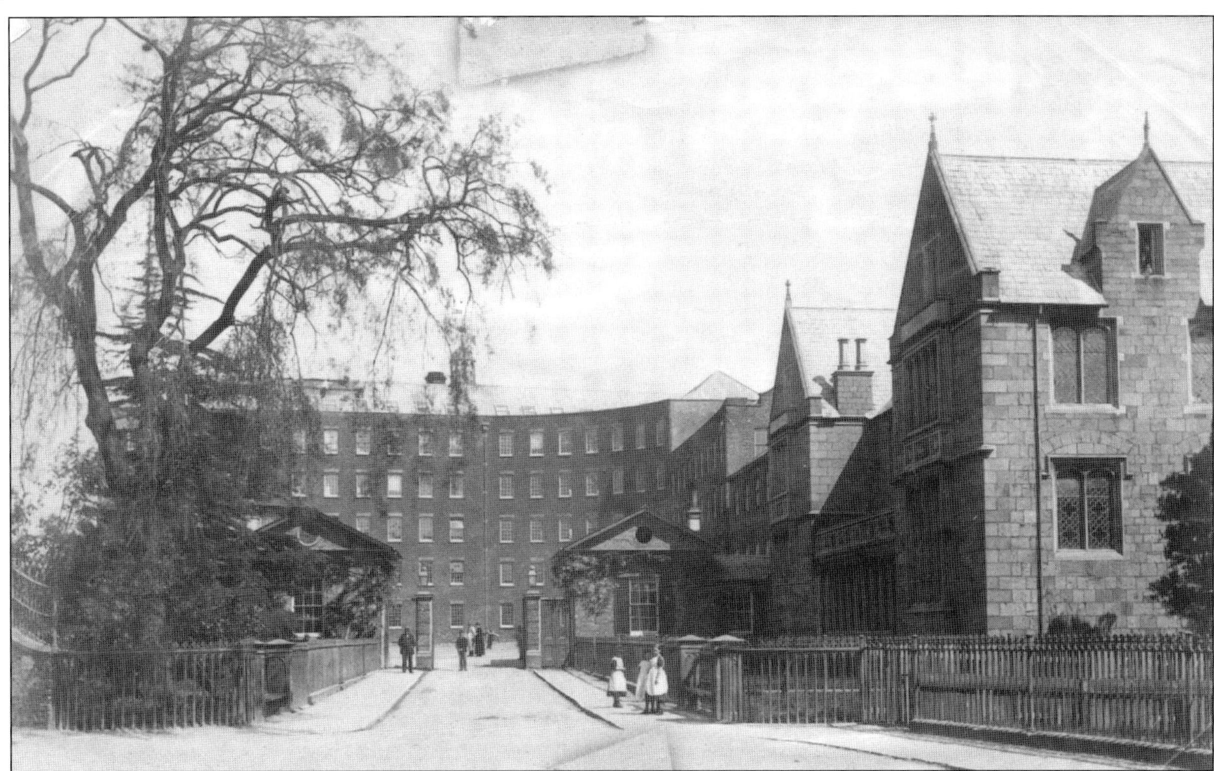

Heathcoat's factory. The school Heathcoat had built at the factory gates was affiliated to the British Society, the Dissenting school body. The pupils on the pavement could have stepped out of the picture below.

MUSEUM COLLECTION

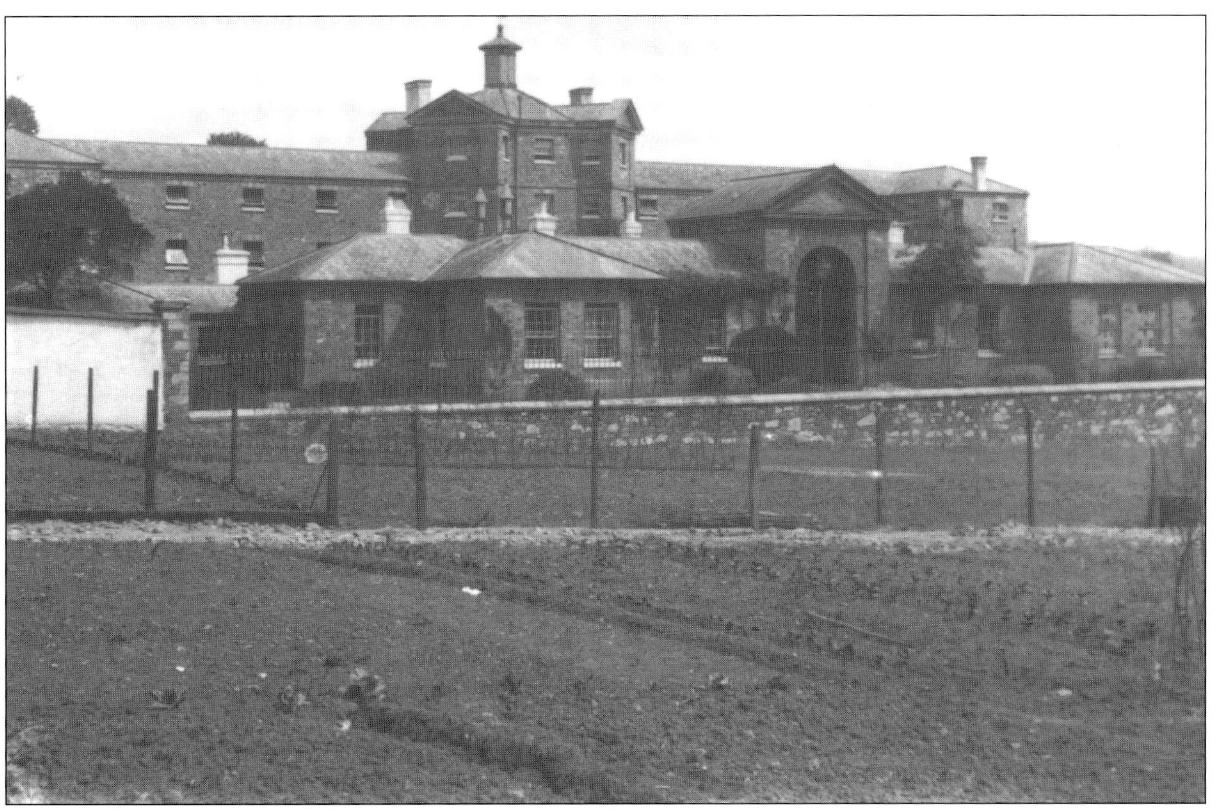

The Union Workhouse, built in the 1830s on the site of the 1698 hospital. It was a looming, fearful presence brooding over the town. As the Poor Law Commissioners stated: The workhouse overseer 'must be the hardest taskmaster and the worst paymaster that the idle and dissolute can apply to.'

MUSEUM COLLECTION

a lake of rural Devon, stretching in a huge arc around Exeter from Uffculme, Bampton and Crediton to Dawlish, with almost 10,000 voters and, although the constituency was still called Tiverton, Parliamentary elections were deprived of their local feeling and, except in times of national excitement such as the 1922–23 elections and the Miners' Strike elections of 1974, lacked much excitement as the new seat was safe for the Tories. The only exception was in 1923 when a by-election was caused by the death of the sitting Conservative and the Liberals had a particularly good local candidate in Francis Acland and won the seat. However, this was only held for a few months before it was lost by three votes in the election of December 1923. Between 1923 and the present day it has stayed 'blue'. Recent boundary changes have left Tiverton on the eastern edge of its constituency.

It is doubtful whether Sir John deserved his baronetcy for his Parliamentary labours, but the family influence on Tiverton was immense. His grandfather and father, the London solicitor Samuel Amory, led the charge against Tory Blundell's. John Heathcoat also funded the Assembly Rooms and later bought the property. In 1844 he offered to lend all of the £3,500 to build the jail. He provided the town's gas from his own plant. He donated the site for St Paul's Church and the cost of the building was shared by the Peard trustees and Ambrose Brewin, Heathcoat's son-in-law, who also built Church Street and the Vicarage. In 1841 Heathcoat provided the money necessary to build the school at the factory gates. He affiliated it to the British and Foreign School's Society, the Nonconformist educational body, as opposed to the National Society, the Anglican body. Significantly, apart from the donation to St Paul's, he was not conspicuous in support of the Church of England. He began a family policy of buying land as it came up for sale. Within the town this was often used for factory housing and in the parish he and Sir John built up a large estate. Between 1869 and 1871 the present National Trust house, Knightshayes, was built on a site purchased from the Dickinson-Walronds. Sir John and his brother-in-law Ambrose Brewin were supporters of Tiverton Hospital. A dispensary had been started at Kiddell's Court in 1852 for the sick poor. In 1865 the Brewins gave the town a new site in Bampton Street and donated £1,250 towards the cost of building an infirmary. Other members of the family gave another £1,000 and Sir John was president of the management committee.

Of necessity, this is an incomplete list of their benefactions, but the main contribution of John Heathcoat to the town was the provision of employment. John Heathcoat had invented a lacemaking machine, which he patented in 1808. He bought the factory and set up work there in 1816 and had soon bought most of the land in northern Westexe. In the 1820s he set up factories in France and in the 1850s in Italy. However, his main focus was at Tiverton where he employed over 1,000 workers, more if the foundry, gasworks and brickworks were included.

An interesting, if unintended, aspect of factory production as opposed to domestic production, or 'cottage industry', was that women began to earn wages in their own right, rather than as units under the 'head of the household', spinners to their husbands' weaving. It was almost entirely due to the wealth generated by the factory that Tiverton's population decline was reversed. Between 1801 and 1851 the population of Cullompton increased by 12 percent, Crediton by 22 percent, Honiton by 45 percent and South Molton by 55 percent, but Tiverton's increased by 66 percent, rising from 6,500 to 11,000.

Not everything was rosy. There had always been poor people in Tiverton; indeed it has been estimated that over half the population in any sixteenth-century town lived from hand to mouth, with no savings or capital to fall back on, at or below the bread line. Innumerable were the bequests to provide the poor with weekly bread. The first bequest in about 1250 was from Countess Isabella of the gift of Elmore so that the poor could keep cattle there. In 1370 Sir Hugh de Courtenay bequeathed the market tolls for the benefit of the poor. In 1517 John Greenway provided houses for some of the poor and a dole so that they could support themselves. Walter Tyrell, John Waldron, Edward Prowse, Joan Prowse, and John Slee all left money for the poor. Sir John Acland left an annuity to supply 12 poor people with a 1d. loaf, weekly, for ever. And that only takes us down to 1614. Others tried to help the poor by leaving money which the poor could borrow in order to set themselves up in a trade. Others sought to endow schools so that the poor could, through education, learn not to be poor. Dunsford lists them down to Benjamin Gilberd in whose will all the various streams of charity are mingled. He gave the interest on £1,000 'to be given annually to such poor people not receiving relief from the parish.' He left £10 each to 'ten young tradesmen of Tiverton about to enter into business there.' He also left £1,500 to Blundell's, £300 to Chilcott's School and £150 to 'the Charity School for boys in the old Churchyard, Tiverton'. Before 1700 there was parish relief, paid for by the poor rate and administered by the churchwardens, and the produce of these charitable bequests, administered either by their trustees or by the wardens.

Dunsford attempted to discover what the poor cost the parish. In 1612 he reckoned £120 a year. His average for the 1680s was about £500 a year. In 1696 it leapt to £950 and in 1697 to over £1,100 a year. This was probably the spur that led the town to seek an Act of Parliament to set up a workhouse on the site of the later Belmont Hospital. The lucky, or perhaps forelock-tugging, poor might get charity and outdoor relief, the less lucky would face semi-incarceration

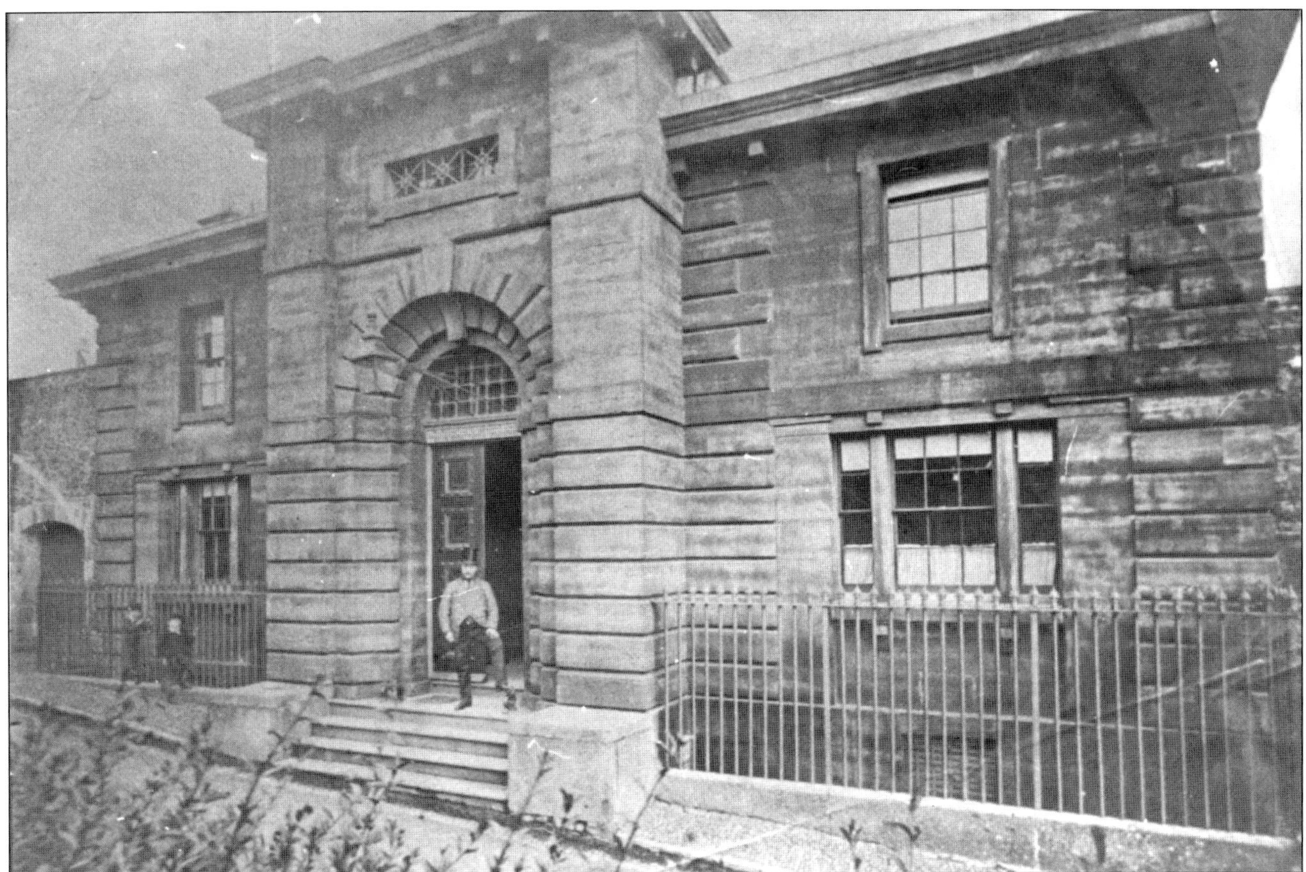

Another deterrent, the gaol and police station in St Andrew Street, built in the 1840s. The population was so well behaved that it was often empty. MUSEUM COLLECTION

in the workhouse, and the able-bodied idle, the Elizabethan 'sturdy beggar' might be whipped round the streets at a cart's tail and sent on his or her way or placed in the Bridewell in St Andrew Street.

The expense of the poor continued to rise. In 1770 it had reached £2,000 for the first time. After 1788 it was never less than £3,000 a year, and in 1816 it had risen to the crippling figure of £7,500. The employment offered by Heathcoat's probably contributed to its fall to £6,500 in the 1820s. The formation of a Tiverton Mendicity Society in 1833 illustrates the problem. It was formed to deal with the wandering mendicants, or beggars. The truth is that the world was not 'local' anymore, people were on the move, into the towns from the pauperised countryside, from struggling decaying towns to the mushrooming towns of the industrial revolution. The problem of the poor could no longer be dealt with by parish remedies and personal charity and in 1834 the government passed the Poor Law, which divided the nation into Poor Law 'Unions'. Tiverton was placed in a 'Union' with 26 other parishes, which included Cullompton, Bampton and Silverton, the germ of the later Tiverton Rural District Council. A new and larger workhouse was built, while outdoor relief was restricted to the sick and old. Into the new workhouse went the economically destitute and, to prevent scrounging, into conditions deliberately kept worse that any normally found outside. Women and children were kept separate from the men. Indeed, pauper children were often apprenticed out as a source of cheap labour. The new workhouses were called Bastilles and lasted until 1926, when the Tiverton Union Workhouse was transformed into the Belmont Hospital. As late as the 1970s the elderly confused were filled with fear at being sent there.

To keep the poor and the criminal under control the Municipal Corporation Act urged the newly elected Council to build a gaol and set up a police force. Every other Devon borough acted promptly and set up their force in 1836 or 1837. Tiverton delayed until 1845, and then the Councillors were so evenly divided, it was won on a casting vote that a force of three constables and a 'super' was set up, operating from a station near the old Town Hall. A new gaol was built on the St Andrew Street site in 1844.

The new Town Council was also strangely dilatory in matters of public health. In response to a public health measure passed in 1848, 260 Tivertonians petitioned that the provisions of the Act should be applied in the town and at the end of 1850, Rammell, a public health inspector, surveyed the town, which had recently been described in *White's Directory* as one of the healthiest towns in Devon. Rammell's report makes horrendous reading. His review of the health of the town in statistics of births and deaths reveals that in the 1840s 25 percent of children died before they were five and that typhus was 'very

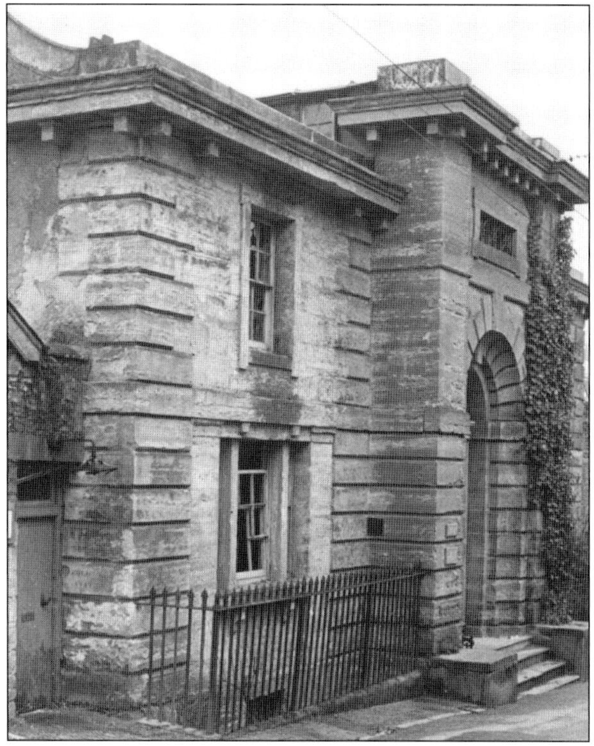

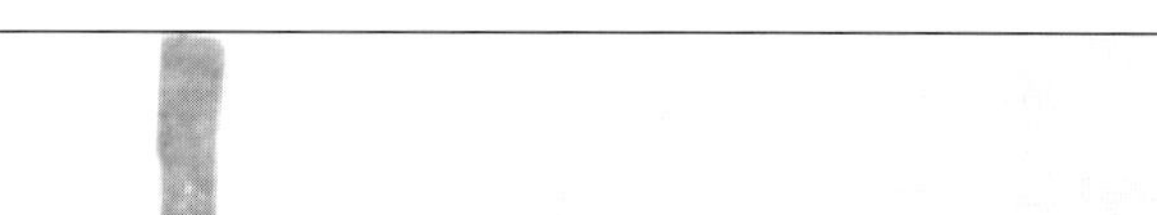

The gaol, derelict in the 1970s. It was suggested that it be knocked down and replaced by a five-storey block of flats, but it was saved by the Civic Society.

MUSEUM COLLECTION

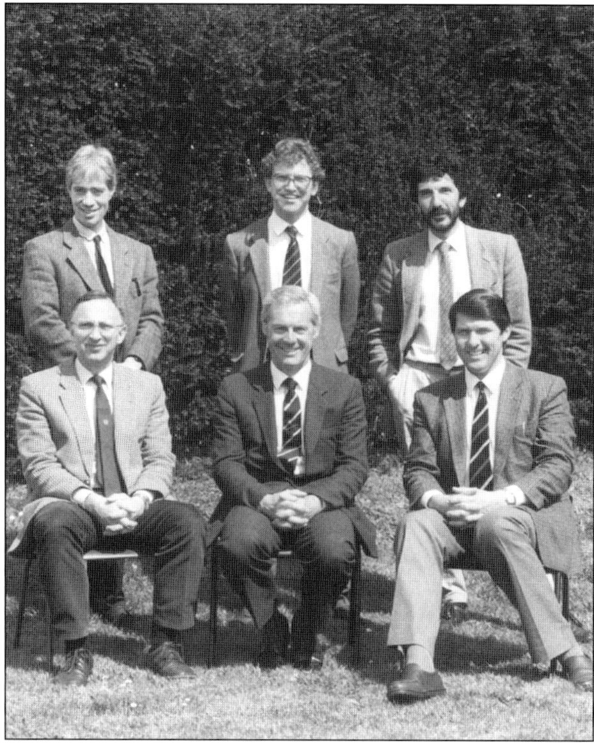

The doctors of Clare House, successors of those medical men who acted on Rammell's report. Pictured are: *Drs Kerr, Grieve, Bloom, Seymour, Peters and Whittlesea.*

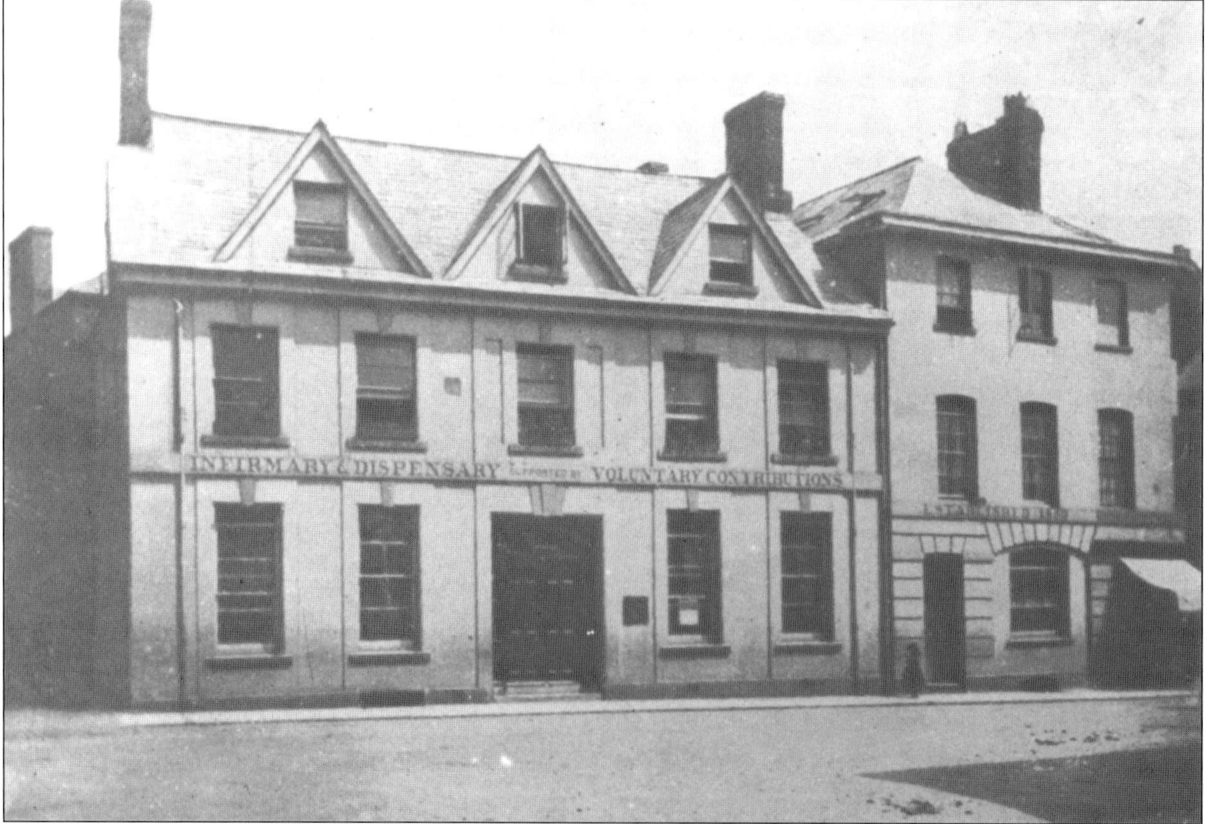

The Tiverton Infirmary in Newport Street, developed in response to Rammell's horrors.

MUSEUM COLLECTION

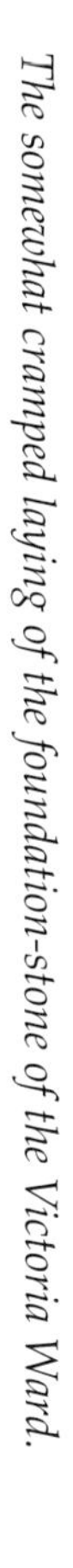

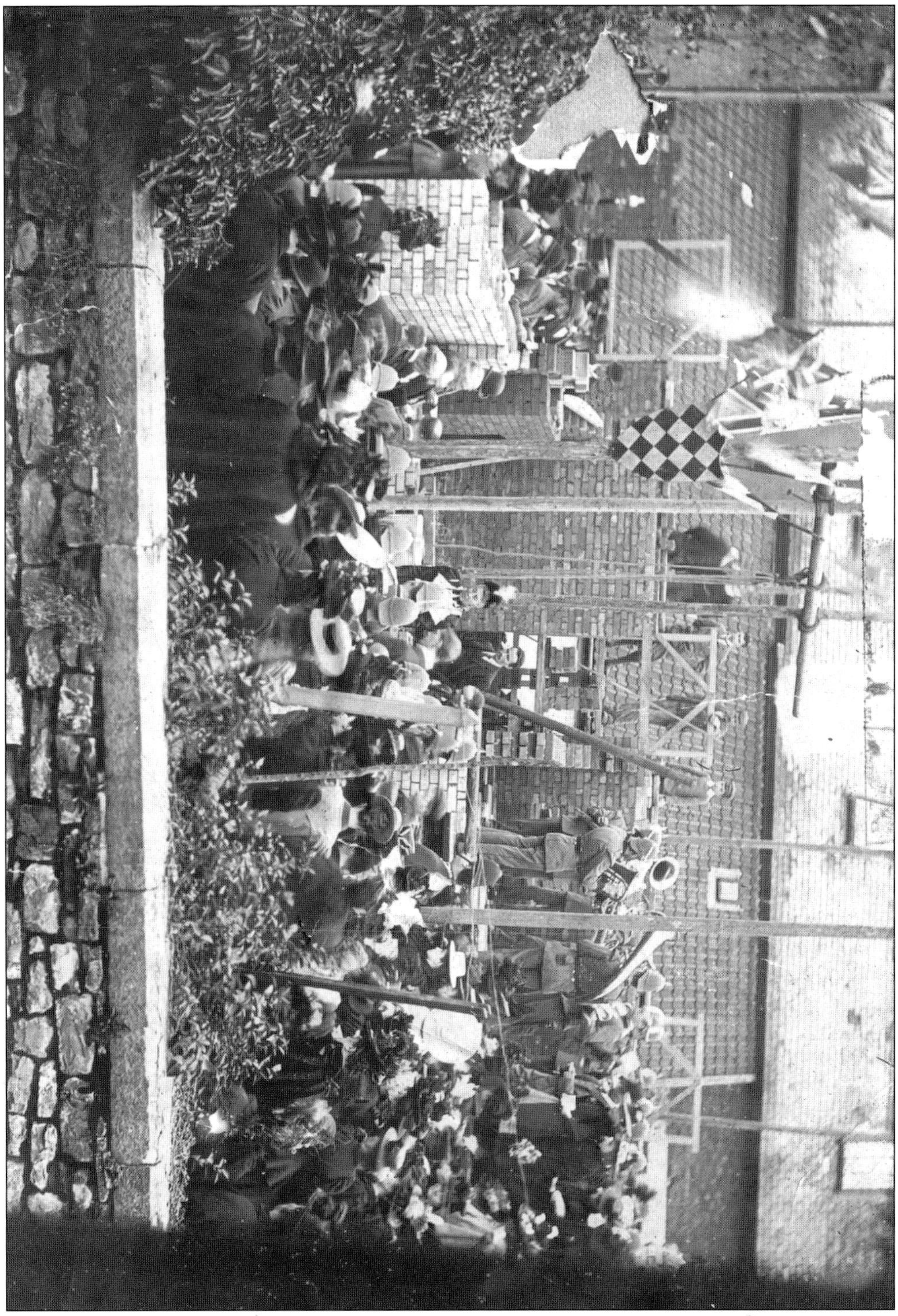

The somewhat cramped laying of the foundation-stone of the Victoria Ward.

MUSEUM COLLECTION

common', particularly in Frog Street and Upper Bampton Street, and that 'in every part of the town there are houses either totally without privies or sharing with up to ten or twelve other families.' He went on to state, 'The medical attendant cannot accomplish his daily rounds without being greeted with offensive effluvia in every variety.' A local doctor gave evidence that the leat served a 'double function of a fountain and a sewer.' The top end of Bampton Street was described as a 'monstrous cesspool'. There were slaughterhouses in William Street, on the corner of Barrington Street and Gold Street, two in Bampton Street, two more in Upper Bampton Street, one in Castle Street and at least two more in courts now demolished. Pigsties were too common to be listed. The two burial grounds, one at St George's, the other at St Peter's, were literally overflowing, so that new graves invariably cut through those containing partially decomposed bodies. A row of houses that then stood along the east side of St George's yard particularly suffered. The number of burials had become so great that the 'earth' in the yard now reached six foot up their back wall and awful fluids seeped through.

Some 20 pages of the report are taken up with an account of his inspection of the town, street by street.

Morrish's Buildings at the upper end of Barrington Street. Five dwellings, 29 inmates. A double privy, seven feet deep, full of liquid matter; one side of the cesspit formed by the back of an adjoining house. The soil removed once a year, first emptied on the surface of the court, where it remains till it is wheeled into the street to be carted away. On last occasion of emptying 10 wagons of soil removed. The pump in this court unfit for use, the water being the colour of urine and smelling offensively... In William Street a row of six houses, having one privy. No back door to any but one house, the passage of which leads to a slaughterhouse behind, the beasts being driven through it to be killed. The liquid of a pigsty falls towards a row of houses beyond... Richard's buildings in the lower part of Barrington Street, five houses with good shops in Gold Street, have one privy in a yard. Within seven feet of the privy is the pump and both are placed against a most objectionable slaughtering room. The drainage of the slaughtering passes through the privy cesspool into the street sewer... Greenway's Almshouses have a sewer conveying the sewage of half the town passing under the lower bedroom windows... Bidgood's premises Frog Street, a row of seven miserable thatched dwellings, near the end of the street, without back door, back window or privy. All refuse thrown into a small gutter beside the leat, except the portion that finds its own way into the leat. All water taken from the leat. The Baptist Minister, who lives opposite, complains of the nuisance from these premises; the children come in front to ease themselves; he can hardly use his front rooms. Higher up the street, adjoining the Bluecoat School is a slaughterhouse with piggeries... The stench about Bartow's Causeway much complained about... Half Moon Court, six houses, one privy. An extremely foul dung pit adjoins the privy and all the drainage flows into the open gutter in Fore Street... Clark's Row [south of Fore Street] 14 houses two privies. The sewage of a portion of the town passes in an open ditch in front. At the end of the row is a fellmongery, reeking with the stench of putrid hides. The mill tail below is three feet deep with black mud. A black ditch full of sewage matter at the back, of which the inmates complained more than of the nuisance at the front.

Every part of the town had its insanitary horrors. Westexe was as bad.

One consequence of the awful state of the water was the consumption of beer and any beverage which contained alcohol in germ-killing quantities. This would largely explain the amount of drunkenness in mid-century Tiverton and also the rise of Thomas Ford. Starting as a one-man-and-a-horse operation out of the Swan Inn, Westexe, he prospered and grew into a partner of Starkey, Knight and Ford, based on a site where the new Council Offices stand. The brewery had bore holes up to 500 feet deep, the pumps powered by water-wheels driven by the Lowman. The company also owned the premises opposite the Palmerston Hotel, where until recently Tesco was housed. Another local brewery, based in Bampton Street, just north of the old hospital, the 'Old Brewery', was taken over by Starkey, Knight and Ford, which was itself taken over by Whitbreads. No beer is now brewed commercially in Tiverton.

The local response to Rammell was partly perverse, partly positive. 'Positively' it no doubt encouraged the development of the infirmary and the hospital, but 'perverse' in that the report was condemned as bad for trade and a large public meeting agreed to send a protest against Rammell's report to the Board of Health. The town remained with too much sewage and not enough sewerage, until a later Act in 1875 made piped water and sewerage connections to each house mandatory. The Aller's water treatment plant was built in 1880 and by 1890 most of the houses in the town had been connected. In the 1890s, to cope with increased demand in dry summers, further supplies were tapped from Warnicombe and Chevithorne. The town should be grateful to John Siddalls, the borough engineer appointed in 1892, after whom Siddalls' Gardens is named.

However, one of the criticisms that Rammell made was acted upon quite quickly. Taking advantage of enabling legislation land was bought from Sir Walter Palk Carew, who held out for the high price of £200 an acre, and the new cemetery was opened in June 1855. In June 1856 Henry Philpotts, the litigious Bishop of Exeter, revoked his licence, because there was insufficient demarcation between the ground for Church of

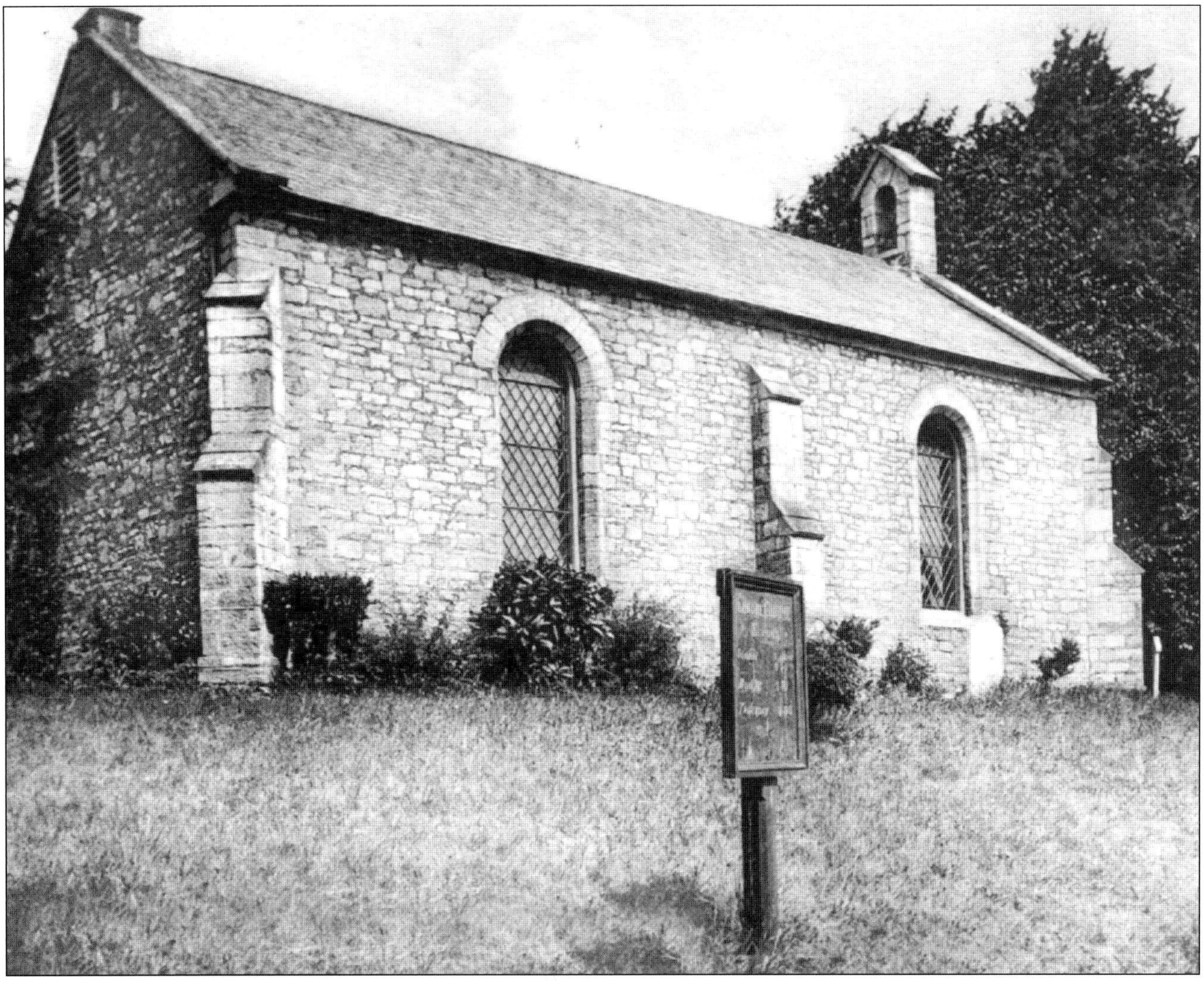

Above: *The expansion of the Congregational Church took place under the leadership of the Revd William Heudebourck. Elmore Chapel opened in the 1840s.*

MUSEUM COLLECTION

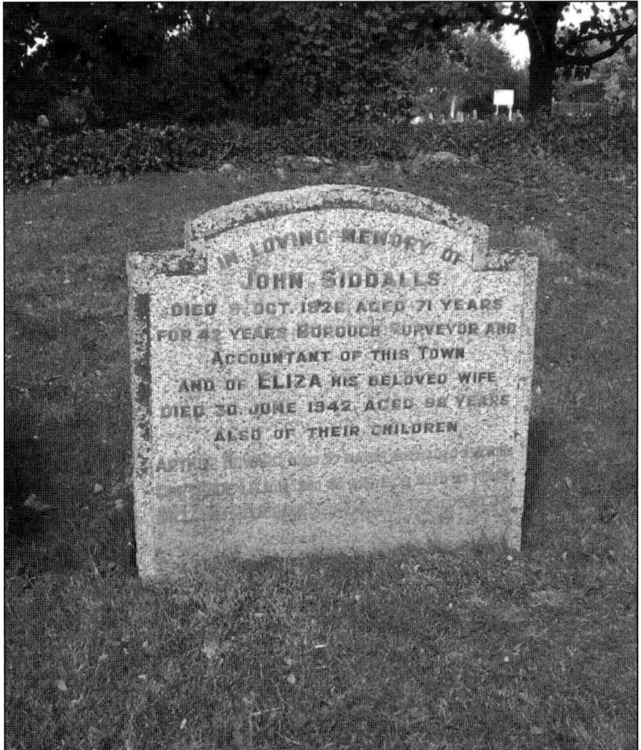

Siddalls' gravestone in the cemetery.

England burials and the ground for burying lesser mortals. The Bishop wanted a wall four foot high. Costly litigation followed and the Bishop only reconsecrated the ground in 1858, the courts having decided that a broad gravel path was all that was necessary to divide the dead destined for heavenly sheepdom from the dead destined for un-Anglican goatdom.

The whole episode illustrates the religious ardour and often religious animosity that affected Tiverton in the nineteenth century. In mid-century all the main churches in Tiverton were rebuilt, enlarged or refurbished. The Anglicans built four new churches, St Catherine's to serve Withleigh and St Thomas' to serve Chevithorne in the 1840s and St Paul's to serve Westexe in the 1850s and a rebuilt Cove Chapel in 1856. The Independents completed their new building in 1837 and built a chapel in Elmore in 1843 and another at Bolham. A Methodist breakaway group, the Bible Christians, obtained the former National School buildings at the top of Ham Place, when they moved over the road to build their big new school,

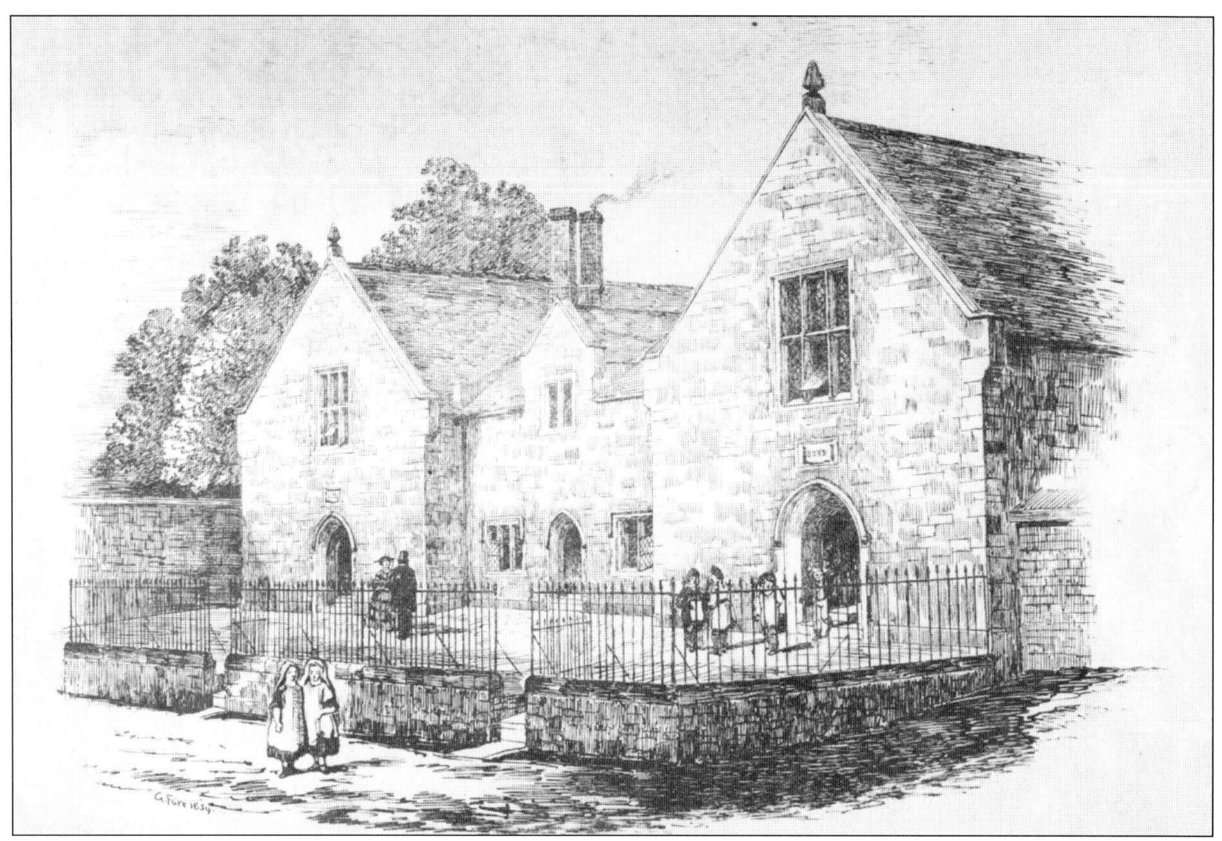

Above: *An engraving of the school built by the Church of England National Society for the 'Education of the Poor in the Principles of the Established Religion' in St Andrew Street. The first National Society School was across the way in the building now used as a chapel.* MUSEUM COLLECTION

Below: *The site now houses the Museum.* MUSEUM COLLECTION

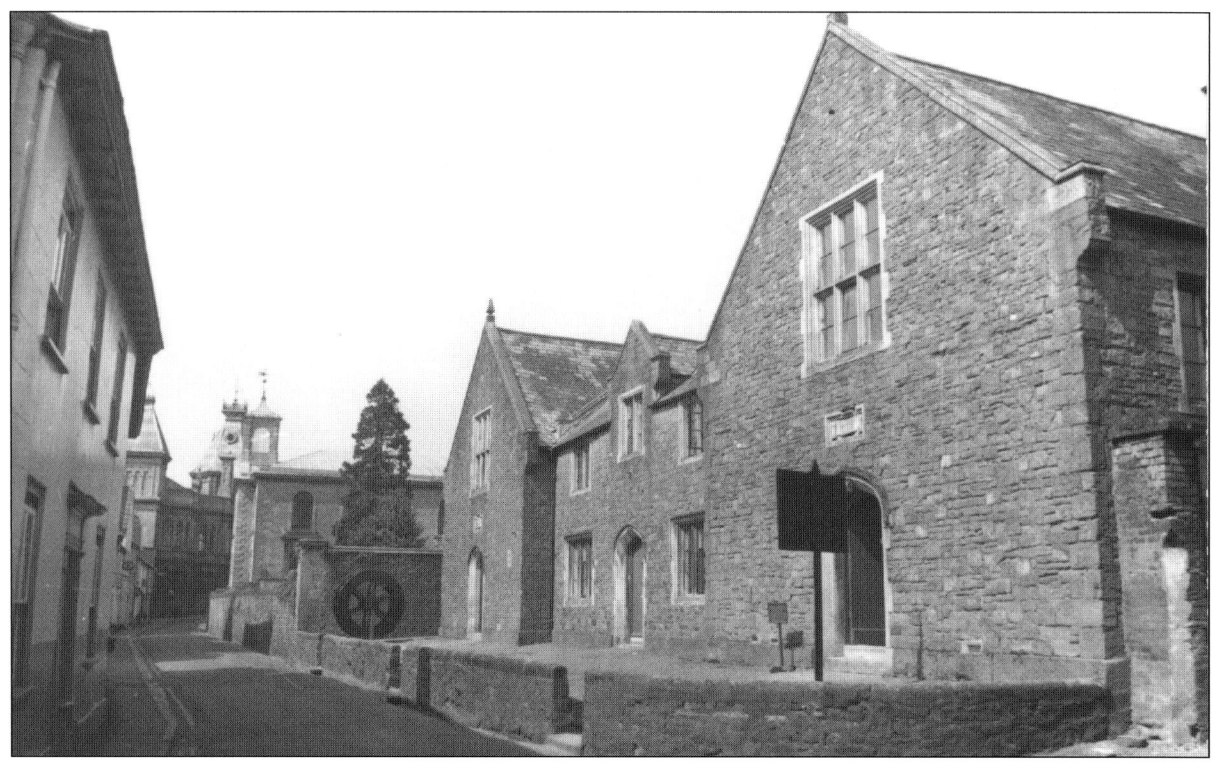

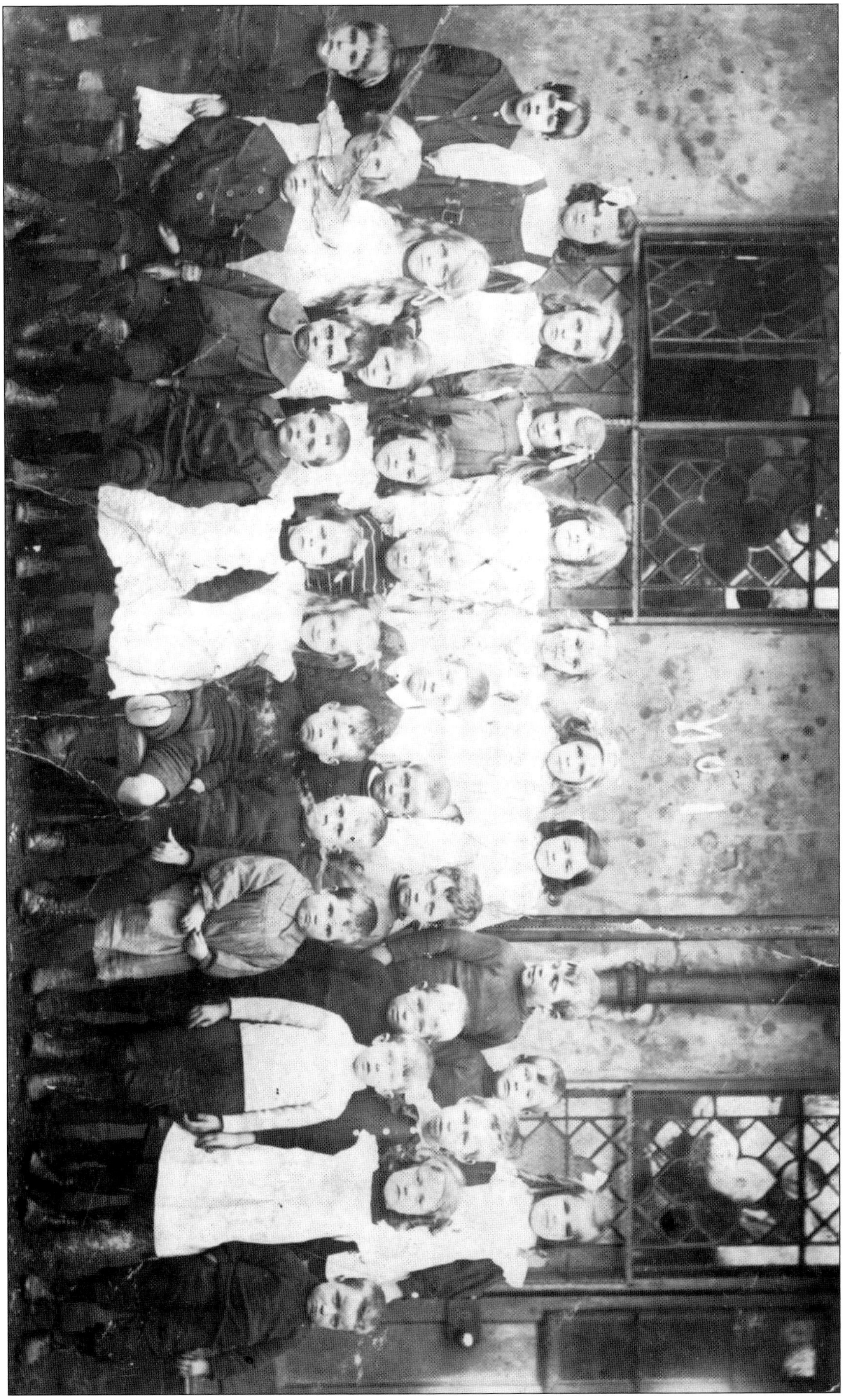

A late-nineteenth-century Infants' Class at Heathcoat's School. Did their boots fit? Probably none of their homes had a bath or plumbed lavatory.

MUSEUM COLLECTION

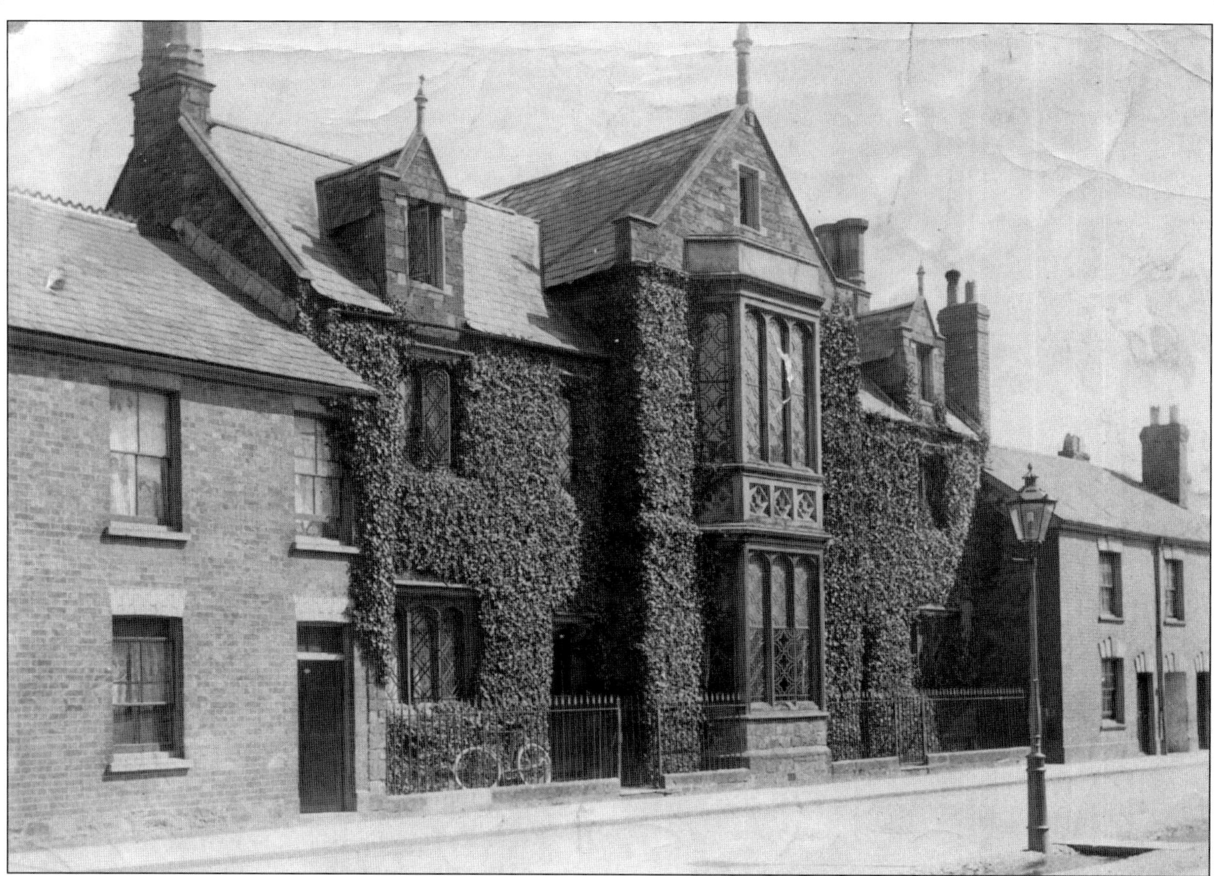

The Middle Schools in Castle Street, where they stayed until the new Middle Schools were built on the 'wilderness' site off Barrington Street. MUSEUM COLLECTION

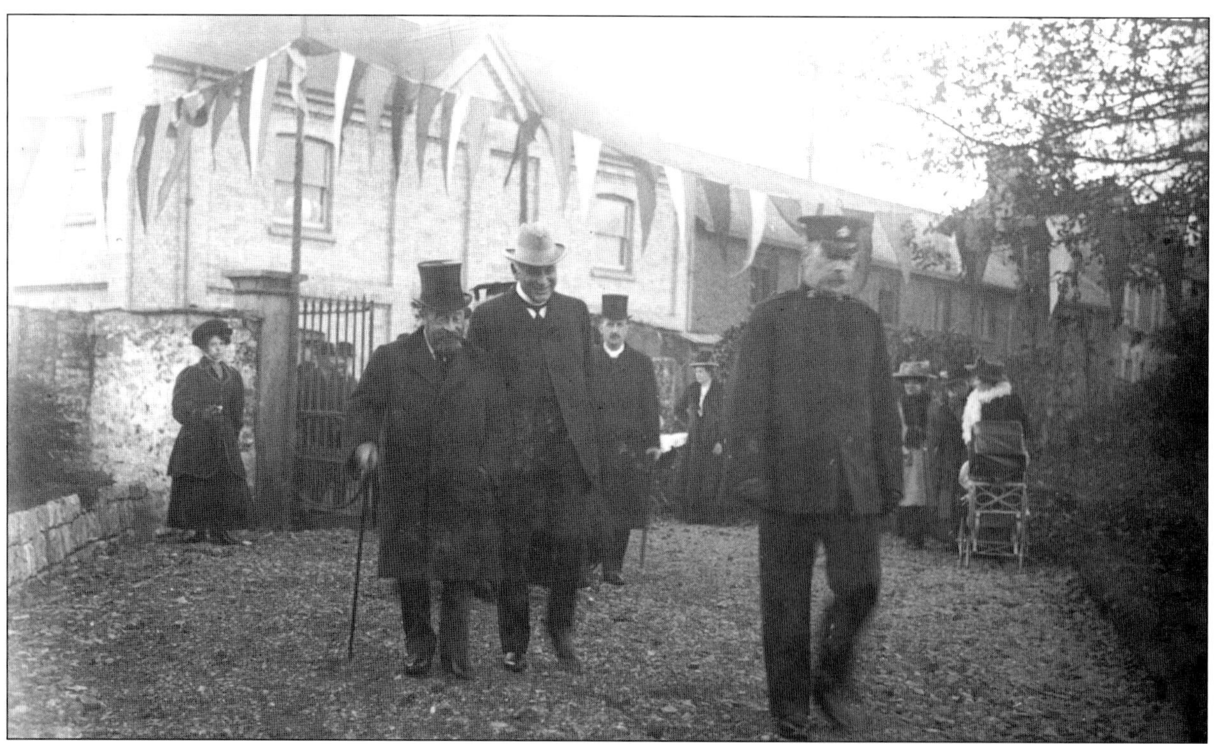

Processing to lay the foundation-stone of the new Middle Schools in November 1909. Wearing a top hat is County Councillor Sir Thomas Acland, accompanied by a Tiverton County Councillor and famous local GP, Dr Mackenzie. Discretely behind them is Revd T. Bewes of St George's. To the fore, Inspector Perry. MUSEUM COLLECTION

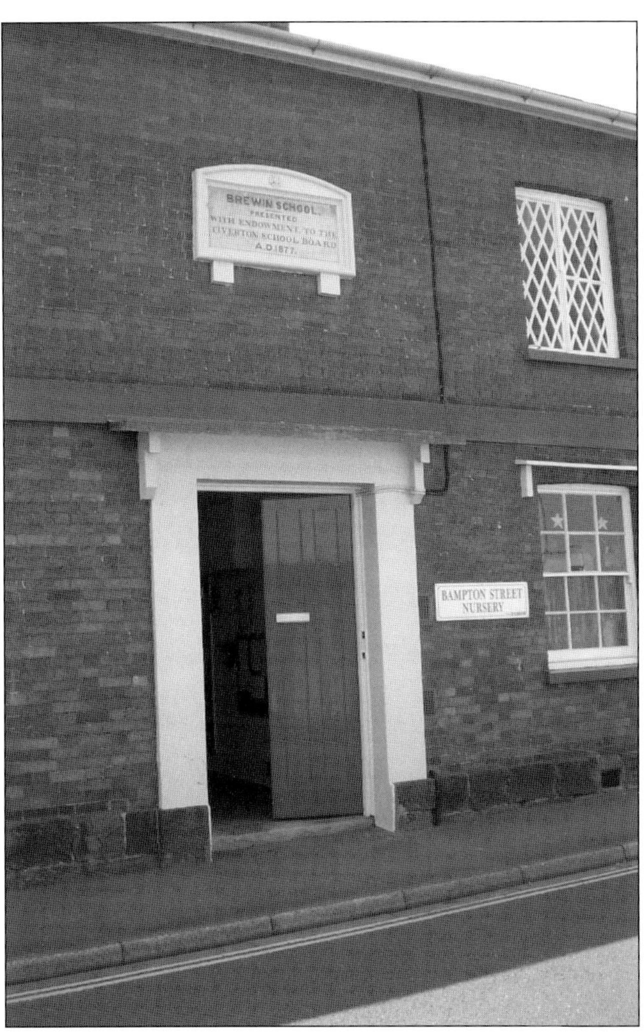

Bampton Street Nursery, endowed by Caroline and Ambrose Brewin. The inscription above the door reads: 'BREWIN SCHOOL. Presented with endowment to the Tiverton School Board AD*1877.'*

which now houses Tiverton Museum. When funds allowed they built a new chapel. The Baptists enlarged their chapel in Newport Street in 1854, but their growing congregation needed more space, so the old chapel was pulled down and the new building opened in 1877. At the opening the whole Corporation, including the Mayor robed and accompanied by the mace bearers, attended. This was the first time that the Mayor had ever attended a Nonconformist chapel in his official capacity. In the 1880s the Plymouth Brethren and the Salvation Army established presences in Tiverton. At the height of the Victorian religious revival the Anglicans had seven functioning places of worship, the Independents three, the Roman Catholics, Methodists, Bible Christians, Baptists, Plymouth Brethren and Salvation Army one each, and that does not include the 'lunatic fringe' of end of the worlders and one man missions to save the world.

The 1880s also saw the end of St Peter's as a Collegiate Church of four rectors. The Rectors of Priors, Tidcombe, Clare and Pitt used to serve St Peter's for one week in four in rotation and then moved to St George's for a week. They were each responsible for ministering to the people in their area of the parish. However, their areas did not include the town centre, called 'All Fours' for which none of them was responsible except in his weeks 'on duty'. Reality was escaping the old system. St Paul's had already been carved out of 'All Fours'. Separate churches had been built for Cove (in Pitt), Chevithorne (in Tidcombe) and Withleigh (in Clare). Ministry to the greater part of the population, who lived in 'All Fours' was in a muddle. In 1884 a new scheme was sanctioned. Withleigh, Cove and Chevithorne became independent parishes responsible for the rural areas to the north and west, and St Paul's was given a wider territory west and south of the river. The urban and suburban heartland east of the river was divided between St Peter's and St George's. St Peter's would be the church for a rector, who would have a new Rectory built nearer the town centre. As the portions fell vacant the scheme was put into operation and the first rector at St Peter's was George Hadow, and the first vicar at St George's was Walter Edmonds. Apart from the demise of Cove, the system is still with us, although the outlying churches are part of team ministries.

A positive aspect of this religious competition was the educational drive of the various churches as they fought for government grants. Apart from intermittent 'private enterprise' establishments and dame schools, in 1800 the full-time schooling available in Tiverton consisted of Chilcott's founded for 100 boys, who paid fees of 7s.6d. a quarter, Blundell's and the Bluecoat Schools in St Peter's churchyard, which taught 60 boys and 50 girls. Part-time schooling was available in the Sunday schools. When godless revolution raged in France it seemed essential to rear children in the principles of the Church of England. Thus the 'National Society for the education of the children of the poor in the principles of the Established Religion' was founded and in 1820 it opened its Tiverton branch in what is now the Salem Chapel in St Andrew Street. After 1833 state funds could swell church funds and in 1842 the school crossed the road into purpose-built quarters, now Tiverton Museum. The Nonconformists were slower off the mark and their educational grouping, the 'British and Foreign Schools Society' had to rely on John Heathcoat, who built them a school at the factory gates in 1841. This was grander and taught 800 children compared to the National Society's 300. His daughter, Caroline Brewin, built schools in Bampton Street and Elmore. In the villages, Chevithorne School was opened in 1857, while schools at Withleigh, Cove and Bolham opened later.

Eventually a state system had to take over to regulate the dynamic, but unco-ordinated efforts of private charity and religious drive. After 1870 various Acts of Parliament led to fundamental changes. In

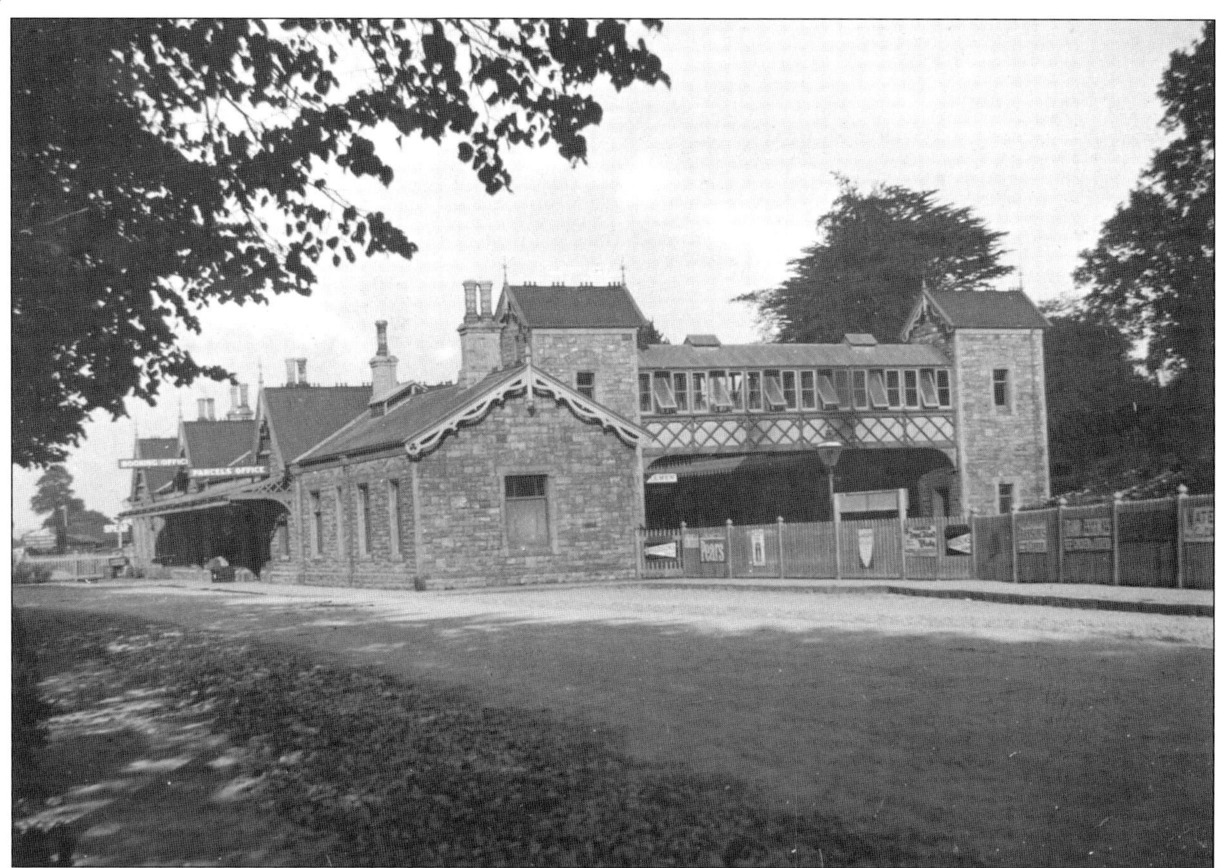

Above: *The second Tiverton Station, built for the Exe Valley line in 1885. The first station was to the northeast.*
MUSEUM COLLECTION

Below: *Beginning to demolish houses in St Andrew Street to start the cutting for the line from Tiverton to Exeter.*
MUSEUM COLLECTION

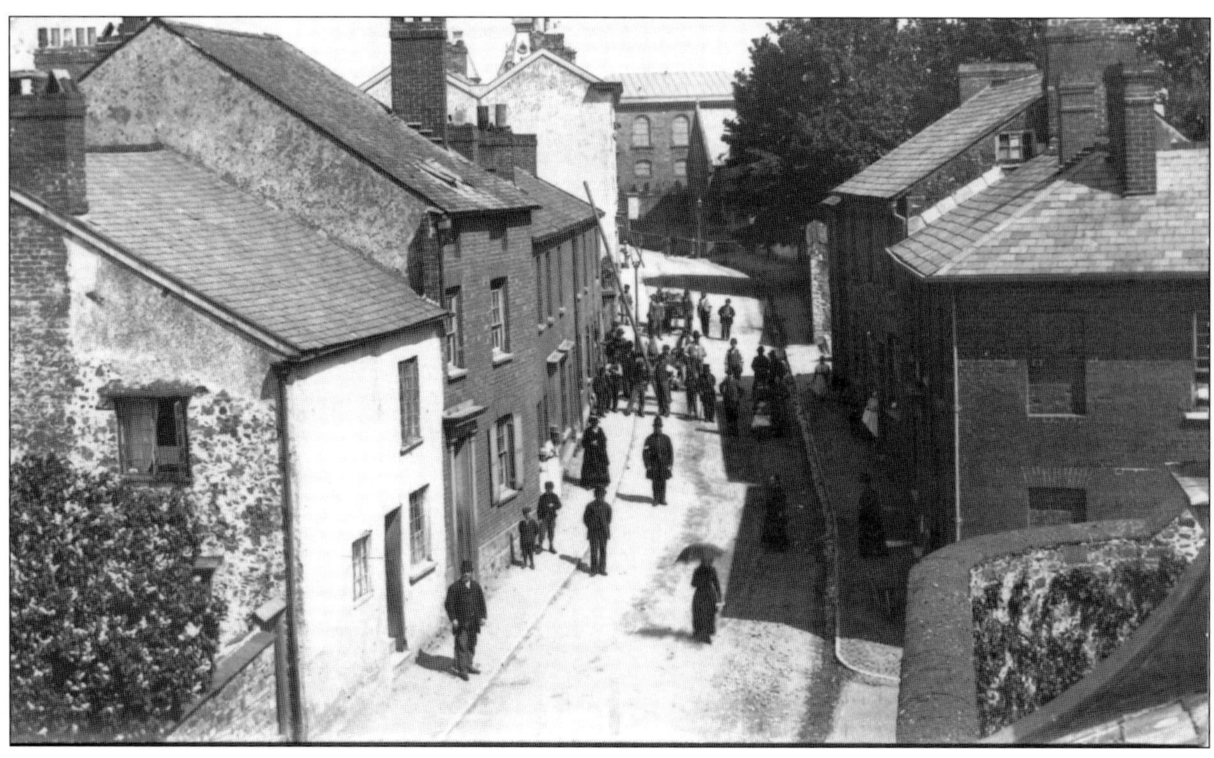

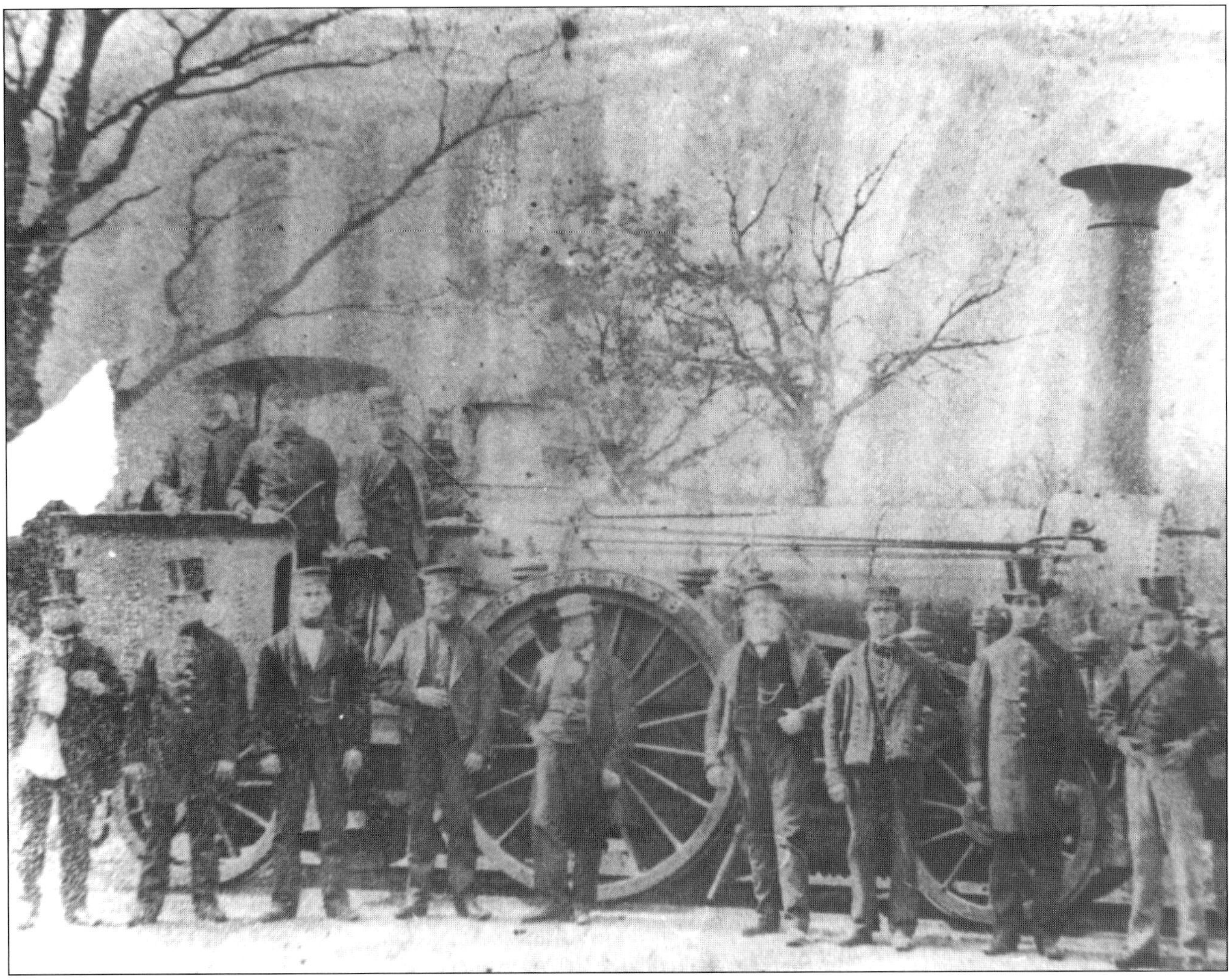

Said to have been the locomotive that first steamed into Tiverton Station in 1845, although one has one's doubts.

MUSEUM COLLECTION

order to earn state grants, denominational schools had to be inspected. Furthermore, in areas where denominational provision was inadequate school boards came into existence to run Board Schools, and in areas where denominational schools were sufficient 'Conscience Clauses' had to be negotiated to exempt pupils from unwanted religious instruction.

William Partridge, a much under-appreciated Tiverton hero, led public pressure and prodded the feoffees into a reorganisation of Blundell's so that it became a boarding and day school, with governors chosen by certain public bodies, rather than the self-perpetuating feoffees as in Peter Blundell's will. To safeguard local interest, four were to be chosen by local bodies. Successive changes have wittled this down and now few of the governors see themselves as spokesmen of local interests. Blundell's may still be an ornament of the town, but it no longer primarily serves the town's children. To be successful as a boarding school Blundell's had to move from its position in a sewage-ridden flood plain, hemmed in by river and railway. With some difficulty Partridge and the new headmaster, A.L. Francis, persuaded the governors to sanction the move to Horsden in 1882. It was hoped that the old buildings would be used for educational purposes, but this did not materialise.

The new legislation led to the birth of the Tiverton Middle Schools, which grew out of the Charity or Bluecoat Schools. They provided post elementary eduction in two schools, one for boys and one for girls, both situated in Castle Street.

To fill in the gaps of primary education the Tiverton School Board (later the LEA) came into existence in 1874, its members elected to serve three year terms. It started by being given the Brewin Schools to run and gradually picked up more schools as denominational funds became inadequate to meet the demands for ever more sophisticated education. Primary education became 'free' in the Board Schools in 1891, which put further pressure on the Church Schools.

An interesting venture began in 1882 when a flourishing art class turned itself into the Tiverton Arts and Science Schools. Public grant and private subscription allowed the purchase of the former Reading Society Rooms (the Athenaeum) in Fore Street. In 1891 central government decided to support technical education so it became called the Technical Art and Science School.

In 1910 the Middle Schools and the Technical Art and Science School merged and opened in new premises. At first it was still called the Tiverton Middle School, although later it became Tiverton Grammar. In 1913 Heathcoat's School moved into a new establishment run by the LEA on a spacious site next to the Westexe Recreation Ground.

This educational narrative has taken us to a time when the first cars appeared in Tiverton, but from the 1840s to the first salvoes of the First World War, Tiverton depended on the railway. It was a misfortune that it took so long to integrate Tiverton into the network. The Bristol to Exeter line opened in 1843 and the nearest station to Tiverton was 'Park', later renamed 'Tiverton Junction' in Willand. The railway directors wanted to put it at Leonard Moor where the new 'Tiverton Parkway' was eventually built in the 1980s. In 1848 a branch line was built from the junction to Tiverton, terminating where Travis Perkins is located at the time of writing. Proposed at the same

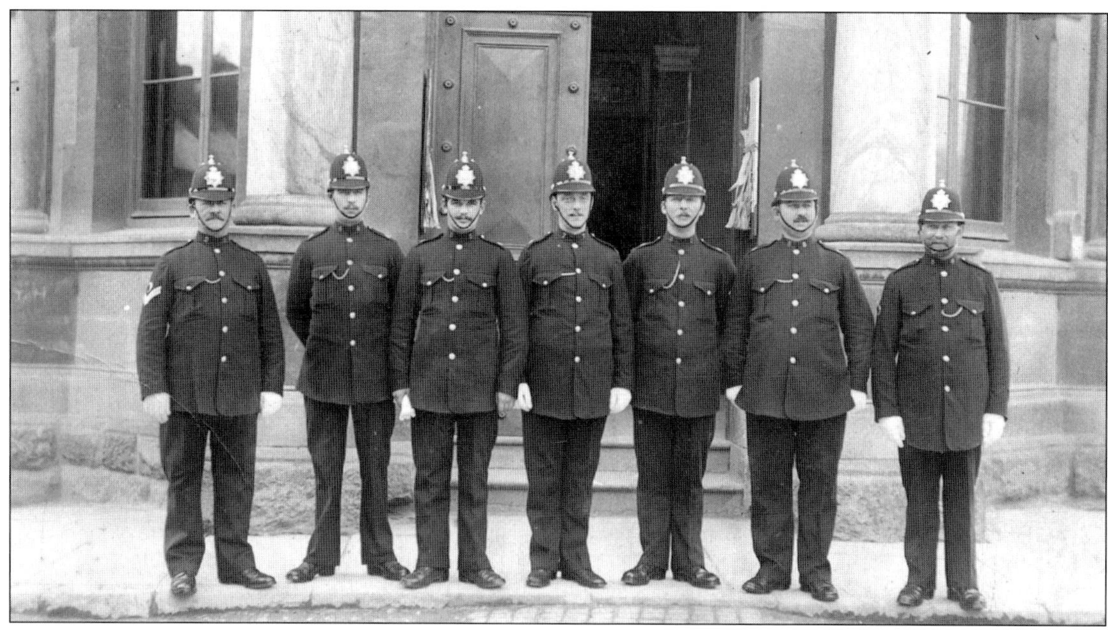

The under-strength, but adequate police force. Pictured are, left to right: *Sgt Takle, PCs Lee, Land, Perry, Stevens, Dunning and Elston.* MUSEUM COLLECTION

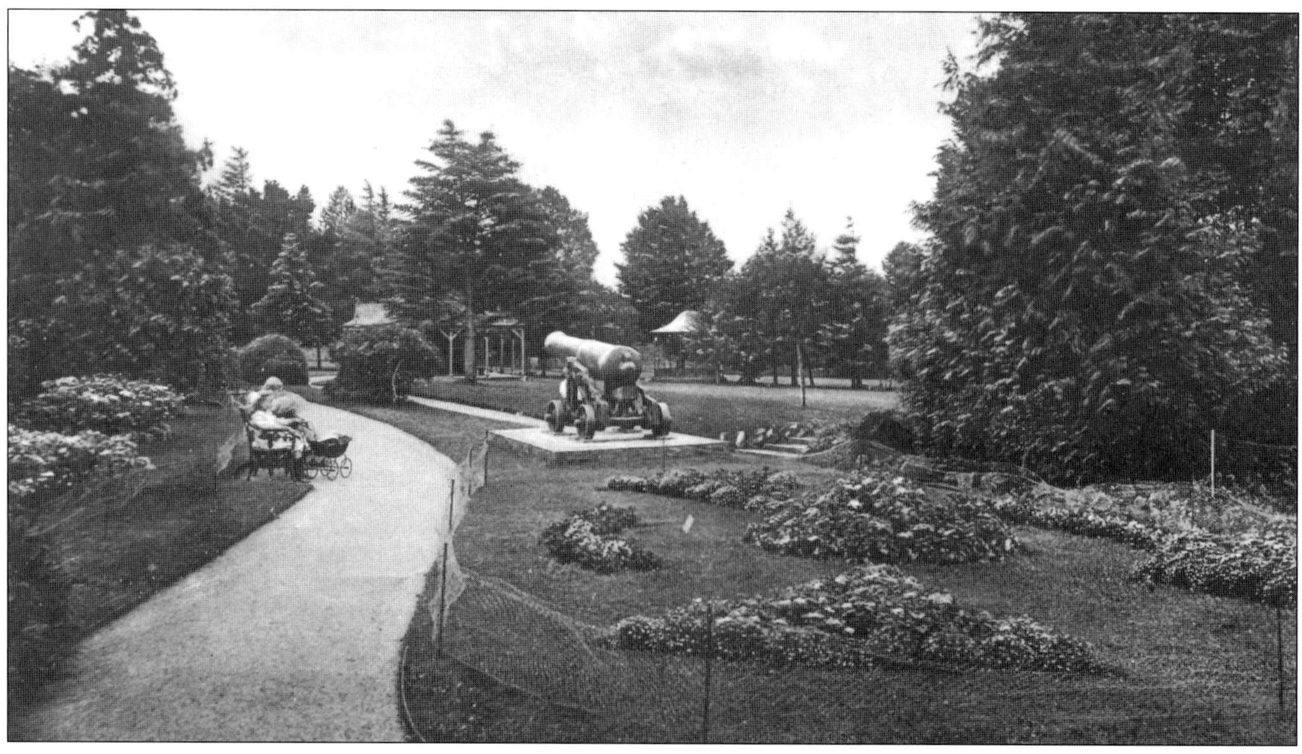

The People's Park, graced by Russian cannon, captured during the Crimean War. MUSEUM COLLECTION

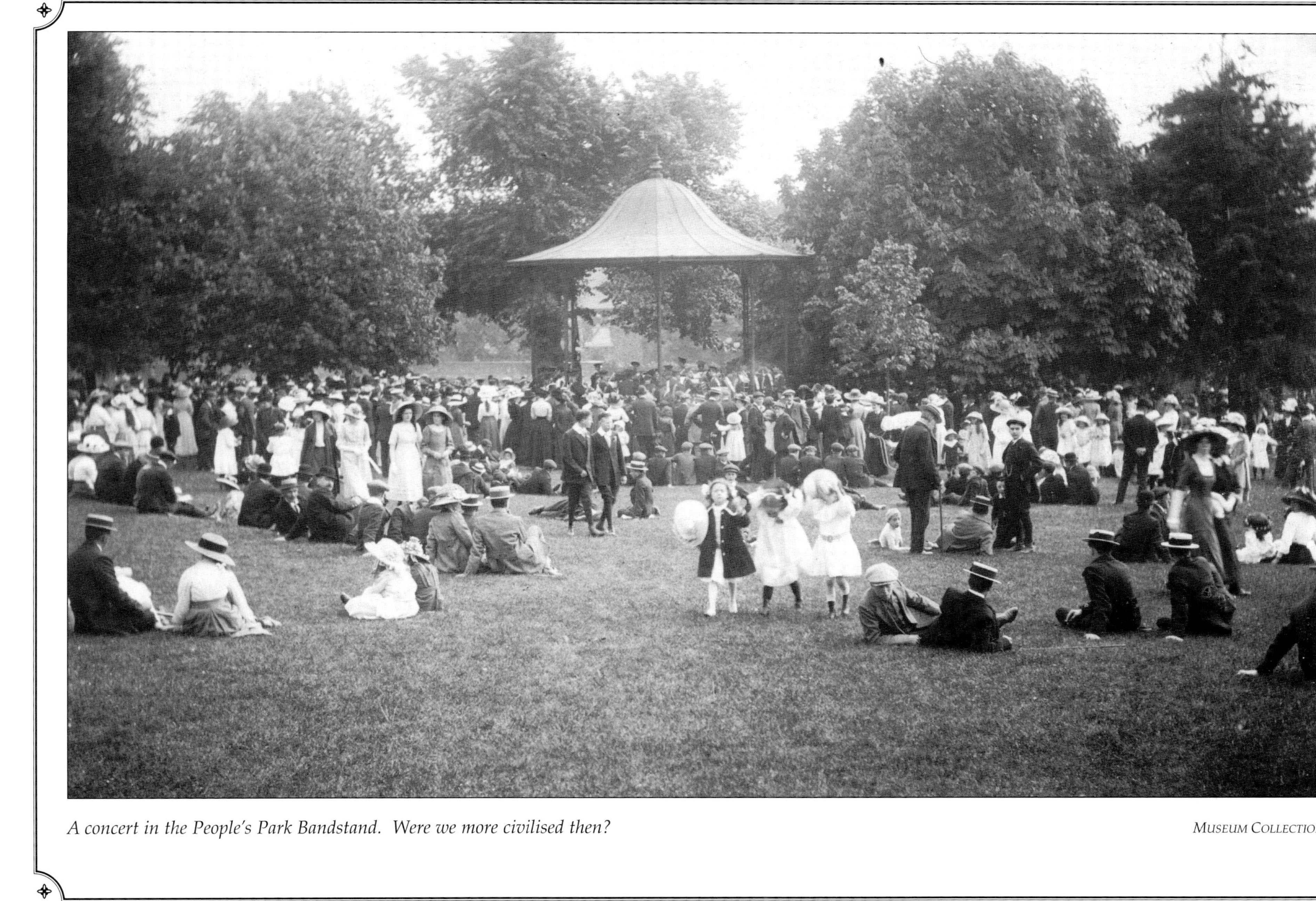

A concert in the People's Park Bandstand. Were we more civilised then?

MUSEUM COLLECTION

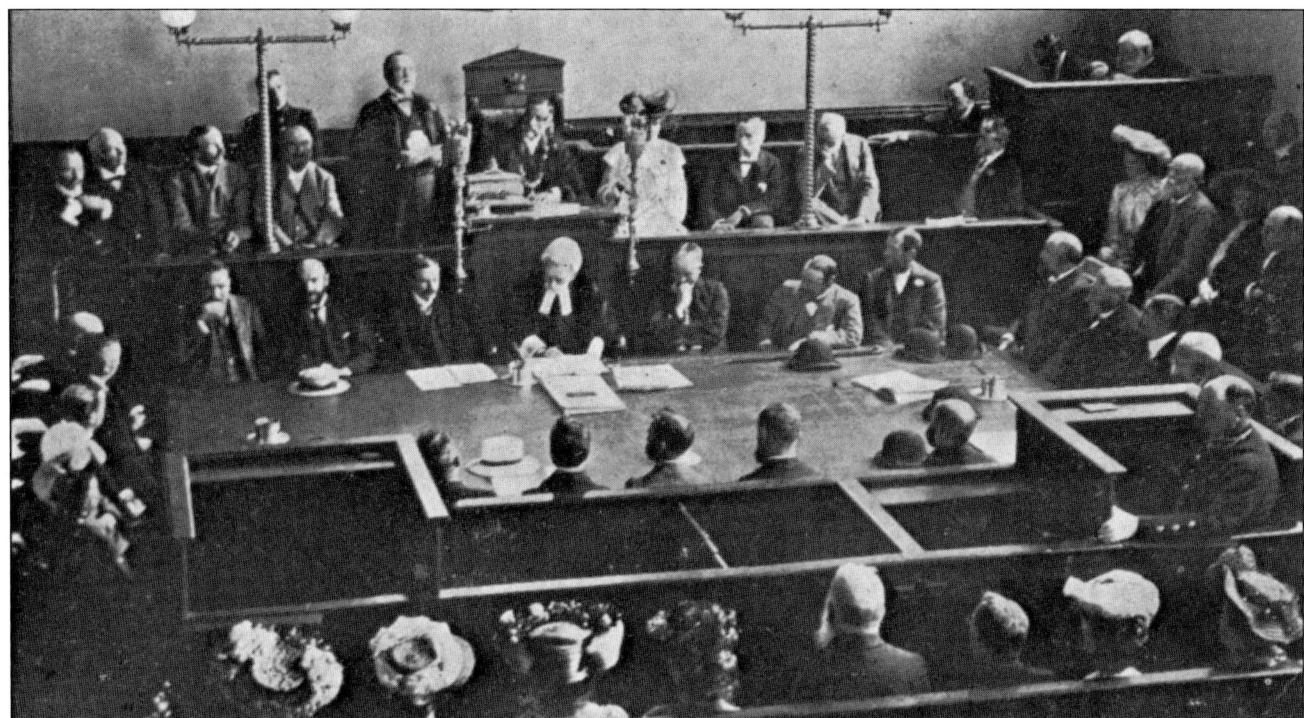

Giving the Freedom of the Borough to John Coles, whose benefactions included generous donations towards the People's Park, the hospital and Blundell's School. Coles is standing on the Mayor's right. 1904. MUSEUM COLLECTION

time was a line from Tiverton to Barnstaple, but it was insufficiently puffed and a line from Exeter to Barnstaple, via Crediton was opened instead. This was a serious blow to the town as it lost most of the traffic between South Devon and North Devon. Further local trade was lost with the completion of the Taunton, Bampton to Barnstaple line in 1863. The railways offered cheap market-day tickets to South Molton and Taunton, and Tiverton's trade suffered. Frantic efforts to link Tiverton with Exeter to the south and Bampton to the north in the 1860s achieved nothing.

The situation was saved by the efforts of William Partridge, 'but for whose efforts it is practically certain Tiverton would never have secured the boon of increased railway accommodation', as Snell orotundly put it. There were still problems as all the landowners along the line to Bampton were in opposition except Sir John. Eventually agreement was reached and the necessary £25,000 of local capital was just raised (thanks to Sir John subscribing £7,000). The campaign to have a Tiverton–Bampton line had started in 1872, but thanks to the opposition it was only opened in 1884 and in 1885 the line from Tiverton to Exeter was completed. However, by then the damage to Tiverton's status as a market town had probably been done. The subscribers never recovered their capital and in 1963 the lines were closed, sadly at a time when local public opinion was inadequate to fight for alternative uses and when the motor car seemed everyone's future.

In the later nineteenth century Tiverton gained more than sewerage, schools and extended railway links. It gained its grand and apparently indestructible Town Hall and the People's Park. Tiverton has endured two local government reorganisations, in 1835 and 1974, and in both cases it has led to new building in order to house the administrators. The new Town Hall was completed in 1864 at a cost of £8,000. The day was observed as a public holiday, bells rang, bands played, the streets beflagged and decorated with greenery. There were many visitors from neighbouring towns. There was a banquet for the gentlemen and a dinner for the workers, a fair in Fore Street and a ball in the Athenaeum. And for the very righteous, a Temperance Gala and two Tea Drinkings.

(In 2002 the District Council crept sheepishly into its new building in Phoenix Lane amid allegations of extravagance.)

In the new building was a basement for coal and stores. On the ground floor, accessed by the lower door facing St Andrew Street, were cells for prisoners awaiting trial and the Magistrates' Offices, as well as offices for the Borough Surveyor and Accountant, a Committee Room, Muniment Room, Police Office and Town Clerk's Office. On the first floor was the Court Room, which doubled up as Council Chamber, Grand Jury Room and Mayor's Parlour.

It is a cleverly designed building making excellent use of a difficult, irregularly shaped 'brownfield' site. The architect was aided by a re-aligning of the top of St Andrew Street, but it is a tour de force in every sense and it illustrates well the vagaries of public taste. Writing in 1847 Harding described the Town Hall's neighbour, St George's as 'heavy, little regard having been paid to architectural beauty in the elevation.' At the end of the century Snell described the appearance of St George's as 'past redemption. Nothing will ever do it any good.' Yet St George's is now regarded as a gem and the Town Hall as a much loved architectural horror, which defies description. Snell tried with the term 'Venetiano-Italian', but had he been to Venice? Others have essayed 'Scots Baronial'. In the same decade the Amorys moved into Knightshayes and perhaps the Town Hall can be seen as 'Municipal Knightshayes'. One hopes that the District Planning Committee, those revered arbiters of taste, may note how wobbly judgements based on taste may be.

The Queen's golden jubilee in 1887 produced for Tiverton a splendid gift. John Coles, a native of Washfield, who had made a fortune in the London insurance market, bought land for £1,200 and handed it over to be the nucleus of a new park. Other adjoining land was bought by other subscribers and the total cost was over £3,700. Coles presented the handsome gates; other donors provided the bandstand, seats and drinking fountains. Coles was to the fore in every good work, especially educational, in the town and was made a Freeman of the Borough. Jubilee Day, 5 July 1887, saw the park open and the Borough Council took over the maintenance, for this was the heroic age of local government. The town ran its own water supplies and sewerage system, its own gasworks, its own police force and gaol, its own hospital, its own schools, it paved its own roads. Intimacy and local control encouraged generous giving and local pride. In the next century most of these powers and services have been sucked away by central government and 'local' government, as it now exists, has come to be seen as a costly and unpopular irrelevance. A great loss to democracy and civic pride.

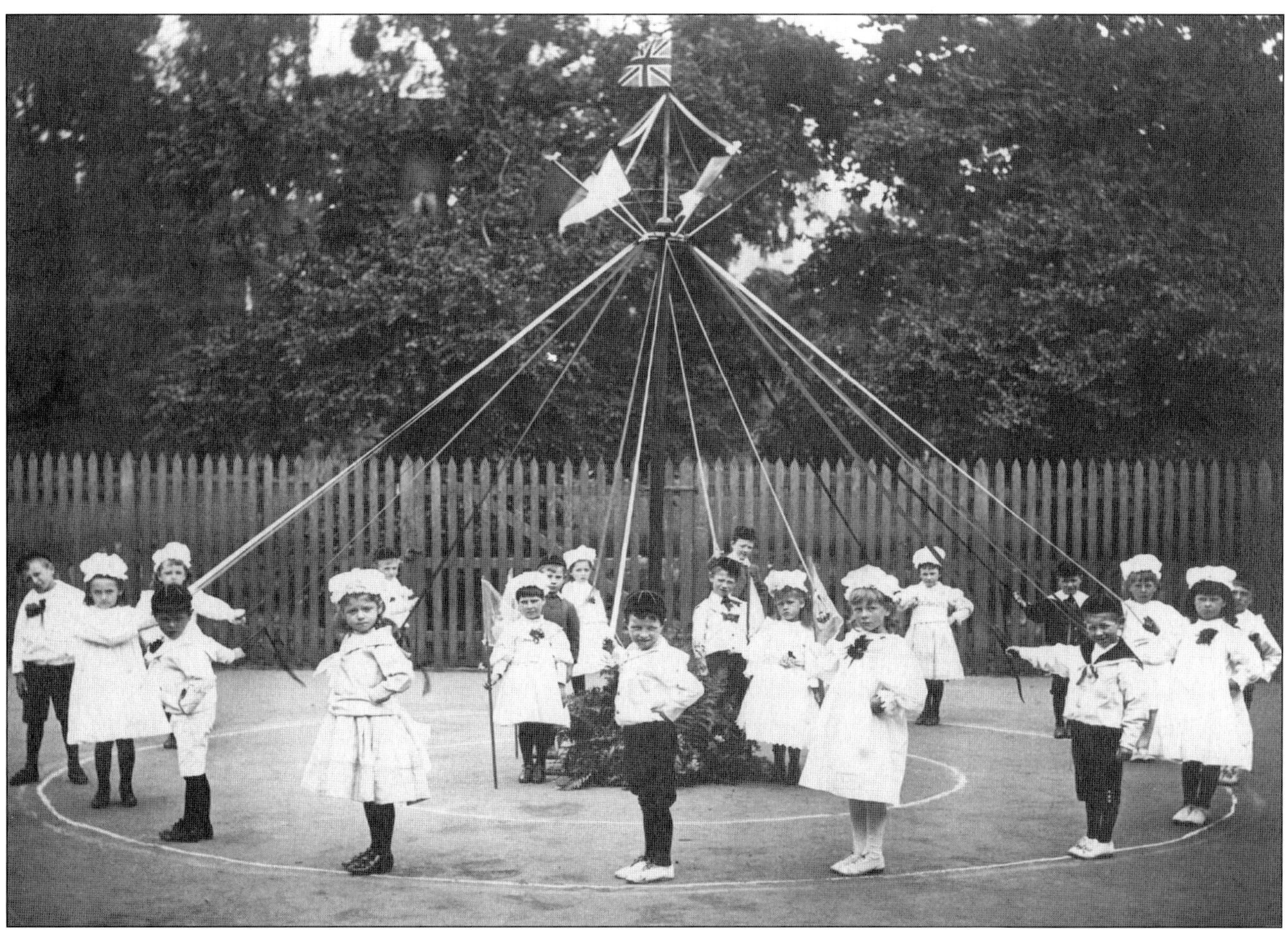

Celebrating Queen Victoria's diamond jubilee rather seriously. An example of a strange British tradition; adult maypole dancing was long since dead, but children were still coerced into doing it. Likewise, daily religious observance had lost its appeal, but schoolchildren still had to get down to it. MUSEUM COLLECTION

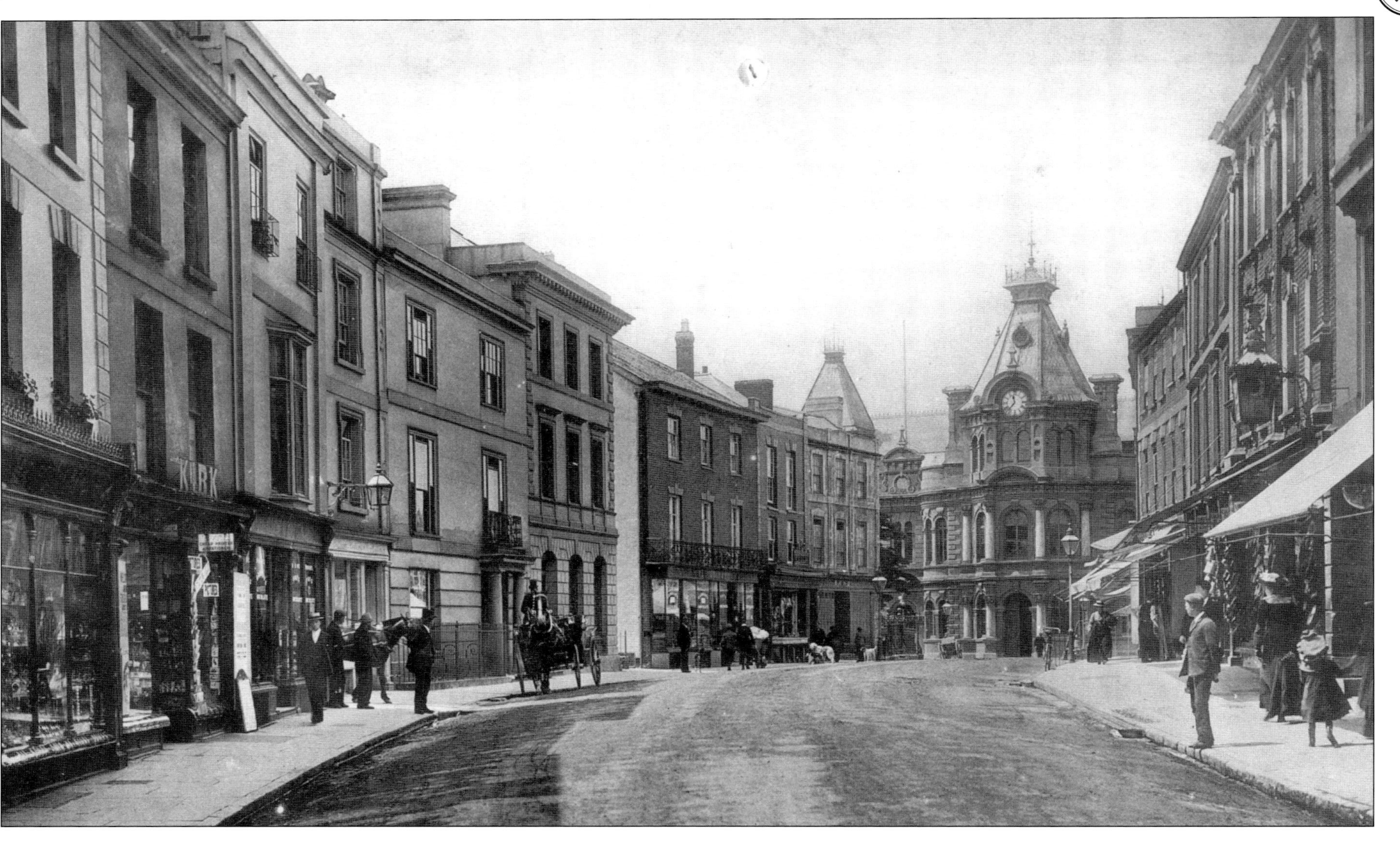

Fore Street and the Town Hall, seat of local power at the end of the great age of local government, pictured c.1900.

Chapter 7

Tiverton in Peace and War, 1900–1918

At the end of the nineteenth century, with its retrospect of unalloyed progress, its running water, sanitation, its railways and steamships, its shops and the novel certainty of supplies, even the prospect of the ending of poverty and want through the processes of agricultural improvement and industrial mass production, the awesome improvements in medicine and science and the pride and security of being defended by a superb navy and being the centre of the largest empire the world had ever known, Tivertonians could face the future confident of their place in an ever more civilised world. In place of the looming poverty that overshadowed 1800, in 1900 thanks to Heathcoat's and Starkey, Knight and Ford the town was prosperous; in place of darkness and the mud of unpaved streets there was pavement and gaslight; in place of cholera, contaminated water and general foulness there was clean water, sewerage and a hospital; in place of a corrupt Corporation there was an elected Borough Council; in place of a two-day journey to London on a stagecoach there was God's Wonderful Railway; in place of a weekly market and fairs there were shops; there were schools for all children, not just a lucky few. There were some sordid little slummy corners still, some poverty, but all was bright with a sense of improvement.

An example of this sense of 'onward and upward' was reported in the first issue of the *Tiverton Gazette* in 1909. In 1908 the Liberal government pushed the Pensions Bill through Parliament and from January 1909 single men and women over 70 would get 5s. a week and married couples 7s.6d., provided that their annual income was under £35.10s.0d. In its issue of 5 January a reporter described the events of the previous Friday:

Not within living memory have there been so many old men and women in the Post Office on 'Pension Morning' as many of the old folk called it. Those who were privileged to witness the joy of the aged poor as they came, some on crutches, some in vehicles and some on the arm of a relative, will never forget the sight. Their faces beamed with delight, as they were handed their pensions by the courteous officials at the main Post Office or the sub Post Office in Westexe South... Some of the pensioners were deaf, and as one heard the high pitched voices of the clerks, one could not help thinking that the government should have supplied them with megaphones and ear-trumpets. The first pension was paid at the Bampton Street Office just after 8.00 and it was not until ten that the old folk turned up in numbers. A pathetic sight was that of an old man, bent nearly double, and hobbling along by means of a crutch and a stick. He was helped up the two steps by Mr Thorne, who happened to be passing. The old man came out smiling and remarked: 'I am 81 years old. I worked on a farm for 70 years, but I never thought I would live to see such times as these. It is beautiful. I've kept off the Parish [charity], because I looked after myself as a young man.'

'Ah! My good old man used to say to me that things

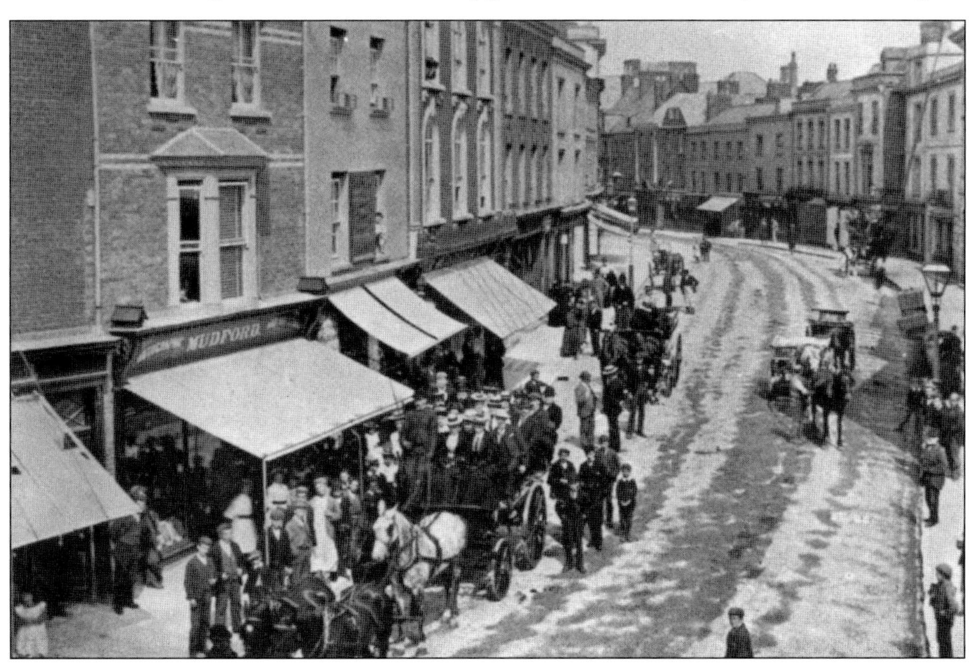

Fore Street before the motor-car. The Mudford family were staunch Liberals at a time when politics were fierce. Henry Mudford was Mayor from 1904–08 and in 1906 was convicted of non-payment of rates, protesting at the fact that they were being used to subsidise Anglican Schools.
MUSEUM COLLECTION

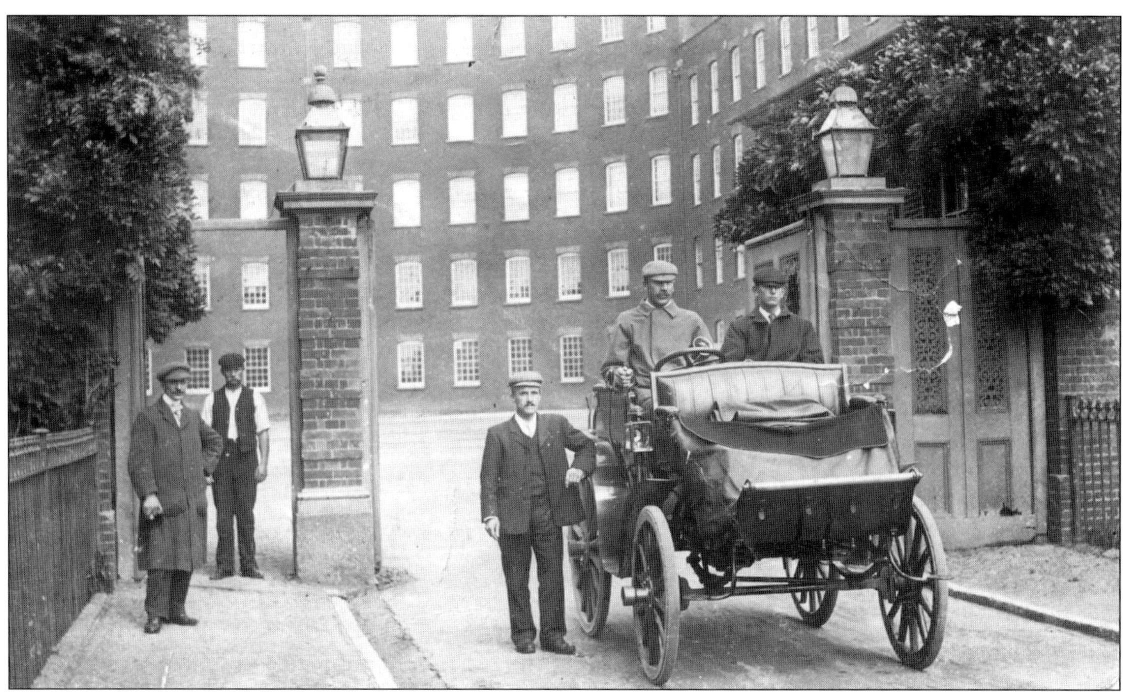

The shape of things to come. Ian Amory setting off for Scotland in 1907. MUSEUM COLLECTION

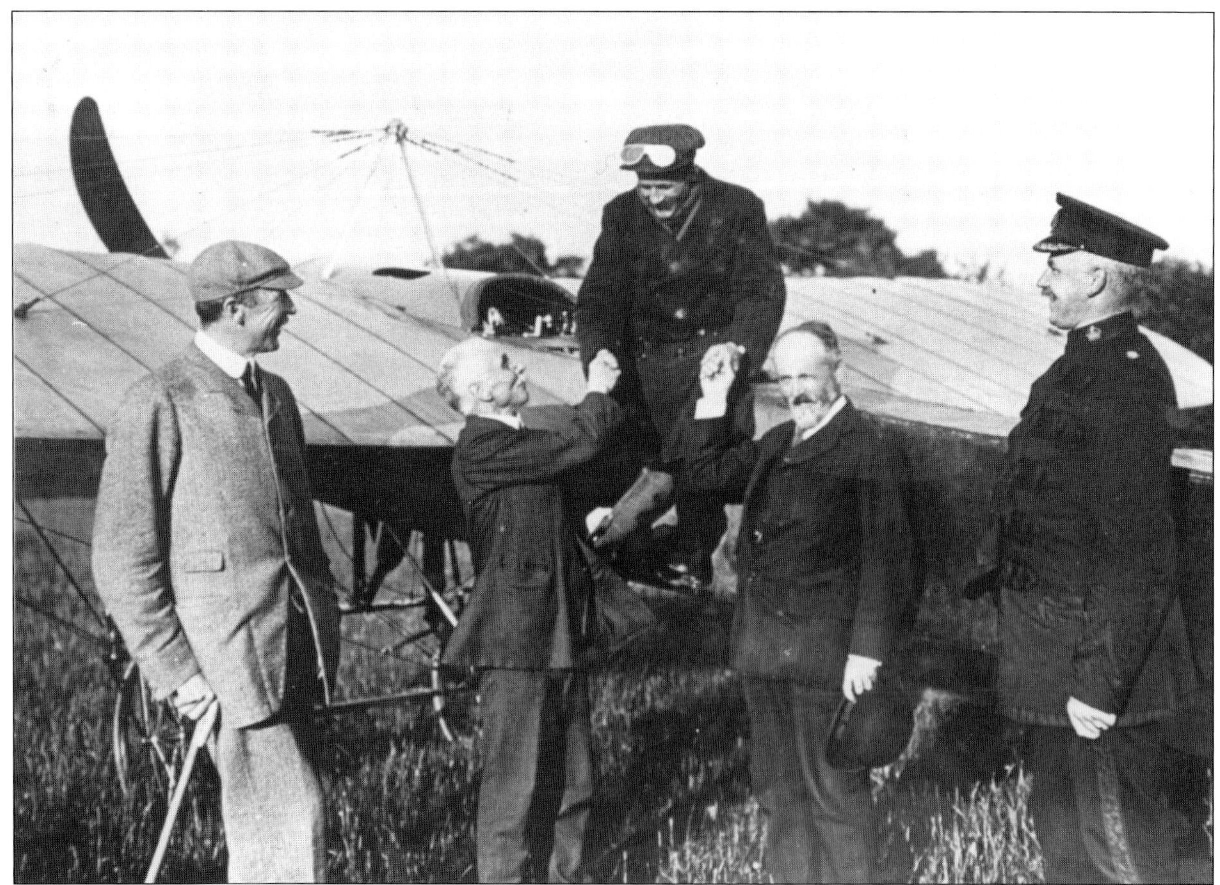

The first aircraft to land in Tiverton, June 1912. The pilot was greeted by Mayor Alfred Gregory, and the bearded Borough Surveyor Siddalls, flanked by Chief Constable Mercer and Ian Amory. MUSEUM COLLECTION

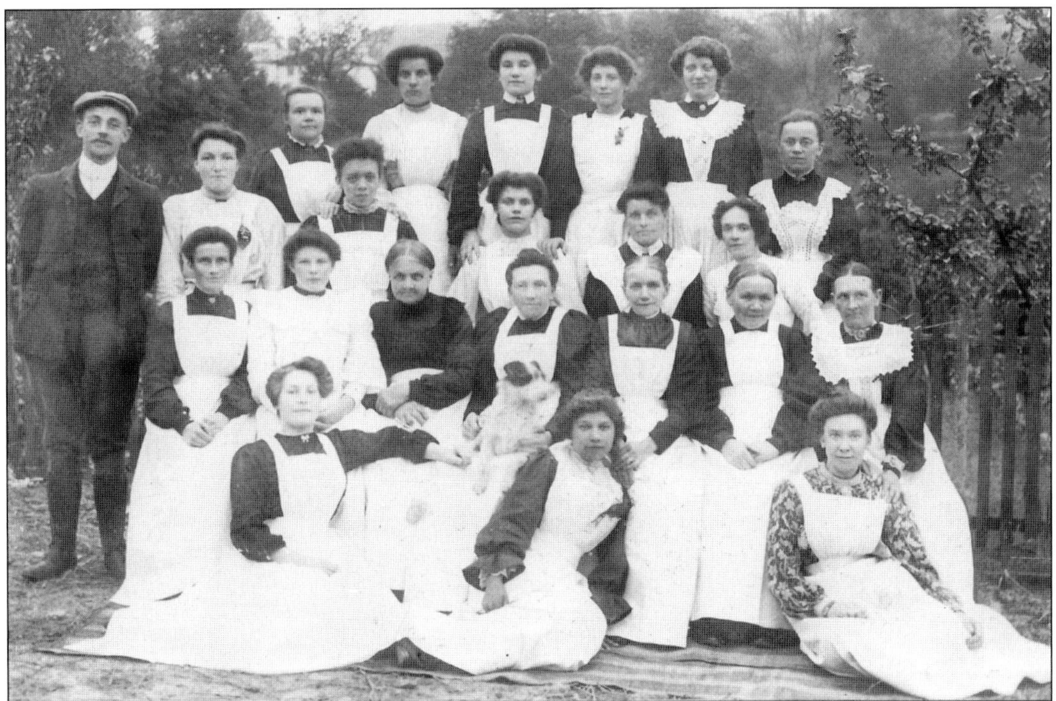

The staff of Tidcombe Laundry, photographed in the garden c.1890. Tidcombe Hall is in the background.The seated women illustrate that, before pensions, you worked till you dropped. MUSEUM COLLECTION

would be brighter by and by,' remarked a woman of 72 summers, 'and 'tis come true. I've just had my pinchen money. Talk about the good old times, people be fools who say 'twas good times in our young days. Mind you I've a good son who has kept me off the parish.' One of the Town Postmen coming out of the Office said to a pensioner: 'Don't forget the Party that gave you your pension.' The pensioner replied: 'I won't forget my friends.'

A buxom dame, who had just collected her pension, said: 'I never had more than seven shillings a week from my man, and on this I had to bring up a family of seven, until two of my eldest went out to work. That was when wheat was five shillings a bushel. They were hard times to be sure. But it seems to me that folks can't bring up a family on less than a pound a week now.'

One applicant was asked whether he thought the scheme should have been contributory. He replied: 'Well, if it had been I would not have a pension now as wages were so low I could not have afforded to contribute.'

On that Friday a flag was hoisted at the Liberal Club. During the day the Town Crier went round the Town making the following proclamation:

This is to give notice that the Old Age Pension Act comes into operation today, and about 150 persons, who have worked hard all their life-time, will benefit by it in Tiverton. I want you not to forget that our present Member, the Hon Lionel Walrond, voted against the Bill in the House of Commons. Don't you forget that at the next election!

The use of a Borough Officer for such obvious political propaganda is an indication that these were times of exciting politics. In the early years of the century the Borough Council had been riven with faction over 'electrification'. A few years previously the Borough had bought the gasworks from the Amory family and was obliged to set up an electric company, which would then be a rival to its own gas company. The Aldermen and Councillors tied themselves up in knots debating the merits of the schemes before them.

In the middle of this purely local spat came an issue of the widest national importance. In 1902 the Conservative government passed an Education Act, under the provisions of which the Borough could hand over its schools to the County Council. That in itself caused heated debate. More heated was the debate over the Act's provisions for the County Council to assume financial responsibility for the schools hitherto run by the National Society and the British Society, while leaving day-to-day control of schools with the religious bodies. As the National Society (Anglican) had far more schools than the British (Dissenting) Society, two cries went up. Firstly that this would lead to state subsidy for teaching the Anglican catechism, and secondly that Dissenting teachers would be denied posts and promotion in 16,000 schools, the maintenance of which they contributed their rates towards. In a violent Liberal party meeting in the Drill Hall in May 1903 Lord Portsmouth attacked the Act as 'enthroning the worst form of sectarianism'. As a supporting speaker Ian Amory was 'glad that the Old Cause was waking up.'

On Sunday 15 November 1903 this political 'violence' hit the streets of Tiverton. The previous

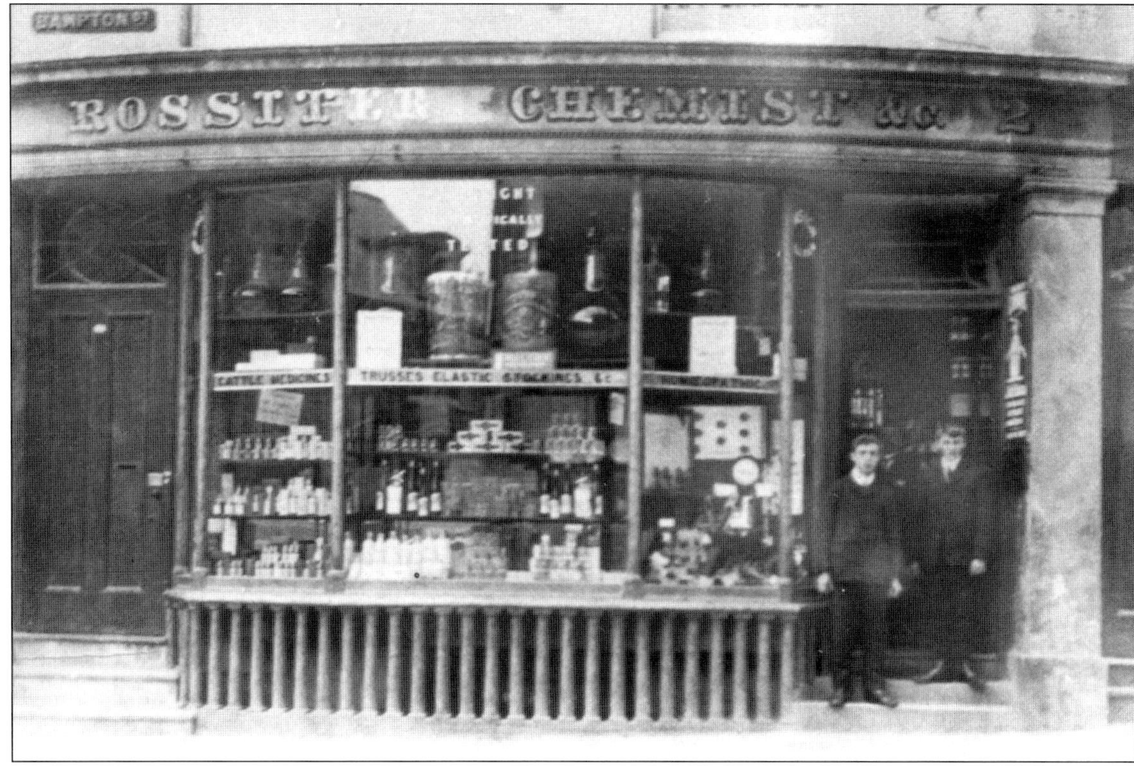

Above: *Rossiters when at the bottom of Gold Street. This was the great age of the independent owner-run shop.* Museum Collection

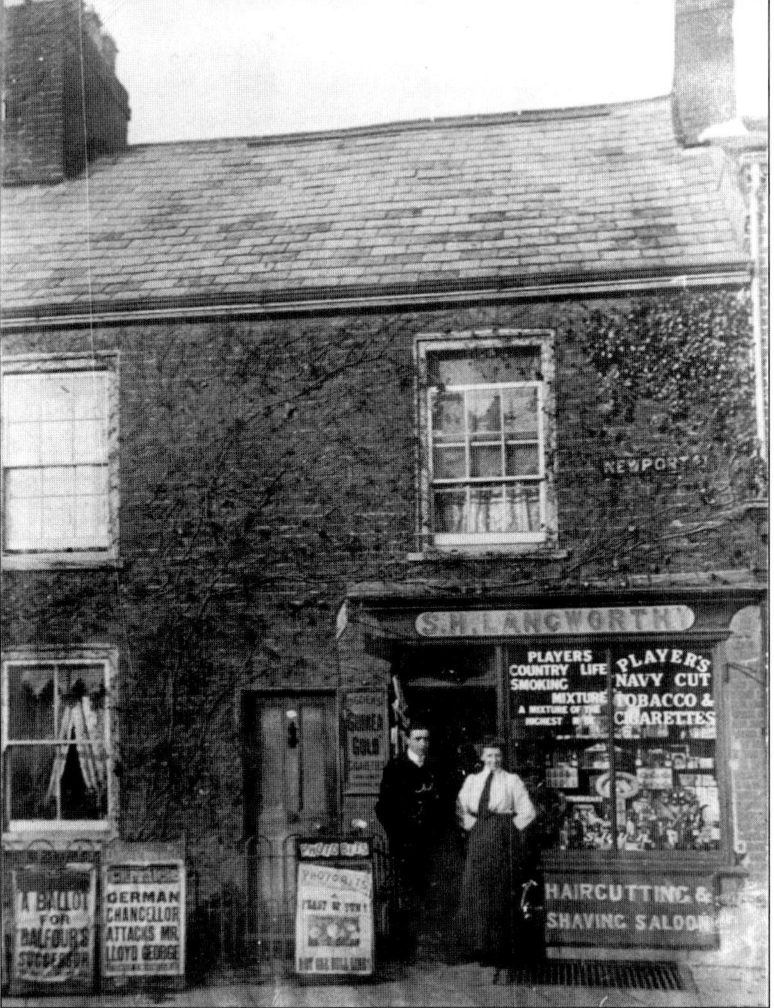

Left: *Langworthy's in Newport Street at the time of Lloyd George's Mansion House speech.*
Museum Collection

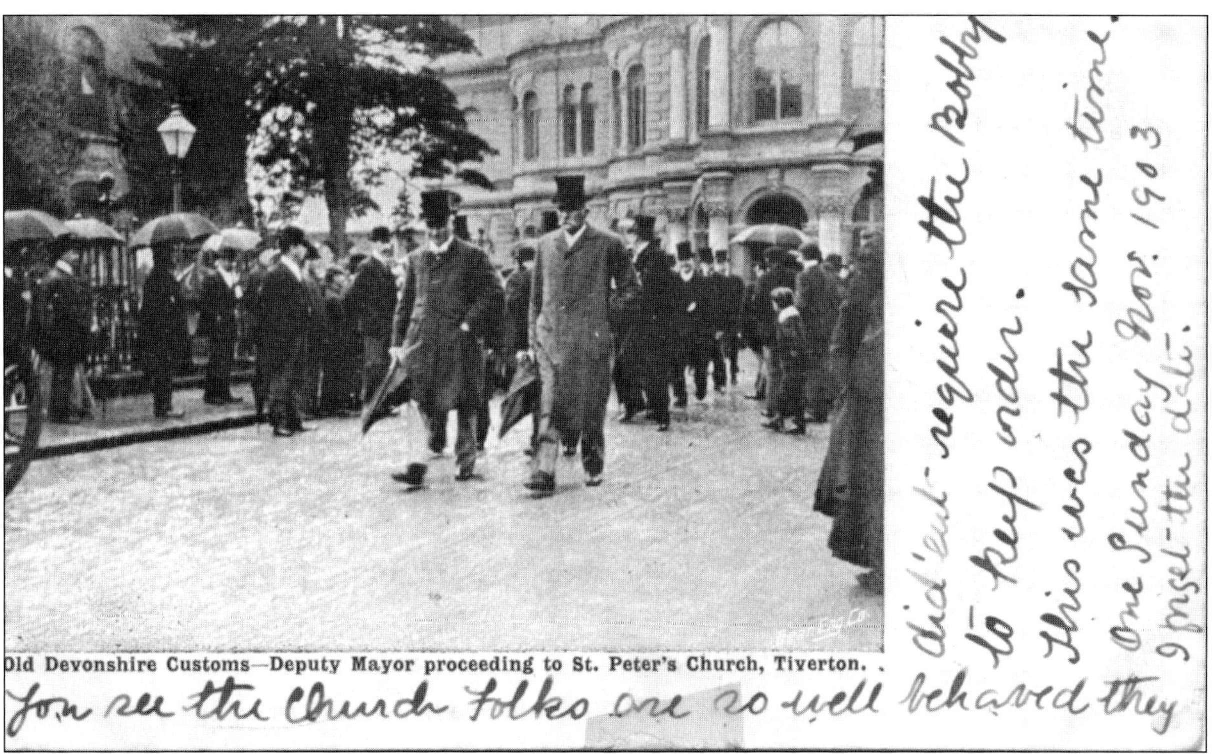

Two postcards illustrating the crisis of 1903. Mayor Lane (below) is striding to the Congregational Church and Deputy Mayor Thorne (above) is heading for St Peter's. The postcard writer is obviously Tory and Cof E!

MUSEUM COLLECTION

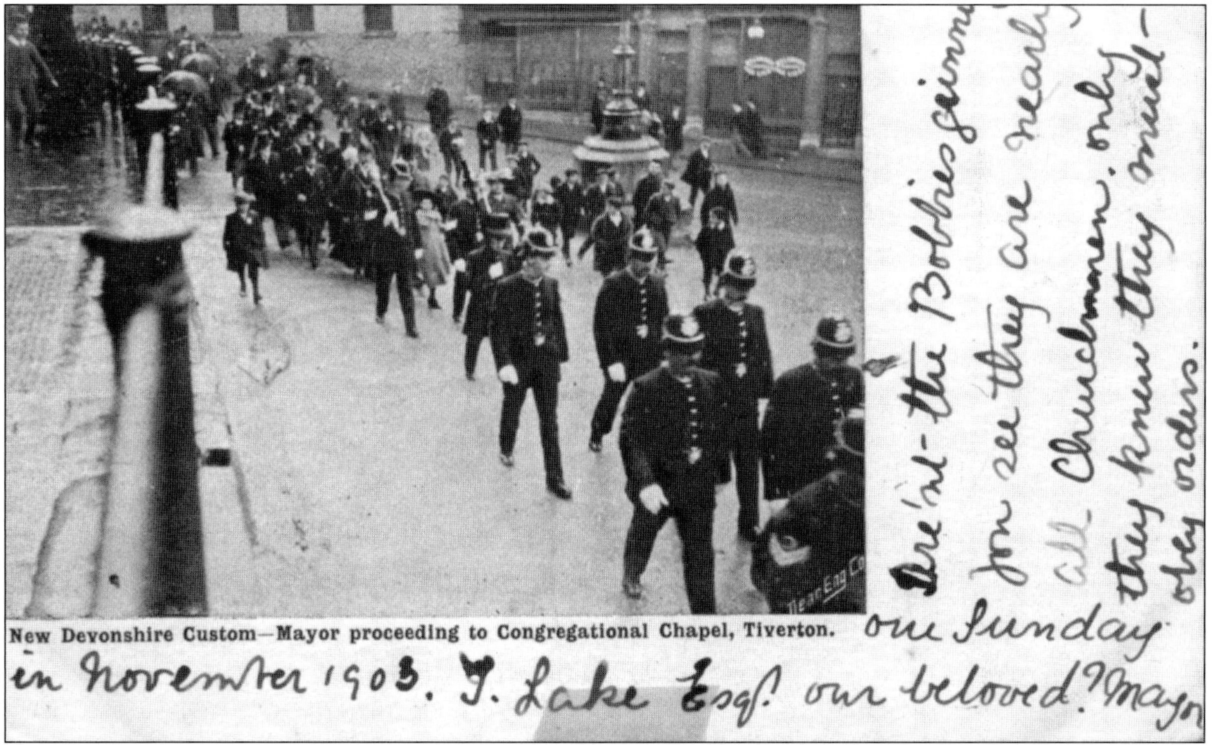

Friday a 'Passive Resistance' meeting had been held in the Congregational Church in St Peter Street, attended by the newly re-elected Mayor, Mr T. Lake and Councillor Mudford and a large number of Dissenters. The decision was taken, as part of a national campaign, to withhold a proportion of rates in protest. On the Sunday morning, as the Councillors collected in the foyer of the Town Hall to form the procession to go to St Peter's for the Mayor's service, it was clear that there had been massive politicking. The *Tiverton Gazette* later reported that a 'Churchman' had sent out letters asking Anglicans to come and support the Deputy Mayor in his procession to St Peter's. 'Be at the Town Hall by 10.45'. In his haste the writer had put inadequate stamps on the letters and all the recipients had been surcharged.

The *Tiverton Gazette* described events in its edition the following Tuesday:

For the good of all concerned it is to be hoped that never again in the history of the loyal and ancient borough of Tiverton will Mayor's Sunday be marred by such scenes as were unhappily enacted this year. It has been the recognised custom for generations past for the newly elected Mayor to attend Divine Service at St Peter's Church in state with the members of the Corporation. For many years the Volunteer Band and the E Company of the 3rd Battalion of the Devon Regiment have accompanied his Worship. Such being the case the decision of Mr T. Lake to attend the Congregational Church in state did not meet with complete favour. Members of the Council who are Nonconformists naturally fell in with the idea, but those who are Churchmen were strongly against the proposed change, though some said they were prepared to accompany his Worship on a subsequent Sunday. Efforts to arrange matters were unsuccessful and two processions left the Town Hall, one for St Peter's, the other for the Congregational Church.

A good number of townspeople were outside the Town Hall to see what happened. Many of them were partisans, judging from the remarks one heard as the Corporation and Officials were assembling in the vestibule. Some approved of the actions of the Mayor. Others spoke out loudly and in by no means complimentary terms of the turn events were taking. Meanwhile last minute attempts to compromise were being made in the Town Hall. Alderman Amory, who had been absent from town on Saturday and only aware of the dissension on Sunday morning, endeavoured to persuade the Mayor for the sake of peace to conform to the old system. At first the Mayor seemed inclined to agree to go to St Peter's, but on the advice of another Alderman he decided to adhere to his former determination.

Thus it was that at 10.50, the Deputy Mayor, Alderman W. Thorne accompanied by Alderman Harwood left the Town Hall for St Peter's Church. Following him in procession were Alderman Pleass, Councillors Grater, Spiller, Liesching, Rowcliffe, Davey, Arthers... As they moved off a derisive laugh was heard. Cheers were in turn raised. There were a few groans. At St Peter's they were greeted by the Churchwardens who, carrying a wand, escorted them to the Corporation pews... Two minutes after the first procession had started, another left the Town Hall. Chief Constable Mercer led it, followed by members of the Borough Police Force. Then came the Town Beadle and the Mace Bearers. The Mayor came next, accompanied by Alderman Winton, followed by the Town Clerk [C. Marshall Hole] and Alderman J. Thorne and Councillors Mudford, Deering, Cottrell, Hill, Steer, Henson and Pinkstone... There was a good deal of hissing and hooting as the procession got under way and there was also some cheering.

Alderman Amory joined neither procession and went home. The military also did not take sides.

The press was full of accounts of the conviction of 'Passive Resisters' and the distraint of their property to meet the full payment of the rates. On 20 September 1904 Councillor Henson was charged with non-payment of £1.5s.0d. The Mayor was on the bench and was reported as saying 'We sympathise with you.' On 27 September the Congregational Minister, G. Ward Siddall, Councillor Mudford and Aldermen J. and W. Thorne were also charged. As Mudford put it, 'I come here in the name of Freedom'. In the same issue their distrained property was advertised for sale.

Mudford was elected Mayor in November 1904 and served for four years, probably the only Mayor to have refused to pay rates on principle. He led a united procession to his place of worship, the Baptist Church, on the following Sunday. He had announced his intention to go to St Peter's for Evensong but 'an intimation was received from the Church Authorities that this would not be convenient.' The bells of St Peter's were not rung in honour of the new Mayor, the reason given being that the health of a Mrs Clarke-Jervoise, would be adversely affected. In November 1905 Mudford again led a united procession to the Baptist Church.

Certainly a glance at the issues of the *Tiverton Gazette* in the first months of 1914 shows a bustling, confident little town. The telephone had arrived; advertisements show that the telephone number of the *Gazette* Office was Tiverton 5 and the Angel Hotel Tiverton 46. The motorcar had also arrived. Ford offered 'Runabouts' for £125. Starkey, Knight and Ford bought a 3-ton lorry with rubber tyres that was capable of travelling at 12 miles per hour, to deliver beer to the coastal resorts. However, it had not been long in use before there was an accident. One of the crew was Thomas Sage, later the winner of a VC, and in July he dismounted to inspect the rear lights. It must have been at the end of a long day, as he slipped on remounting and the wheels went over his right leg and side.

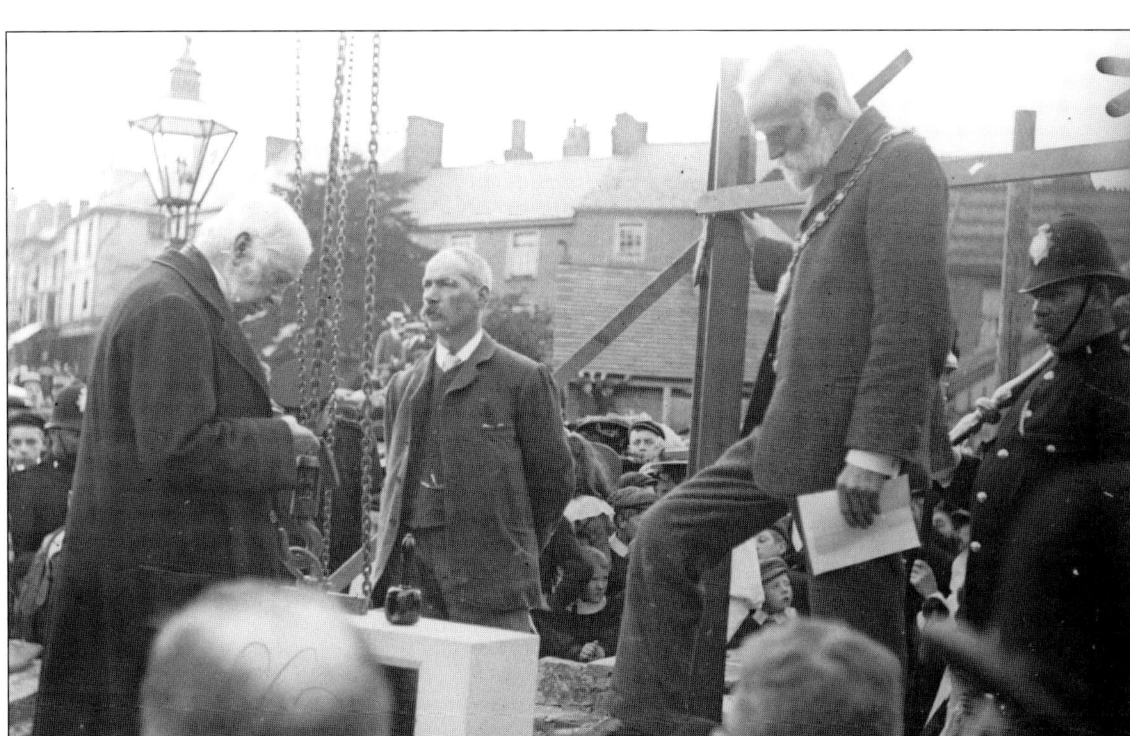

Above: *Civic pride: Mr Ford lays the foundation of his Clock Tower at Lowman Green with Mayor Mudford looking on, 1907.*

MUSEUM COLLECTION

Right and below: *Unveiling the statue of Edward VII, before and after. When one considers the statue-worthy in Tiverton's past – Greenway, Blundell, Fairfax, John Heathcoat, John Coles, Lord Palmerston and Viscount Amory – one is puzzled by this choice of one of the least worthy of the House of Saxe-Weimar-Windsor.*

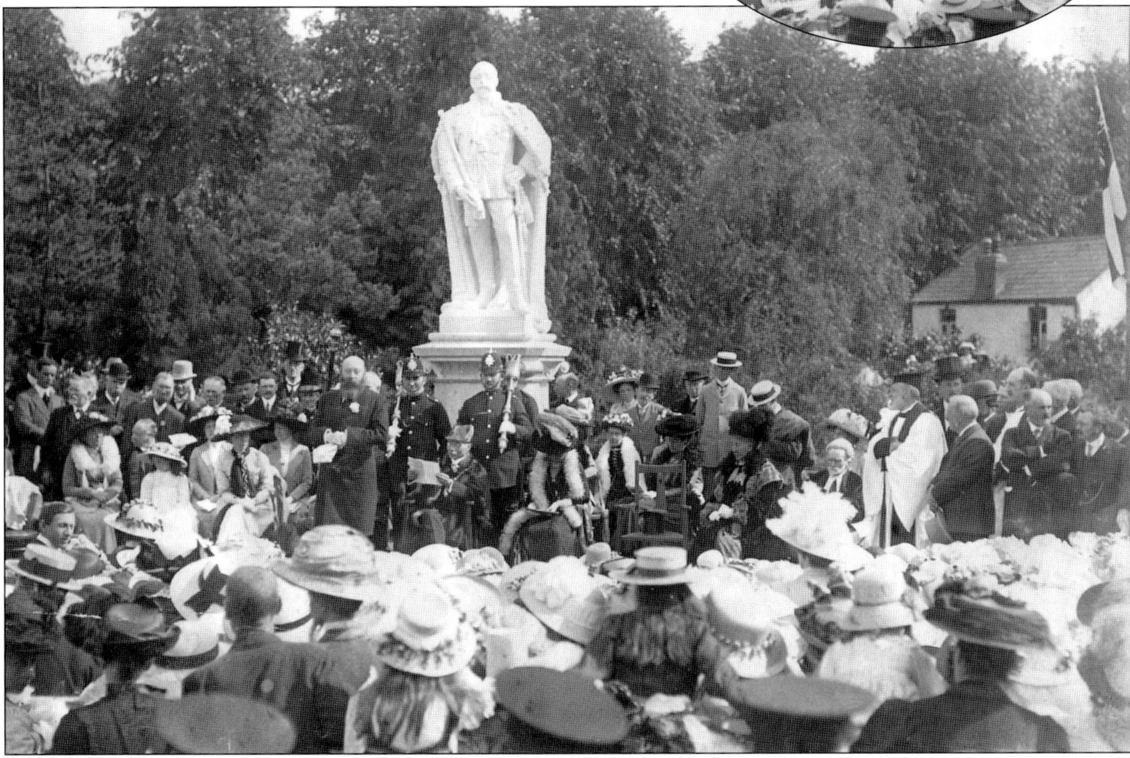

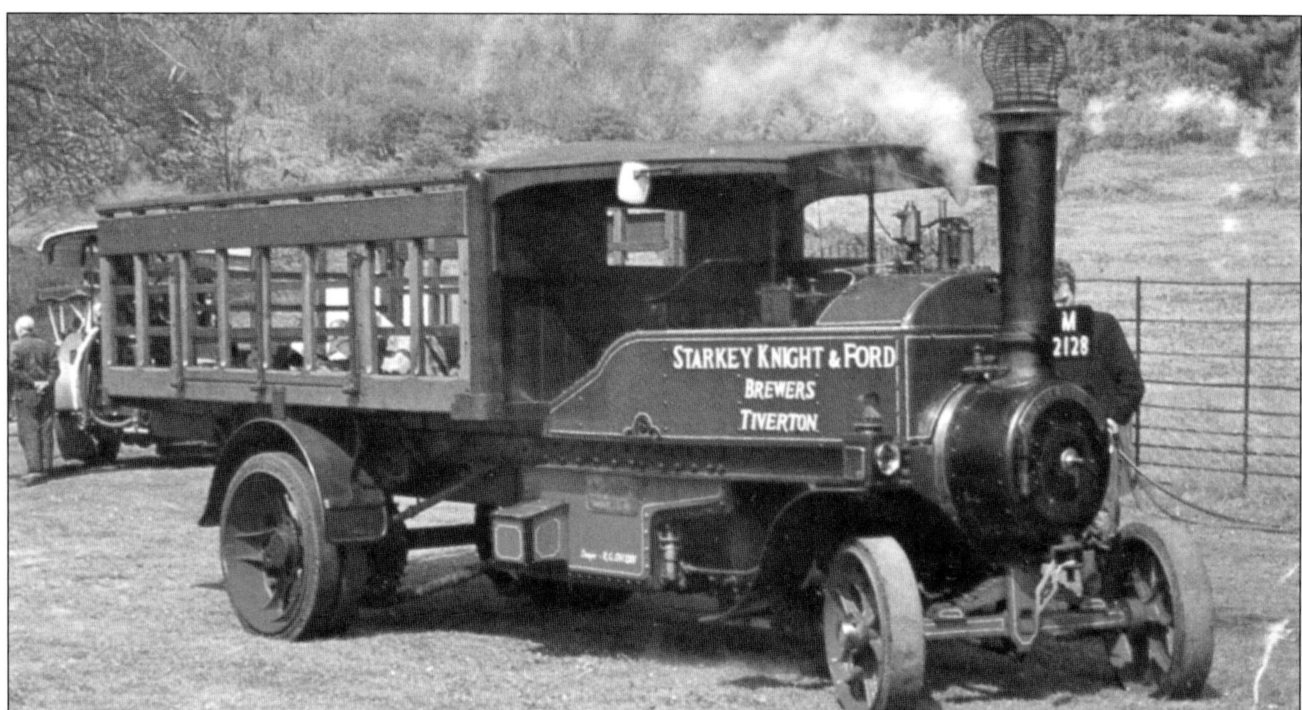

A reconditioned Starkey, Knight and Ford vehicle, but probably not of the type that ran over Thomas Sage.
MUSEUM COLLECTION

Motoring allowed group excursions, but they were still so much of a novelty that the *Gazette* gave them full coverage. The Methodist Choir outing was by 'wagonette' to Ilfracombe, the journey taking two and a half hours. In January 1914 places on a Daimler wagonette that took people to and from the pantomime in Exeter cost 3s. The choir of St George's hired two charabancs to go to Cheddar Gorge and Caves, Wells and Glastonbury. They left at 8.30 a.m. and returned to Tiverton at 10.30 p.m. They saw an aeroplane giving demonstration flights as they went through Taunton. The Borough Council took a charabanc for a lunch at Sidmouth and tea at Seaton. It carried the Mayor, two Aldermen, six Councillors, Mr Siddalls, the Borough Surveyor, Mr Pugsley the Clerk, Mr Deeks the Accountant, Mr Pethick the Veterinary Inspector, Mr Jeffrey the Gas Manager and 11 municipal employees.

Other expeditions travelled by train. The 14 workers at the Roller Mills left at 6.20 a.m. one Saturday in 1914 bound for Plymouth, where they took a boat trip to Looe and got back just after midnight. On 7 July of the same year the combined Sunday school pupils of St Peter's, St George's and St Paul's, 901 of them, went to Teignmouth by special train, leaving at 8.45 a.m.

The suggestion from these expeditions that workplace and place of worship were central to social life is not misplaced. St Paul's and St Peter's ran cricket teams, as did Heathcoat's. St George's and St Peter's ran football teams, as did Heathcoat's and the Tiverton Youth Institute. There were also teams called Tiverton Green Shields, founded in 1908 and Tiverton Athletic. The year 1914 was the centenary of Tiverton Methodist Church and the Town Council attended the festivities. In June the Free Churches did their bit at the start of a National Campaign to encourage people into church every Sunday.

Even for the very poorest inhabitants of Tiverton, life was improving. Children over three were no longer to be found in the workhouse, but were in Elm House at Shillingford; married people over 60 had a statutory right to live together in the workhouse; pensions for the over 70s had reduced the fear of geriatric destitution and full employment meant the Poor Law Guardians could report that there were no able-bodied men in the workhouse, though there were some foul-mouthed women. The first council-houses, eight of them in Chapel Street, were ready for occupation in the summer of 1914. Although the Tiverton police force was considerably below strength, according to the national yardstick of 'Peelers' or 'Bobbies' per 1,000 population, the Council decided not to recruit more as crime was 'negligible'. Crime certainly got short shrift. In May a man was drunk

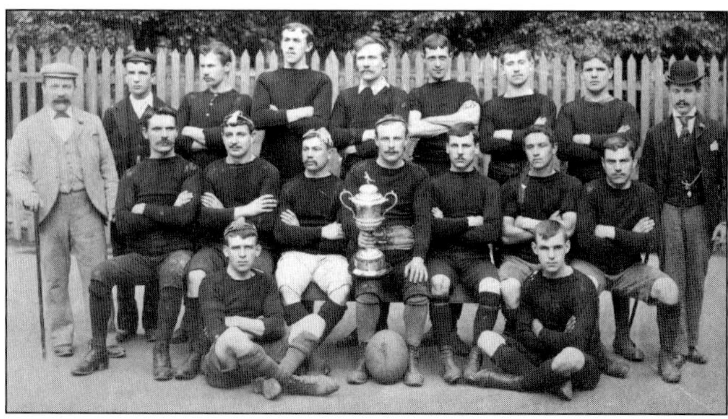

A rugger team of 1892. Team games were an invention of the later nineteenth century. MUSEUM COLLECTION

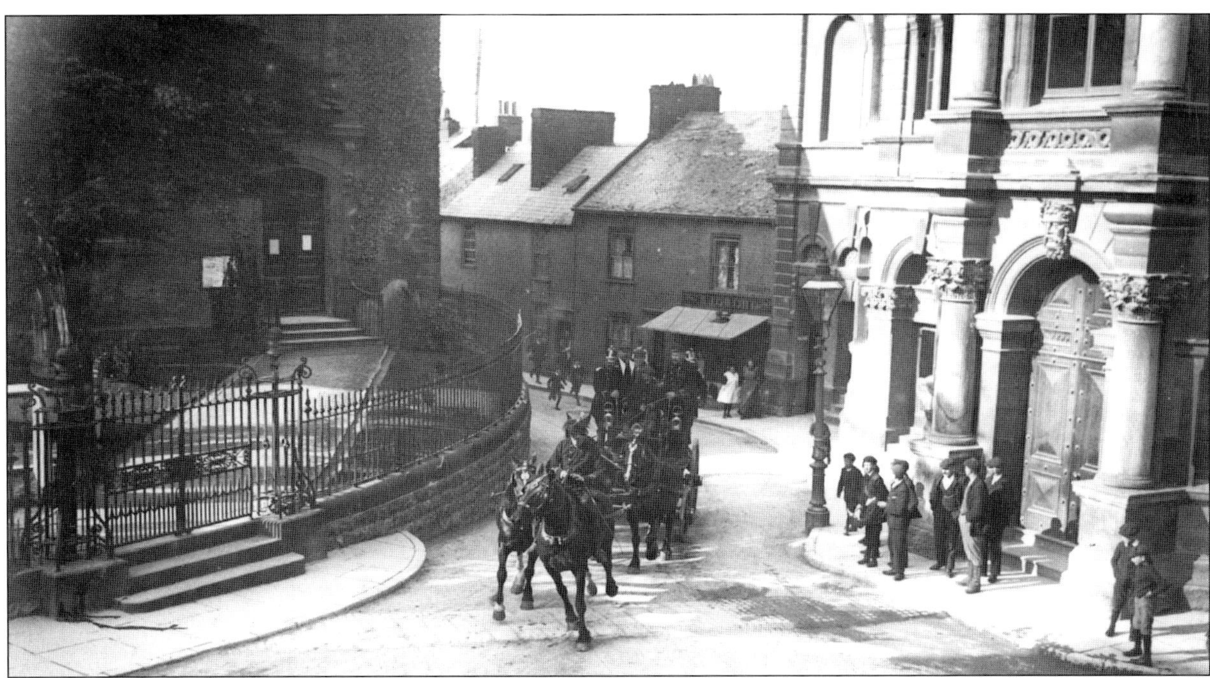

Above: *Our gallant fire brigade galloping out of St Andrew Street to a fire in May 1909.* MUSEUM COLLECTION

Below: *Our motorised brigade outside the St Andrew Street garage, next to the prison. Chief Constable Mercer is in charge.* MUSEUM COLLECTION

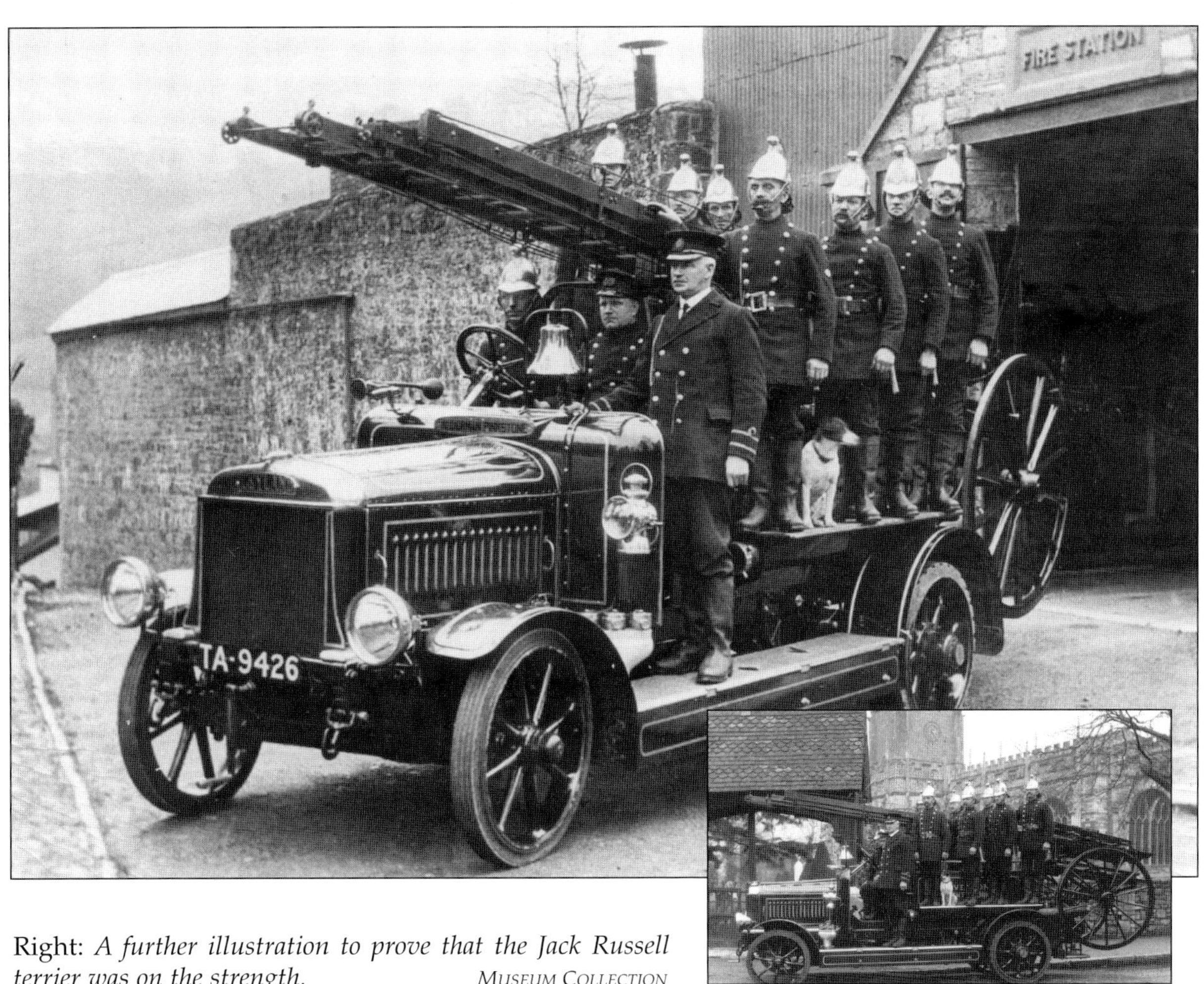

Right: *A further illustration to prove that the Jack Russell terrier was on the strength.* MUSEUM COLLECTION

and foul-mouthed in St Peter's Street and was promptly given 14 days of hard labour.

When news was in short supply the *Gazette* fell back on light relief. In April 1914 it reported at length the 'Bullock in Fore Street Affair'. Mr Pope, a butcher who had a shop on Angel Hill and a slaughterhouse at the bottom of St Andrew Street, being in danger of running out of beef, arranged to buy an animal from Farmer Joslin of Cruwys Morchard. A Charles Phillips of Pinkstone Court was commissioned to meet the animal at Withleigh and drive it to the St Andrew Street slaughterhouse. All went well until halfway down St Andrew Street, when the animal stampeded back up the street, across the bridge and through Westexe North, before doubling back to Fore Street, where it knocked down and injured Mr Drew of Barrington Street, knocking out some of his teeth. The 'bullock' roared up and down before going into Beck Square, where it charged and chased Albert Govier. Eventually it was boxed into the Square and three other cattle were driven in to calm it down and it then proceeded quietly to the slaughterhouse. The case came up in court at the end of May and raised some neat legal issues. Phillips was accused of driving a bullock without due care and attention in contravention of a by-law of 1889, and pleaded 'not guilty' as the beast had been totally under control, until it stampeded. Mr Pope claimed that the beast was not his until it had been slaughtered and weighed. Poor Mr Drew's evidence was treated with great levity, the Chairman wondering if he had been wandering about without care and attention, as he had not seen the animal coming. The case collapsed when Counsel for the Defendant pointed out that the 1889 by-law only mentioned 'bullocks' and this animal had been a four-year-old cow!

The *Gazette* also reported at length the campaign of Mr Athelstan Corderoy to be elected one of the six Poor Law Guardians. Corderoy, who lived in Exmouth in a beach hut named 'Noah's Ark', ended his election address with the ringing words:

> *I have the honour to be, so long as you back me up in fighting for God and His Empire, Your faithful Soldier, Servant and Leader to Victory or Death, Athelstan Corderoy.*

There were only seven candidates for the six places, but it must be odd that our Athelstan was elected. Having been elected our Athelstan sent 'a long telegram and an even longer letter' to the Board of Guardians questioning the legality of the whole election and refusing to take his seat. (It is a perennial hope of the author that the Tiverton electorate might take more care about whom they choose.)

At the end of May Sir John Amory died and his obsequies make a fitting summary of this time of high hope and past achievement. He had been born in 1829, before the Reform Bill, his mother being Anne, a daughter of John Heathcoat, his father Samuel Amory from a London legal and banking family. He had been a member of the reformed Borough Council from the early 1850s to 1892, being Mayor twice, in 1857 and 1862, aged 28 and 33 respectively. He was a JP for both town and county and one of the first County Councillors from 1889–92. He was a Liberal MP from 1868 until the town's 'disenfranchisement' in 1885, and for services to the party was baronetted by Gladstone in 1874. He had been a governor of Blundell's School for 50 years, and for many of them chairman. For half a century he had been President of Tiverton Hospital. He was granted the Freedom of the Borough in 1908.

During all this time he had been the real or nominal head of the firm, but perhaps he had been more squire than industrialist. He had enlarged and beautified Chevithorne Church. He had developed Chevithorne Rifle Range as part of his support of the Volunteer movement. He and his family ran the Tiverton Foxhounds, the Tiverton Staghounds and

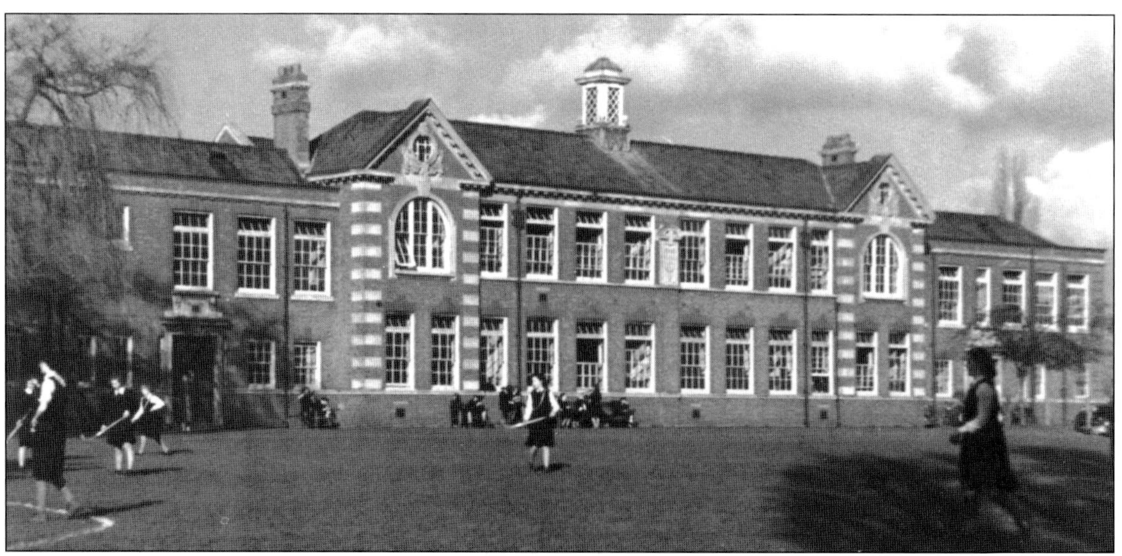

The Middle Schools which opened in 1910 on the 'wilderness' site. MUSEUM COLLECTION

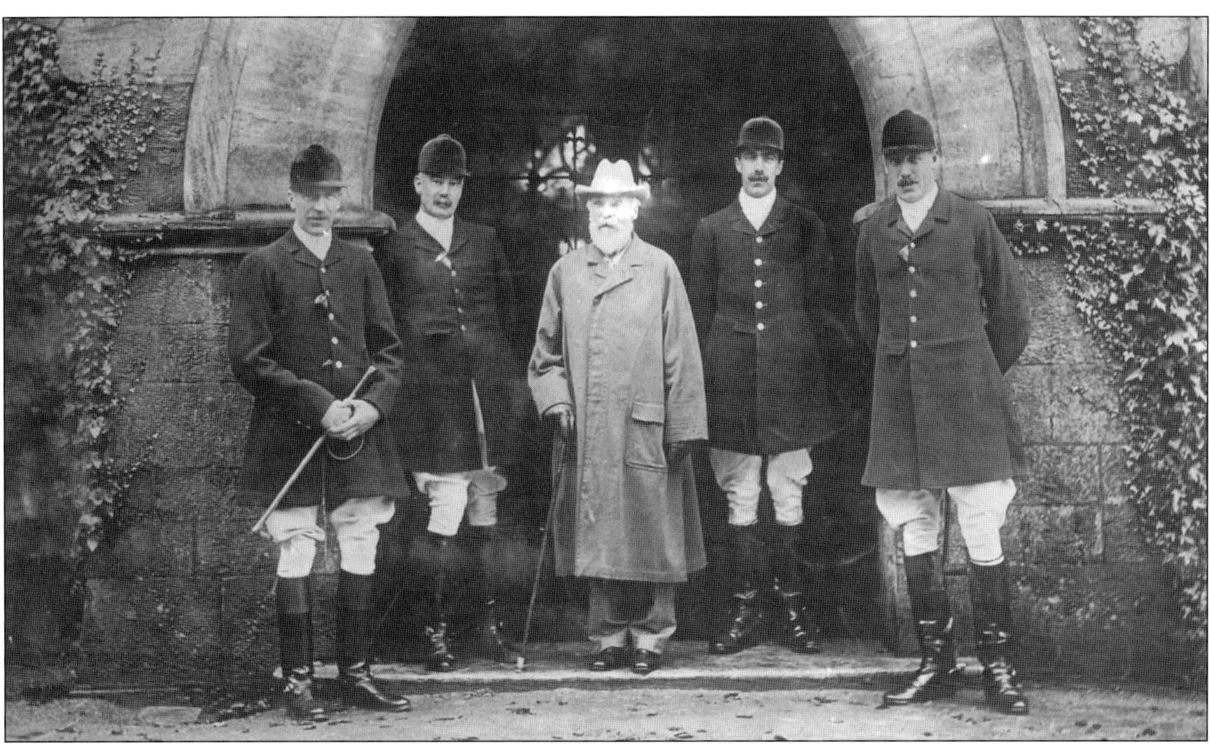

Sir John Amory and his sons in the doorway of Knightshayes. Left to right: *Ian H. Amory Esq.* MFH, *C.R.S. Carew Esq.* MH, *Sir John Amory* BART, *Ludovic H. Amory Esq, Captain H.H. Amory* MSH. MUSEUM COLLECTION

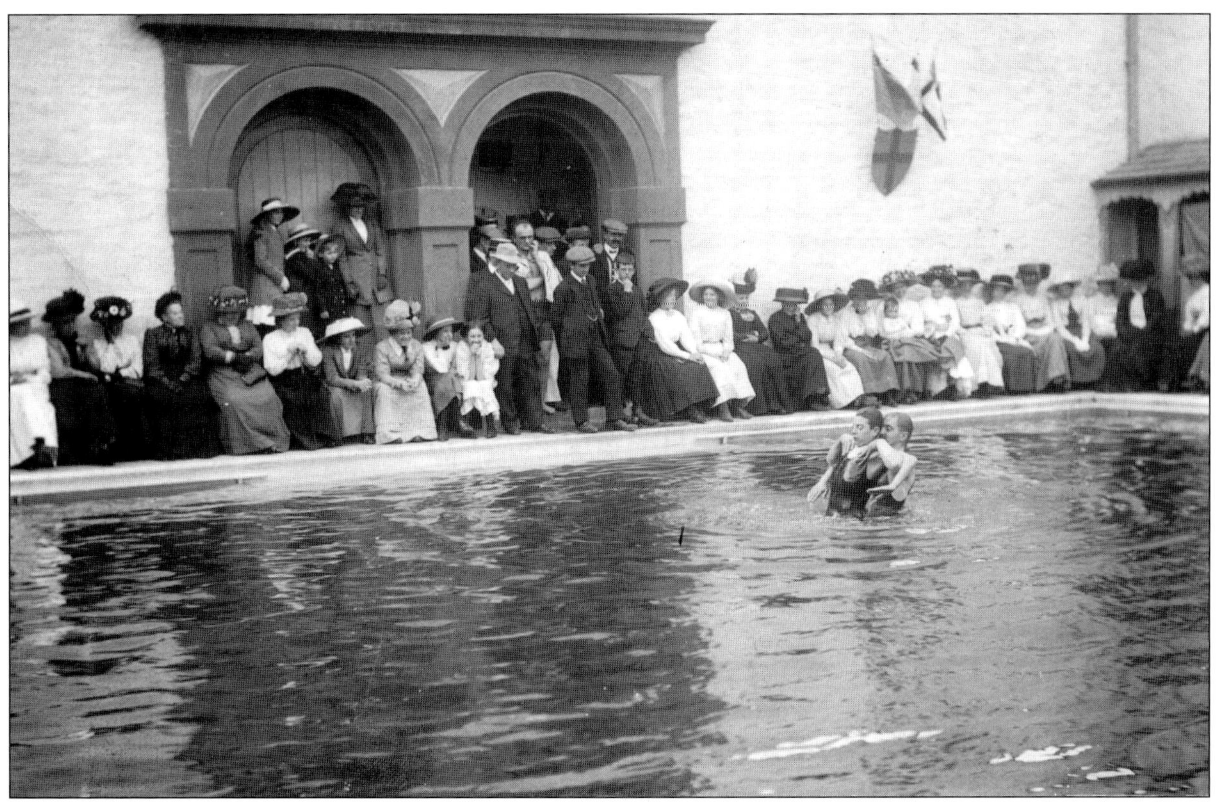

The St Andrew Street Baths on the other side of the prison. A hot bath could be purchased on the site until after 1945 – a necessity as most houses had no hot water or bathroom until the 1950s. MUSEUM COLLECTION

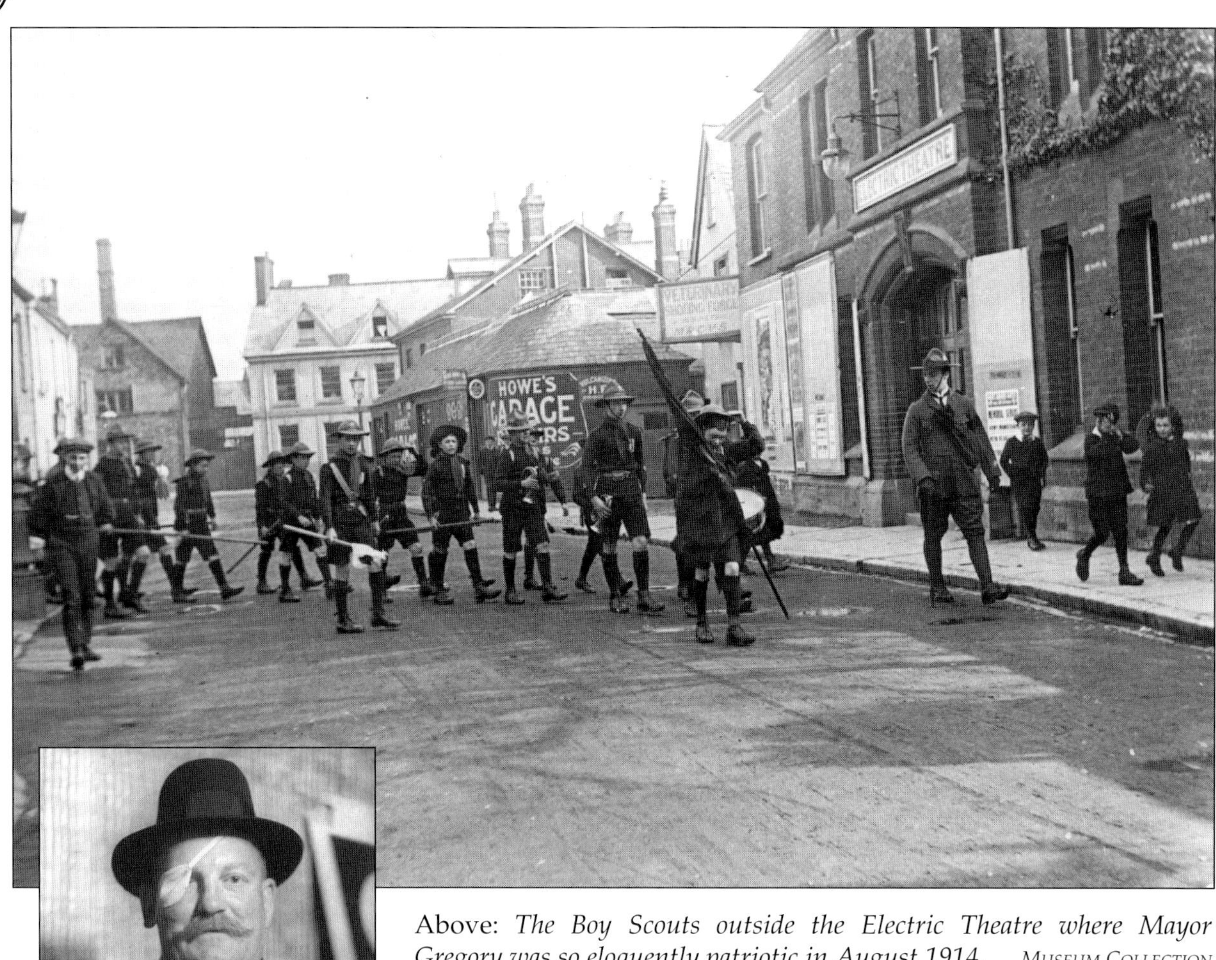

Above: *The Boy Scouts outside the Electric Theatre where Mayor Gregory was so eloquently patriotic in August 1914.* MUSEUM COLLECTION

Left: *Corporal Thomas Sage* VC. *A road in Wilcombe is named after him.* MUSEUM COLLECTION

Below: *For King and Country. The Devons parade on Angel Hill, October 1914.* MUSEUM COLLECTION

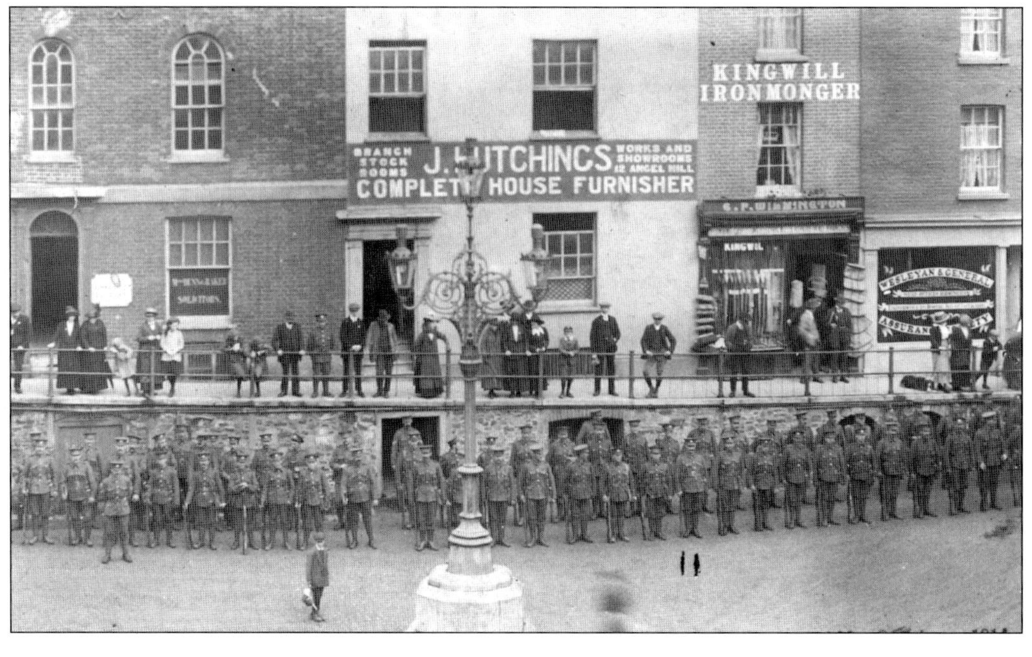

the Tiverton Harriers. He had acquired a grouse moor in Scotland and a fishing river in Norway. He possessed a prize flock of Devon Long Wools, and the roll of farmers attending the funeral of their landlord shows that the family had come to own a very large proportion of the parish.

When he was buried in early June 1914, the *Tiverton Gazette* was full of an impending crisis, but until the very end of July the crisis word is the headline for articles on the Ulster problem. Only in the issue of 28 July was it applied to the Continental situation. When war was declared on the evening of 4 August local excitement was at fever pitch. On the evening of Thursday 6 August Mayor Gregory called a public meeting for 6 p.m. at the Electric Theatre:

> *The Hall was filled. It is estimated that over 800 men of all classes were present, including clergy of all denominations, county gentlemen, magistrates, professional men, traders, farmers, artisans, young men fresh from school; and six ladies, especially invited by the Mayor – namely Lady Heathcoat Amory, the Hon. Mrs Lionel Walrond, the Hon. Mrs Lesley Butler, Mrs C. Carew, the Mayoress and Mrs Pugsley, the wife of the Town Clerk.*

As the men crowded in, each was given a printed card on which to indicate the form of service he was willing to undertake in the National Reserve, the Territorials, the Civic Guard, as Scout or Dispatch Rider, in the Control of Provisions, in the Distribution of Relief or in any other capacity.

A few minutes after 6 p.m. the Mayor led the ladies to the platform, followed by Aldermen Thorne, Mudford and Lake and most of the Councillors. Also on the platform were the massed ranks of the clergy and a sprinkling of military men led by Major General Bowles and including the officers of the Blundell's Officer Training Corps. Mayor Gregory then began by greeting the meeting and mentioning some absentees who had sent their apologies, including Mr Girdlestone of Bradley Down, who was organising sentries to guard the local railways against a surprise German attack. He went on:

> *We are met together in the interests of public safety... I am here to ask your help. You know that we are up against an extremely big job, the biggest job that this nation has had forced upon it since a hundred years ago we vindicated the liberty of Europe and crushed despotism on the field of Waterloo. [Cheers] In that respect I think it is extremely possible history will repeat itself. [Loud cheers]*

For a few moments he then reviewed events leading to the outbreak of war:

> *What are we to do in the position in which we find ourselves? First let us count the cost. Reckon it up amongst yourselves, ye men of Tiverton; and I am sure the women will be no less brave. [Cheers] There must be in front of us for some time to come tribulation, distress, hardship, those are the things that test the manhood of people. [Cheers] We must be calm and pull together. Thank God that for the time being party spirit is dead. [Prolonged cheers]*
>
> *Come the three corners of the world in arms,*
> *And we shall shock them; nought shall make us rue,*
> *If England to itself do rest but true. [Cheers]*

Then followed an exhortation not to waste provisions, nor to hoard food or to profit from temporary high prices:

> *I am sure that in this time of emergency we shall all try to bear one another's burdens. The strong will help the weak and the rich will help the poor. And so we shall all get through, and no man in this town shall suffer want as long as I am Mayor and have a sovereign in the Bank or the power to appeal to other people. [Vociferous cheers] I have issued the cards, which you have in your hands, for you to indicate your offers of service. I hope to raise in this town what I shall call a Patriotic Fund for those in need and particularly for the wives and families, who may happen to run short.*

At this point, the Hon. Mrs Walrond, the wife of the MP, passed him a cheque for £100 (at least £10,000 in modern terms) for the Fund, which was received by deafening cheers.

Gregory then described the purpose of the Civic Guard, which was to protect the town and the local railways from attack by any Germans who might descend from airships. Then there were announcements about the availability of training, tributes to the patriotism of local women and the Mayor led the meeting in a prayer which ended with the words:

> *... that God will watch over this land of ours, and I say to you, let your prayers rise up to God like a fountain night and day till this tyranny be overpast. [Loud cheers]*

The National Anthem was then sung, with the Hon. Mrs Walrond leading off with the first verse. After 'Three Cheers for the King' many men stayed on to sign up for the Territorials, the National Reserve, the Civic Guard or as Dispatch Riders. 'Drilling began next day at the Drill Hall, morning and evening.'

Patrols were sent out to guard strong points against the possibility of surprise attack. It is impossible to belittle the response of Tivertonians to the demand of war, but their efforts are part of the national story. Gregory remained Mayor for nine years; there were no elections; suffragettes who had been active in the town before the war were quiescent; Knightshayes became a VAD hospital. The war years thus represented a pause in development.

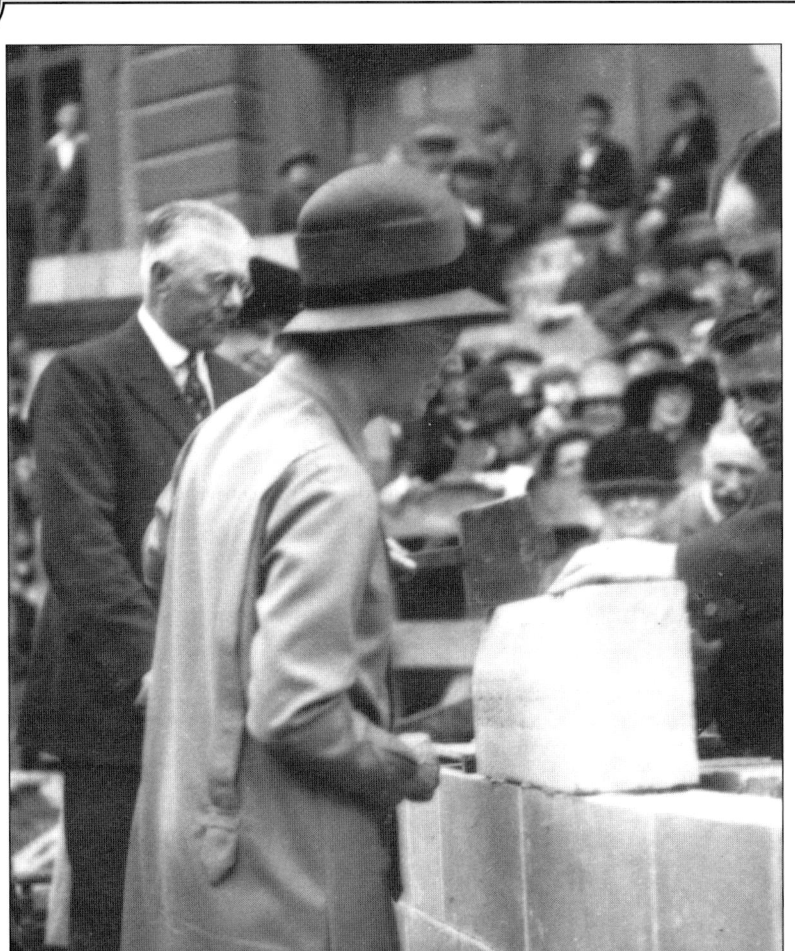

Left and below: *Kate Lazenby, a remarkable Tiverton lady, given the Freedom of the Borough in 1943 for her public work, particularly within the field of education, lays the foundation-stone of the War Memorial building in 1927. She opened her house on Saturday mornings to any child who wanted to come and read in her library. She was a keen British Israelite.*
MUSEUM COLLECTION

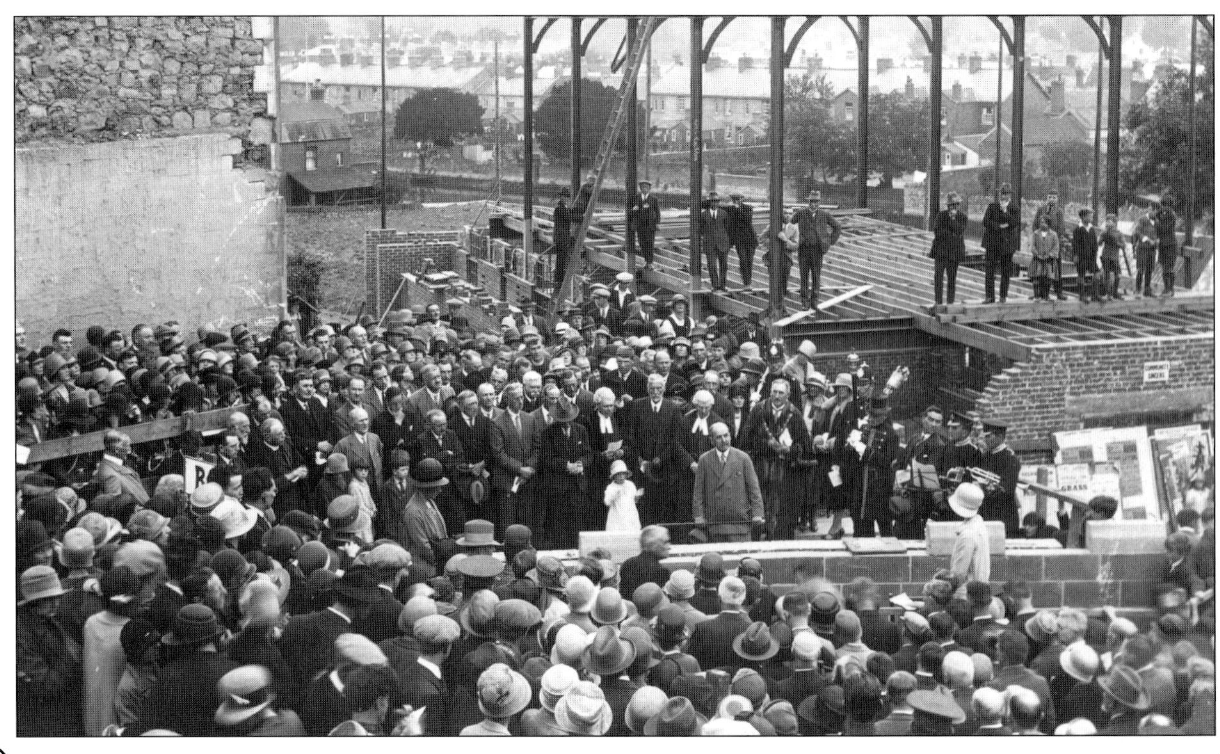

Chapter 8

Peace and More War, 1919–1945

'What is our task? To make Britain a fit country for heroes to live in'.
Lloyd George, November 1918.

'Do not let us speak of darker days; let us rather speak of sterner days'.
Churchill, October 1941.

Victory and sacrifice called for celebrations and memorials. The oddest celebration came in August 1919 and took place before Colliepriest House. An enormous pageant took place with 400 performers and a choir of 140, the whole written by Mayor and *Tiverton Gazette* editor Alfred Gregory. It told the history of Tiverton, albeit very selectively. Episode 1 was entitled 'The Gift of Water, 1250'; Episode 2 was 'The ending of the Manor, 1538' and had a young Peter Blundell promising to build a school to make good the loss of monkish education. Episode 3 was 'The Granting of the Charter, 1615' and Episode 4 was 'The Departure of the French Prisoners' with the 1919 head-master of Blundell's playing the 1814 head, Dr Richards, and prophesying the arrival at Blundell's of the young Frederick Temple, who in 1814 had not yet been born.

In 1920 two birds were killed with one stone. The Angel Hotel was taken over, which allowed the road to be widened on Angel Hill and a War Memorial Library and Hall to be erected in its place. The north aisle of St Peter's Church became a Memorial Chapel.

Progress towards creating a land fit for heroes was at best steady. For many years, politics were conducted in the shadow of the Russian Revolution in an atmosphere of frenzied hope for some and of abhorrent dread for others. In 1923 great excitement led to the election of Tiverton's last Liberal MP, Francis Acland, but he lost his seat within a year. Most progress towards a better Britain was done to provide more adequate housing. The earliest council-houses had been begun in 1912 at the top of Chapel Street and were called Council Gardens (later renamed Siddalls' Gardens after the Borough Surveyor), but the majority of them were finished in the early 1920s. The houses in Park Road, opposite the People's Park, came next as part of a nationally subsidised scheme of houses for sale. In the 1930s stronger powers to demolish and rebuild enabled the Council to draw up a slum clearance plan, but little progress was made until after 1945. In 1936 a start

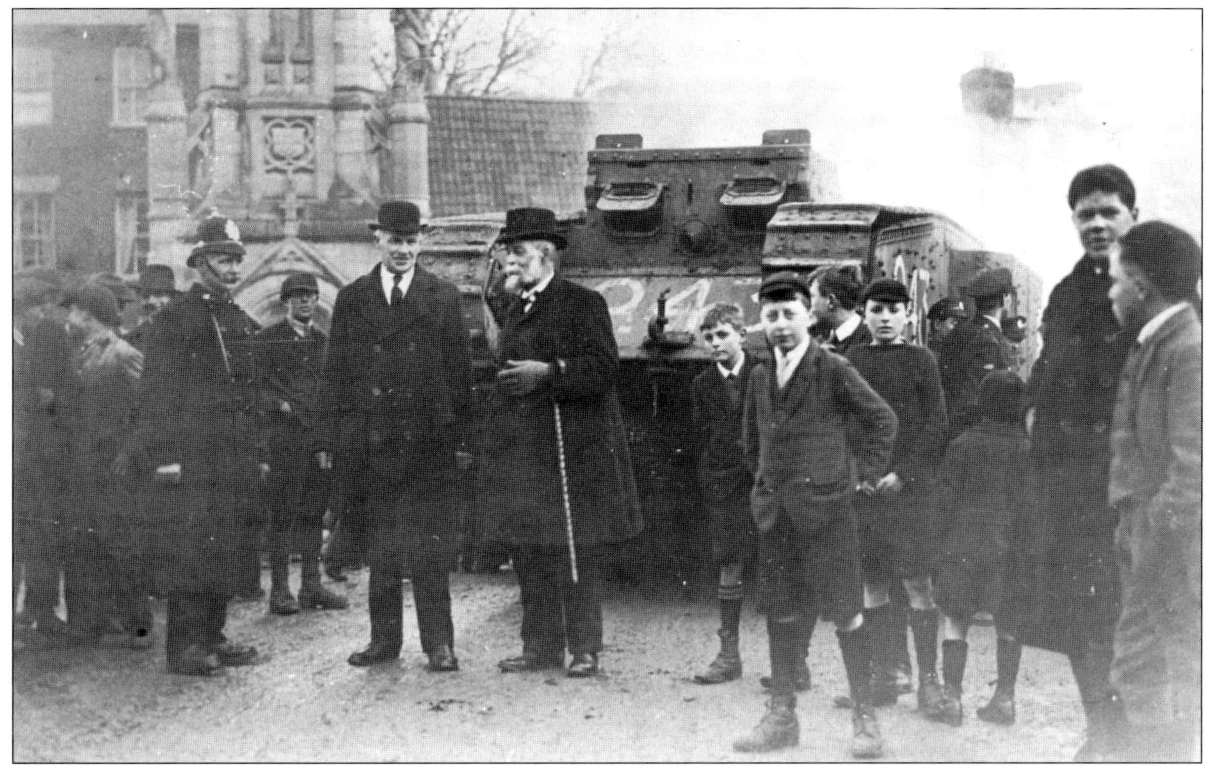

In 1919 a British tank was placed on Lowman Green as a symbol of victory. In 1940 it was sold as scrap and paid for the bus shelter. Pictured are: *PC May, Chief Constable Mercer* (in bowler hat) *and Mayor Barrons. Eventually all the other trophies of past wars were also scrapped.* MUSEUM COLLECTION

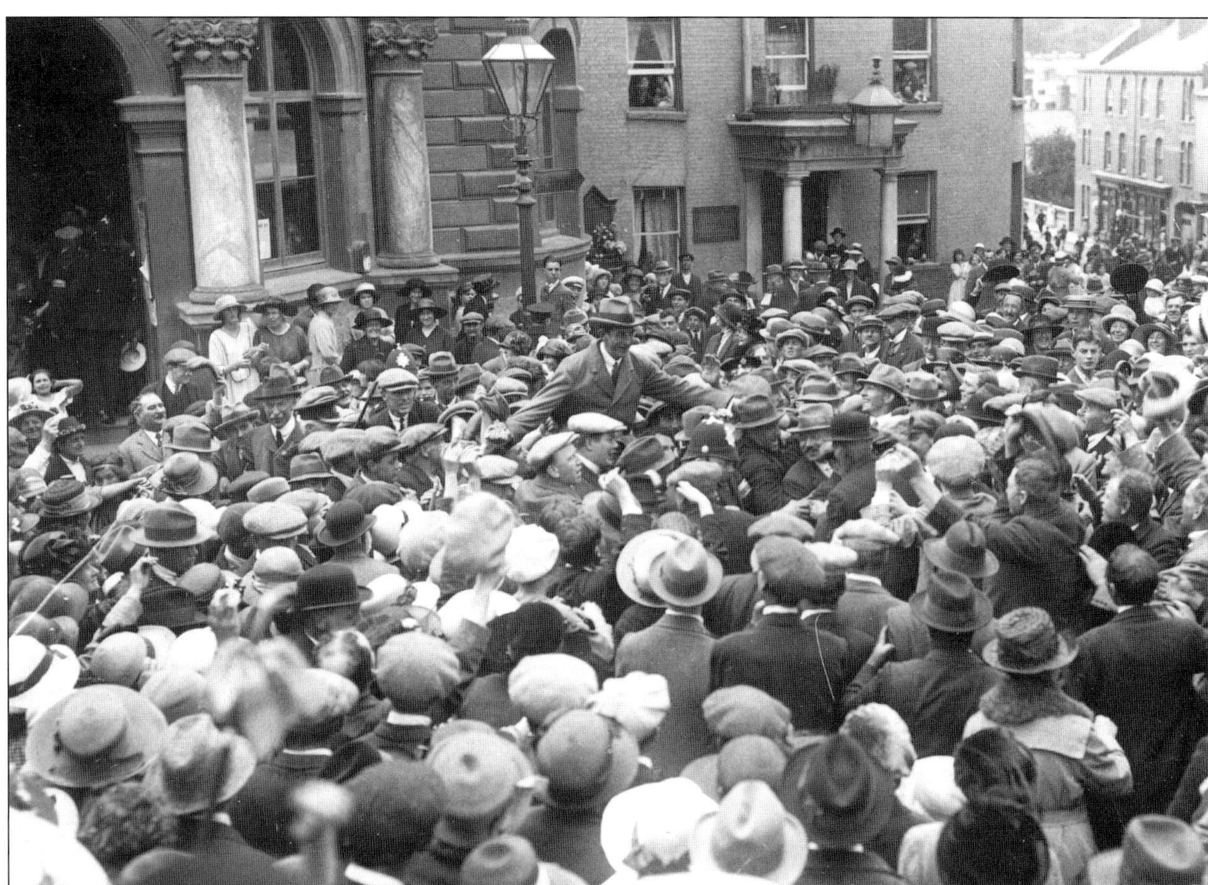

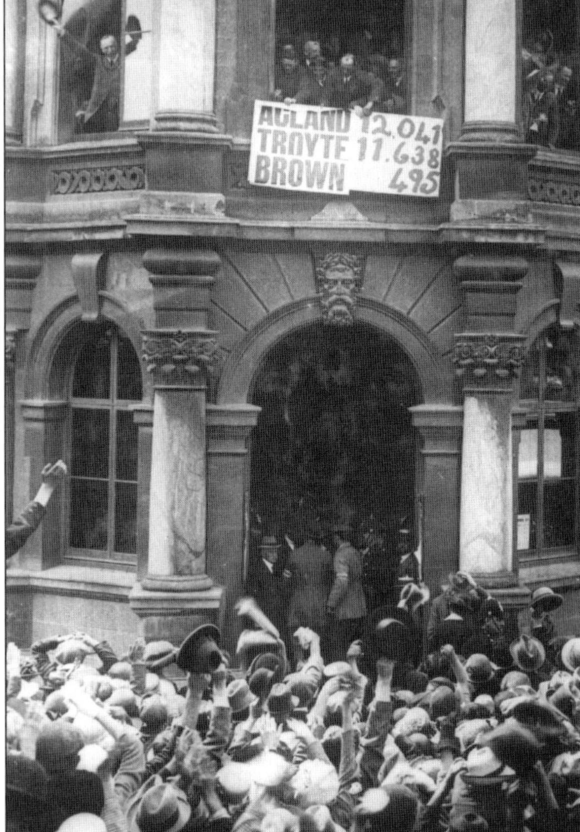

Above: *Chairing the candidate, Francis Acland, to the Liberal Club, then in Bampton Street. Note the Angel Hotel, soon to be demolished.* MUSEUM COLLECTION

Left: *The last Liberal election victory in Tiverton in 1923. The jubilant gent in the left-hand window is Sir Ian Amory, his family still being Liberal supporters.* MUSEUM COLLECTION

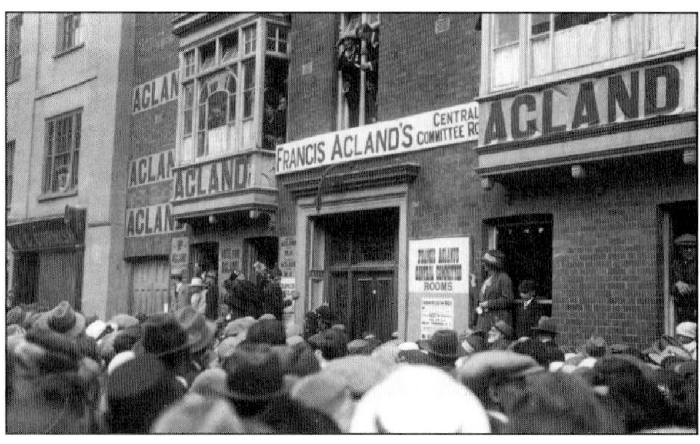

Above: *Acland addressing the crowd from the Liberal Club. He lost his seat within a year.* MUSEUM COLLECTION

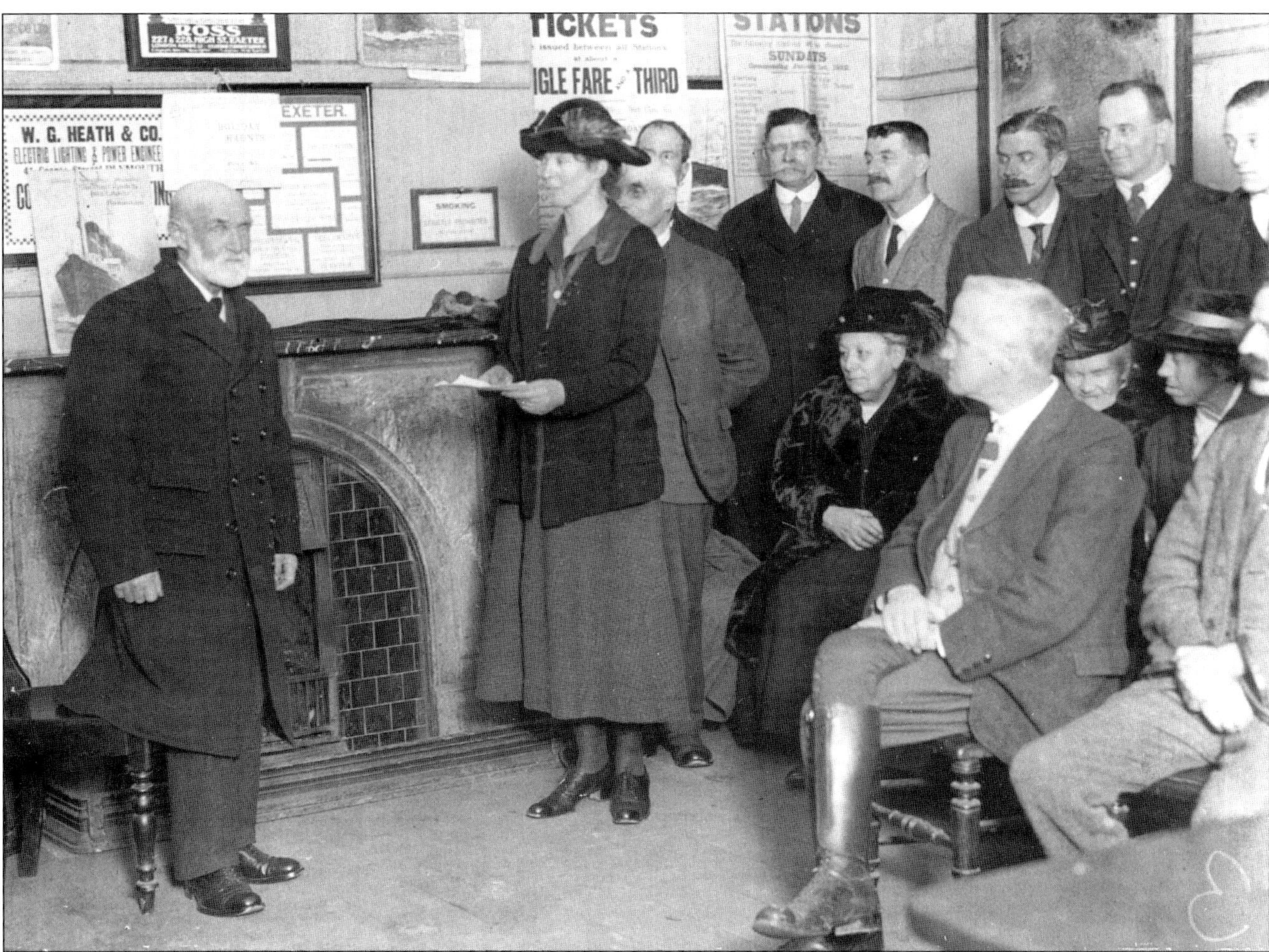

Miss Lazenby making a presentation to Railwayman Slee for long service. A period piece from 1922. MUSEUM COLLECTION

was made on council-housing at Shillands and Watery Lane, and in 1939 plans were announced for over 250 council-houses in Westexe South.

Useful pieces of tidying up were the removal of abattoirs from housing areas and the carrying out of very necessary street widening as more and more cars came into the town. In the 1920s it had been decided to provide a municipal slaughterhouse at Horsdon, where the cattle market would be relocated. Indeed, into the 1950s cattle would still be driven up Bampton Street on market days. By the mid-1930s abattoirs on Canal Hill, Broad Lane and St Andrew Street had been closed.

In the interwar years important developments took place in what we now call 'utilities'. Electricity became properly established in Tiverton. The generator was built on part of the site where Tesco now sits and had a customer base of just over 100 households by 1925. Very soon almost every house was connected and the sales of electrical gadgets, particularly radios, soared. The Electric Theatre became a cinema and the town's second cinema, the Tivoli, was opened in 1932, built by Gregory Eastmond, who also built the very modern house on the hill behind. The Council was still responsible for the supply of gas and electricity and in the 1930s had its own showroom for the sale of white goods at the top end of St Andrew Street. The high hopes that the wireless and its successor, the television, might produce an ever more enlightened and knowledgeable nation have been sadly unfulfilled. The town's water-supply was by now inadequate for modern needs and the Allers works were fed from extra sources in a scheme begun in 1935. Regular flooding demonstrated that there was plenty of water about.

In the interwar years Tiverton's fortunes were still mostly decided locally by Tivertonians. In the 1930s there were interesting developments at the hospital. It was decided to expand northwards along Bampton Street in order to achieve more ward space, and a local system of health insurance was introduced. Tivertonians were invited to cover their hospital and nursing costs by joining the scheme at the rates of 2d. a week for wage earners, 6d. a week for the better off and 1s. a week for the wealthier. It was still up to patients to negotiate with doctors and surgeons and to pay their fees. A local management committee still ran the hospital, still largely funded by charitable donations and bequests. Its funds were held in a local bank and it published an annual report. Almost every issue of the *Tiverton Gazette* conveyed the thanks of the matron for individual gifts of flowers,

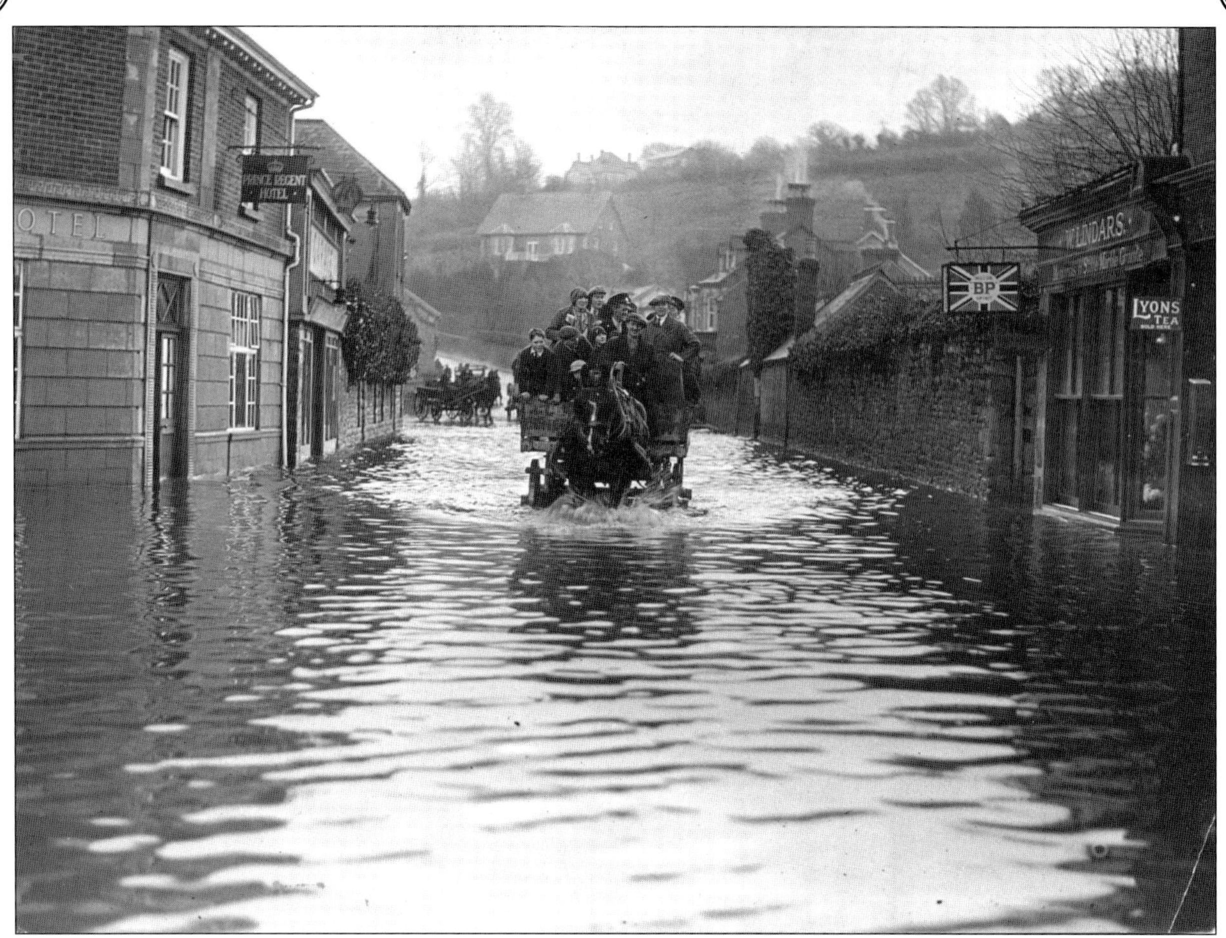

The floods of 1929 outside The Prince Regent. Unofficial water-supplies were often copious. MUSEUM COLLECTION

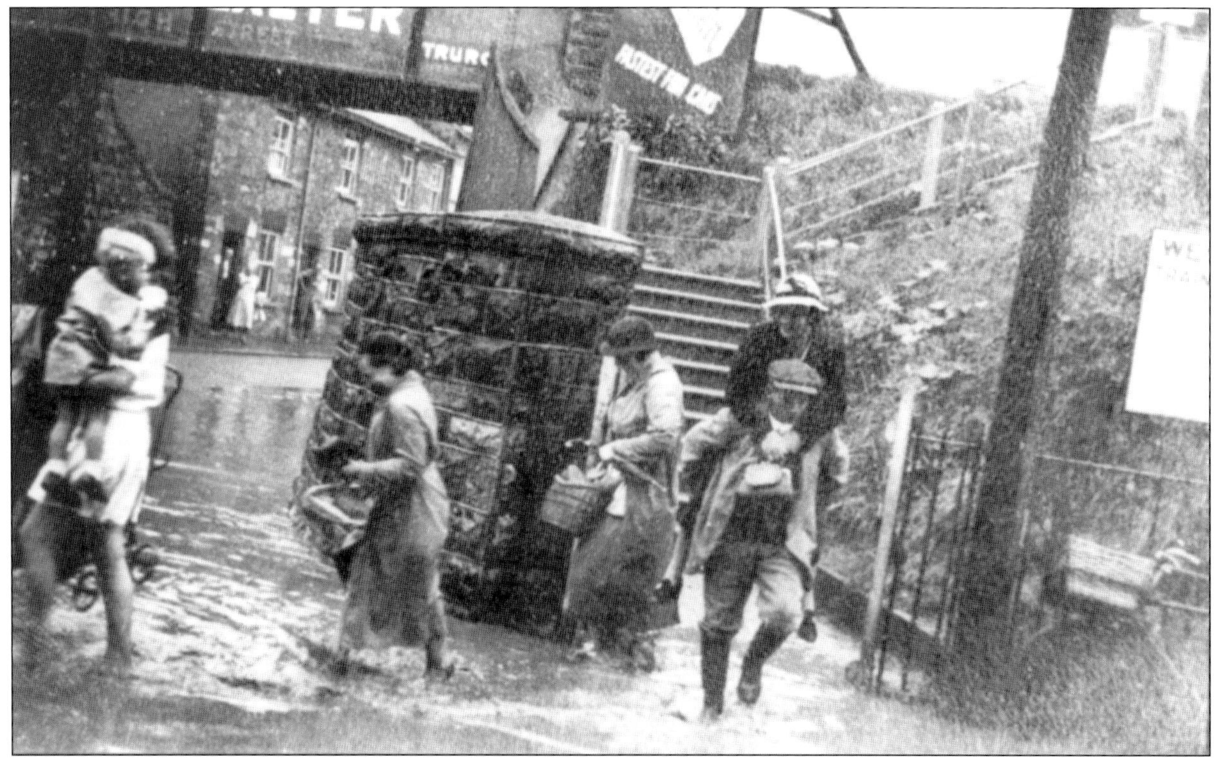

Passengers alighting from Westexe Halt during the floods of 1929. The railway bridge was demolished in the 1980s. MUSEUM COLLECTION

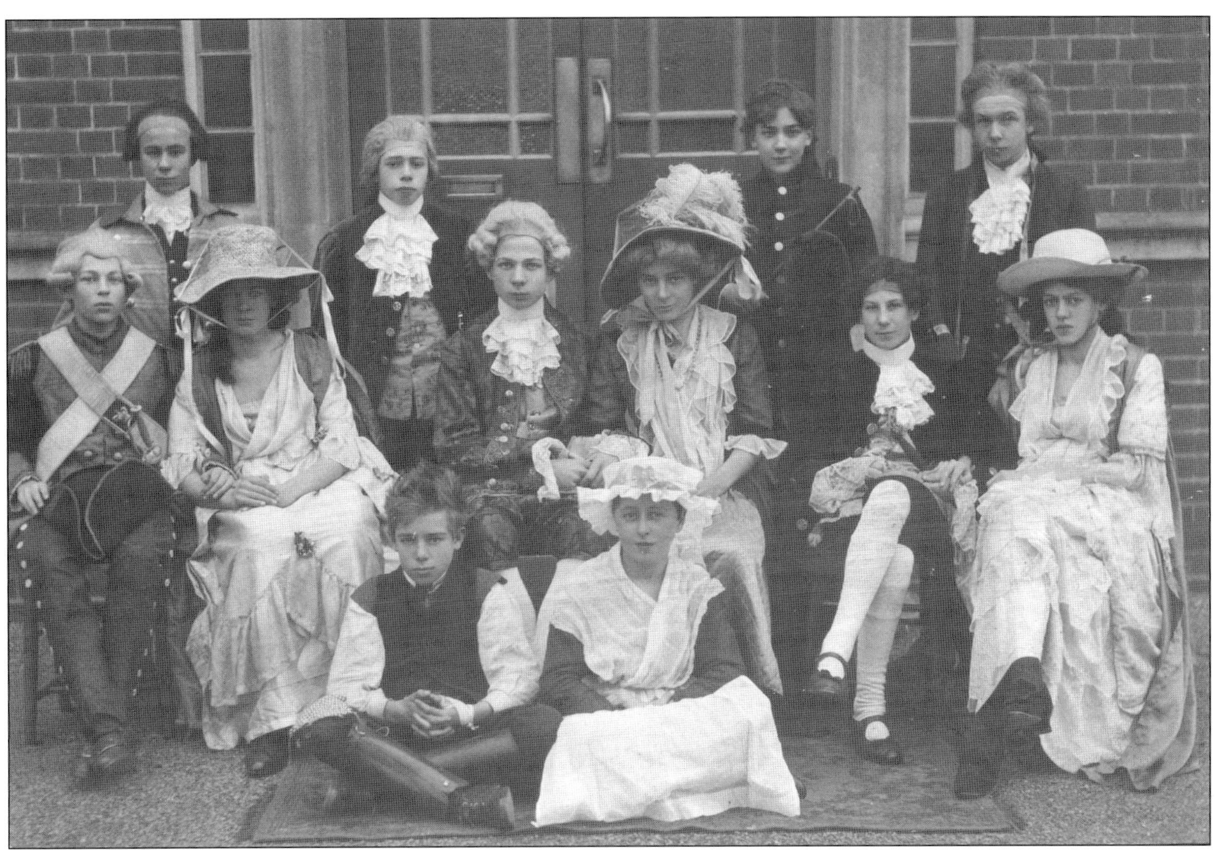

Tiverton Middle School Boys perform The Rivals, *c.1921.* The picture includes: *S. Jordan, ? Melhuish, P. Soundy, ? Farrant, C.J. Bending, A. Manning, K. Bareham, ? Greenslade, E. Munday, J. Johnson and L. Lee. Carl Bending, the 'man' in the middle, was in the Lowman Green tank photograph.* MUSEUM COLLECTION

Right: *Heathcoat's Tennis Club 1929.* MUSEUM COLLECTION

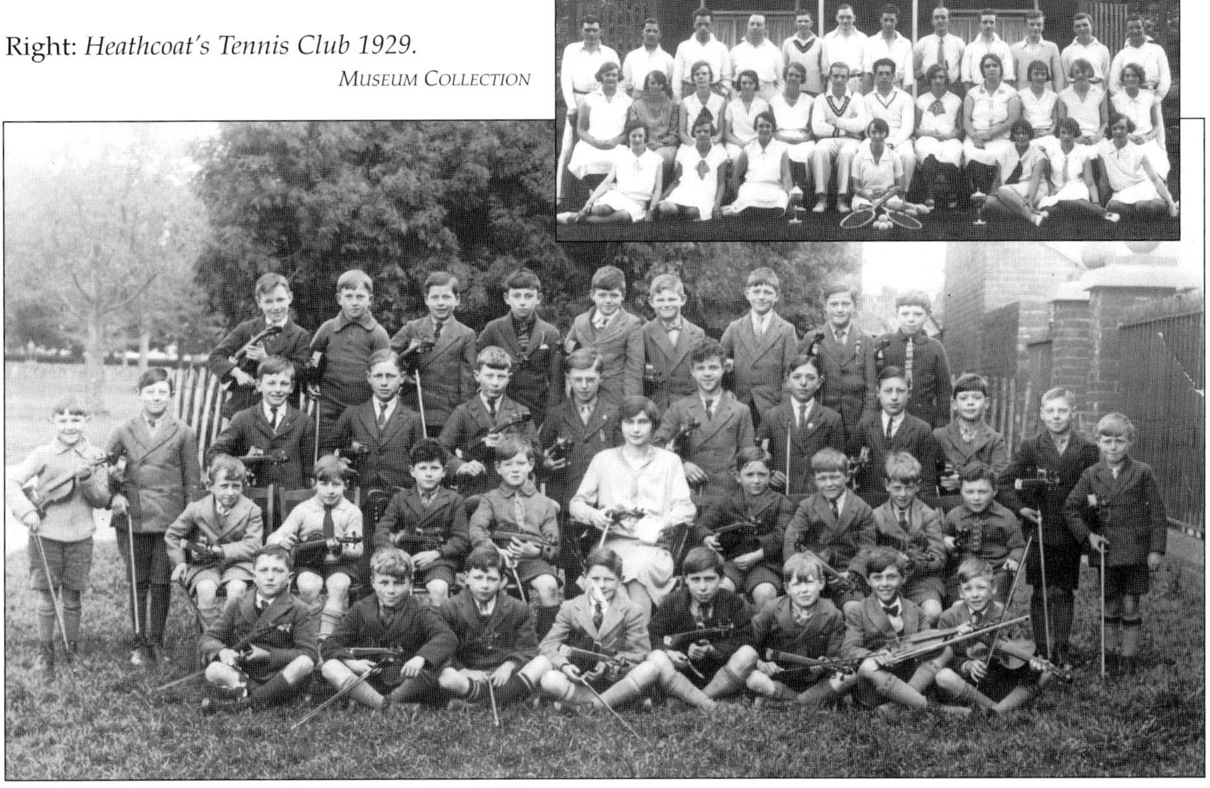

Heathcoat Boys' School Orchestra in the 1920s, when music was music. The teacher is Miss Marjorie Woodward. MUSEUM COLLECTION

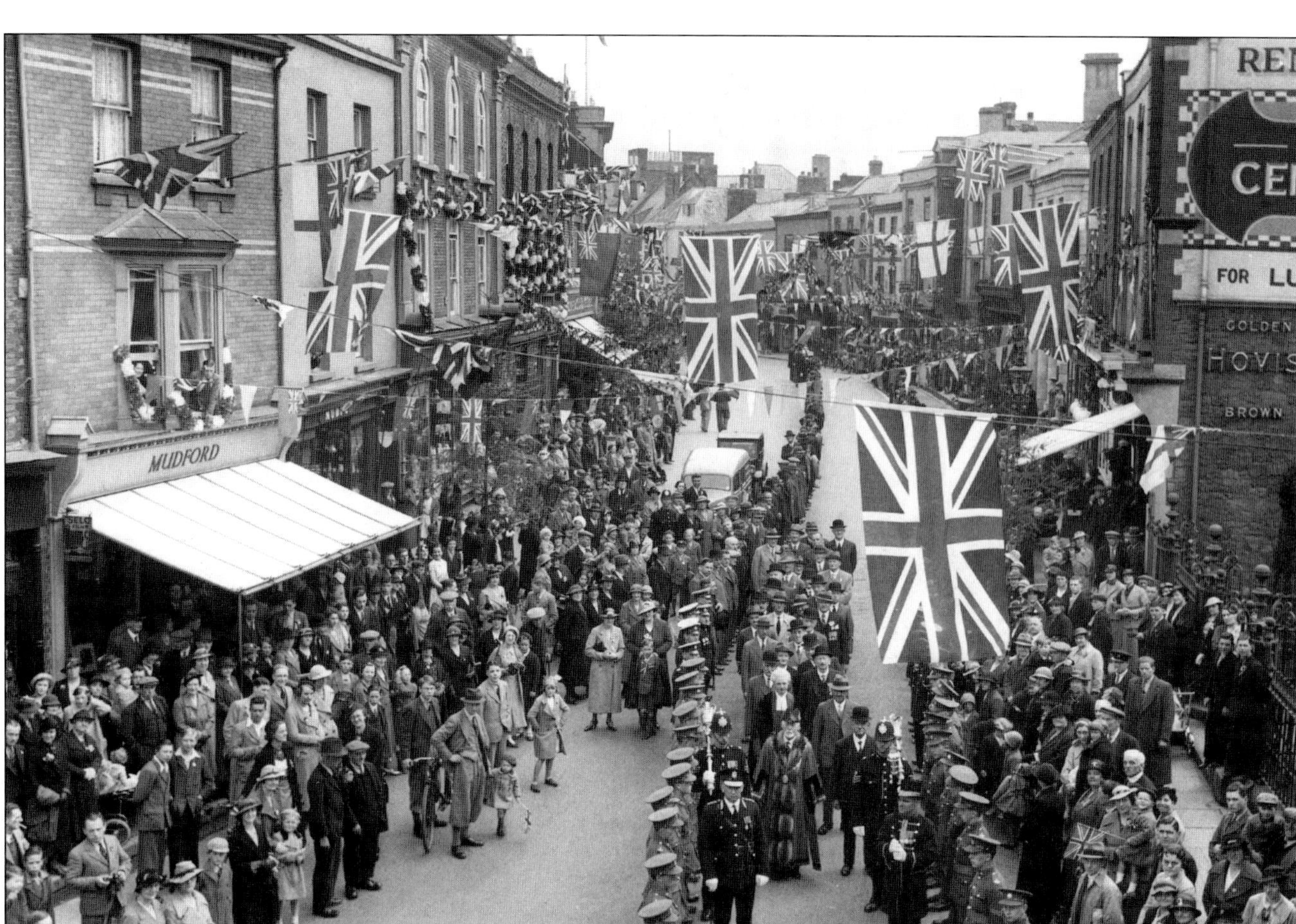

Above: *Procession in celebration of George VI's coronation, 1937. Mayor Wakefield and Town Clerk J.F. Pugsley are in Fore Street.* MUSEUM COLLECTION

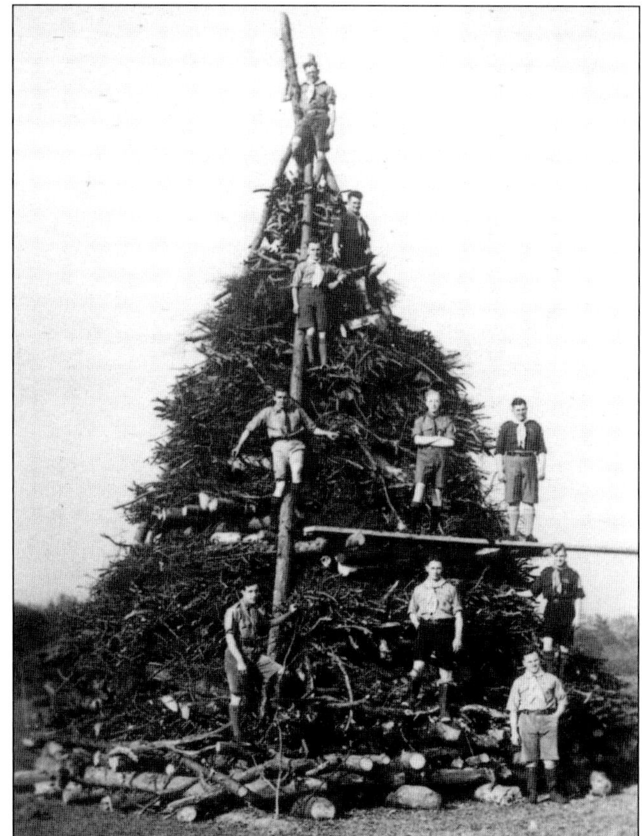

The bonfire for George V's silver jubilee in 1935. MUSEUM COLLECTION

eggs and vegetables to the hospital. Running its own hospital was one of the ways the community worked together. Over the next half-century these links would become ever weaker and fewer as central government took over more of the things that had been run locally.

In the mid-1930s the Black Shirts were active in Tiverton. In March 1935 they held a very well attended meeting at the Heathcoat Hall, addressed by William Joyce, later known as Lord Haw Haw and executed in 1945 for his war work for Germany. He ran through the usual Fascist policies: economic protectionism, the corporative state, abolition of the Lords, defence of the Empire and his analysis found two threats to world peace: international Jewish finance and international Bolshevism, the same bogeys that Hitler blamed for the outbreak of war in 1939. The local leader seems to have been Mr Hooper of Hartnoll Farm, who was still writing letters to the *Tiverton Gazette* in 1940, extolling the virtues of the party.

Less controversially, in May 1935, the Scouts constructed an enormous beacon fire at Gogwell Farm, to celebrate King George V's silver jubilee. Its framework of four larch trees stood at over 40 feet high.

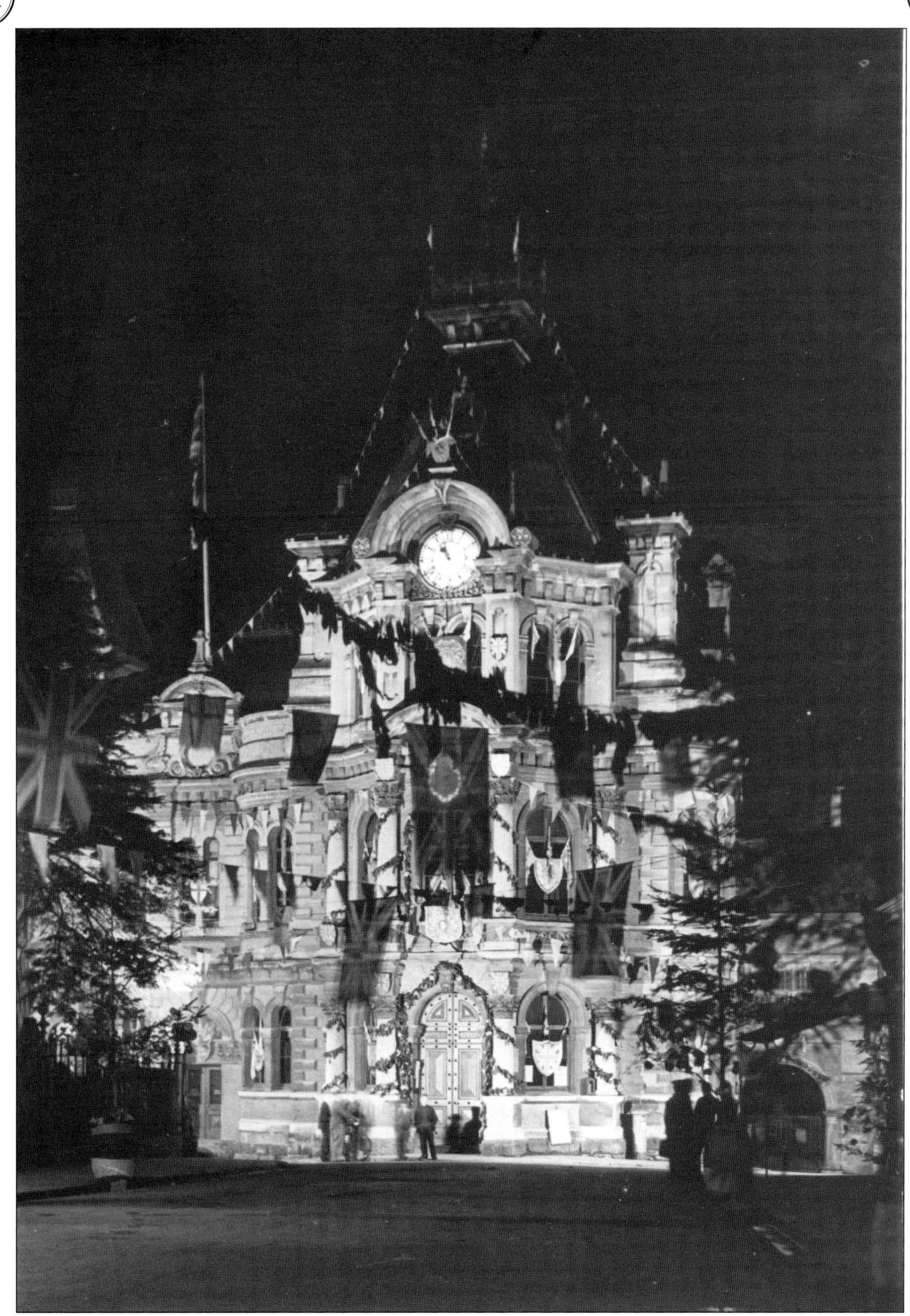

The illuminated Town Hall. Electricity was still a novelty. MUSEUM COLLECTION

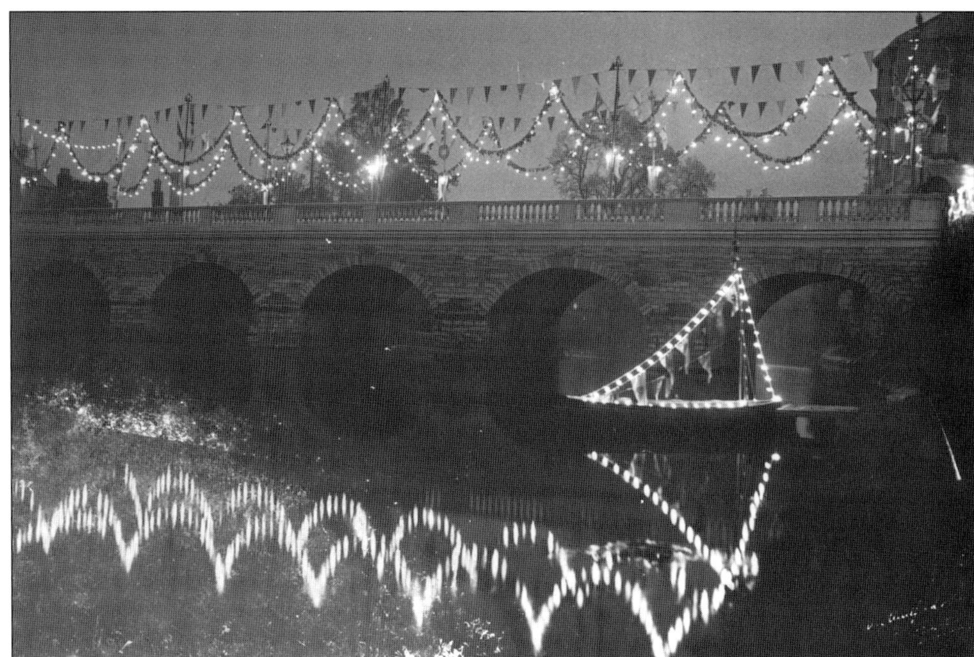

The Exe Bridge jubilee illuminations. Did those who received their 2s.6d. get similarly lit up? MUSEUM COLLECTION

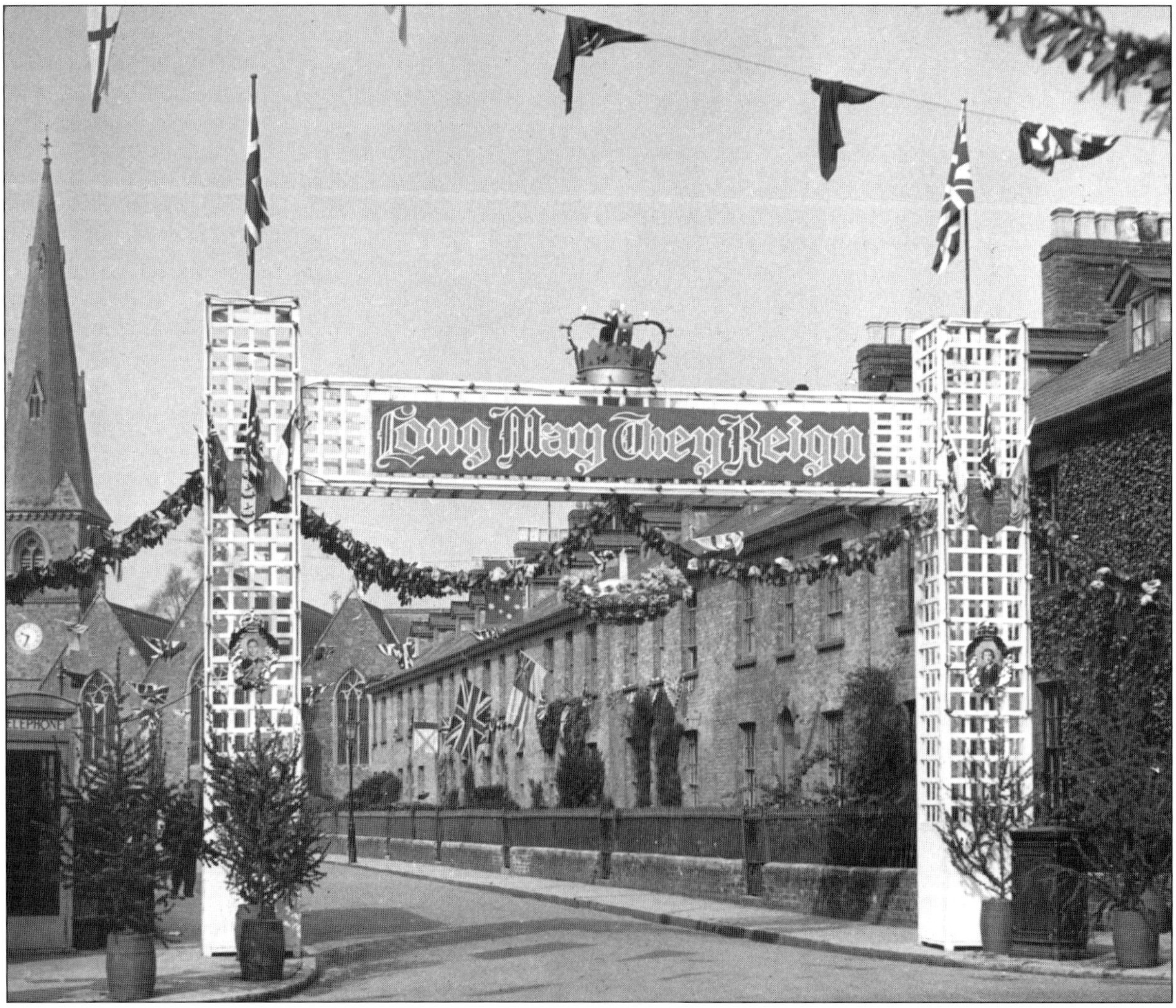

The Church Street jubilee arch, which reappeared at the next two coronations. MUSEUM COLLECTION

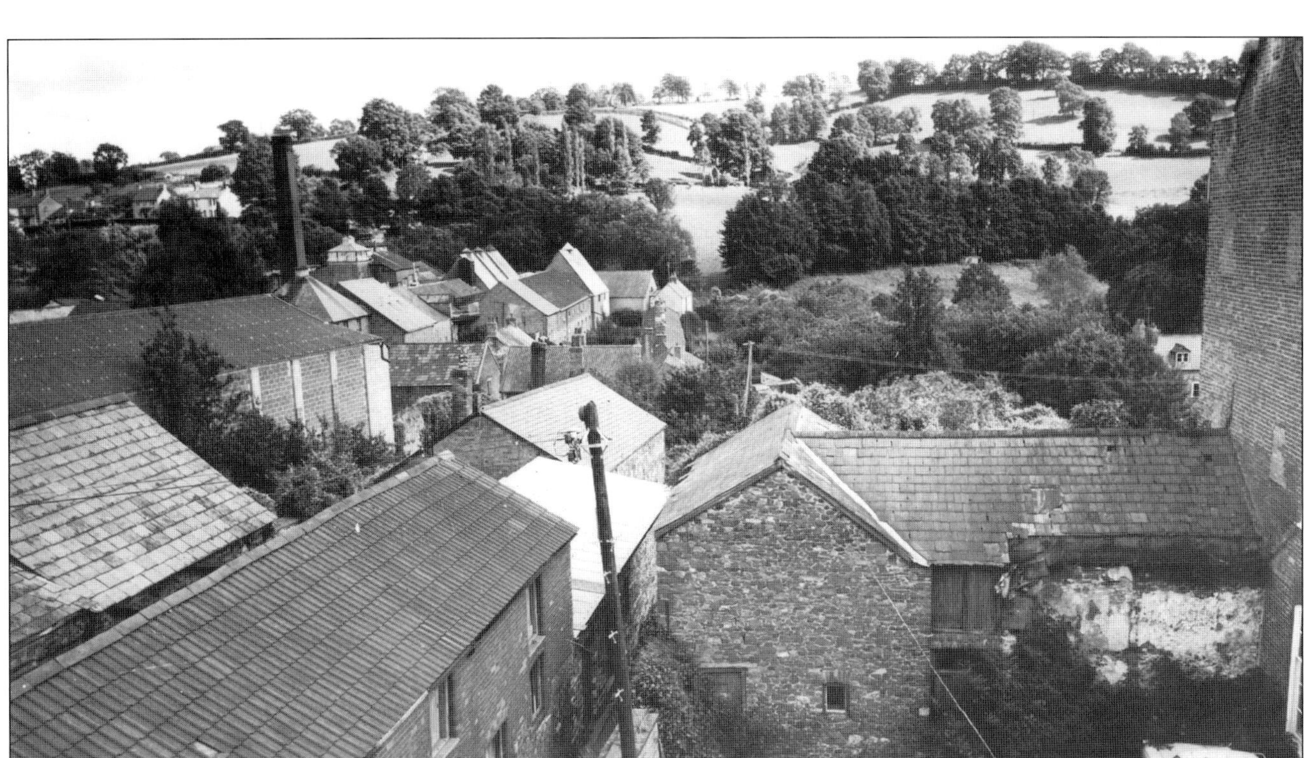

The Starkey, Knight and Ford Brewery, where the Mid Devon District Council offices now stand, no doubt suppliers of refreshment for the jubilee. MUSEUM COLLECTION

At 10 p.m. on the night of the jubilee, it was lit by the Mayor, Cllr Ford. Simultaneously a crescendo of large rockets flared into the sky. Within minutes the spectators could see about 20 other beacons pricking the night sky. This was the finale of a day that had included church services, children's sports and teas, a firework display and a display by the Tiverton Physical Culture Club at Amory Park. Every unemployed and recipient of outdoor relief was given half a crown with which to celebrate and the pubs were granted an extension from normal closing at 10 p.m. to 11 p.m.

Another silver jubilee in 1936 was the celebration of 25 years of Tiverton Middle School, which ten years later was to metamorphose into Tiverton Grammar School.

1936 ended with a severe fire at the factory. The morning after the fire things may have seemed disastrous, but by July 1938 all was repaired and in full production. Throughout the next war Heathcoat's was advertising for workers. Women were offered £2–£3 a week, boys 25s. and girls 21s. An attraction was the canteen that served lunches at 9d., tea at 1d. and buns at 1d. Free bus transport was also offered.

The old Tiverton faced the outbreak of the Second World War more soberly for, throughout the 1930s, the British people had been exposed to a continuous run of news items about the horrors of bombings in China, Abyssinia and Spain. The first ARP (air raid precaution) lecture was held in January 1936. So seriously was the danger taken that the government had ordered over a million coffins to cater for the expected bombing casualties. Tiverton prepared itself in timely fashion. In January 1939 there was an ARP stocktake. There were three first aid parties, a first aid post, four ambulances, three casualty cars, one light rescue squad, one heavy rescue squad and a decontamination squad (gas bombing was seen as a serious threat). Many Tivertonians had already received first aid training, 6,700 gas masks had been issued and more were available from a local strategic reserve kept in the Thorverton Drill Hall. There were

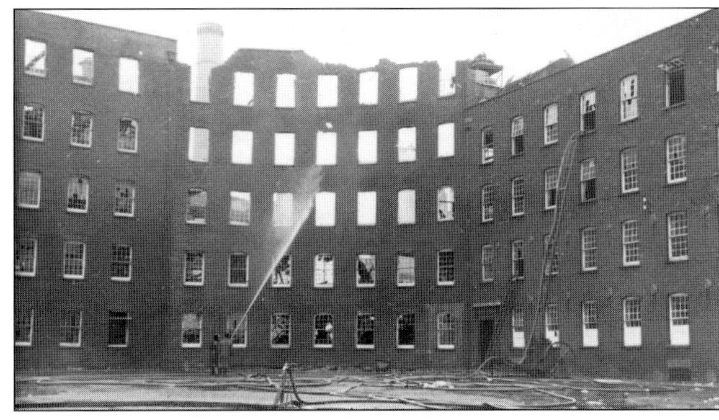

The factory fire of 1936. It was repaired and ready to work again in 1938. Full employment lasted until 1960. MUSEUM COLLECTION

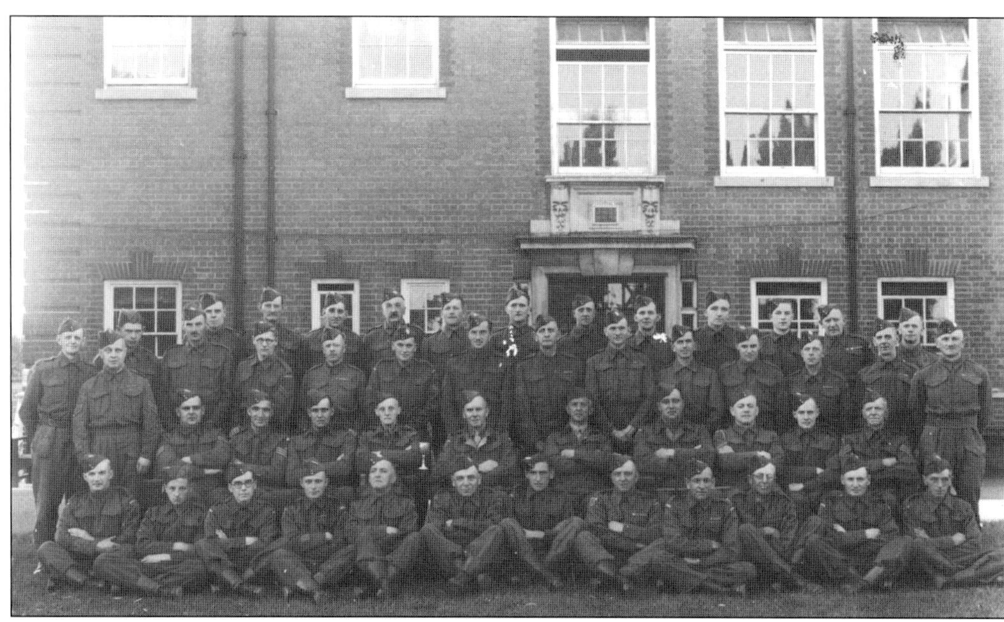

No 3 Platoon, Tiverton Home Guard outside the Middle Schools, probably on the eve of stand down in December 1944. Left to right, back row: *Ptes Emmett, Andrews, Bird, Carpenter, Willman, Habgood, Wilkins, Kerr, Allen, Montandon, L. Cpl. Hookway, Pte Payne;* third row: *Ptes Leaworthy, Frankpitt, Cpls Searle, Gardiner, Mogridge, Gale, Sgts Day, Cook, Cpls Greenslade, Davey, Hicks, L. Cpl Legg, Ptes Ayshford, Matthews;* second row: *Sgts Marker, Bicknell, CQMS Ellicott, 2nd Lt P. Bicknell, Lt Heal, Capt. Warren, Lt Jenkins, Lt B. Bicknell, P/Sgt Cox, Sgt Beck, Wills;* front row: *Ptes Poole, Paul, Edwards, Jones, Fewings, Forward, Snow, Green, White, Mills, Lanchbury, Goff.* MUSEUM COLLECTION

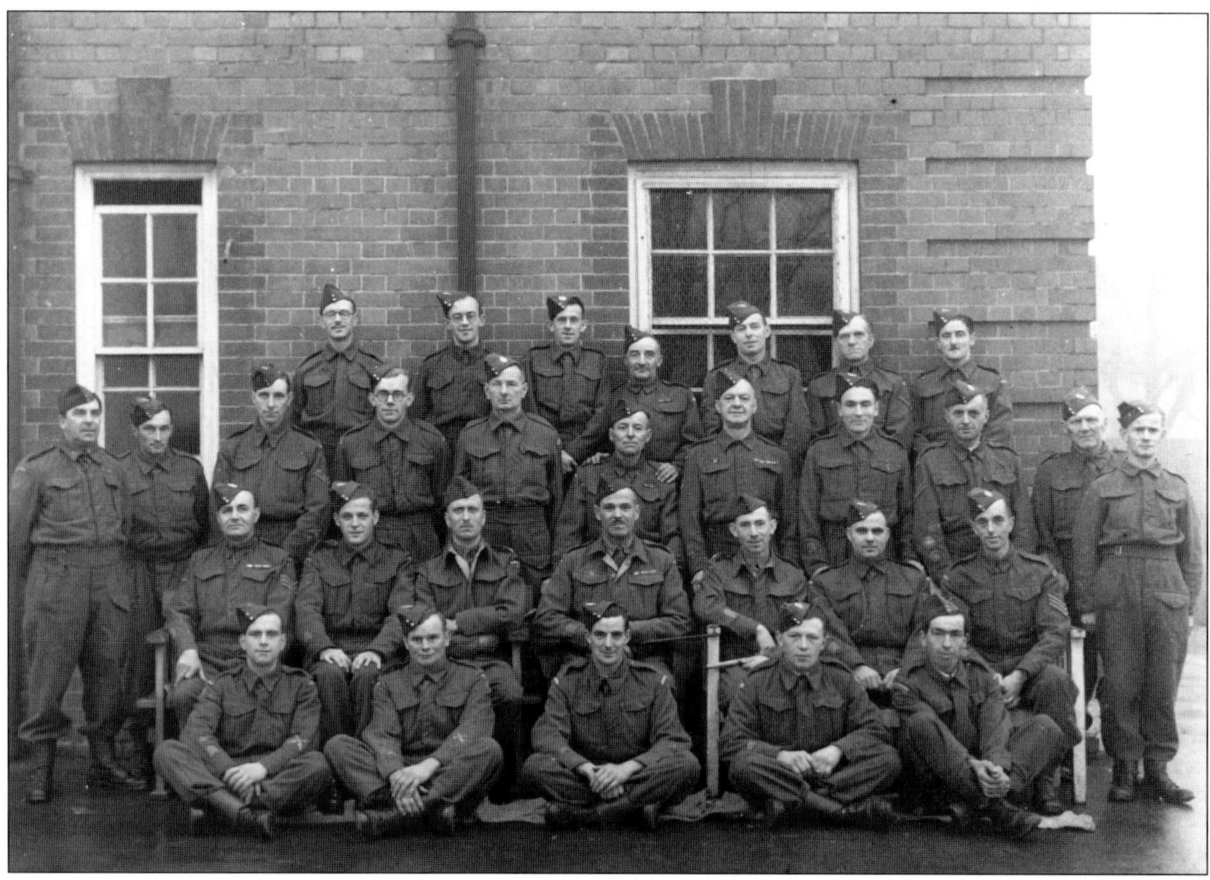

No 4 Platoon, sadly without names. Same time and place. Sadly too there are no photos of the WVS, who did equally sterling work. MUSEUM COLLECTION

60 trained ARP wardens based in St Paul's Schoolroom, the Palmerston Hotel and Carpenter's Coal Depot near the station. Blundell's had its own ARP organisation. In its first issue after war broke out *Tiverton Gazette* carried a prominent front-page advertisement asking for stretcher bearers who had to be over 41, of good physique and experienced in their craft. This issue carried notices that all cinemas were to be closed as well as refresher instructions on how to wear gas masks. There was also a patriotic exhortation to 'Start Knitting Now' for the troops, but that was inserted by Kirk's, a haberdashery in Fore Street. The *Gazette* reported that there was no excitement; 'Tiverton went about its business with a calmness which was remarkable.'

To prepare for the onslaught of the bombers the government had organised a programme to evacuate mothers and young children from London. Hosts would receive 10s. for the first 'guest' and 8s. for subsequent ones. The quota for Tiverton and the surrounding area was 2,600 who would start arriving on the fourth day of the war, but a canvas of the town and district showed a readiness to take in 4,000 evacuees. Typically the CPRE (Campaign to Protect Rural England) hoped that Devon would not be swamped by them. As it happened the first 140 evacuees arrived on 12 September as an overflow from those destined for Sidmouth. They were mothers and children under five from the Walworth Road, a slum area of Southeast London. The Mayoress, Mrs Lewis, appealed for prams and cots and the mothers complained that Tiverton lacked entertainment. Over the winter of the Phoney War many of them drifted home.

It was a bitter winter. In January a temperature of minus 3 degrees Fahrenheit was recorded in Cullompton. There was skating on the canal and the Exe froze. There were certainly more casualties from motor accidents in the blackout than from enemy action. Ration books were issued and everyone had to register with a butcher to get their meat ration. There was a drive for scrap metal, which swallowed up the First World War tank that stood on Lowman Green, its 40 tons of metal paying for the bus shelter there. The howitzers in the People's Park soon followed. In March a ministry placed advertisements exhorting farmers to plough land and even to plough at night. Col Troyte, MP for Tiverton, fiercely condemned the Committees who exempted 'Conchies' from military service as too soft, he wanted members of the Peace Pledge Union to be treated as traitors, and all enemy aliens to be interned. Reflecting the servant shortage, the *Tiverton Gazette* carried advertisements for a detergent unhappily called 'SOAKO'.

Things began in earnest in May 1940. In response to Eden's request for Local Defence Volunteers, 300 enrolled at the police station and 80 were originally selected led by Borough Surveyor Colonel Duncan Arthur and Captain Sir John Amory. Volunteers from the Hunt organised mounted patrols to look for enemy paratroops. The public were told to phone the police if they saw the enemy descending. In June the LDV became the Home Guard and was organised in patrolling platoons. An enthusiastic unit of the Blundell's Home Guard arrested Sir John Amory and refused to release him until proof of identity was provided.

Civilians were exhorted to 'Eat more Potatoes', and less bread and to grow more food. In a more militant vein, the town began a Spitfire Fund to raise £5,000 to provide the nation with a machine. Some of the more timid Council tenants, living in whitewashed houses, begged the Council to repaint them more drably, so that they would be less visible to bombers, but they were told to keep their upper lips stiff.

Evacuees now began to arrive in earnest. They were met and registered at the station, then taken to the market for refreshment and onward distribution. Some 700 London children from Ilford, Daggenham, Barking, Paddington and Kilburn, with their accompanying teachers, arrived in mid-June. The *Tiverton Gazette* stated:

> *A pathetic feature of the Registration was the considerable number of family groups. Little mothers aged 8 or 9 came forward with brothers and sisters of 5 and 6 by the hand, ready to supply the necessary information for their less articulate charges.*

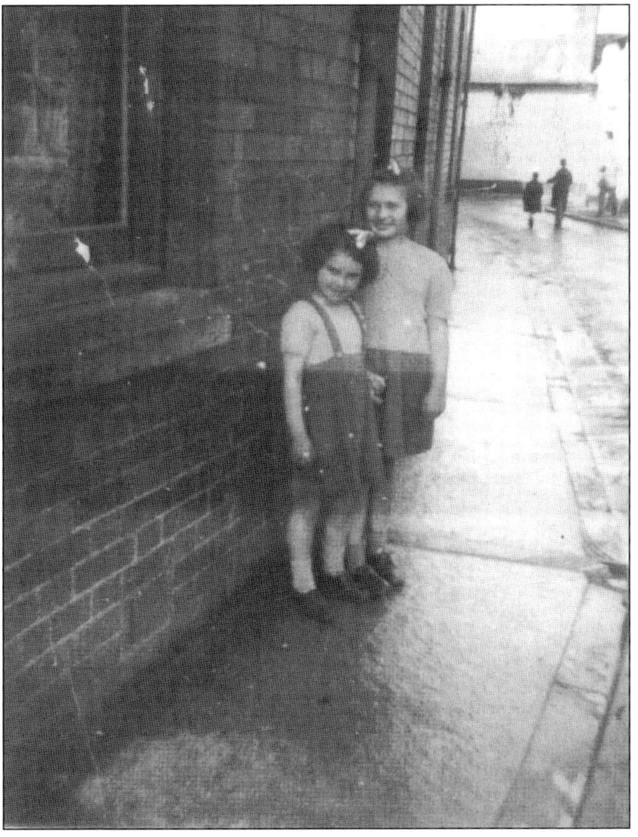

Mary Willis with her evacuee, Leslie Keeley, in Silver Street, 1943. COURTESY OF MARY WILLIS

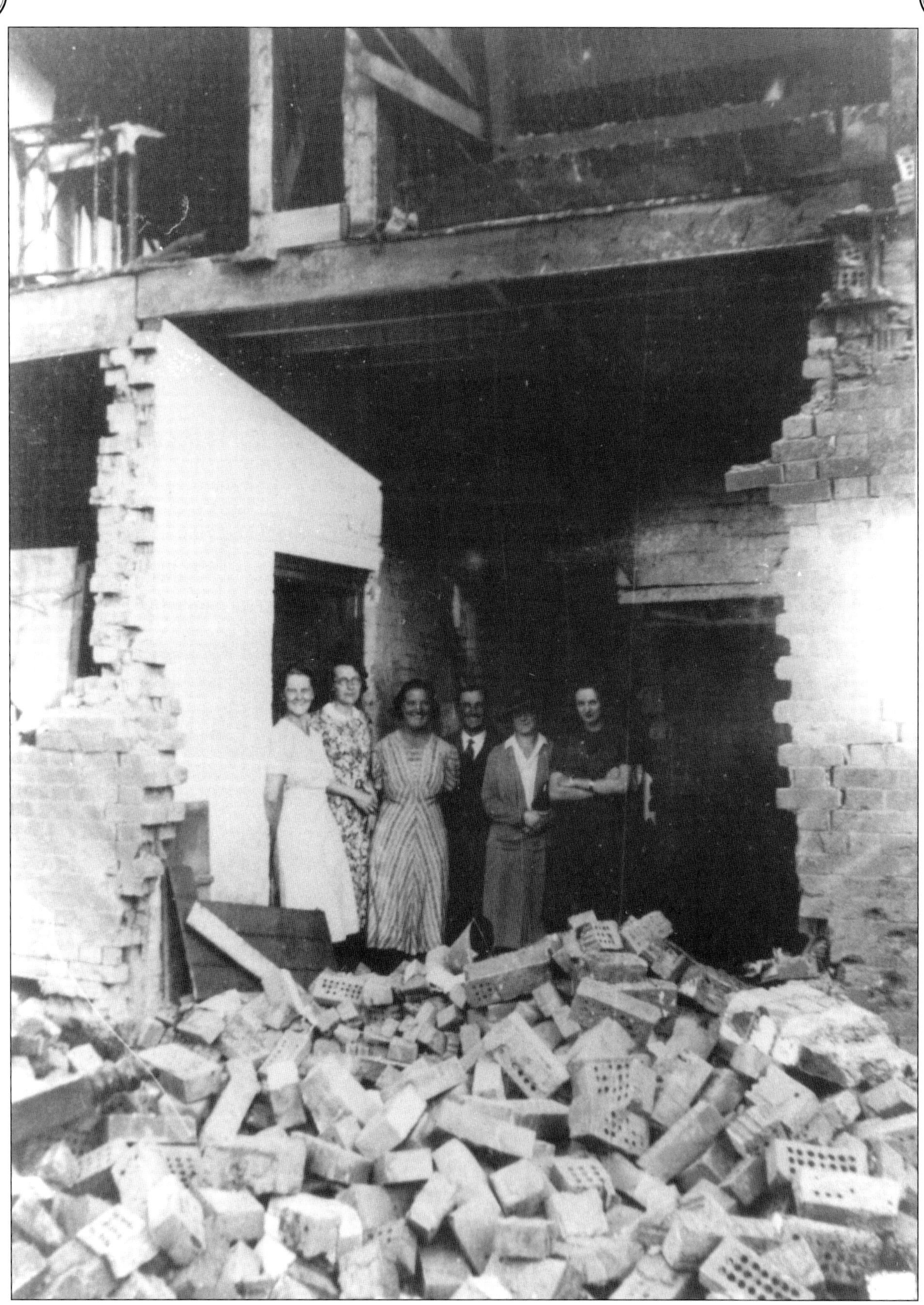

Tiverton's only bomb damage: Belmont Road, July 1940. The people in this picture have not been identified but may be the Hill family. How modern Health and Safety would fret at this photo. MUSEUM COLLECTION

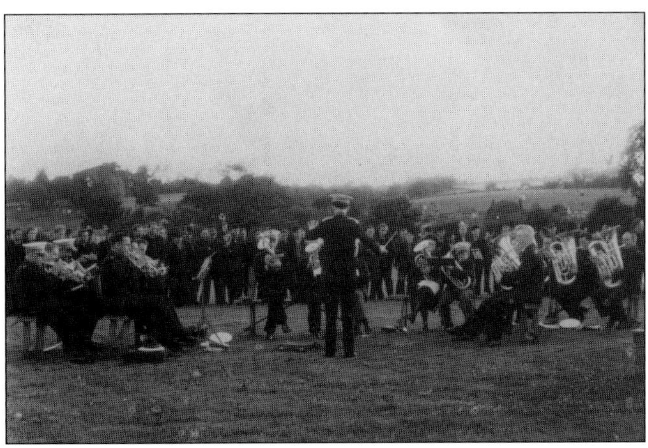

"Blessed are the Peacemakers". The Salvation Army Band plays to German PoWs, probably in 1945, at the PoW camp at Bolham Rd.

Later in the month another 796 arrived. In July another 200. In October came two parties that altogether contained 400 mothers and children. The immense task of greeting them, organising them and then finding homes for them was achieved by Chief Billeting Officer, F. Langmead and the ladies of the WVS (Women's Voluntary Service), who laid on daily lunch for evacuees in the St Peter Street Masonic Hall for 6d. The general standard of housing in the town is revealed by the complaint that there were not enough lavatories. In response the Council made the ladies' public lavatories free for the duration. It was estimated that there were 1,100 evacuees living in Tiverton by the end of 1940, the remainder having been dispersed to the villages.

The schools had to find places for almost 400 extra pupils and appealed to the churches for extra space. All responded with offers of help, except the Plymouth Brethren, whose rooms could not be used for so secular a purpose. However, the Salvation Army went the extra mile and organised three Christmas parties for the evacuees and over 250 attended each. They were helped by a donation of £105 from Sir John Amory, who, with Mayor Lewis, attended them.

Evacuees came and went according to the fluctuations of war. In March 1942, Miss Tibble, who had taken over as Chief Billeting Officer at a salary of £4 a week, presented a report to the Council. Between November 1940 and February 1942, 2,624 evacuees had been received in Tiverton and their average stay had been five months, though 267 children and 158 family units were still in their original billets. A 156-strong Devonport girls school, was being hosted and would stay until 1945, to the delight of many local lads. Every billet was visited monthly. Naturally there was a clothing problem, especially after clothes rationing began in June 1941. Lady Amory ran a clothing depot in Westexe; the WVS mended innumerable articles of clothing and a mobile laundry did washing. Boot repairs were tackled by a boys' class in Heathcoat's School. Meath House was an evacuee childrens' hostel and Ashley Court a hospital for evacuee children. The indefatigable Miss Tibble had started a girls club, the 'Happevacs' which met on Mondays. The boys had a club on Wednesdays.

Further evacuees would come and receive temporary help when Exeter and Plymouth were later bombed. To cater for them and for those workers who needed lunch, the Council opened a British Restaurant

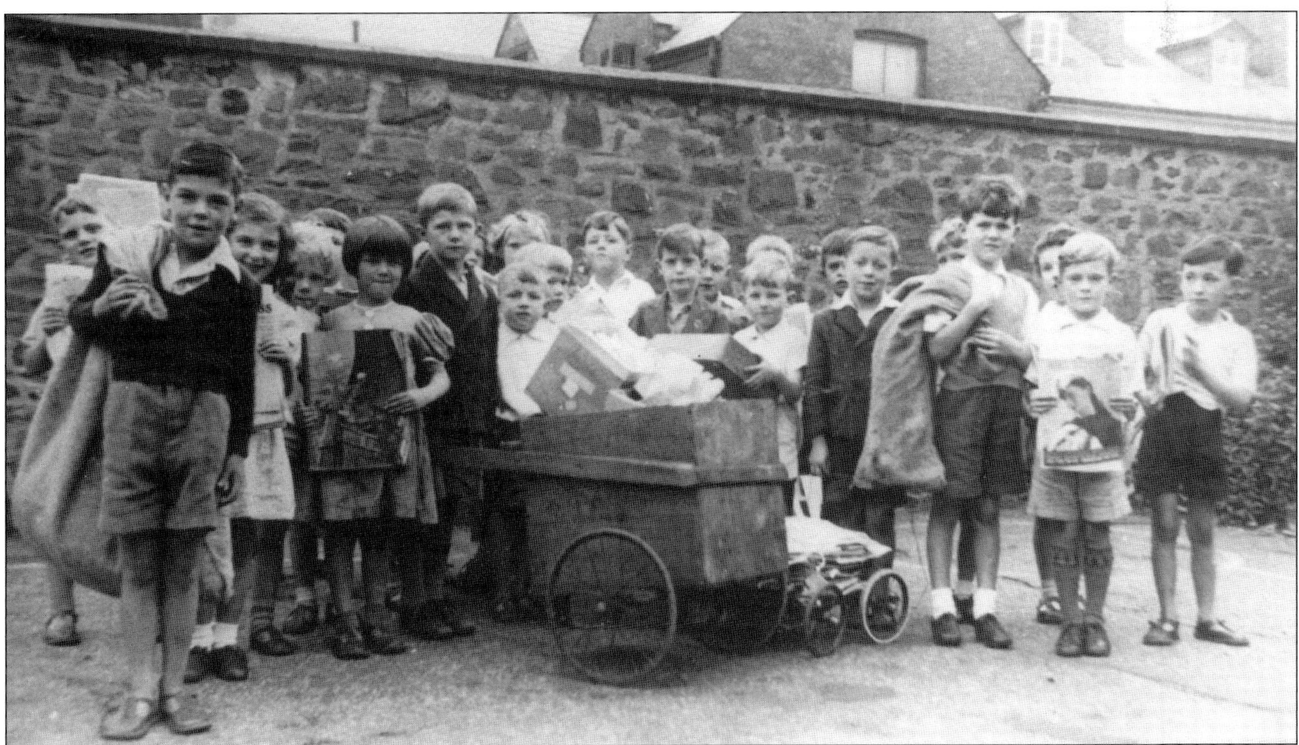

The young do their bit in one of the salvage drives organised by the WVS. MUSEUM COLLECTION

in the Pannier Market, which provided soup for 2d., meat and two veg for 8d., sweets for 2d. and tea for 1d., with children under ten years old charged at half price. In 1943 it provided a daily average of 150 lunches and consistently made a small profit. Probably the only time that building has done so!

The war was ever-present. There were continuous exhortations to save, periodically dressed up as campaign weeks. There was a Weapons Drive Week in 1941 when groups were allotted monetary targets equivalent to bits of kit or hardware. For example, Cove WI's target was four bombs and the residents of Council Gardens a tommy gun. In May 1942 there was Warship Week when the town raised £179,000 in National Savings, which enabled HMS *Bluebell*, a flower-class corvette, to be 'purchased' for the war effort. She was the town's adopted ship until she was sunk in February 1945. In the autumn there was a Tank Drive, while in May 1943 it was Wings for Victory, which exhorted Savings for Spitfires with a full week of events beginning with a mass meeting at the Electric Theatre addressed by a Squadron Leader MP. On the Thursday of the same week there was a huge parade of the RAF Regiment, the WAAF, ATC, Red Cross, WVS, Civil Defence, Blundell's JTC, Army Cadet Corps, Home Guard, Girls' Training Corps, Naval Cadets, National Fire Service, Women's Land Army, the Scouts and others. A total of £266,000 was raised. In May 1944 it was Salute the Soldier Week, when £189,000 was raised.

These may have been the big events, but the pressure was unrelenting. There were many overlapping drives for salvage. The Lowman Tank and the antique ordnance in the People's Park had already gone. All railings were removed by the end of 1942. In May 1942 the WVS visited every house to encourage the public to eliminate waste. In July there was a Waste Paper Drive, in August Scrap Metal Week. Earlier in the year shopkeepers had been forbidden to wrap anything but exposed food.

The Exeter Blitz caused a redoubling of Air Raid Protection efforts. Local authorities gained the powers to compel 12 hours of fire-watching a week, the clearance of lofts was ordered and every household had to make arrangements to admit firefighters at all times.

Morale was not neglected. From 1941 onwards a series of lecturers came to explain war aims, peace aims, how super Russia was and when the Second Front would open. In 1942 and 1943 the Council

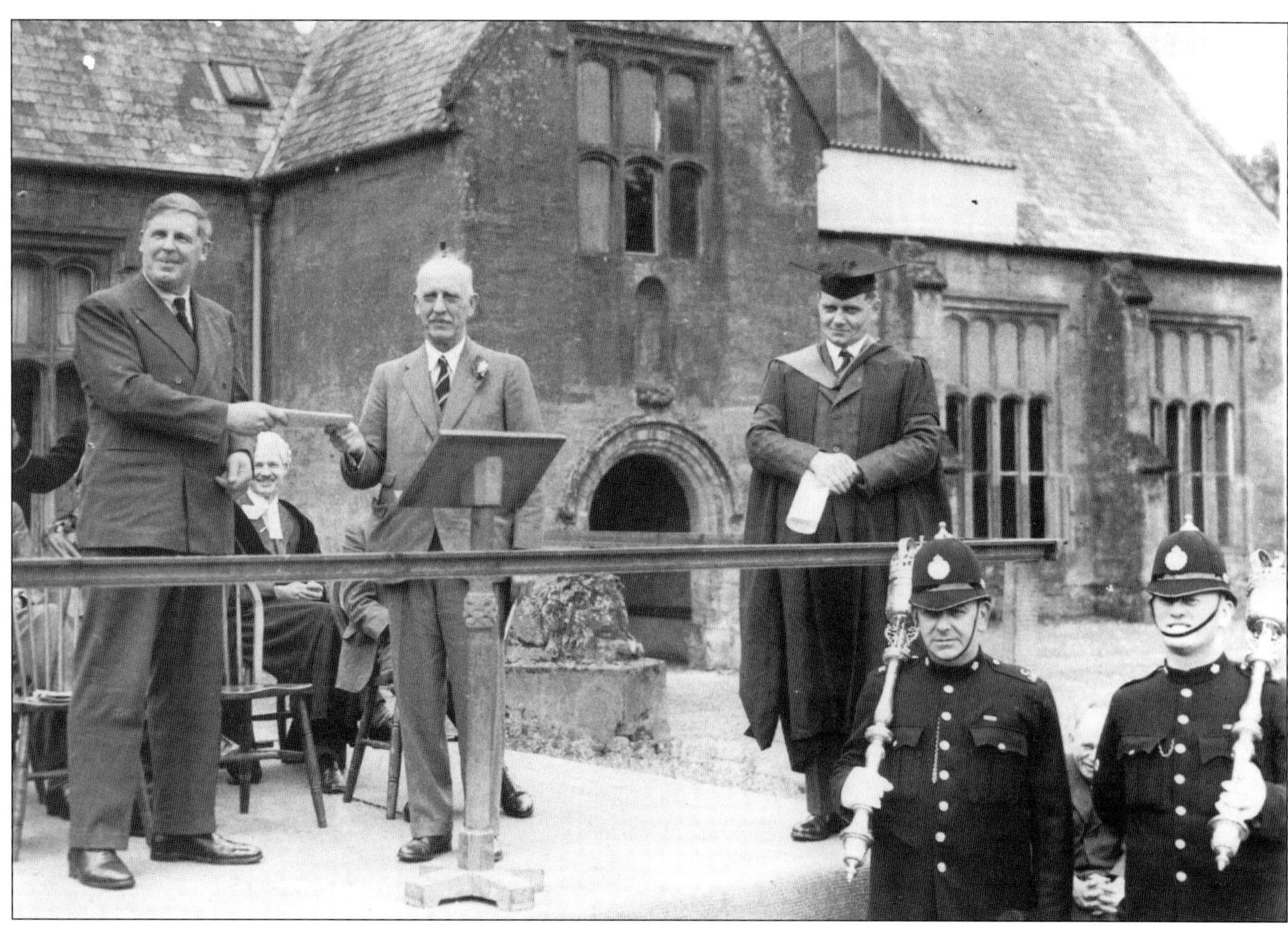

Another type of war damage. Part of Old Blundell's was destroyed by a fire started by billeted soldiers. This is Old Boys' Day, June 1946. The Old Boys had raised money to buy Old Blundell's and are handing it over to Sir Jack Amory, chairman of governors. Town Clerk Pugsley and mace bearers Squire and Chidgey are also present.

MUSEUM COLLECTION

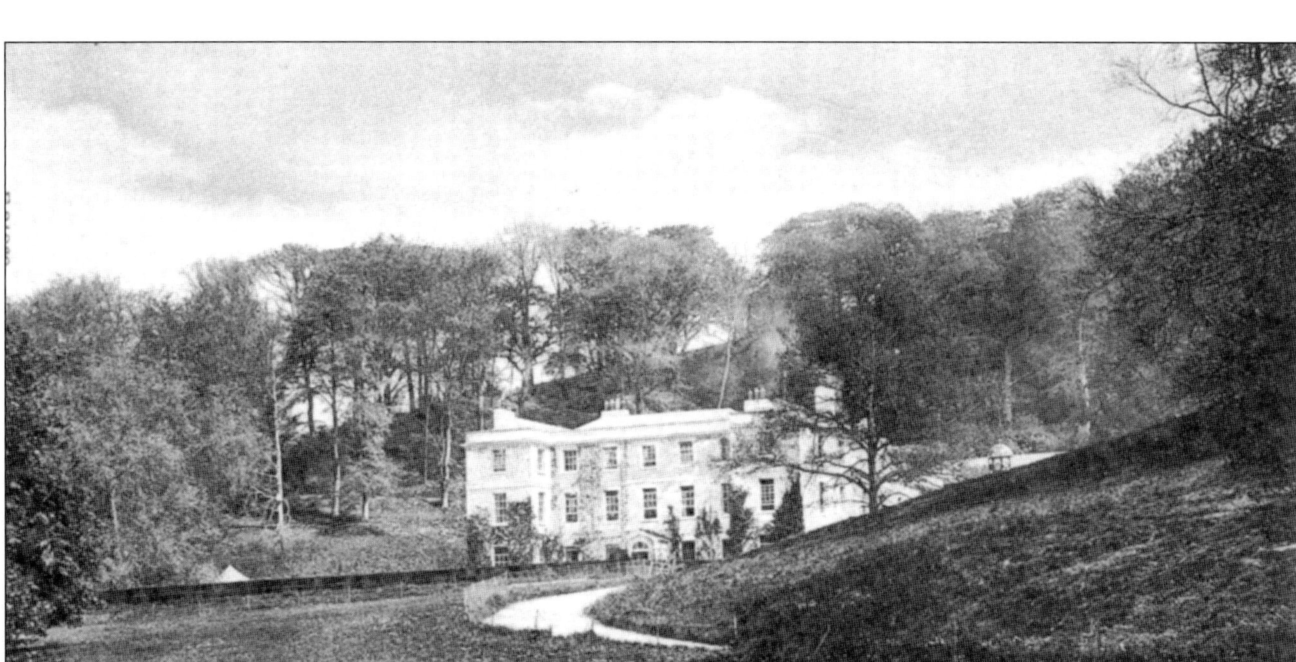

Colliepriest House, the headquarters of the American Army in Tiverton, 1943–44. The house was built by the Blundell family, 'modernised' in the eighteenth century and later lived in by the Palk Carews. By 1970 it was derelict, then developed into flats. MUSEUM COLLECTION

organised Holidays at Home Week in early August as travelling away for a break was at this time impossible. The weeks started with a united service in the People's Park. Usually the week was enlivened by performances by our own Salvation Army Band and a Service Band. The Services would put on unarmed combat displays. There were cricket matches, sports and swimming galas, dances and children's carnivals.

The 'good' Tivertonian would be in the Home Guard or Civil Defence, a 12-hour a week fire-watcher. He would have an allotment and be growing as much food as possible, attending lectures, raising funds for Russia in whist drives and dances, coping with evacuees at home, collecting salvage and working flat out at his job. His wife would also be undertaking most of these tasks as well as juggling rations to create effective meals, plus knitting and mending to eke out the clothing ration, helping the WVS in their multitude of tasks or as a member of another organisation. The war was one of the few times when the Blundell's staff did their bit in the community; two housemasters helped with the Army Cadet Corps founded in June 1942 and one, W.W. French, was chairman of the Youth Service Committee.

Eventually, towards the end of 1942, the war turned towards victory. In September an article appeared in the *Tiverton Gazette* advertising a talk on 'how to be nice to Americans', but it was not until January 1944 that the newspaper mentioned their actual presence, though given the nature of the coverage they must have been here earlier. In fact in early 1943 a small group of Americans ran a Naval Store from the factory and were well liked. However, the arrival of a Texan Infantry Division in the run up to D-Day was a different story and it is obvious that their presence was not without problems of the 'Over-paid, Over-sexed and Over here' variety. Speaking in an agitated Borough Council meeting in January 1944 Alderman Thorne regretted seeing so many children drinking with US soldiers on Sundays. 'We must stop this rot'. It was suggested that opening the cinemas on Sunday evening might be the lesser evil. Another Councillor complained of GIs sitting on the doorsteps of Fore Street on Sunday afternoons. Even Sir John Amory opined that there was 'more immorality on Sunday afternoons and evenings than any other time of the week.' In February of the same year, Superintendent Beynon complained of sales of alcohol to the young and particularly of the over-consumption by young girls. 'Every girl is the daughter of someone and stopping this will make a difference to the homes of England.' The plan to allow each GI to take one companion into cinemas on Sundays was found to be illegal, as they had to be open to all or closed to all. In spite of the Sabbatarian scruples of two Councillors our cinemas were to be opened on Sunday evenings and attempts to close them after the GIs had gone failed. The ever-conscientious Miss Tibble started a register of Tivertonians prepared to invite GIs into their homes.

This was not the only unhappiness connected with

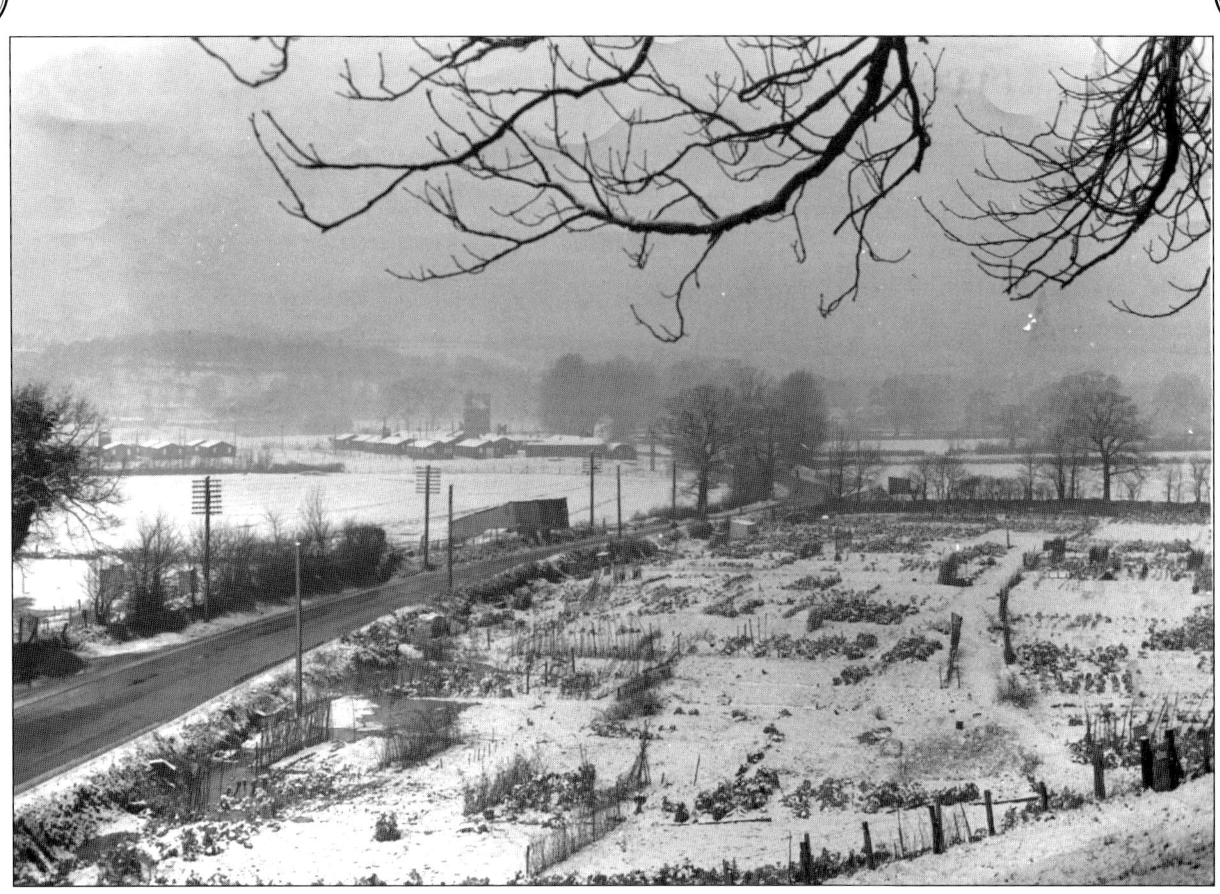

The camp for German prisoners of war on Bolham Road, probably photographed in the winter of 1944–45. Note the allotments on the site of the Exe Valley Leisure Centre, where Tivertonians 'Dug for Victory'.

MUSEUM COLLECTION

Victory tea party in Middlemead Road.

MUSEUM COLLECTION

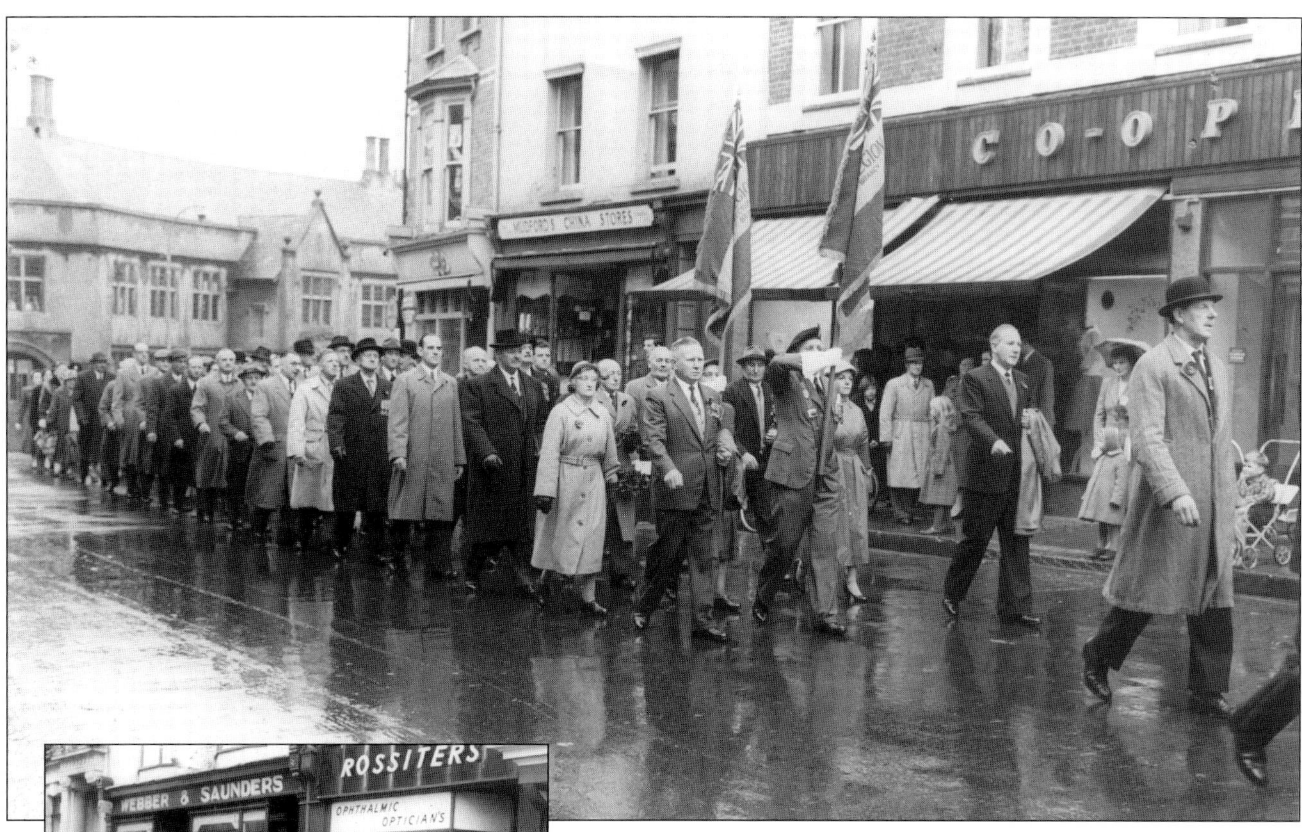

Above: *Not a victory parade, but the Remembrance Day parade of 1960. The veterans of 1939–45 include the Chancellor of the Exchequer, Derick Amory, veteran of Arnhem and Colditz, about six files back.* MUSEUM COLLECTION

Left: *Mayor Charlie Skinner leading the parade with Alderman Carpenter, followed by Aldermen Stagg and Lee and Councillors Bill Dunsford, Harold Shapland, Bill Trickey, Bill Authers and Victor Broomfield.* MUSEUM COLLECTION

the Tiverton sojourn of the US 4th Division. In March 1944 the *Tiverton Gazette* reported the murder of an American Sergeant by a drunken GI. However, a more revealing incident was reported to the author by two prominent Tivertonians, who in 1944 were going to school by way of a bridge that then crossed the Exe from Colliepriest to the southern end of Westexe, but found their route barred by police investigating the body of a black GI allegedly murdered by white GIs for the crime of going out with Tiverton girls.

After the bulk of the American Forces had left for France a plaque was presented to the Borough by US Major Hart. In his speech he made the semi-apologetic statement that 'our adjustment [to Tiverton life] was not completely successful', which in army-speak seems to have been a confession of disaster. No doubt there had been some pleasant episodes and a number of friendships made.

It was a great disappointment that the war was not over by the end of 1944. The efforts of Total War ground on with only slight relief. England's south-east and London were suffering V1 and V2 attacks and the WVS organised yet another collection, this time of furniture and kitchen utensils for the new ranks of the bombed out, which was rushed up to London by lorry.

A small sign of better things to come was the standing down of the Home Guard in a final parade on 3 December at Blundell's. In February 1945 Ron Davey gathered together the Tiverton Youth Orchestra and in March the Council completed the purchase of 12 acres of Cottey Farm for housing. There was also a big educational conference at the Town Hall to discuss the implementation of the Butler Act. In the Drill Hall was held a Youth Hobbies' Exhibition, with 700 exhibits arranged in nine categories: Art, Craft, Woodwork, Embroidery, Cooking, Collections, Photography, Literary and Miscellaneous.

In May the awful war in Europe came to an end, but Japan was not defeated until August. The lights came on, there were bonfires and fireworks. For three weeks the *Tiverton Gazette* carried photos of street parties, all of which had been spontaneously organised by residents. The evacuees silently went homeward and the British Restaurant closed. Tiverton had risen to the challenge, done its duty and endured.

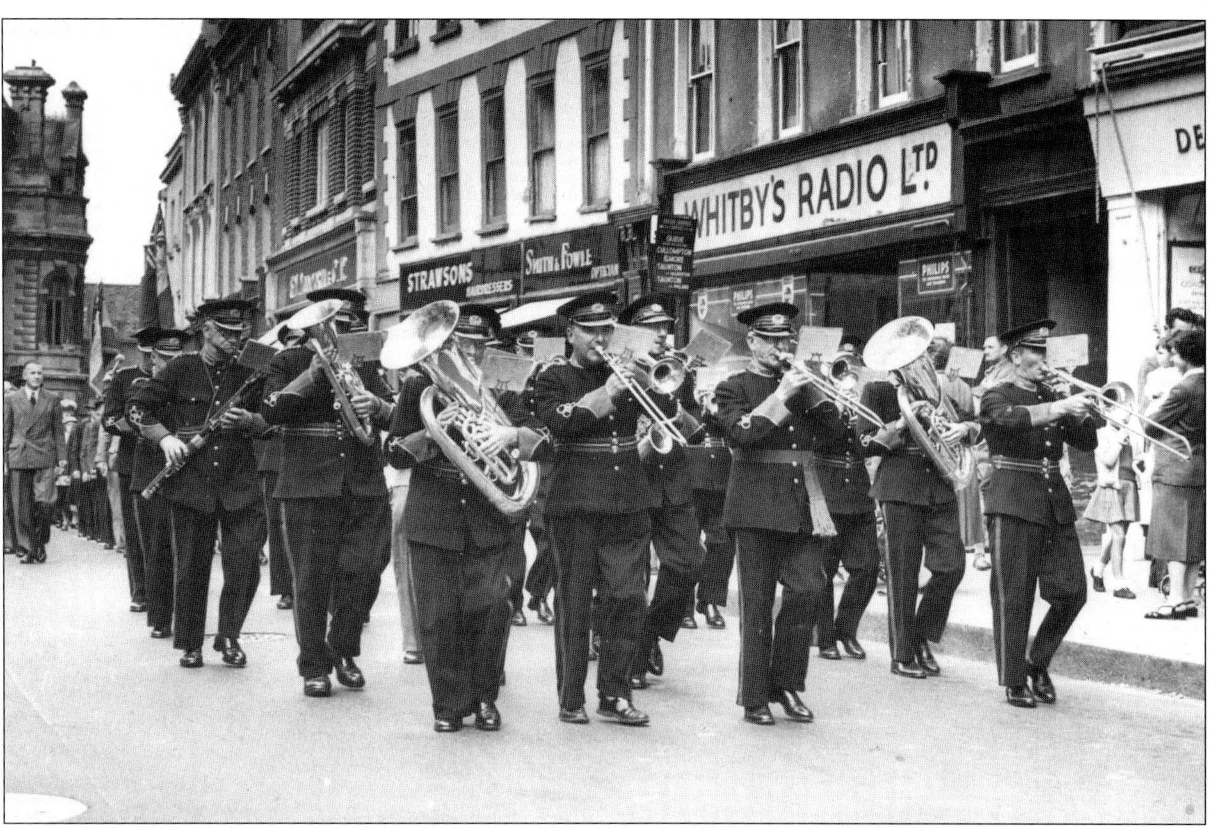

Tiverton Town Band in what may have been a victory parade. MUSEUM COLLECTION

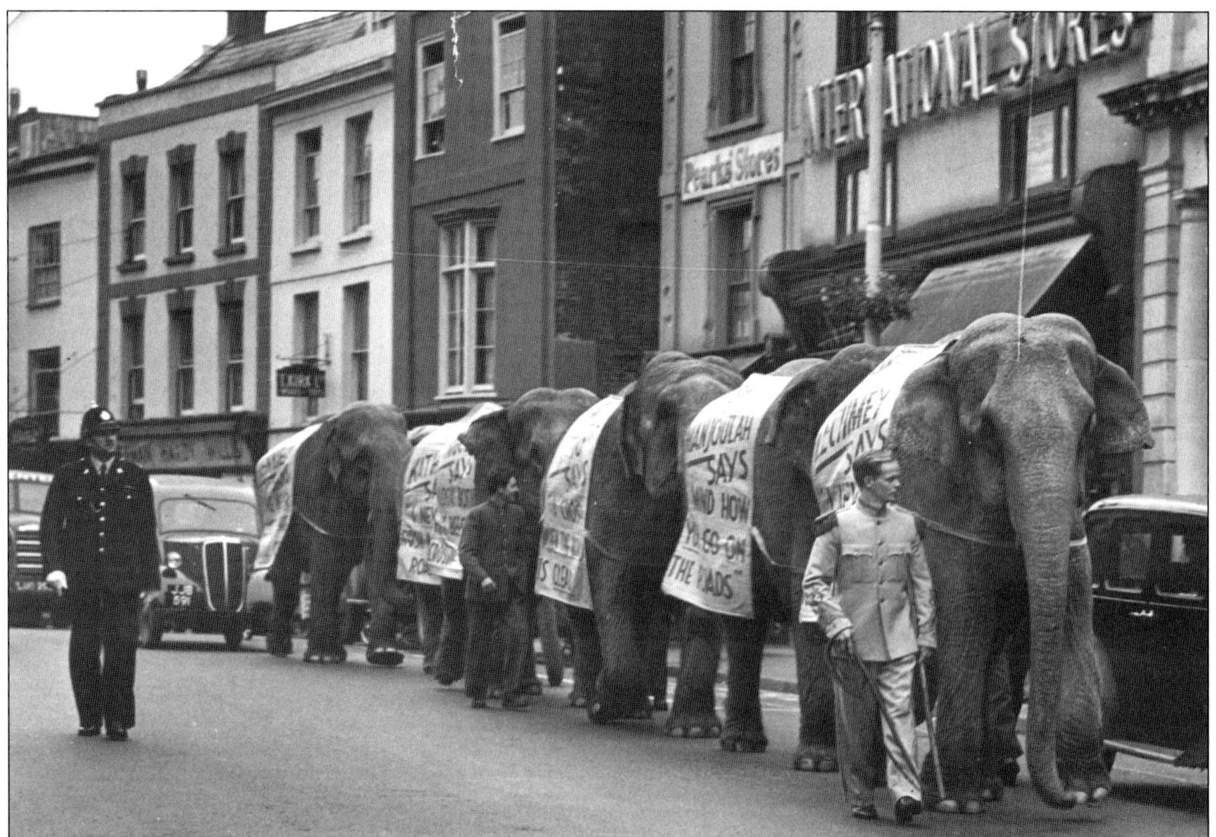

Another procession accompanied by PC Stuckey. MUSEUM COLLECTION

Chapter 9

The Last Years of the Borough

'What's not destroy'd by Time's devouring hand?
Where's Troy, and where's the Maypole in the Strand.'
Rev'd James Bramston 1694-1744

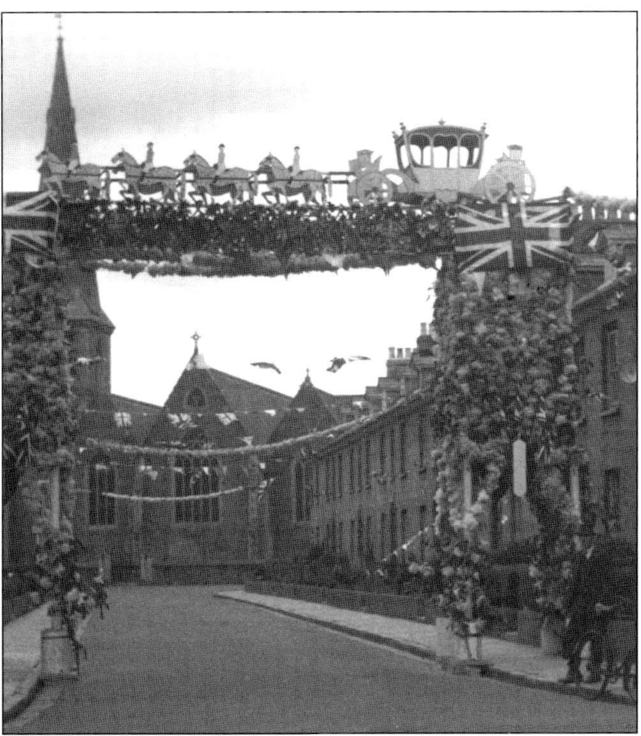

The Church Street arch reappeared for the coronation of 1953. Is the arch in storage somewhere for re-use? MUSEUM COLLECTION

The transition from war to peace was not immediate. The Bolham Road prisoner-of-war camp lost its last prisoner at the very end of 1948 and it is often forgotten that the worst years of food rationing were 1947 and 1948. Rationing was only ended in the mid-1950s. Even bread was rationed in 1946 and National Service continued until the mid-1950s. However, a new sense of optimism developed after the coronation of Queen Elizabeth II in 1953.

The big achievement of the Borough in these post-war years was its vigorous approach to the housing problem. The Council had recognised a serious housing problem in the 1930s and this had been exacerbated by the hiatus in building during the war. An emergency solution was the erection of 'prefabs', and the granting of permission to the caravan park to house such structures at Underhill, below the castle. 'Proper' houses soon followed in Westexe South, Cotteylands, the Walronds and Cowleymoor, where Queensway's name commemorated the 1953 coronation. The 500th council-house was completed in 1951 and the 1,000th in 1956, by which time another 540 were planned for Wilcombe. In the 1960s and 1970s further council-housing was built in Wilcombe and Tidcombe, so that at the time of the 1971 census there were 2,005 council-houses as well as 1,225 houses rented from private landlords, mostly from the factory. Only 1,995 houses were in owner occupation and out of a population of 15,565 just over 10,000 Tivertonians lived in the rented sector.

The new estates were not particularly well planned and were uniform to the point of being drab, with not a pub, church or a park in sight. Nor were the houses well maintained. A canvasser in 1974 found almost every house on Queensway seriously defective, the window frames so rotten that a finger could be pushed right through. It could also be argued that a combination of ample council-housing and factory houses at low rents encouraged a dependency culture. However one should not forget the genuine idealism that had led to this expansion of the town's housing stock, and one should also not forget how the existing houses were improved. The 1951 census reveals that 26 percent of houses had no internal lavatory and 50 percent had no plumbed-in bath, so that the Borough Bath House in St Andrew Street was still much needed. By 2001 the census was more interested in the number of houses without central-heating and the number of lone parents.

Estates of private houses were built on Pinnex Moor in the early 1960s and uphill of the canal, between St Aubyn's Villas and Tidcombe Lane. The Glebelands estate was also begun in the early 1960s. Sadly the fashion of those years favoured the bungalow so that the town's footprint expanded enormously. In 1931 the census gave Tiverton's population as 9,610, in 1951 it was 10,869 (about the same as in 1851) and by 1971 it had risen to 15,565. In 1991 it had grown to over 17,000 – a rate of growth only paralleled in its history by that between 1570 and 1620.

The new estates needed new schools. Cowleymoor Primary School opened in 1953, while Roman Catholic St John's in a big breeze block shed in Melbourne Street opened at the same time. St John's existed in this shed for 30 years and the niff of many woolly bodies on a wet February afternoon will be long remembered. Elmore School, which had existed grimly in Chapel Street, was moved to new buildings beside Cowleymoor School in 1968. Wilcombe School was opened in 1963, Sunningmead followed in 1975 and Tidcombe School in 1979. Heathcoat's School re-opened in new premises in 1960. To meet the

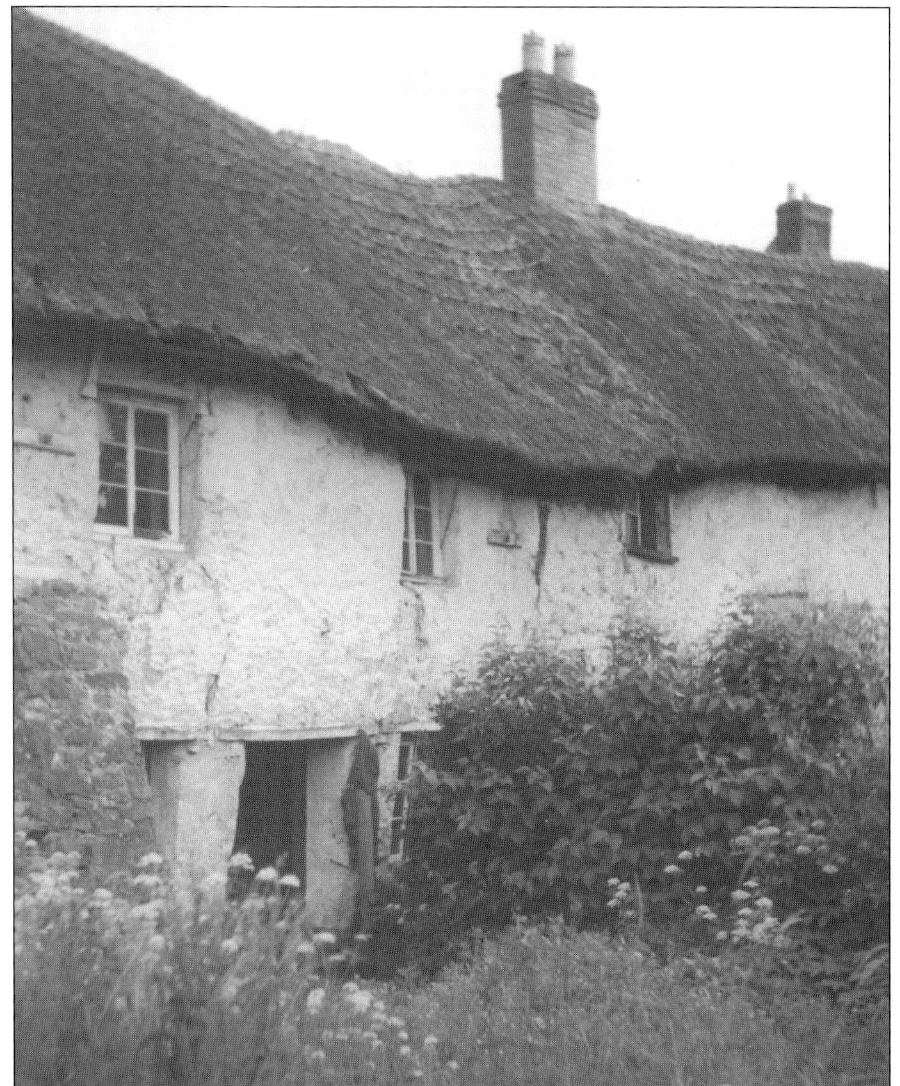

Left and below: *The sort of housing that still existed in parts of Tiverton until the late 1960s. Little Silver at the bottom of St Andrew Street in 1907* (below) *and 1953* (left), *slums in a semi-rural style.*
MUSEUM COLLECTION

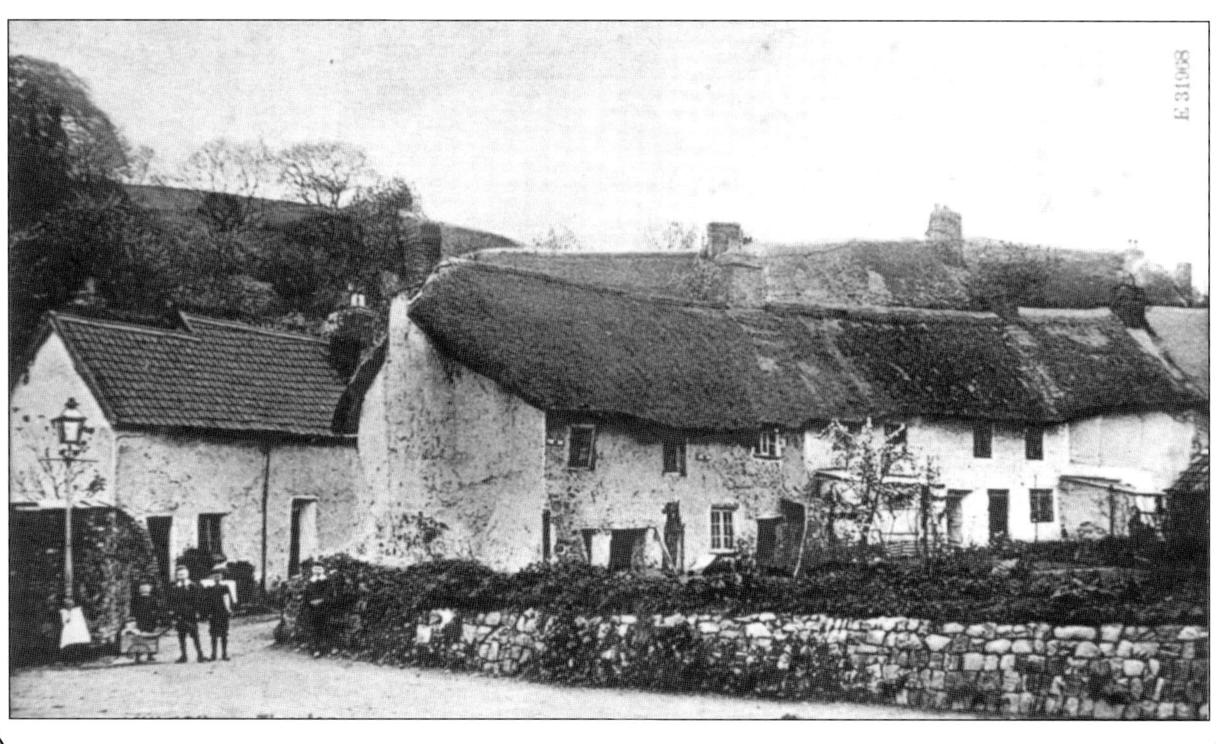

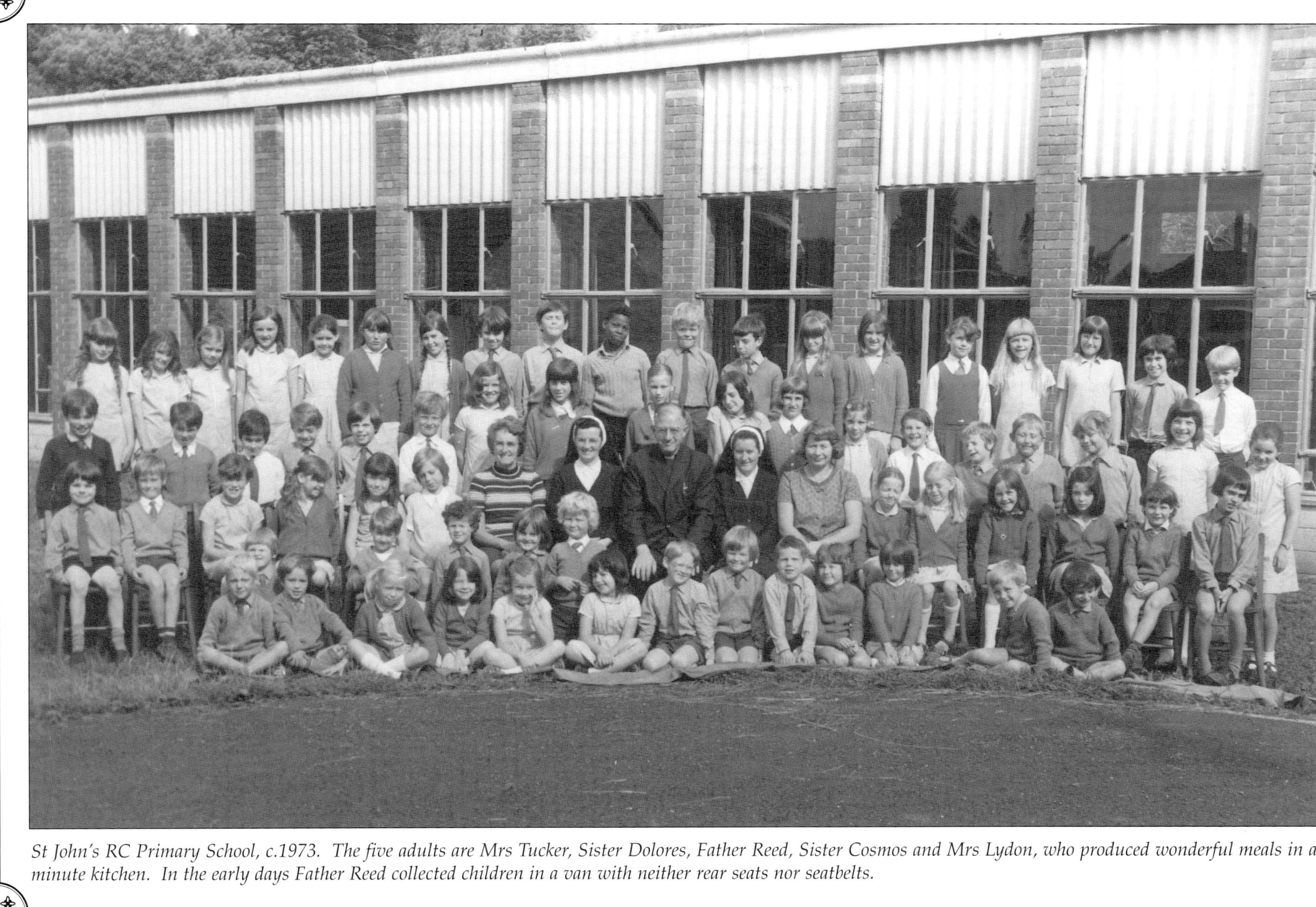

St John's RC Primary School, c.1973. The five adults are Mrs Tucker, Sister Dolores, Father Reed, Sister Cosmos and Mrs Lydon, who produced wonderful meals in a minute kitchen. In the early days Father Reed collected children in a van with neither rear seats nor seatbelts.

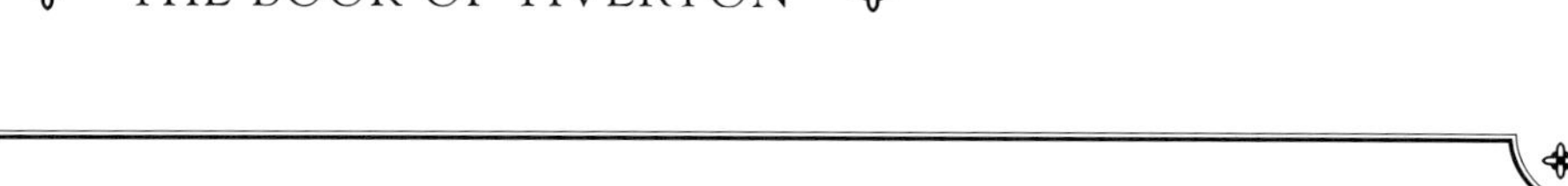

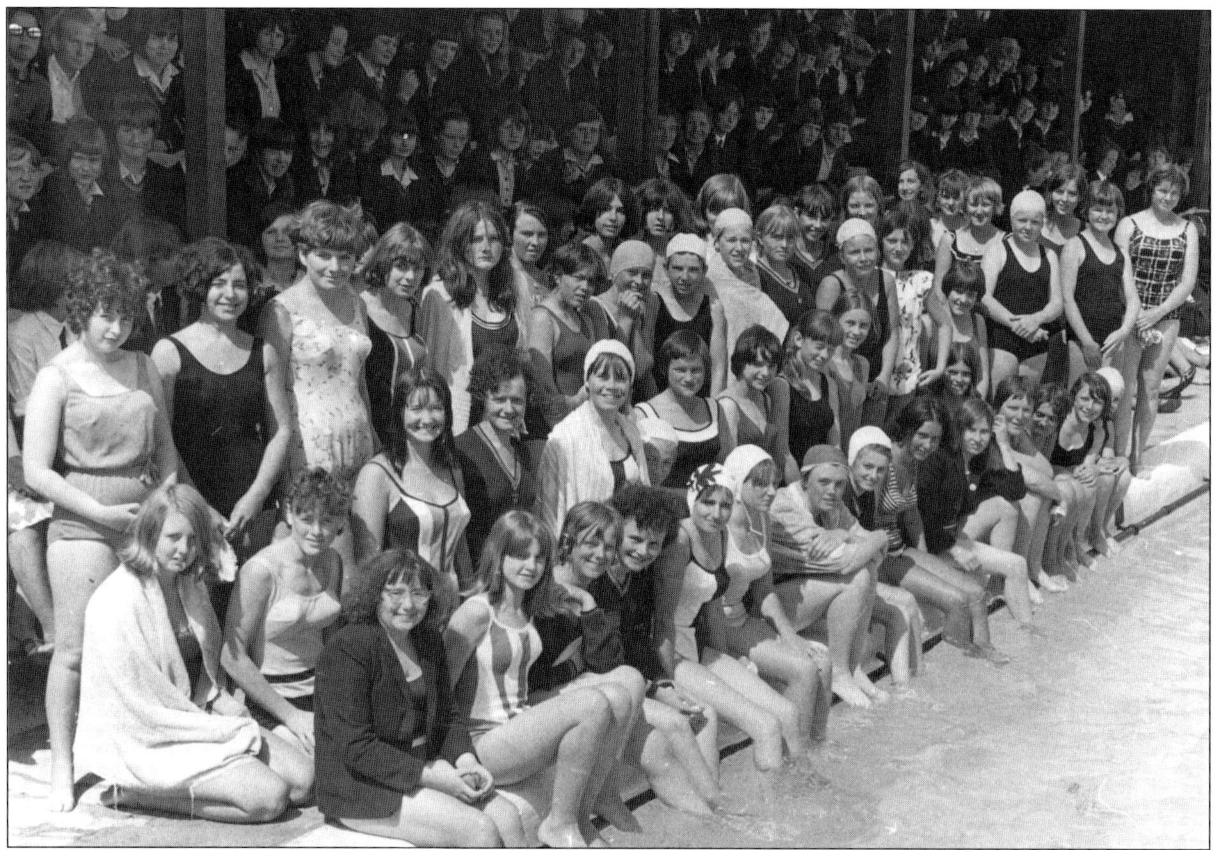

Tiverton Girls' Grammar School Swimming Sports at the Leat Street Baths, mid-1960s. MUSEUM COLLECTION

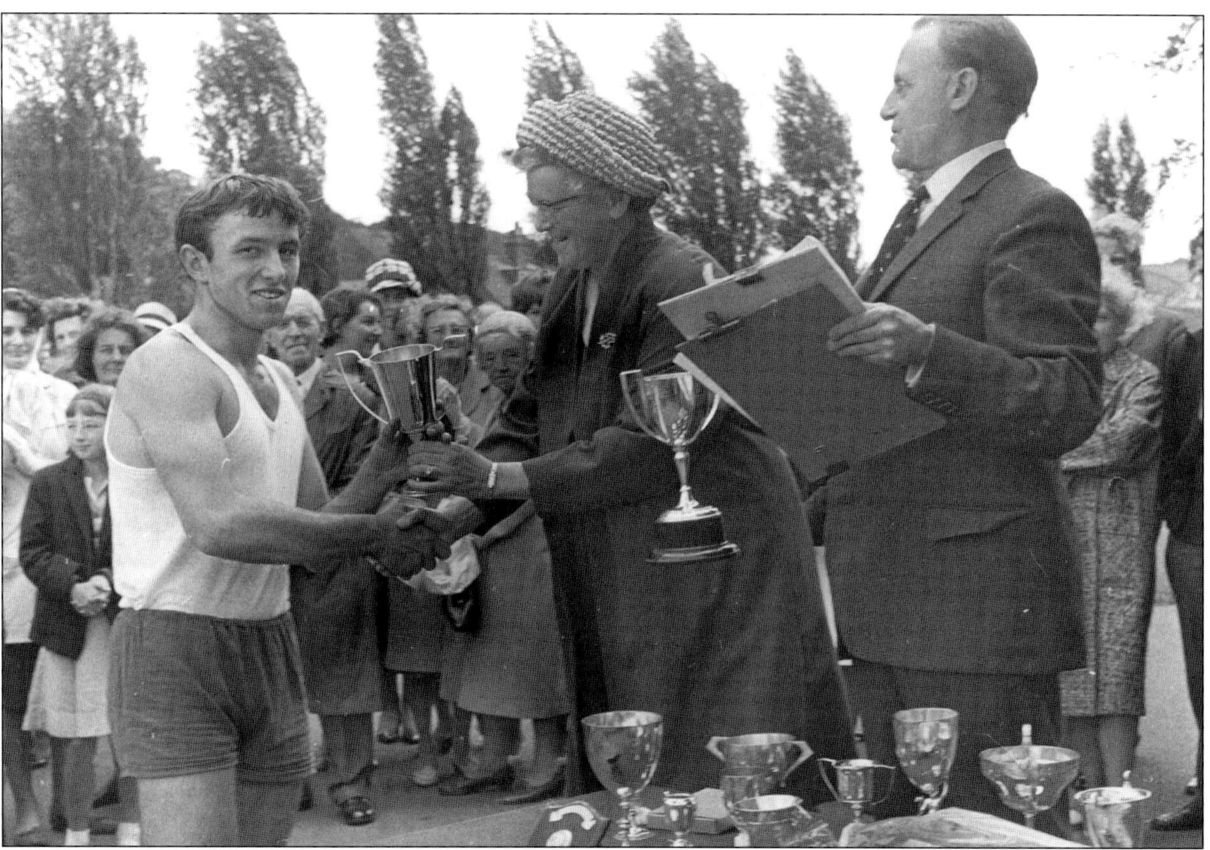

Tiverton Grammar schoolboy, Pope, collects a prize from Mrs Pugsley. Headmaster Norman Bradshaw is also pictured. There must be a training camp for Headmasters where they can learn the right body language. MUSEUM COLLECTION

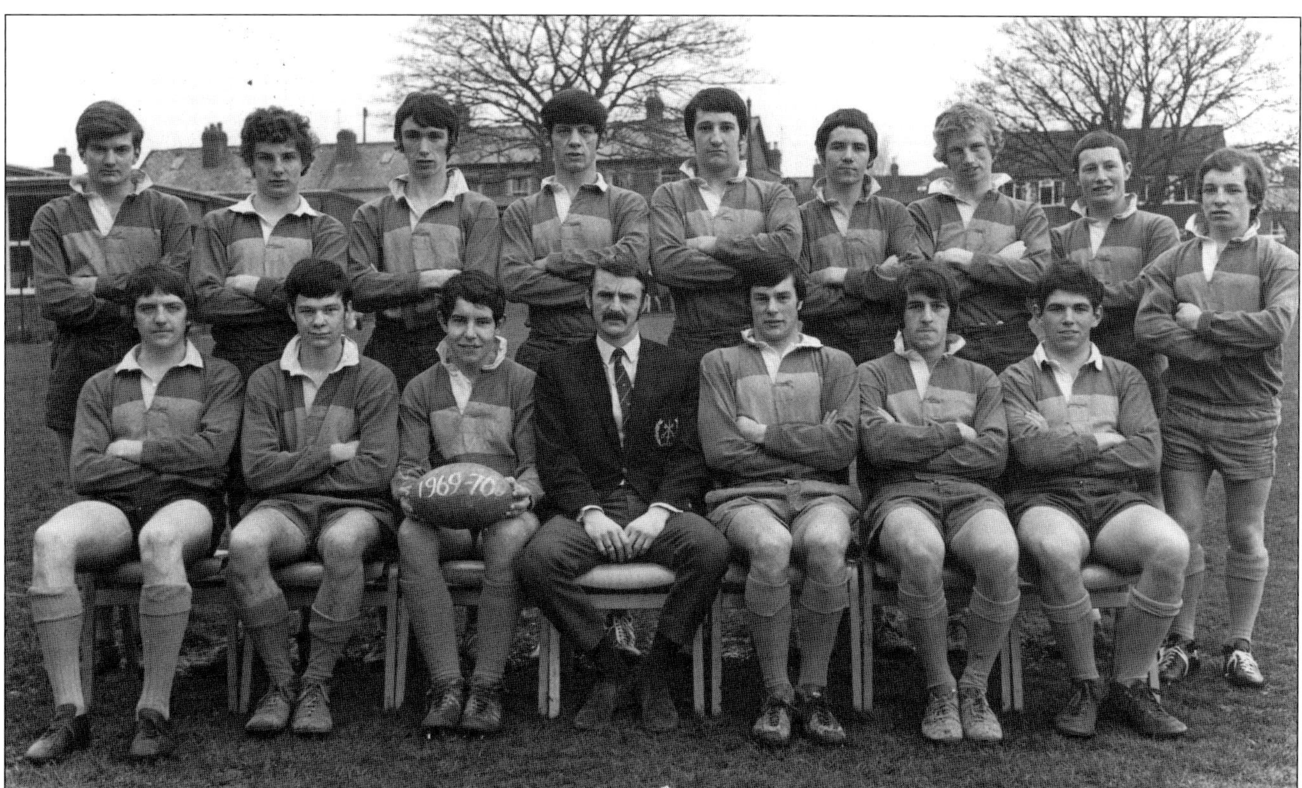

Tiverton Grammar School rugby team, 1969–70, with coach Terry Townshend. Left to right, back row: *Saunders, Coombe, Burrows, Milden, Buncher, Bryant, Lindsay, Batting, Hill.* Seated: *Cole, Hyde, Prout, Terry Townshend, Lydon, Hancock, Williams.* MUSEUM COLLECTION

demands of secondary education, the old Middle Schools became Tiverton Grammar School and a new Secondary Modern opened on the site of the prisoner-of-war camp on Bolham Road in 1960.

No sooner were these schools in existence than 'Comprehensivisation' reared its head. The new Secondary Modern at Bolham Road was earmarked as the new Comprehensive and the former Grammar School would become Castle School.

The most interesting and most successful part of this late 1960s reorganisation was the Middle Schools. The heads of the three largest existing Primary Schools, Ewart Champion (Elmore), Wilcombe (Norman Annett) and Heathcoat's (Norman Holbrook) worked very closely together and steered the County Council into developing their schools as Middle 'Secondary' Schools for pupils aged nine to 13, thus attracting more generous facilities and specialist staff. Each of these four Middle Schools (the Grammar School buildings were taken over by Castle Street Middle School) was fed by a cluster of First Schools teaching children aged four to nine. Thus initially the new Comprehensive mirrored Blundell's as a school for pupils aged 13–18.

This was an excellent system; sadly the County Council took it apart. Perhaps its demise stemmed from the poor planning decisions of the 1950s and 1960s – all those bungalows. Whoever moved into them as first occupiers, second and third occupiers tended to be retired people, so that school rolls, which peaked about 1970, subsequently fell. Largely as an economy measure the Middle Schools reverted to primaries for children under 11, while the Comprehensive became a school for those aged 11–16 and all preparation for A Levels was shifted to the new Technical College. These changes were seen as a disaster by many parents. Local demand for day places at Blundell's suddenly doubled to over 100 and overnight the state system lost many of its keener pupils and more committed parents.

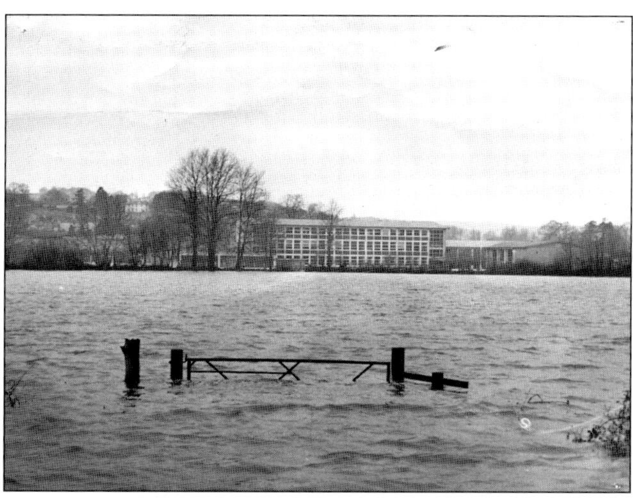

The new Secondary Modern at Bolham Road during the floods of 1960–61. This becoming the nucleus for the new Comprehensive sent out the wrong vibes and the day boy element at Blundell's School immediately doubled.

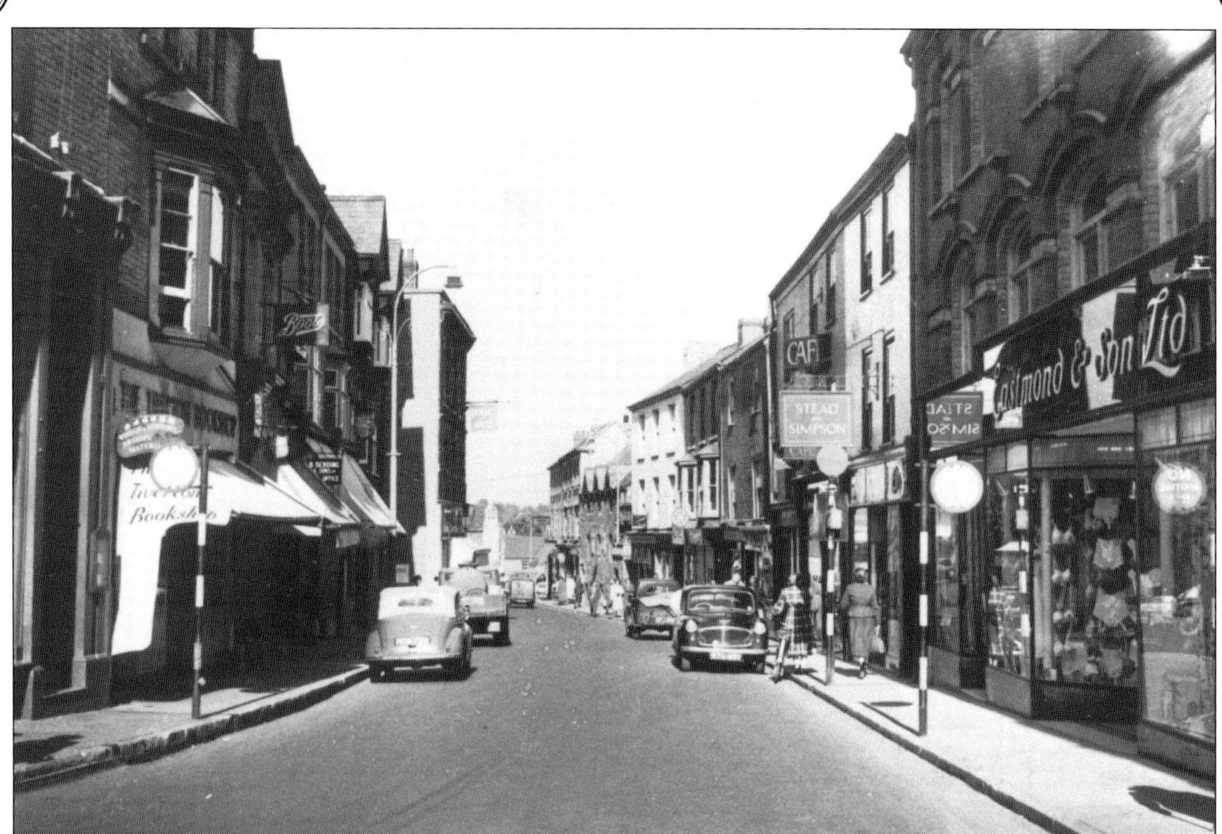

Two-way traffic in Gold Street. MUSEUM COLLECTION

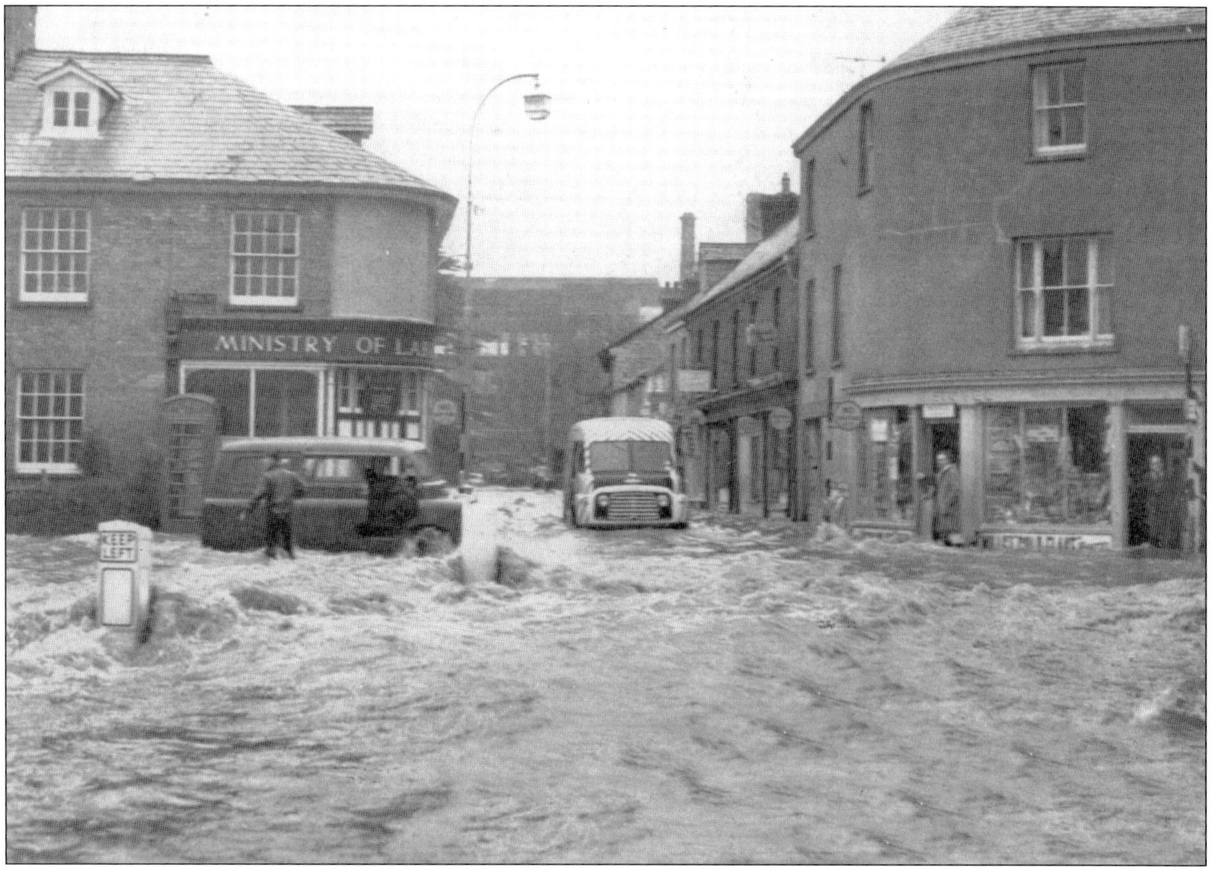

Westexe under water in the floods of the 1960s. MUSEUM COLLECTION

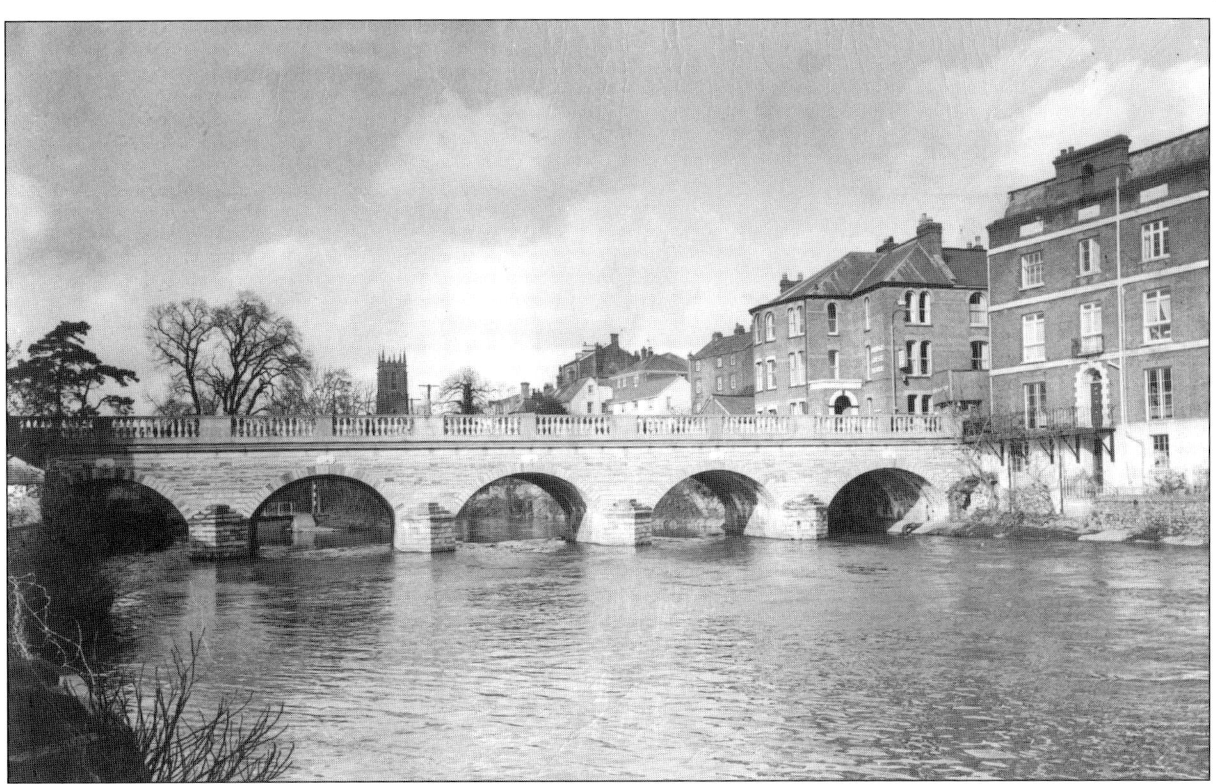

The 'old' Exe Bridge, a dignified structure. MUSEUM COLLECTION

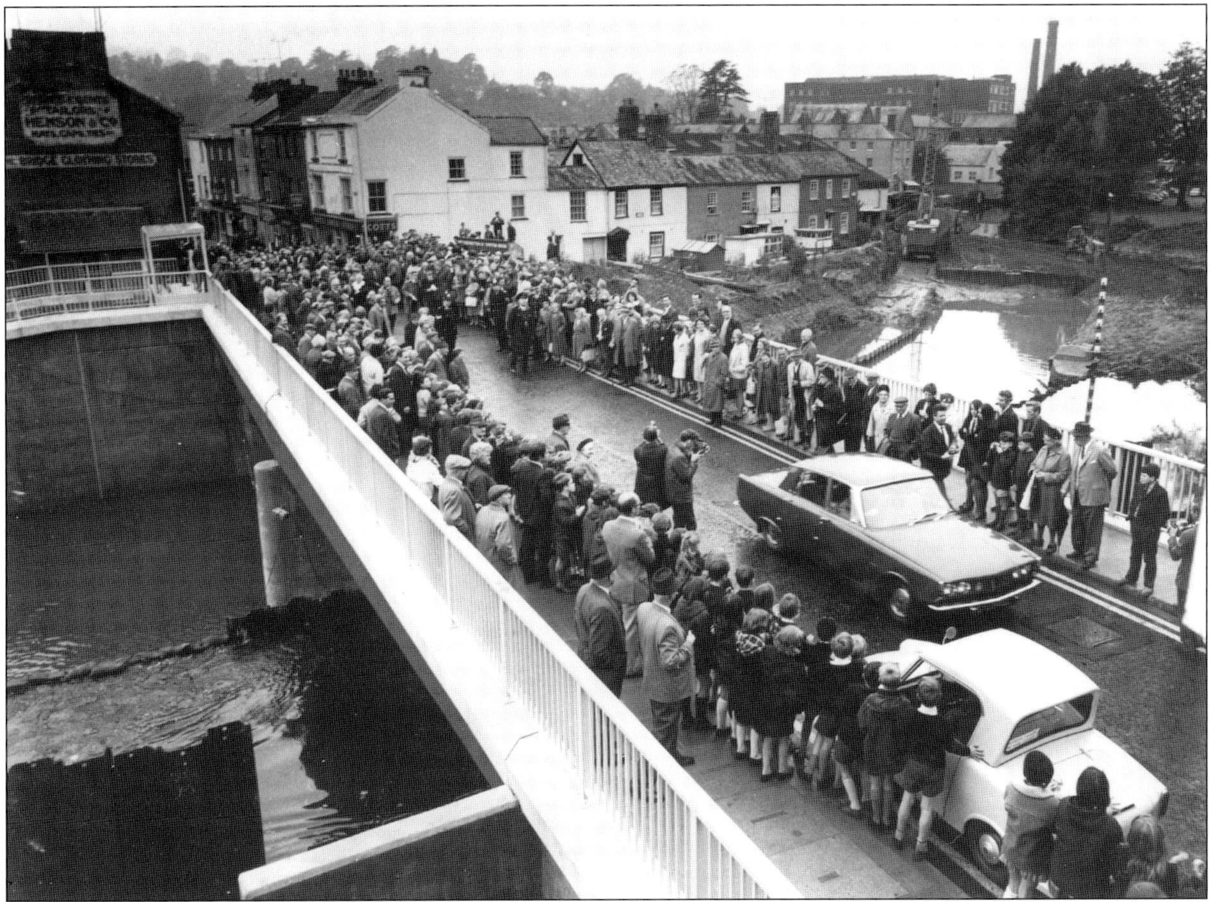

Opening the new bridge while the flood-protection scheme was still being built. MUSEUM COLLECTION

The new estates gave many families a decent, modern home, though some of the Cowleymoor and Wilcombe council-houses developed concrete cancer in the 1980s. However, the layout made for traffic problems. Cars from Pinnex Moor and Cowleymoor could only reach the outside world via Chapel Street and Bampton Street. Wilcombe and Tidcombe were slightly better off with egress over Newte's Hill to Cullompton and two other exits: Tidcombe Lane and Canal Hill. Traffic flows in the centre of town had been improved by the replacement of the Angel Hotel with the War Memorial Library and Hall set back so that the road width was doubled. Westexe South was widened by the demolition of all the houses on the western side in 1957. The south side of William Street was knocked down in 1960 to widen that road and a new entrance was made to the market from Newport Street – previously the only vehicular access was from Bampton Street and, even after the war, cattle would be driven up the street to auction. None of the council-houses had garages and by the 1970s estates were clogged with parked cars. There was still only one bridge for road traffic over the Exe and the Saturday holiday traffic could back up as far as Post Hill.

A second bridge was built in 1965 in Kennedy Way, but it took disastrous floods to push its approval through the system. Severe flooding of Westexe in October 1960 and again in December caused plans to be drawn up but they were then shelved. Further severe flooding in 1965 led to their being put into practice. The Exe Bridge would be rebuilt to allow a less impeded flow, flood walls would be erected, but first a new bridge at Kennedy Way would have to be built, for only on its completion could the old bridge be dismantled. The new Exe Bridge was completed in 1968 and the brutal, but effective, flood walls in 1970.

This brutalism, sadly, was not confined to the river bank. In the early 1960s the junction of Gold Street, Fore Street and Bampton Street was changed out of all recognition. To the south the old and dignified retail outlets of Starkey, Knight and Ford, the Co-op Stores and Timothy Whites, all based in grand old buildings comparable to any in the town, were replaced by the present Superdrug, Eastmonds and the former Tesco buildings. On the Gold Street/Bampton Street corner the dignified late Victorian pile that housed Thorne's the ironmongers was pulled down and replaced by concrete Rossiter's. Finally the Palmerston, formerly the Three Tuns, was also pulled down and replaced with what you see today, the only rival to the Half Moon as the town's ugliest building.

The misplaced energy that rebuilt this part of the town was the dark side of the prosperity of the 1950s and 1960s. For 25 years after the war Tiverton's economy flourished. Almost every wartime issue of the *Gazette* carried an advertisement asking for recruits to join Heathcoat's workforce. In 1946 the firm expanded at Carn Brea in Cornwall and built more weaving sheds in Westexe. In the 1950s there were plans for expansion into Australia and New Zealand. The engineering firm, Stenner's, which had opened in Tiverton in the later nineteenth century, had a very successful time making and selling machine saws around the world. Later Medland Sanders and Twose developed farm machinery and the Globe Elastic Thread Co set up an office and factory, where the new hospital is now located.

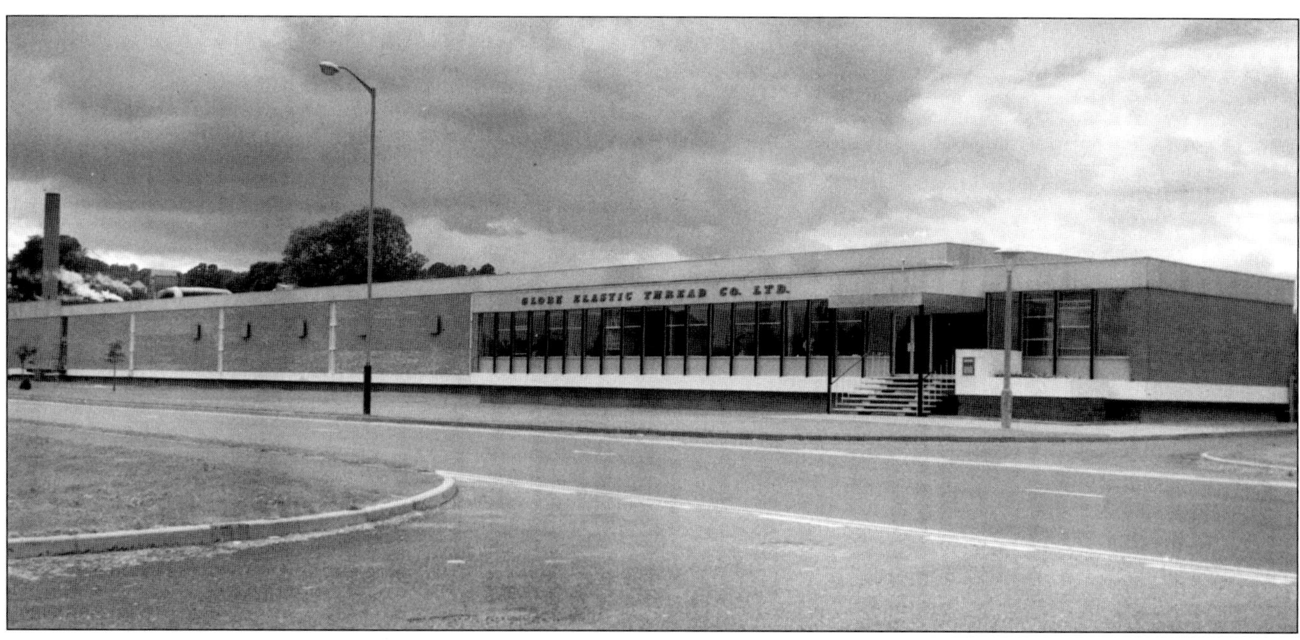

The other new bridge at Kennedy Way opened up more sites for industry, including that for Globe Elastic, where the new hospital now stands. Globe Elastic gave off quite a whiff, but it was only air-born acetic acid (vinegar). Some frantic Councillors later claimed the site was 'polluted' and unfit for a hospital, but the 'pollution' was simply a few old tyres and a diesel spill or two. MUSEUM COLLECTION

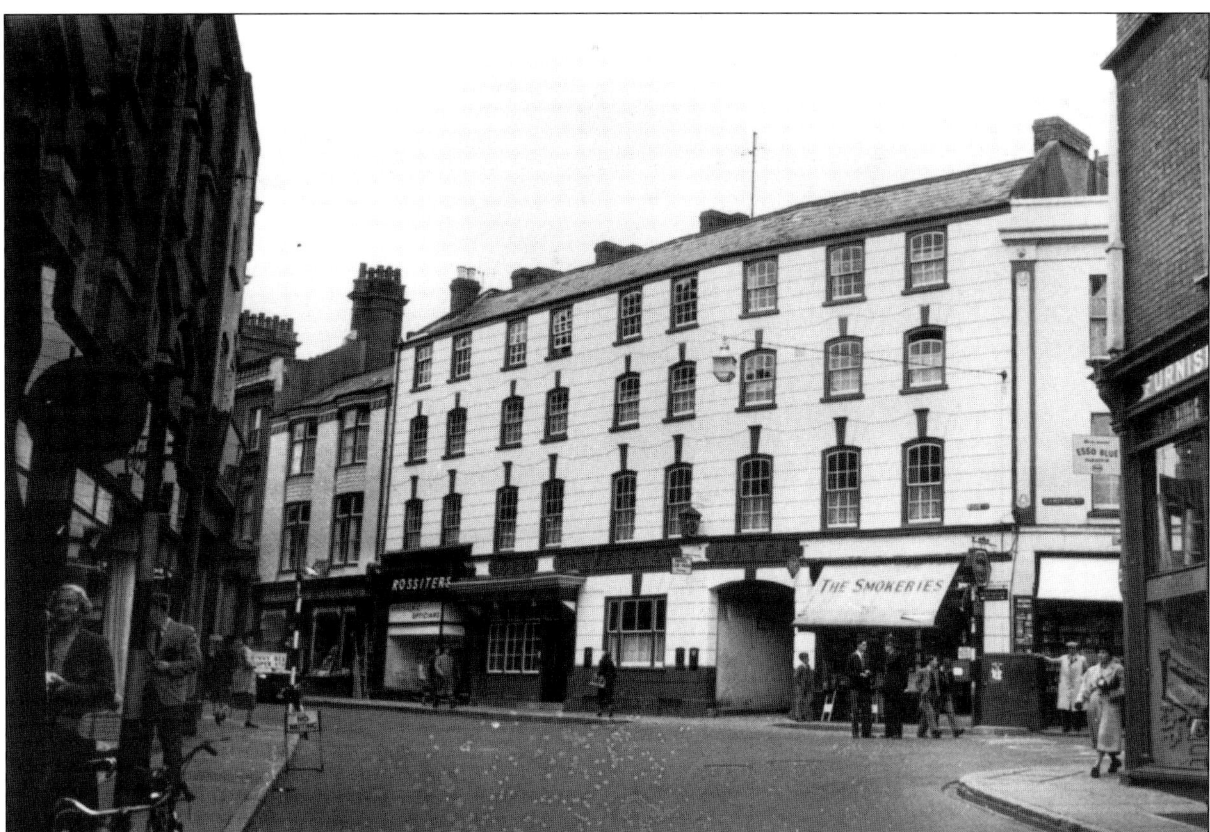

The Palmerston Hotel in the years before its destruction. MUSEUM COLLECTION

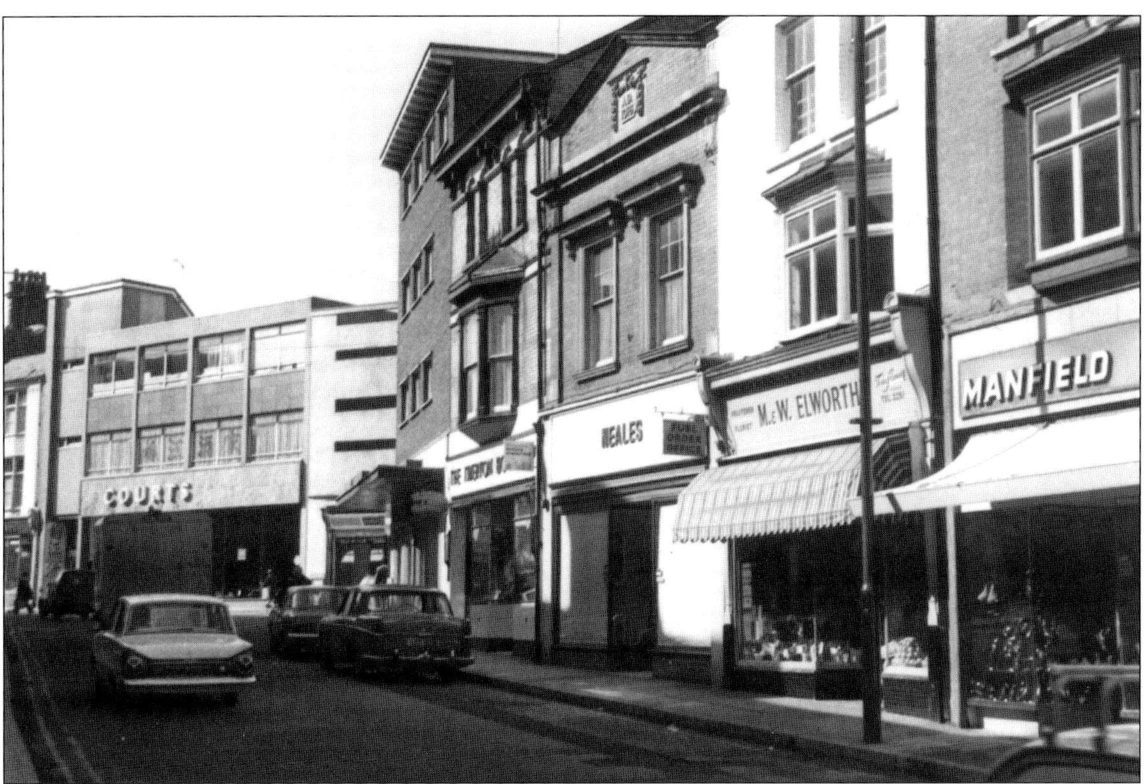

The Palmerston's replacement, now W.H. Smith's. MUSEUM COLLECTION

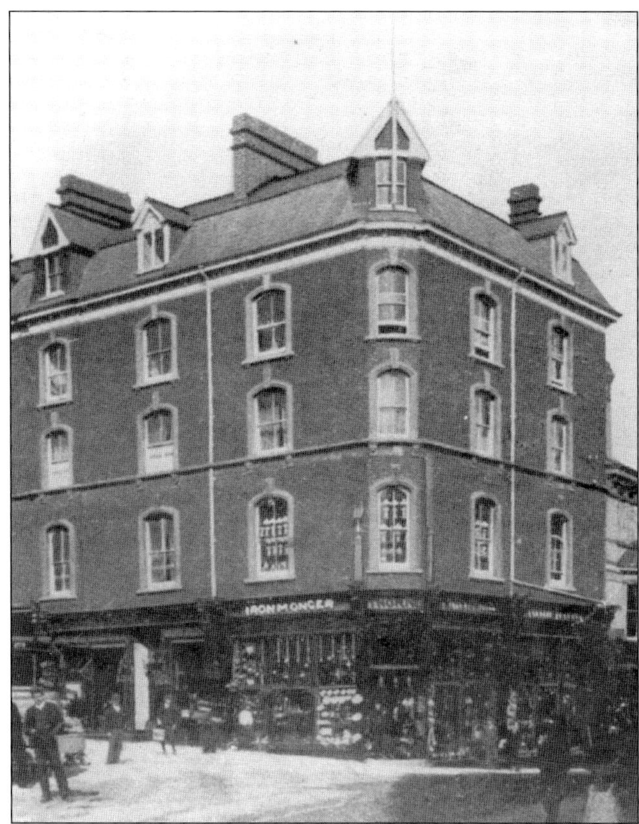

The dignified late-Victorian pile of Thorne's on the corner of Gold Street and Bampton Street. MUSEUM COLLECTION

Starkey, Knight and Ford were still brewing on their site between Greenway's almshouses and the end of Phoenix Lane. That another Heathcoat Amory was also MP for Tiverton and a Cabinet Minister seemed to confirm that the good times were here again.

But things were not really the same. The old bonds were dissolving, for good or ill. A small straw in the wind, Tiverton's version of the opening scene of the film *I'm all right, Jack!* was reported in the local press. When many Sunday school children were given the 'treat' of watching a lengthy religious film they greeted the raising of Lazarus with howls of derision. 'Little savages' opined the Vicar of St George's. The plates were shifting. By the 1960s there was universal concern among the clergy about 'the state of the young'. In response, the Youth Centre was opened on Bolham Road in 1964 and the Drop-In Centre more recently. The debate in Council about the granting of planning permission to the Drop-In Centre revealed how strong NIMBY oppostion to the scheme was and how wide the gulf has become between the young and the rest. The centre, led by Mark Day, does excellent work.

Between 1962 and 1974 the changes came thick and fast and Tiverton's self-contained world was shattered for good. The first of the town's employers to be taken over was Starkey, Knight and Ford which was acquired by Whitbread's in 1962. The old brewery was closed and the local base moved to Howden; no more beer was brewed in the town. In 1969 Heathcoat's was taken over by Coats Paton, under whom the labour force was run down and the enterprise was only saved by a management buy-out led by Reg Waddington. Globe Elastic did not survive the industrial crises of the 1970s. There are now only a few hundred working in the textile industry; in 1950 there were almost 2,000.

Matching these changes was the end of the railway. The extent of the town's rail links can be illustrated by a story of the winter of 1962–63. A factory employee who lived at Brushford found her usual rail route blocked by snow. So she went to work via Barnstaple, took the train to Exeter, then to Tiverton Junction. She then took a train as far as Halberton. As the last stretch to Tiverton was blocked, she

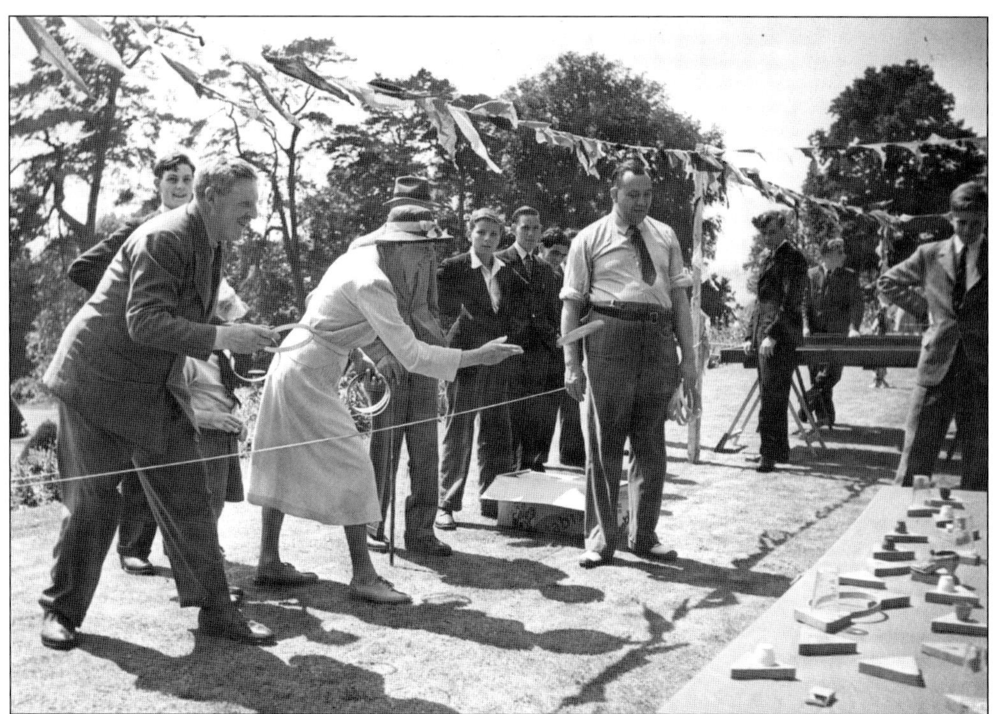

Sir John and Lady Amory at a Conservative fête at Knightshayes in 1950. The election of Derrick Amory as a Conservative MP in 1945 had marked the family's switch from Liberal to Conservative. MUSEUM COLLECTION

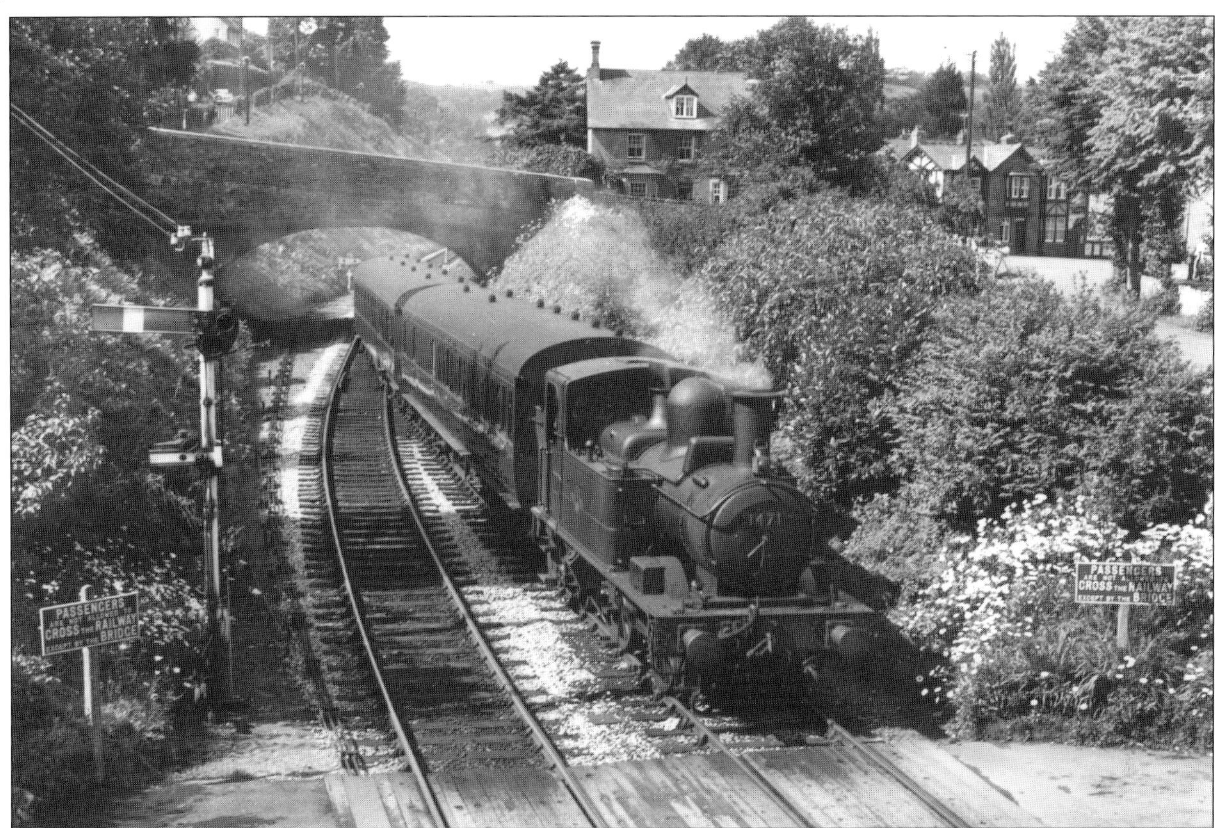

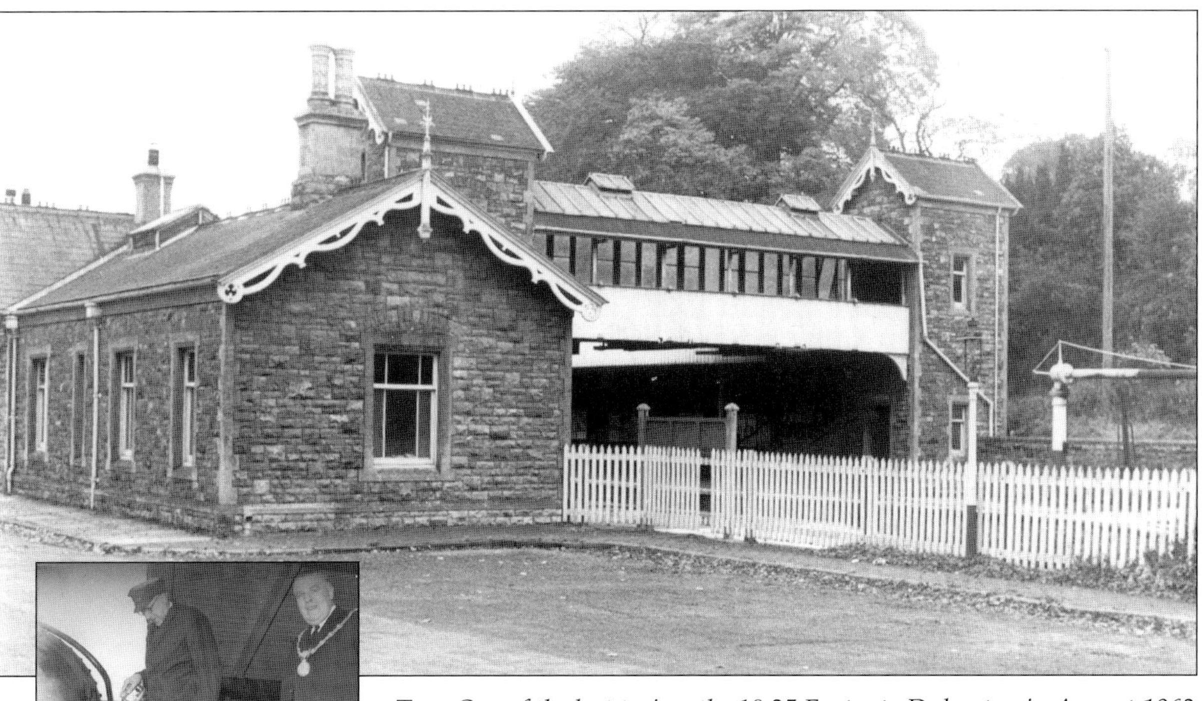

Top: *One of the last trains, the 10.25 Exeter to Dulverton in August 1962 going under the old Canal Road bridge and entering Tiverton Station.*
MUSEUM COLLECTION

Above: *Tiverton Station from the Old Blundell's end.* MUSEUM COLLECTION

Left: *Engine driver Lord Amory and Guard Mayor Authers prepare to steam from Tiverton Junction to Tiverton in 1964 for the 'last run'.*
MUSEUM COLLECTION

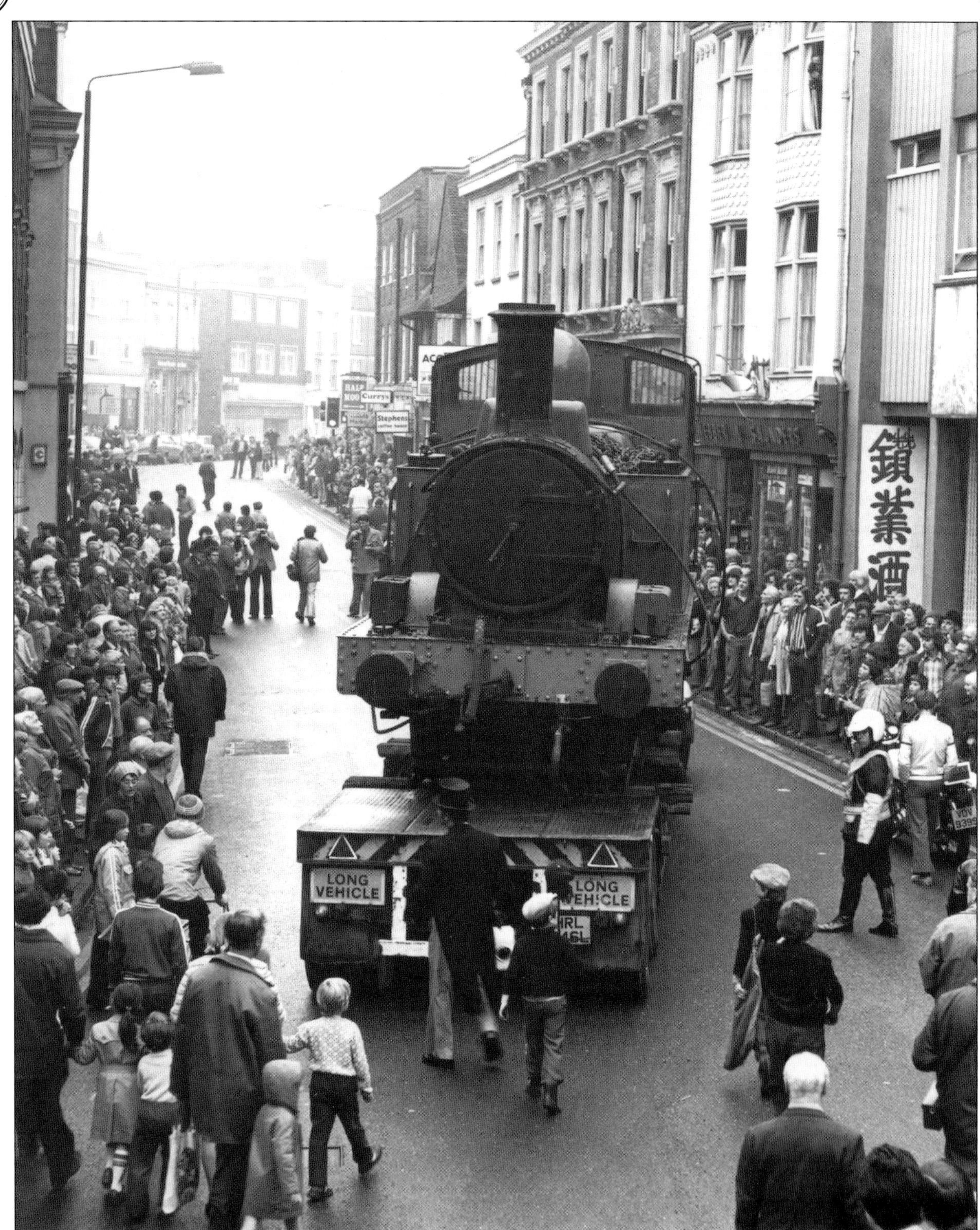

Above: *The Tivvy Bumper going backwards down Fore Street to its final home in the Museum.*
MUSEUM COLLECTION

Opposite page, top: *Taking the Tivvy Bumper from its temporary base outside Medland Sanders and Twose to its final home at Tiverton Museum.* MUSEUM COLLECTION

Opposite page, bottom: *The Bumper in the Museum.* MUSEUM COLLECTION

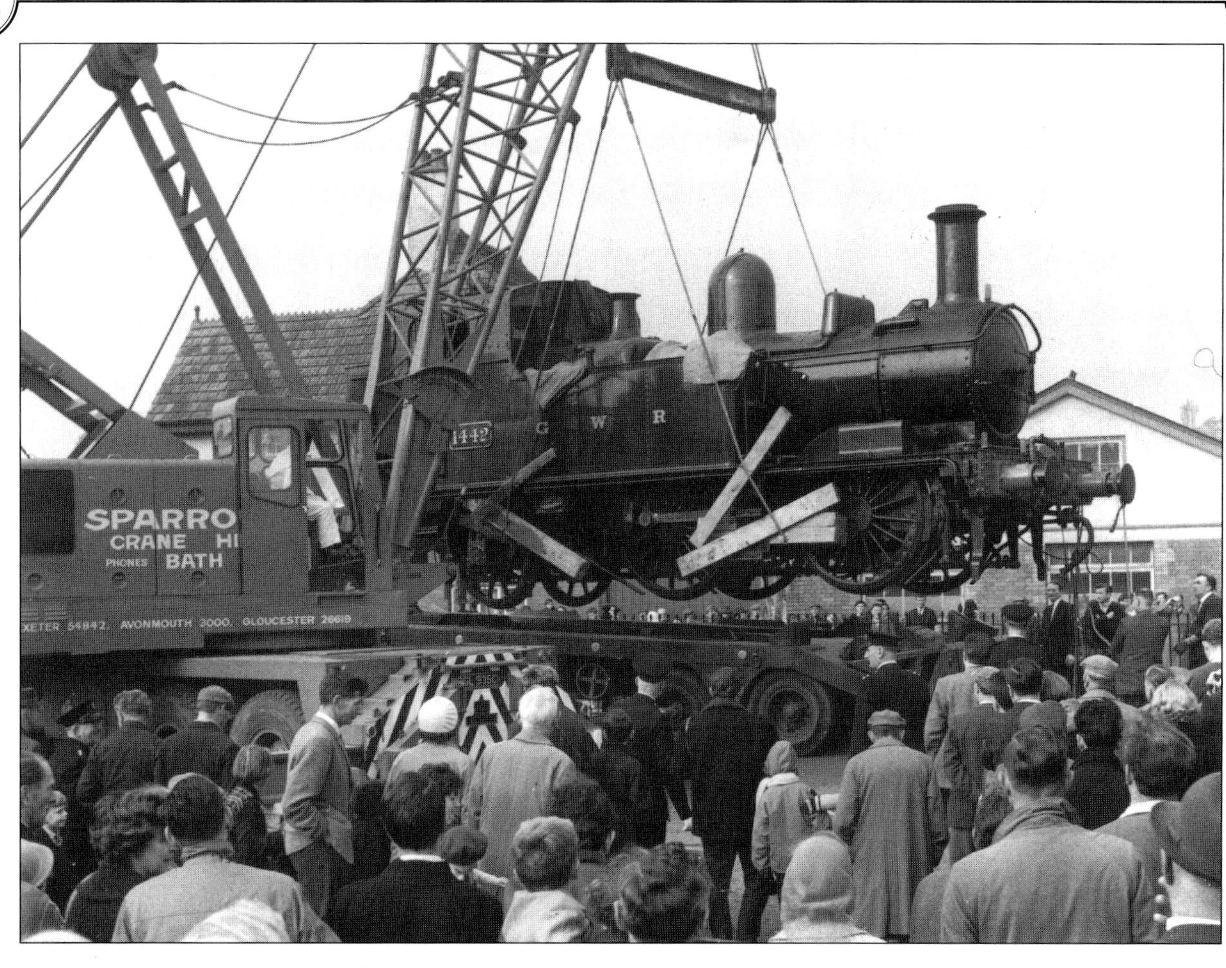
SPARRO
CRANE HI
PHONES BATH
XETER 54842, AVONMOUTH 3000, GLOUCESTER 26619
1442
G W R

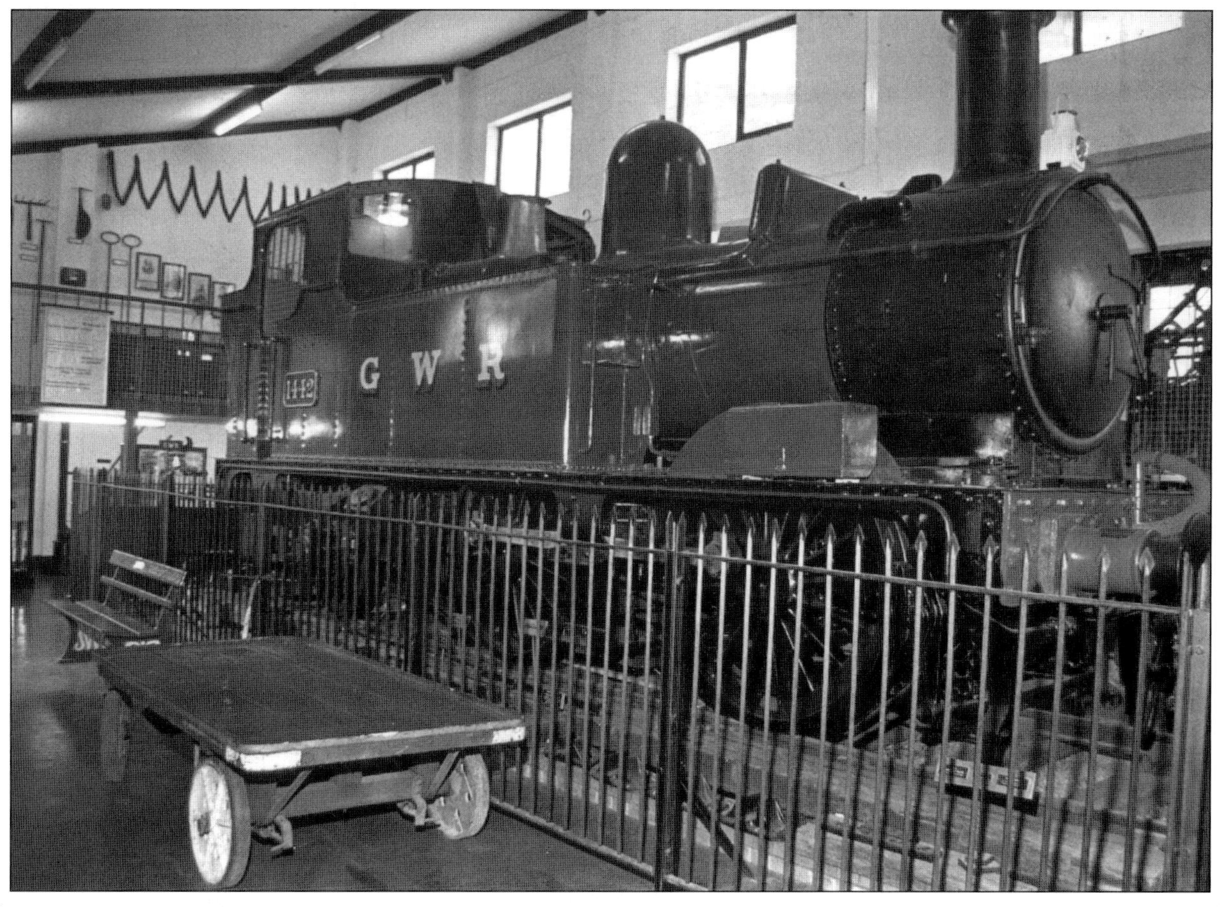
1442
G W R

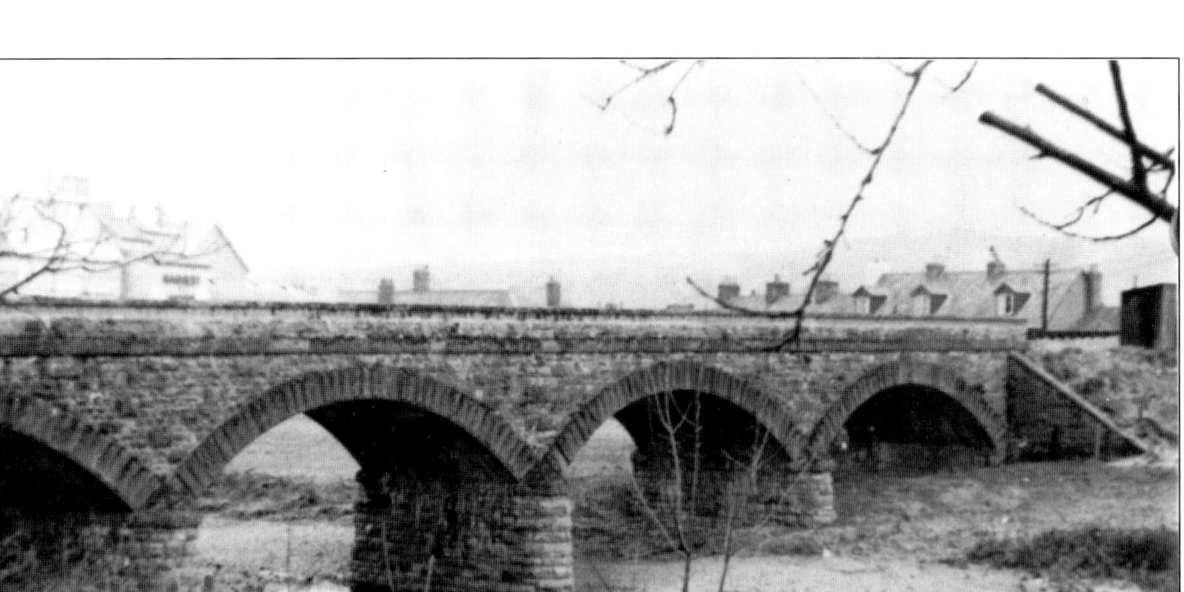

Another bygone landmark: the old railway bridge now replaced by the Southern Relief Road. MUSEUM COLLECTION

walked in from Halberton, to find that the factory had closed because workers could not get in! The Valley Line went first and then in 1963 came the announcement that the Tiverton to Tiverton Junction spur would also close. One of Sir John Amory's many generous gifts to the town was his purchase of the Tivvy Bumper, now in Tiverton Museum.

Conversely, the relatively useless Grand Western Canal was 'saved'. The spur from Burlescombe to Tiverton had long been isolated from the rest of the canal and forgotten, except as an occasionally mentioned route for a southern bypass. Then in 1966 Bill Authers and Dennis Harwood started a campaign to turn the largely derelict canal into a country park. With vigorous local support they succeeded in getting joint funding from the Borough and County Councils. The whole project depended on the hard work of local volunteers. Once the canal was cleared, a horse-drawn barge began to give tourists one of Devon's mellower experiences. It was a pity that the railway did not attract a similar body of support as the railways up and down the Exe Valley might now be run by 'retired' volunteers. When one observes the happy engine-drivers, stationmasters and guards who man the Minehead to Bishop's Lydiard line, one sighs for the loss of a similar occupation for Tiverton's 'Third Age', who could have run steam trains up and down the Exe Valley until called upon to run that greater branch line in the sky.

The salvation of the canal in the mid-1960s reflected a sense that the past was slipping away. Many prominent Tivertonians became determined to save what could be saved. In the early 1960s the Palmerston Hotel went with little protest, but plans to demolish the police station and gaol and build four- or five-storey flats on the site were successfully halted, and when what is now Raymond Penny House was scheduled for demolition in the mid-1970s the protest was immediate and effective. A decade earlier Gotham House had been rescued. The organisation that marked this change was the Civic Society, founded in 1968, largely organised by its indefatigable Secretary, Margaret Allen, and supported by Bill Authers. Perhaps its birth may have been encouraged by a one-man crusade by Sir John Amory to preserve the last Victorian street light on Angel Hill.

The most significant work of historic salvation was the founding of the Tiverton Museum. Since the 1890s legislation had empowered local government to fund museums and libraries, but the Borough Council refused to take up those powers. In 1901 the Council decided a clock tower at Lowman Green would be a better memorial to Queen Victoria than a library. A library was set up in 1920 in the War Memorial Hall on Angel Hill, in quarters that must have been pokey from the start. With inadequate support from the Borough Council, but strong support from Derick Amory, and thanks to the drive of Bill Authers and others a small museum was opened in two rooms of a house on Angel

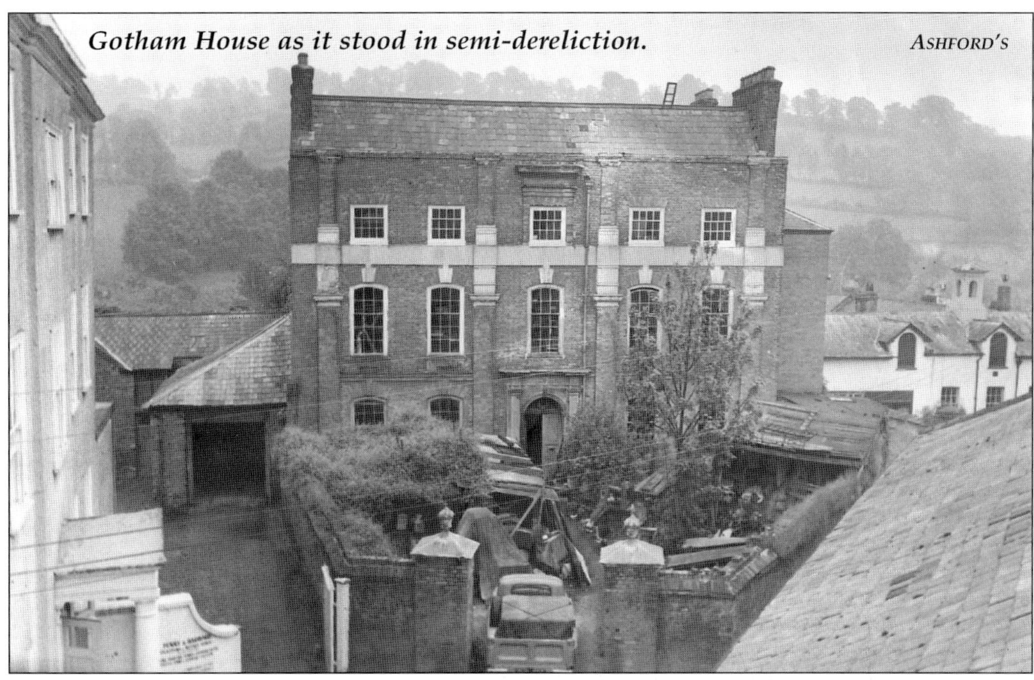

Gotham House as it stood in semi-dereliction. ASHFORD'S

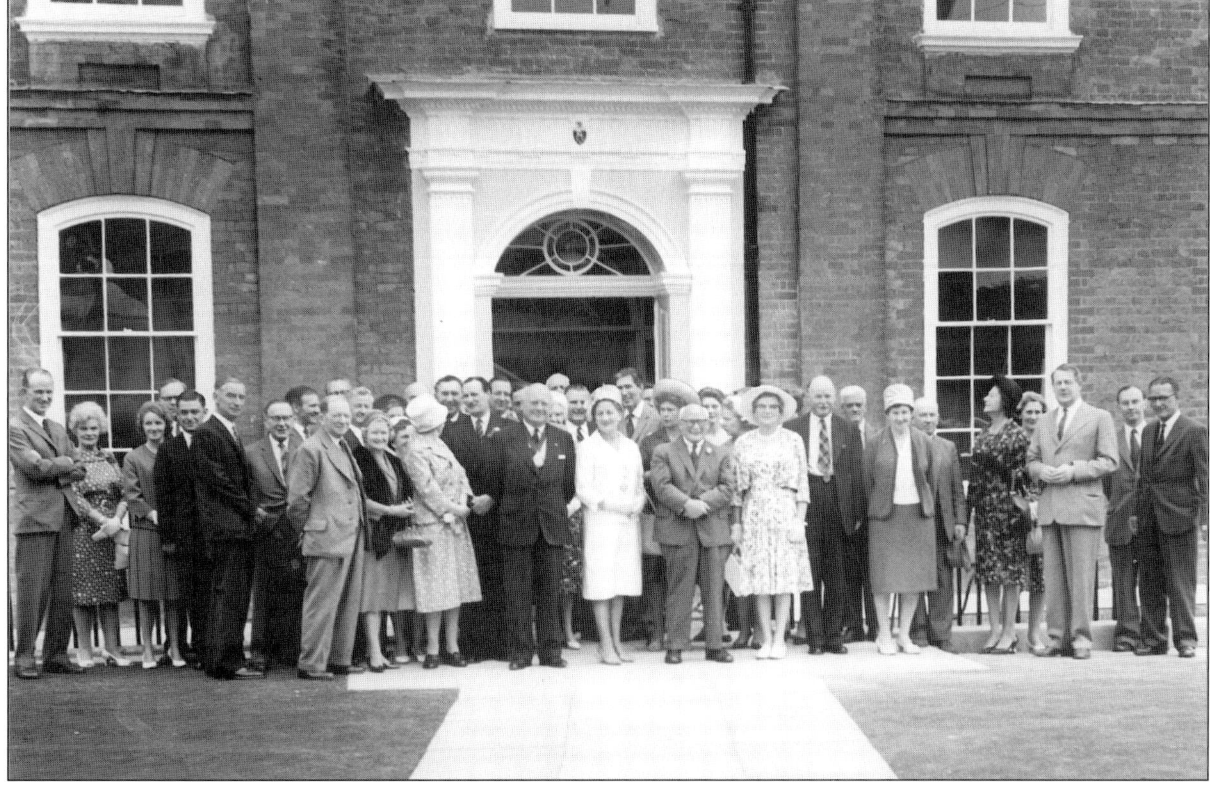

Gotham House in its glory, opening as the offices of Penny and Harward. The photograph includes, from left: *Mr Johnson (carpentry teacher at the Secondary Modern who rebuilt the staircase), Mrs Johnson, Cllr and Mrs Brian Homer, Frank Suter* (behind), *black-suited Tom Peters (Borough Engineer) and Mr Croxton (treasurer), Cllr Viv Scott* (looking right), *Alderman Ford, Mr Coleman (builder) and Mrs Harward, Mrs Ford* (looking behind her), *Dennis Harward, Cllr Dennis Nott, Mayor Bill Dunsford* (centre), *Mrs Authers, Bill Authers, Mrs Dunsford, John and Mary Palmer, Senior Partner Arthur Raymond Penny, Mrs Scott, Mrs Pugsley, Town Clerk Pugsley, Alderman Carpenter (a coal merchant after whom Carpenter Close is named), Mrs Penny. In the group of five on the right are Mr and Mrs Pettit and an unknown lady, Tom Penny and Clement Toy. Toy was the gifted architect who also designed the Westexe South Council Houses and Shillands.* ASHFORD'S

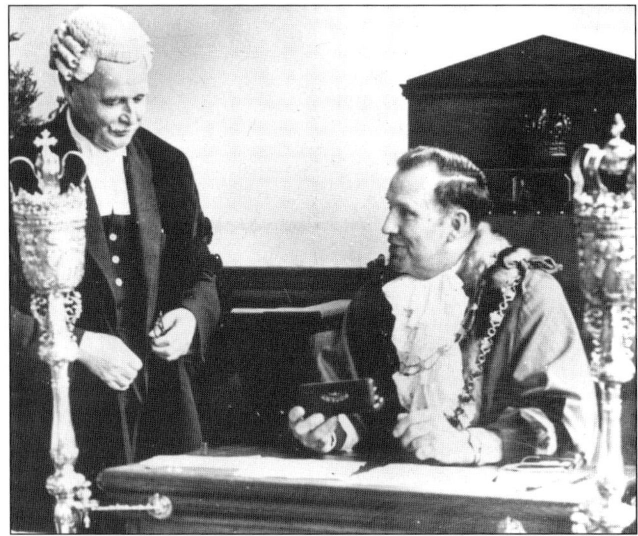

Civic pomp. Mayor Ayre (1967) and Town Clerk Pugsley (1937–67). An applicant for a post on the Borough returned home to Norwich to find a quotation from Henry Ayre's removal firm in his post the following day. Only a week later did he get offered the job. Pugsley's father had also been Town Clerk (1914–37), as well as Clerk to the Rural District Council, the Borough and County JPs, Blundell's, the Poor Law Guardians and Coroner.

MUSEUM COLLECTION

Hill. Later it was moved to Chilcott School and finally to the former Church of England Primary School in St Andrew Street, where it has grown and flourished into the Museum of Mid Devon Life.

Although the Borough Council celebrated its 350th birthday in 1965, a year after the last train service that ran in October 1964, it was in retrospect a swansong. A portent of change was the ending of the connection of the firm of Hole and Pugsley with the governance of the Town. Marshall Hole had been Town Clerk from 1867-1914, followed by John Follett Pugsley from 1914-37 and William Pugsley from 1937-67. Less than ten years later, a local government reorganisation merged Tiverton with three other local authorities, reducing the Borough Council to the level of a parish. One of the last acts of the old Borough was to twin with Chinon. There was considerable debate whether it would be wise to continue with a Town Council after reorganisation, as a Mayor presiding over a Council with no powers would be a significant anticlimax after 359 years of local effectiveness. In its last century the Borough had lost its two MPs, its own borough electorate perhaps only a quarter of the constantly changing new constituency. In the next election Tiverton will be on the eastern fringe of its constituency. In 1900 the Borough used to run its gas, electricity, sewerage

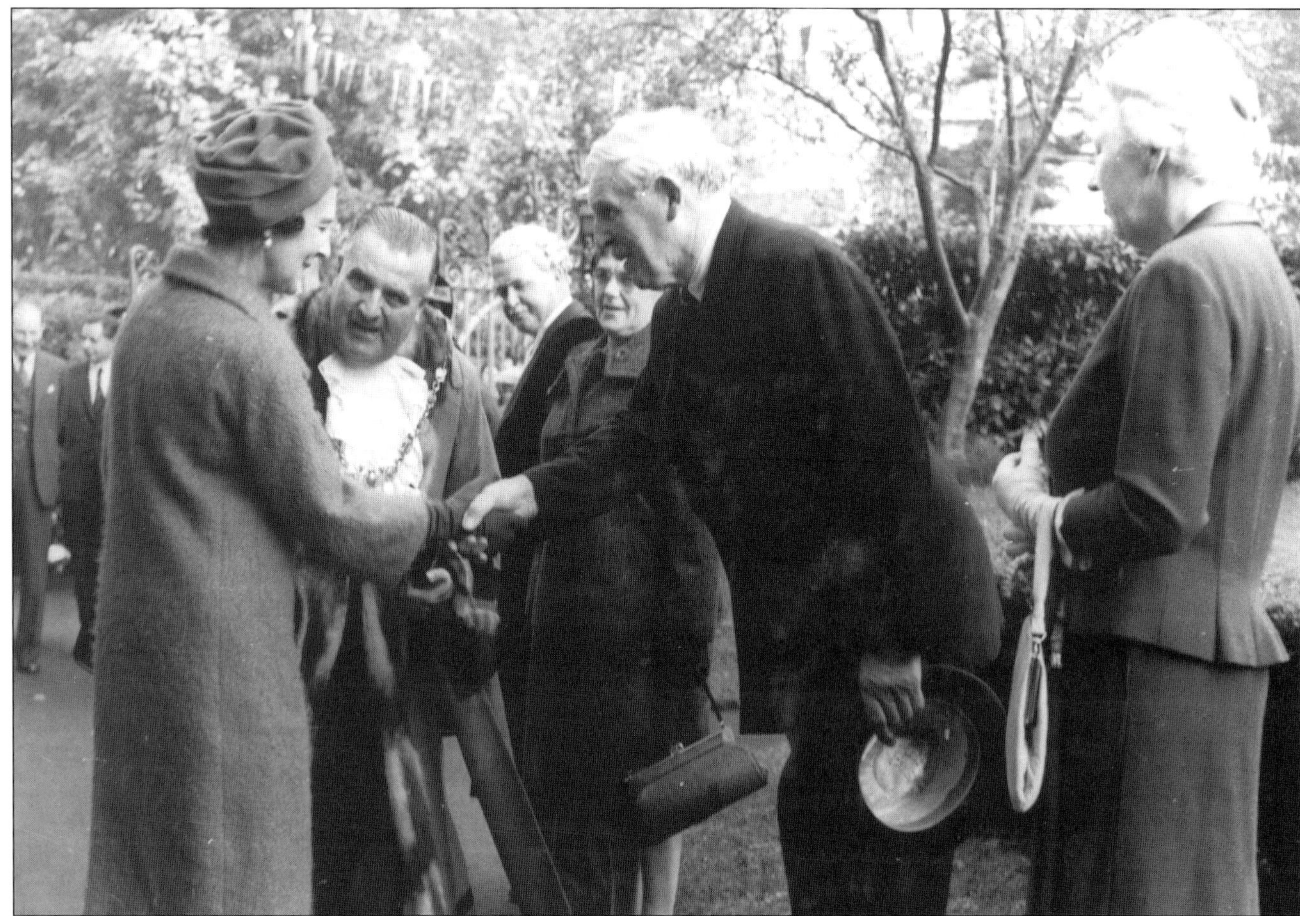

Bill Authers introduces Sir John Amory to Princess Marina. Lady Amory, the Town Clerk and Mrs Pugsley look on.

MUSEUM COLLECTION

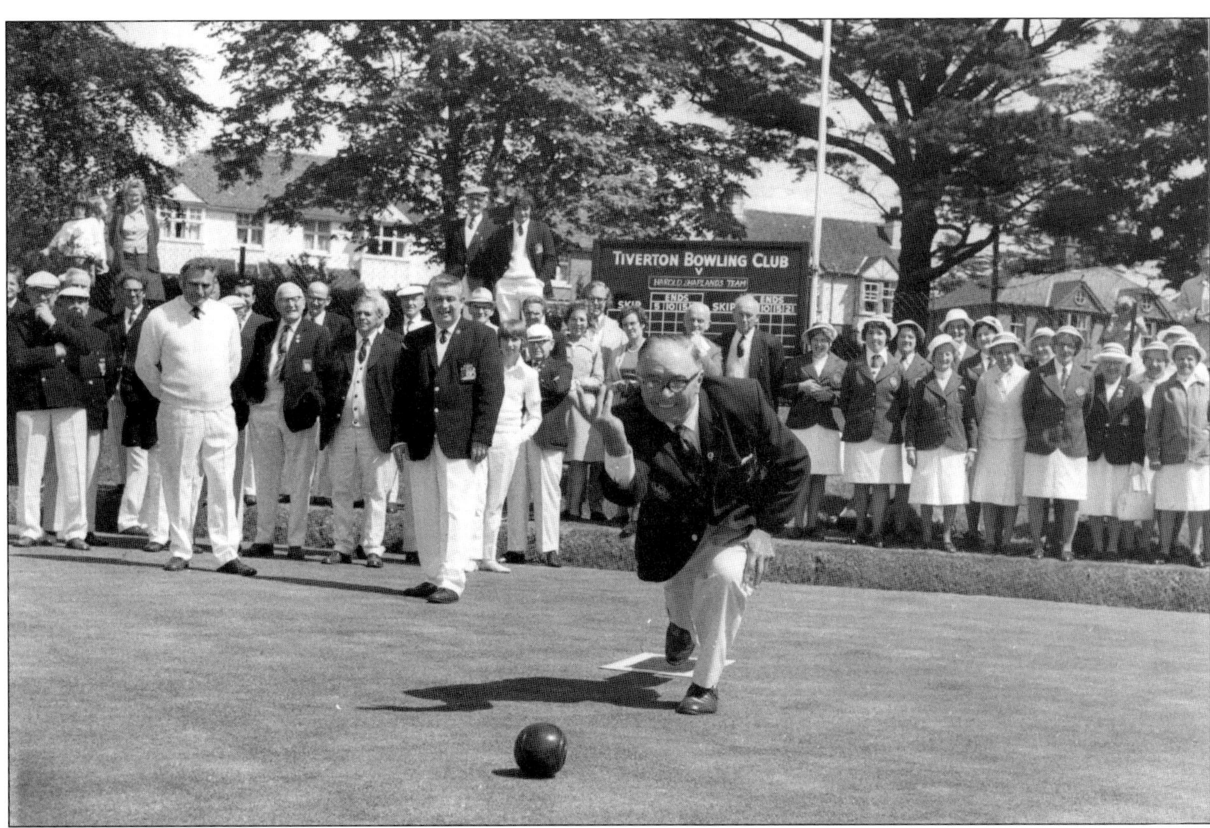

Above: *Alderman Harold Shapland bowls in front of the men and their dutiful ladies, c.1970s. Harold was a formidable local politician. His father, himself and his son, Eric, were all Mayors.* Museum Collection

Below: *Twinning with Chinon in 1972. Mayor Viv Scott, the new Town Clerk, Colin Greensmith, Alderman Bill Dunsford* (left) *and Eric Shapland (behind Clerk Greensmith's right ear) flank the Chinon representatives.* Museum Collection

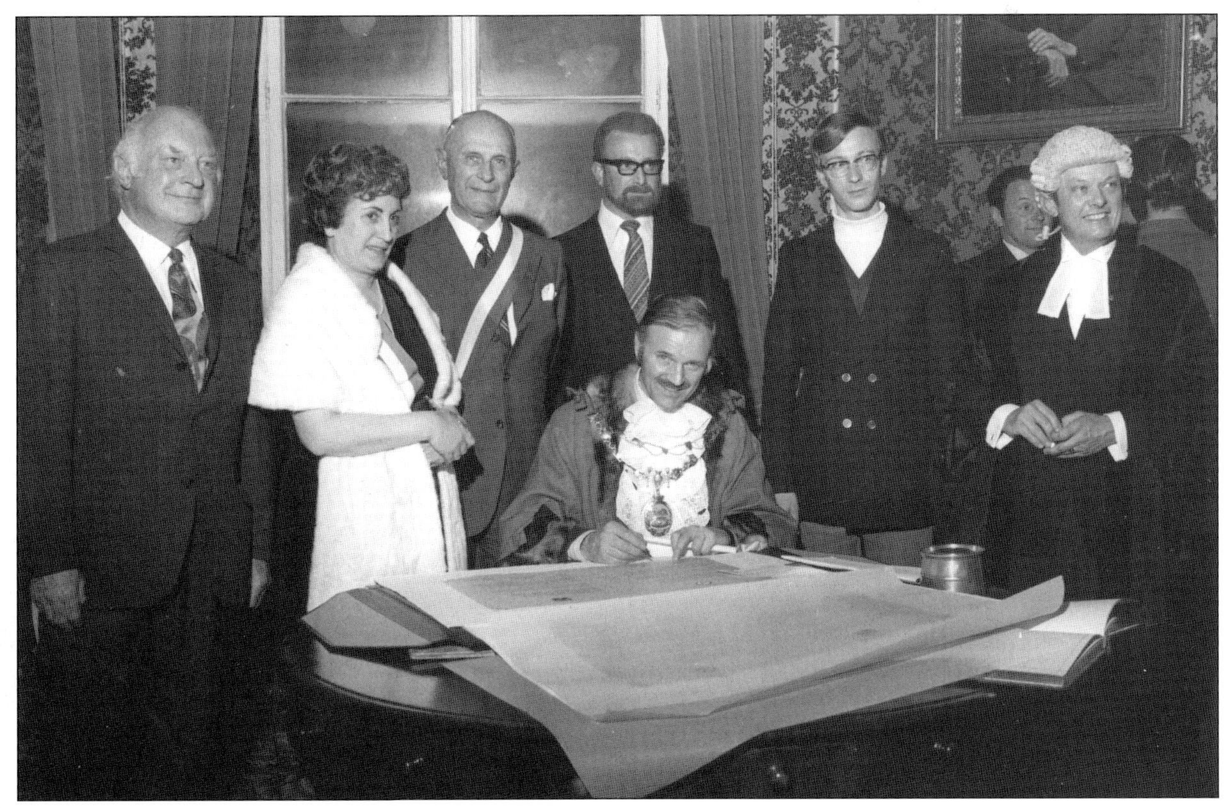

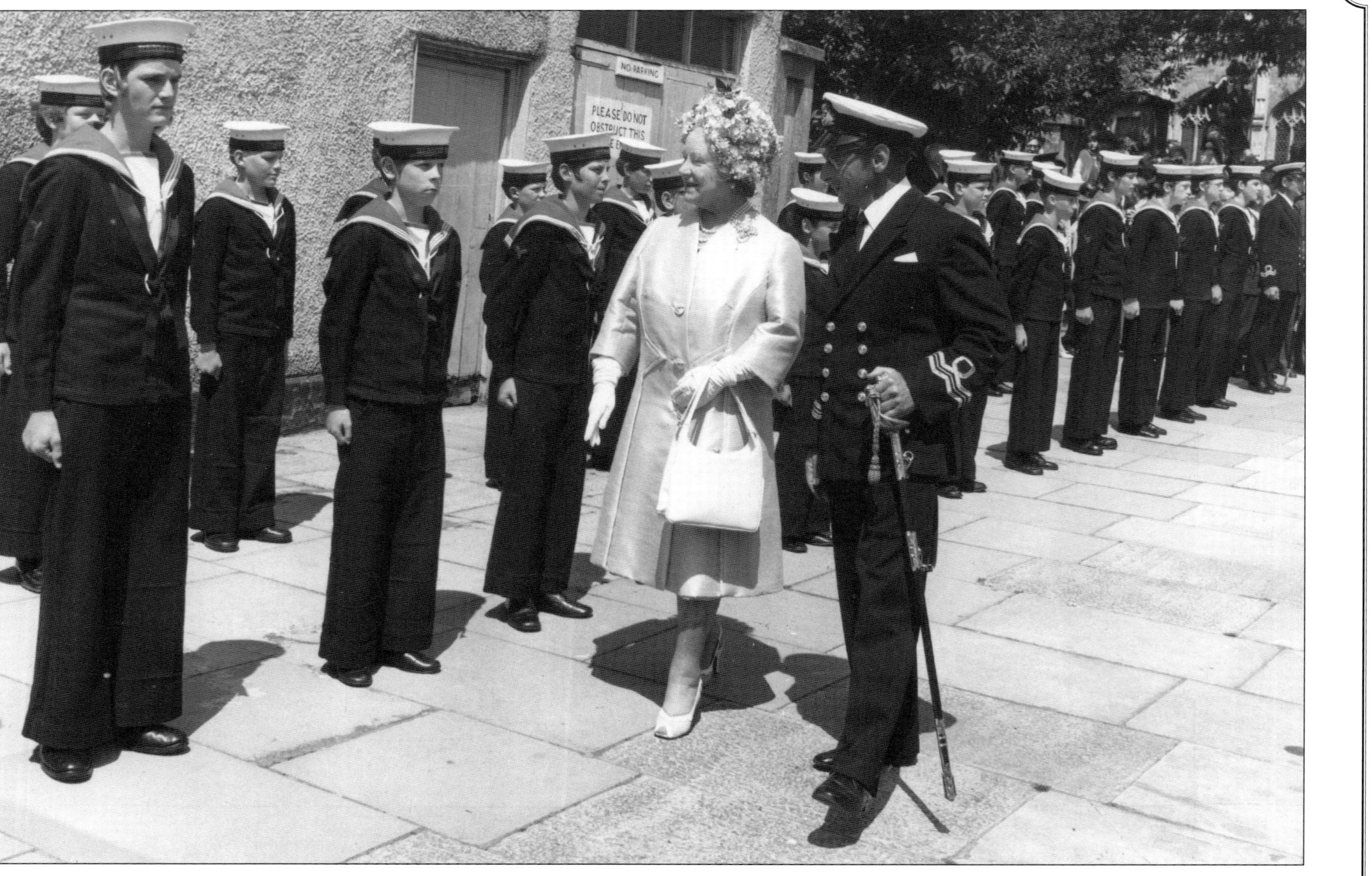

The Queen Mother inspecting the Sea Cadets in 1973 at St Peter's 900th anniversary. MUSEUM COLLECTION

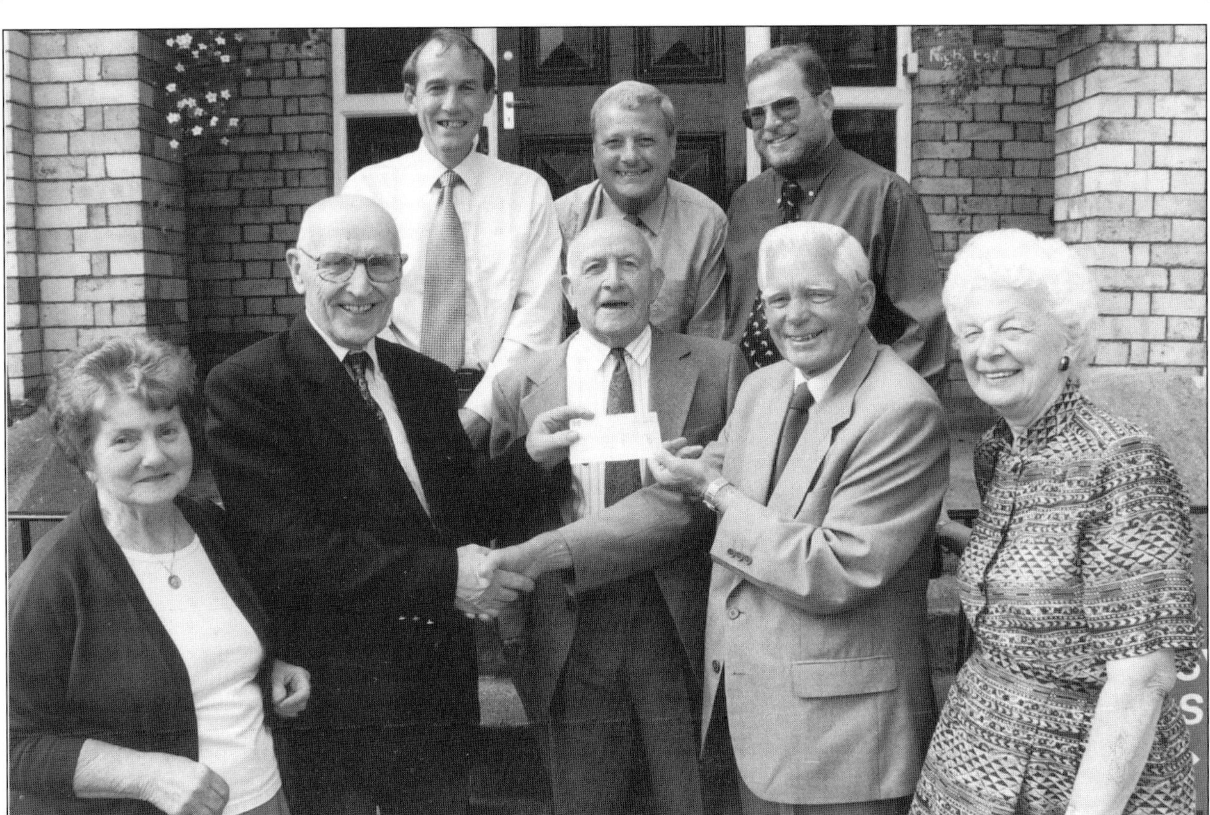

Bill Trickey, chairman of the Friends of Tiverton Hospital, receives a cheque from the Licensed Victuallers.

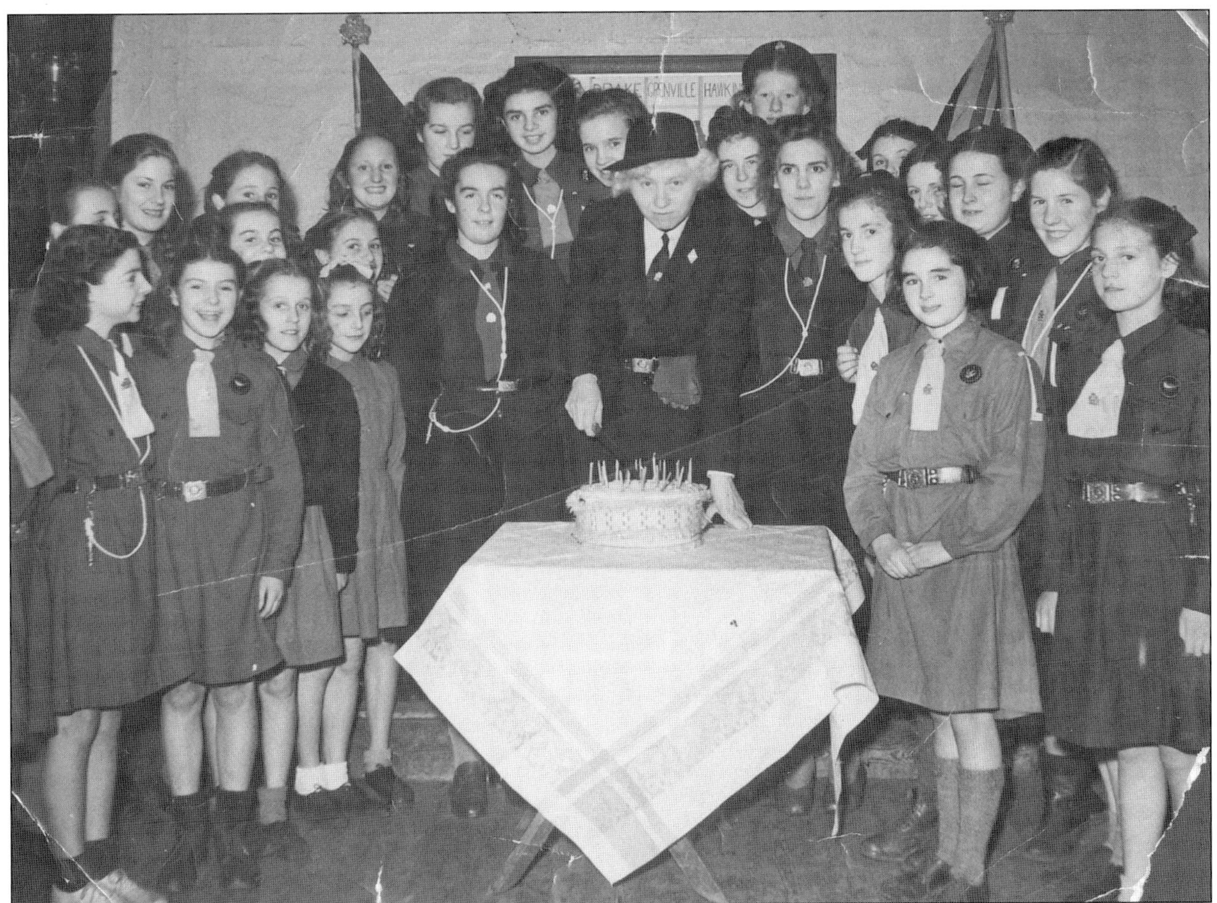

Joyce Wethered, Lady Amory, with a postwar Guide Group.

and water systems. It was responsible for its police, schools and roads. All the major firms giving employment in the town were controlled locally and in 1900 the vast majority of the shops were owned and run by local families.

The hospital was run locally too. The last chairman of the Hospital Committee was Bill Trickey, who became a board member of the National Health body based in Exeter, which managed the area's hospitals. He then moved on to be one of the founder members of the Friends of Tiverton Hospital, who have done yeoman work in raising funds so that as much could be done in Tiverton as possible, to avoid the trek to Exeter hospitals. When the new hospital on the Globe Elastic site was planned, the Friends raised £500,000 towards the cost of equipping it.

Sir John Amory, 1894–1972.

Sir John Amory had died in the summer of 1972. He had been born in 1894 and inherited in 1930. After weathering the slump and the fire of 1936, under him Heathcoat's prospered until the European textile industry succumbed to foreign competition. His benefactions were legion. He donated land for the extension of the old hospital in 1931, and he bought Bradfield Farm as the site of Tiverton Golf Club in the same year. He set up the Heathcoat Trust with a gift of £100,000 in 1940. He gave Alexandra Lodge for the care of the elderly, bought the Tivvy Bumper for the museum, restored the lamp-stand on Angel Hill. He lent the land for the old swimming baths beside the leat and with his brother gave £100,000 towards the first pool on the Bolham Road site. He was a Borough Councillor, Alderman and County Councillor and second in command of the Tiverton Home Guard. He developed the Knightshayes Cricket Club and captained Devon. He was for many years a JP until increasing deafness made the task too difficult. One story sums up his humanity. Sitting on the bench with John Lake, they had to sentence a young man who had caused alarm and dismay by mucking about with fireworks in a public place. The young man was an employee of Lake's and so the bench took his advice as to the level of fine that would be appropriate. Later Sir John sent the 'criminal' a letter enclosing some money as he thought the fine had been too high. With his brother Derick, then Chancellor of the Exchequer, he was granted the Freedom of the Borough in 1959. During the ceremony, in his speech of thanks Sir John said:

> *The family have always regarded ownership of the business not as personal property but as a trust for the welfare of those employed in it and for the borough of Tiverton.*

One wonders if such a career will ever be possible again, as it seems to have depended on a combination of great public spirit with the economic and political independence of small towns, the latter now a thing of the past.

Chapter 10

Postscript

'The best way to suppose what may come, is to remember what is past.'
George Saville, Marquess of Halifax, 1633-95.

There are many problems in tackling these recent years; most of the traditional strands of Tiverton's history have been cut. Its traditional textile industry is not the dominant strand it once was and, although the Amorys still have a local presence, they are no longer the main employer and Knightshayes is part of the National Trust. The Town Council and the Mayoralty does its best to perform an integrative function, but, shorn of its powers, it is a shadow of its former self. There are few things now that affect Tivertonians that are decided in Tiverton. We are light years away from the days when Peter Blundell, in his will, could refer to those not born in Tiverton as 'foreigners'. Probably the majority of Tiverton's voters have not voted for the winning MP since the 1880s, except when Acland won and when Derrick Amory was MP after 1945. Mid Devon District Council has not filled the gap, and with its limited powers and its concerns spread from Bow to Hemyock and from Bampton to Thorverton, it is probably unable to do so.

A pessimist might say that a sense of local government dysfunction has spread. There is no local co-ordination, only loss of empowerment. The ability to solve housing problems through local democracy ended in the 1980s and the 'Right to Buy' has reduced the town's council-housing from over 2,000 to under 1,300. Housing Associations have not filled the gap as house prices have rocketed. A large terraced house in St Andrew Street, that could have been bought for under £6,000 in the early 1970s, sold recently for over £300,000, three times a teacher's salary in the earlier date, ten or 11 times now. The housing problem may not be as bad as that

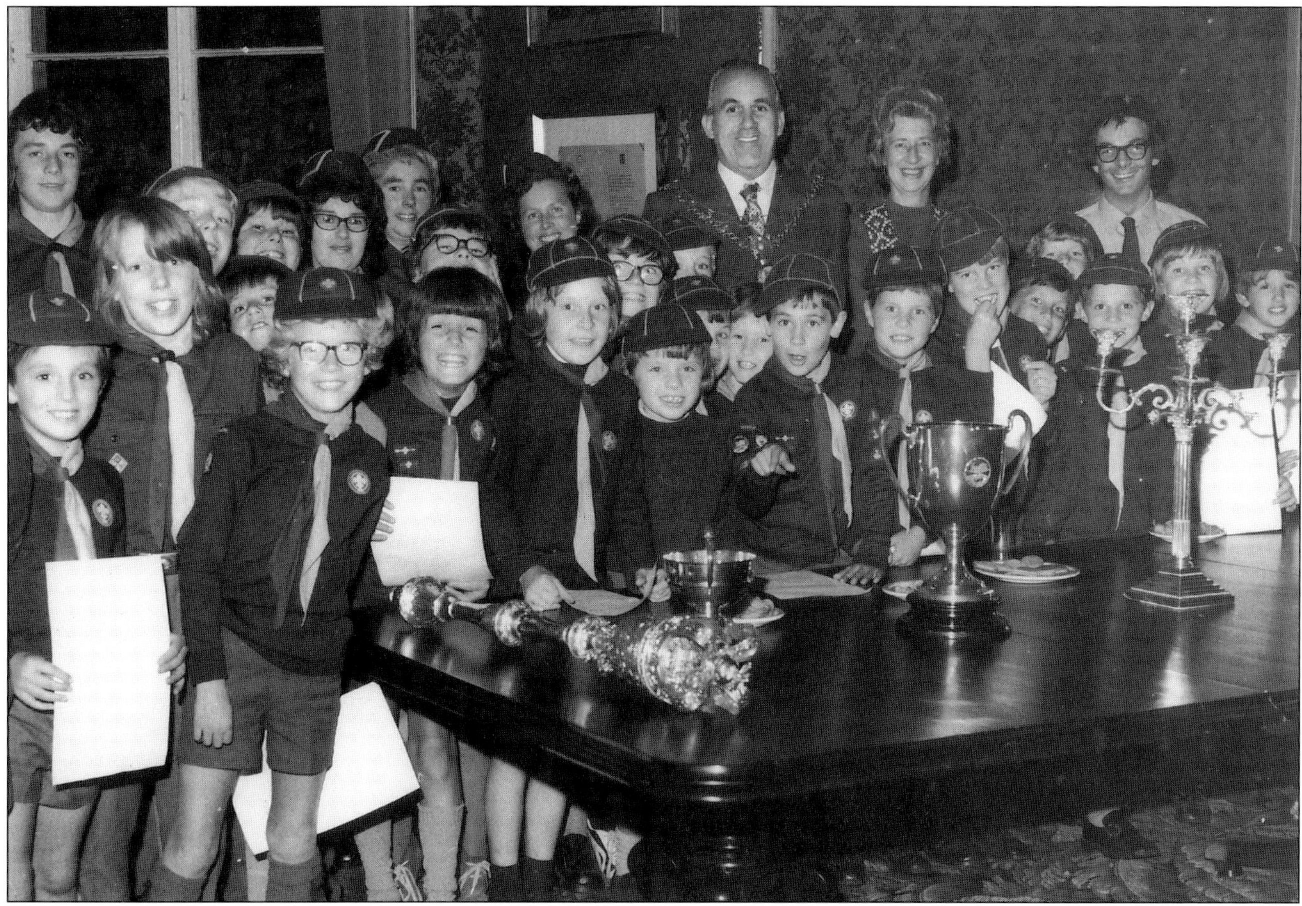

Mayor Cecil Phippen and Mrs Phippen showing Mary Willis' Cub Pack the Parlour and the Regalia, 1975. As a lad Cecil was one of Brian Homer's gang, The Dirty Works, who took on the evacuee gang, The Snapes. Please help with the names of the cubs!

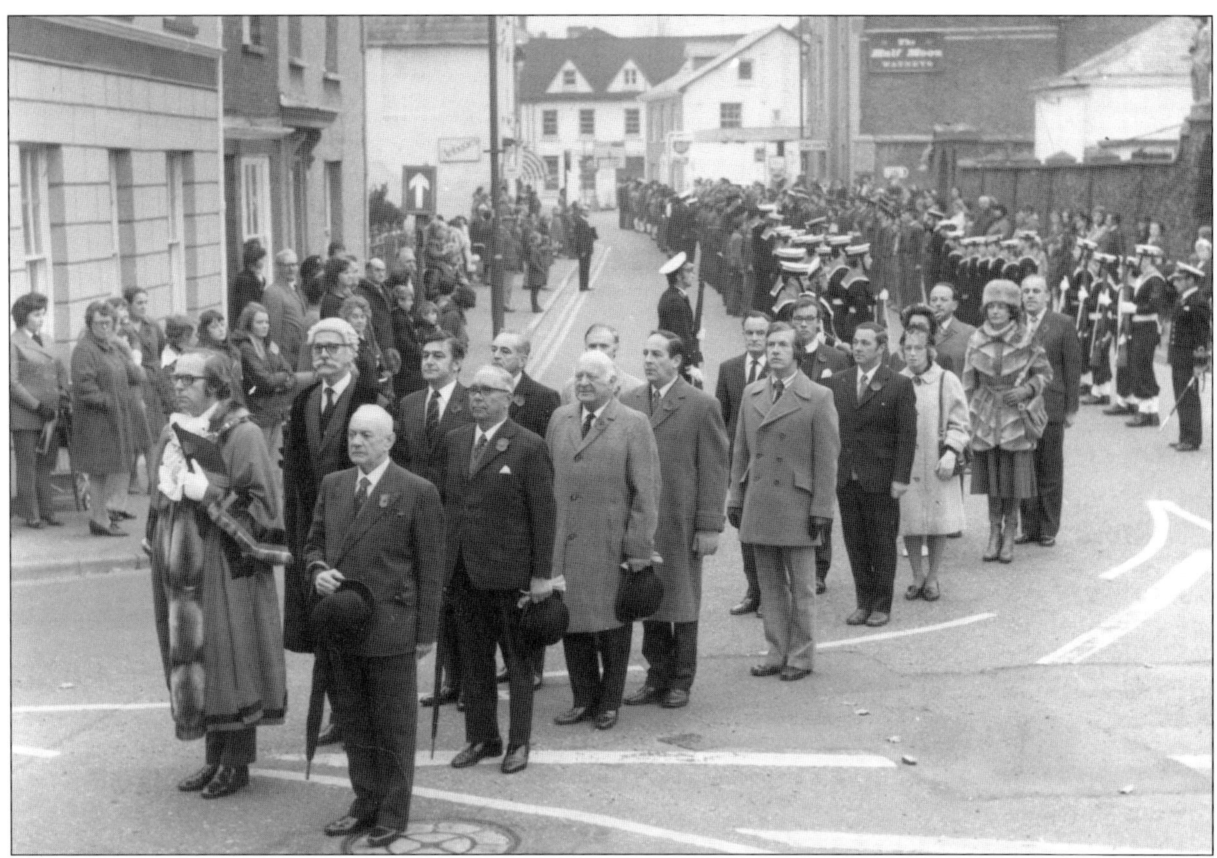

Mayoral parade, 1975, soon after losing Borough status. Mayor Frank Suter said 'We have lost an Empire and not found a role.' The procession includes, from left: *Mayor Suter and Sidney Cox, Clerk Camfield and Harold Shapland, Brian Homer and Bill Dunsford, John Lake and Ewart Champion, Viv Scott and Ken Greenslade, Derek Coulthard and Eric Shapland, Charles Noon and Margaret Allen, Mary Turner, Cecil Phippen and Bill Jones.* *MUSEUM COLLECTION*

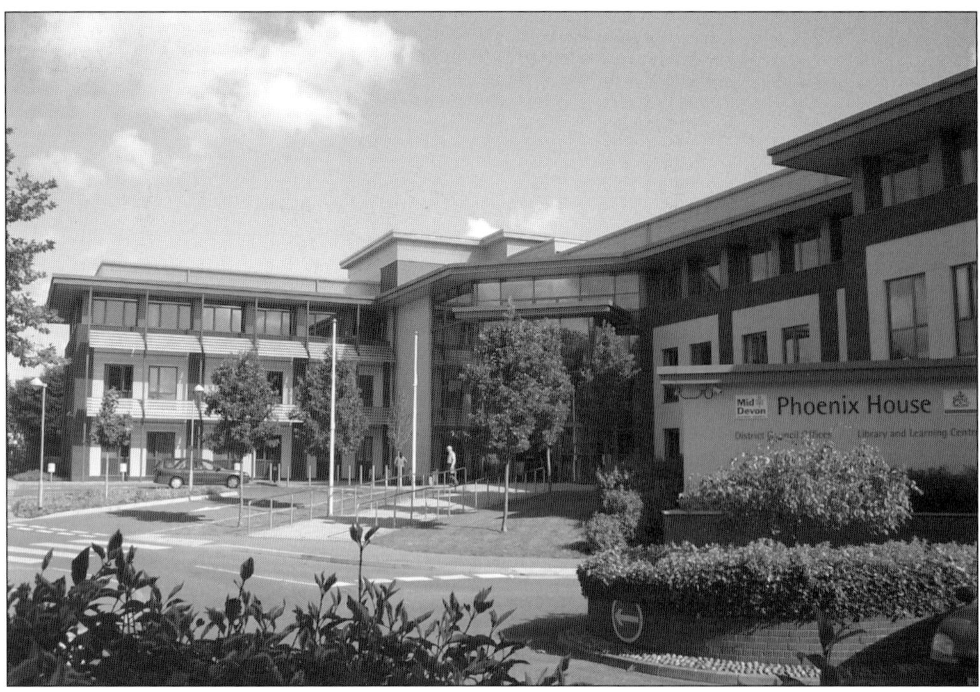

The New District Council offices. Previously the Council was housed in different buildings all over town, mostly rented, and the rationale was that building its own would be cheaper. The building was opened sheepishly in contrast to the outburst of pride that accompanied the opening of the Town Hall in 1864.

facing the Borough Council in 1945, but it is 'bad', and local government has not the powers to cope. Tivertonians are largely impotent receivers of National Health services; they feel that the police are distant; that the financing and running of their schools is beyond their control; they have to pay the fire service and water 'taxes' without any democratic controls; and the system of 'poor relief', or Social Security, is a mystery to them. A century ago all these were under local control: the local fire service and police force, Tiverton School Board, the Poor Law Guardians and the Tiverton Hospital Committee are just a few examples.

For a contemporary Tivertonian to have a coherent input, similar to a 1930s Borough Councillor, he or she would have to be a member at the least of the District Council, County Council, Primary Care Trust, Police Authority, and South West Water. Genuine local government has been made impossible and is not often a focus of local patriotism. Certainly the local press regards it as a whipping boy, which is a shame as the people working in these posts are usually well-intentioned folk coping with a difficult system not of their making.

The statistics produced by central government show that Tiverton has areas of serious deprivation, so deep that they are rated in the worst 20 percent of the whole country, but the local means to remedy the situation seem lacking.

What has given the last 30 years dignity are the efforts made by a multitude of individuals and groups to hold the community together in an age when governments have tried to restrict us to being individual 'customers', 'consumers' or 'stake-holders' and when even a Prime Minister has denied the reality of community. To try to tell the story of these efforts will result in a piecemeal account and the 'History of Tiverton' will have become the 'History of the Friends of Tiverton Hospital,' the 'History of Tiverton Museum', the 'History of the Civic Society', the 'History of the Greenway Trust' and the histories of all the organisations that make the town tick. There may always be a sad feeling that theirs has been a noble rearguard action and a sad guess that the underlying dominant theme of the recent history of Tiverton has been the story of increasing globalisation, disengagement and even alienation. On the other hand two individual contributions might be mentioned. Ron Davey's heroic work with the Tiverton Youth Orchestra, which culminated in his hiring the Albert Hall and taking his musicians to play there in 1977. And in the same year Mary Turner as Mayor almost single-handedly championed the silver jubilee celebrations.

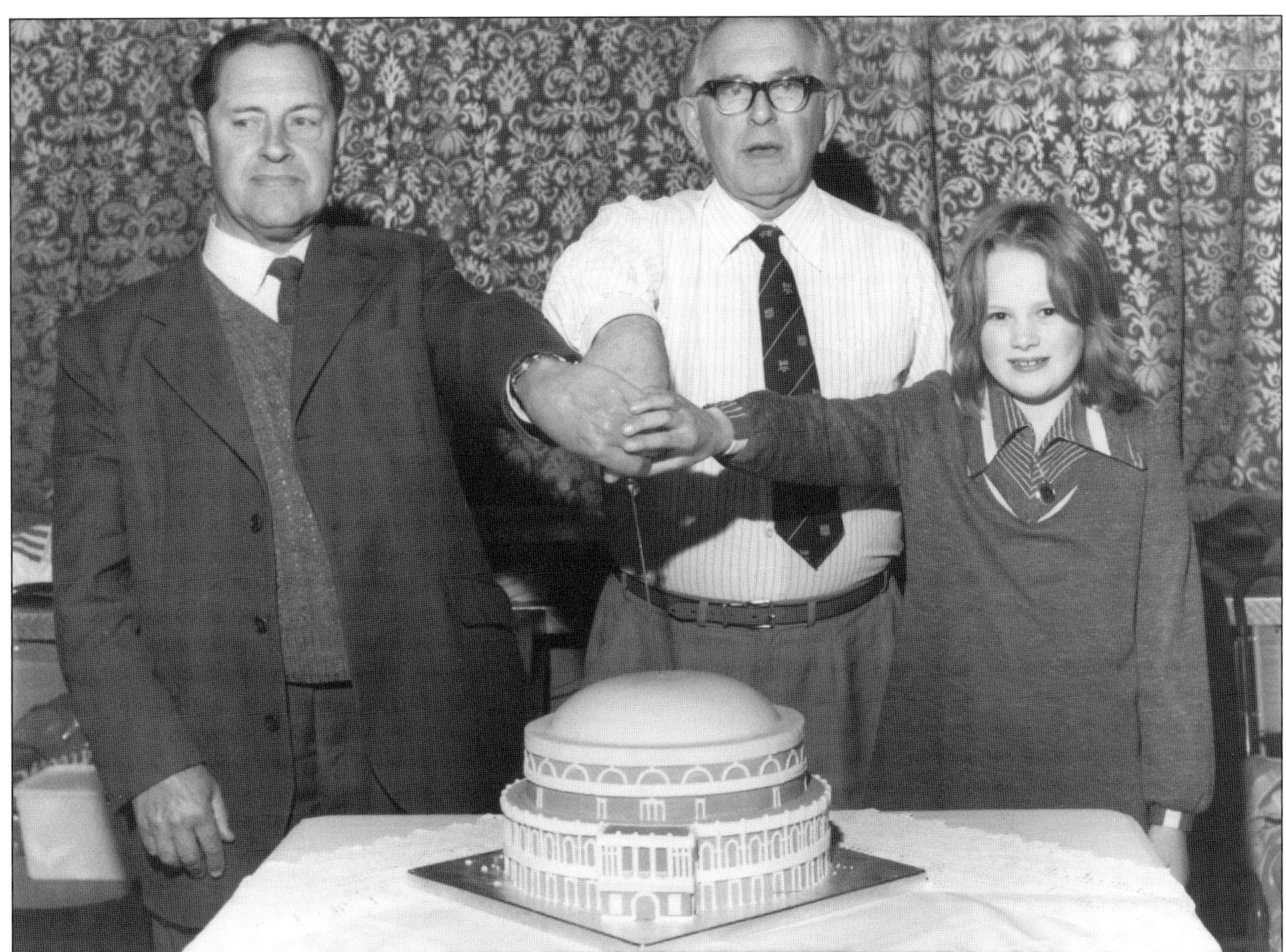

Ron Davey, the inspirational leader of Tiverton Youth Orchestra and his Albert Hall gateau, 1977. He took his orchestra to play in the Albert Hall! MUSEUM COLLECTION

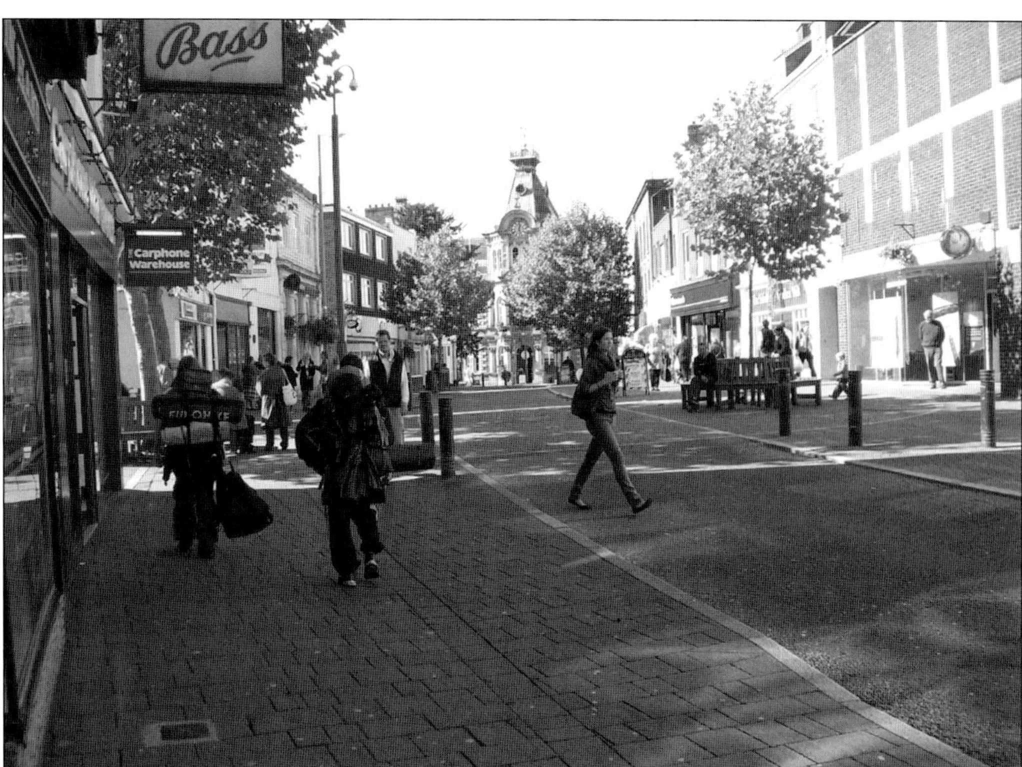

Fore Street pedestrianised. Has it been a 'good move'? It was certainly vehemently opposed by Tiverton traders.

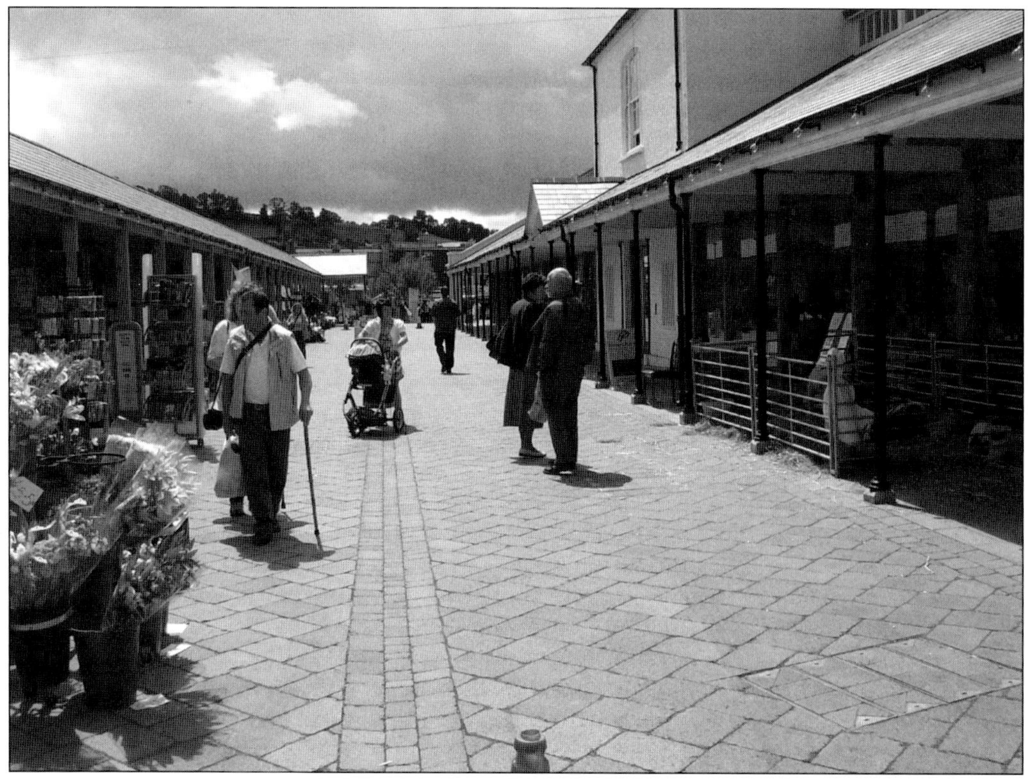

The outside stalls of Tiverton Market and a view of Cranmore Castle in the distance.

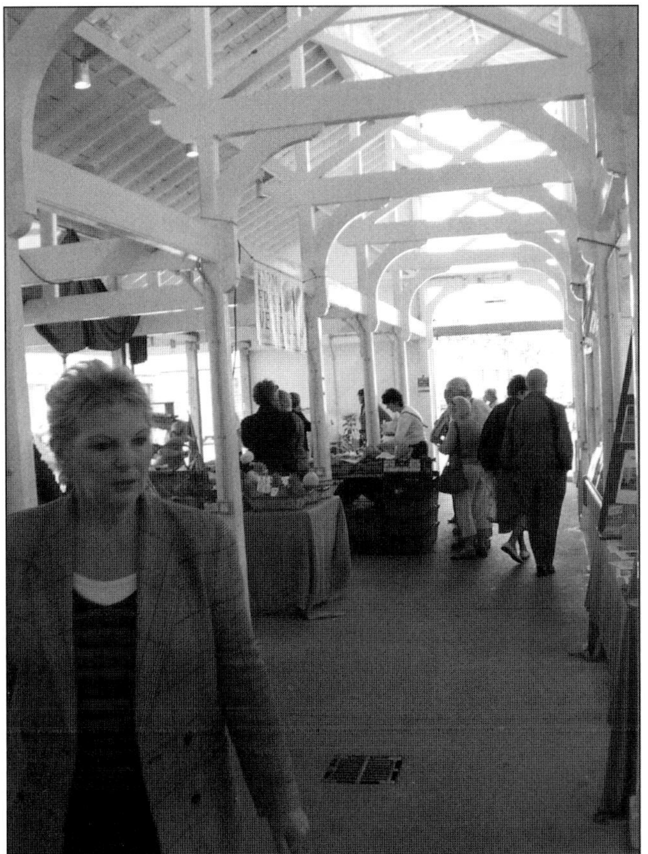

The new Pannier Market, largely financed by European Union money.

The District Council has produced some good things: the pedestrianisation of Fore Street, achieved against the opposition of much local opinion; the improvement of Castle Street; the development of the market, with the help of European money; and new recreation facilities at Bolham Road. On the other hand, confusion in local government destroyed the Tennis Club that operated behind the old Town Hall and destroyed the Tiverton Cricket Club that played at Amory Park until the mid-1970s. The planning system may infuriate individual applicants, but it provides a protection for the past that was lacking in the 1960s. The 'system' only prevented the demolition of Raymond Penny House in the mid-1970s by a whisker of a casting vote. Raymond Penny House was named after a solicitor, who did much good work for the hospital and other charitable trusts.

Perhaps that will be the role of local government, to be an umbrella organisation that holds the ring through the planning system and oversees services such as refuse collection and other public health measures, leaving the 'doing' to those organisations that are increasingly making the town work and supporting the efficient with grants. Support for young people seems to be being provided more effectively by organisations such as the Drop-In Centre in the market. Housing problems may be being tackled (but not solved!) more effectively by such organisations as the Tiverton Almshouse Trust, the Church Housing Action Team and Housing Associations. Some 30 years in local government gave me a respect for the ability and good intentions of most local government officers, but the system now largely confines them to a reactive rather than a positive role. The Citizens' Advice Bureau often provides more relevant help and is of great use to those with problems, but must have a grant to support its organisational skeleton.

One should remember that in the centuries after the Norman conquest Tiverton grew from just another large Devon village because of the economic effect of the castle and the spending power of its great household and garrison. In medieval terms, Tiverton grew because it became a centre of 'government'. It is fashionable to moan about the numbers of local government officers and to complain about their salaries, but the District Council is one of Tiverton's largest employers and, while the town remains a centre of government, this one element of its prosperity remains secure. Any further local government reorganisation, which might tend to remove local government offices from Tiverton, must be seen as a serious threat to local prosperity.

One facet of the last 50 years has been the enormous growth of the town's 'footprint'. In 1945 Tiverton's place on the map had grown since Dunsford's time, but not by much. There had been the graceful development of Church Street and St Paul's Square in Westexe, as well as the building for factory workers in John Street, Melbourne Street and Alexandra Terrace. There was also a dribble of gentrified development to the north of Townend Corner. The railway station and the post-1882 Blundell's had encouraged little accretions around them. All of this, except the Post Hill satellite, was within walking distance of the centre. In 1931 the population of the whole parish was 9,610, well down on the 1851 figure of 11,144. (Much of the fall was probably depopulation in the large rural areas of the parish, the town population probably holding its own.) By 1971 the population was 15,548 and in the 2001 census 18,621, thereby doubling in 70 years. To Westexe South have been added Cotteylands, and Palmerston Park. Elmore, Pinnex Moor, Wilcombe, and Glebelands have been added to the east. More recently houses have covered the large area out to the Link Road and estates have grown to the north and south of Westexe, as well as large in-fills around Blundell's, as the school sold land to finance expansion. Few of these areas are within shopping/ walking distance of the town centre.

Households too have changed. In 1945 there was genuine overcrowding. In 2001 there were 7,952 households and 2,437 of them, 31 percent, were single adult households, and about a quarter of the children are now living in single parent households. The jury is still 'out' as to whether these changes are significant and what they may mean for life in towns

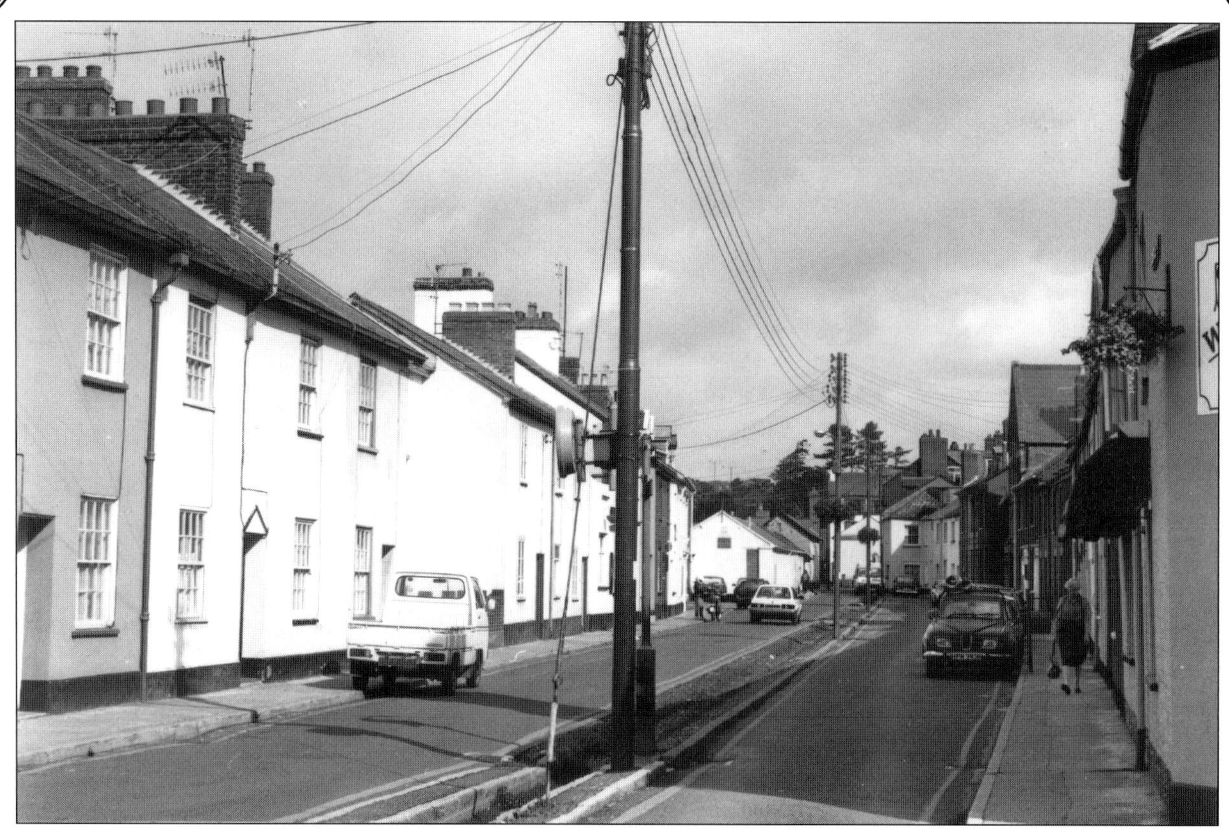

Castle Street before (above) *and after* (below) *cosmetic surgery. Well worth it!* MUSEUM COLLECTION

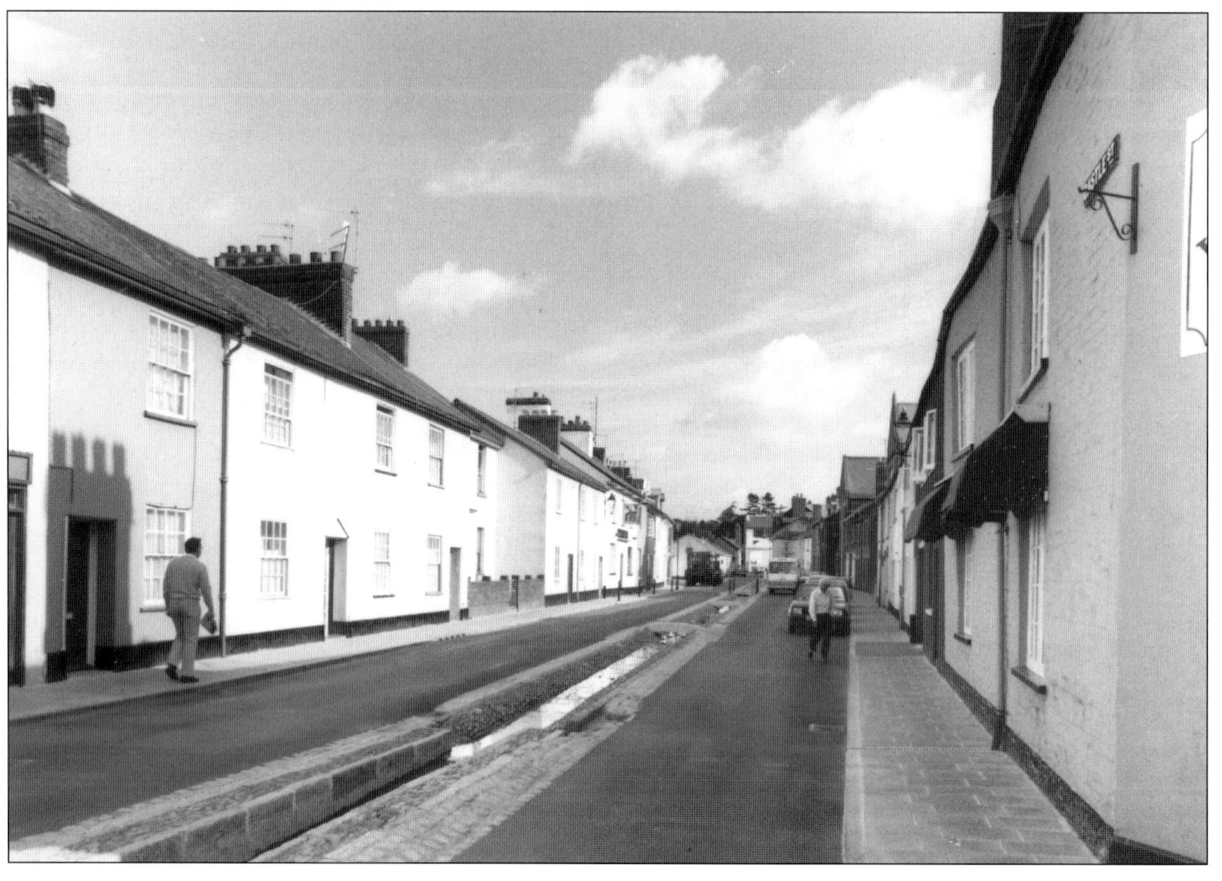

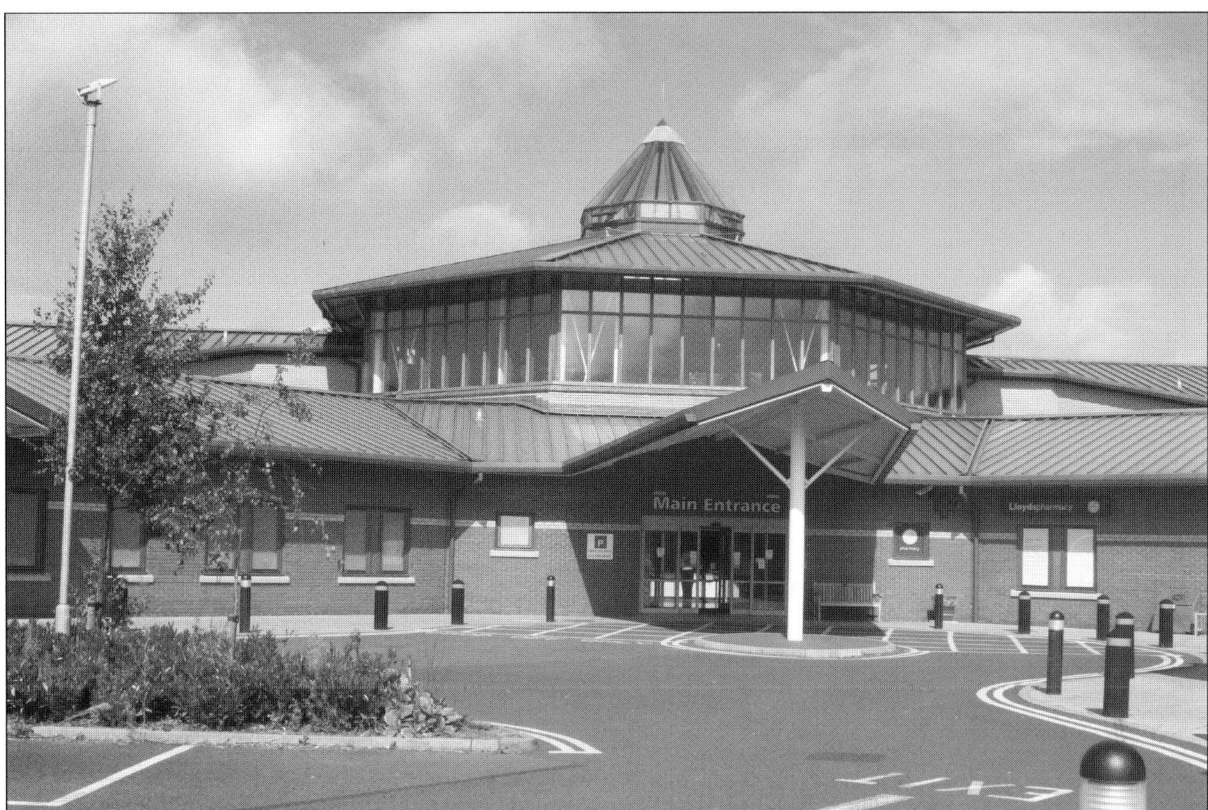

The new hospital. COLIN WHITE

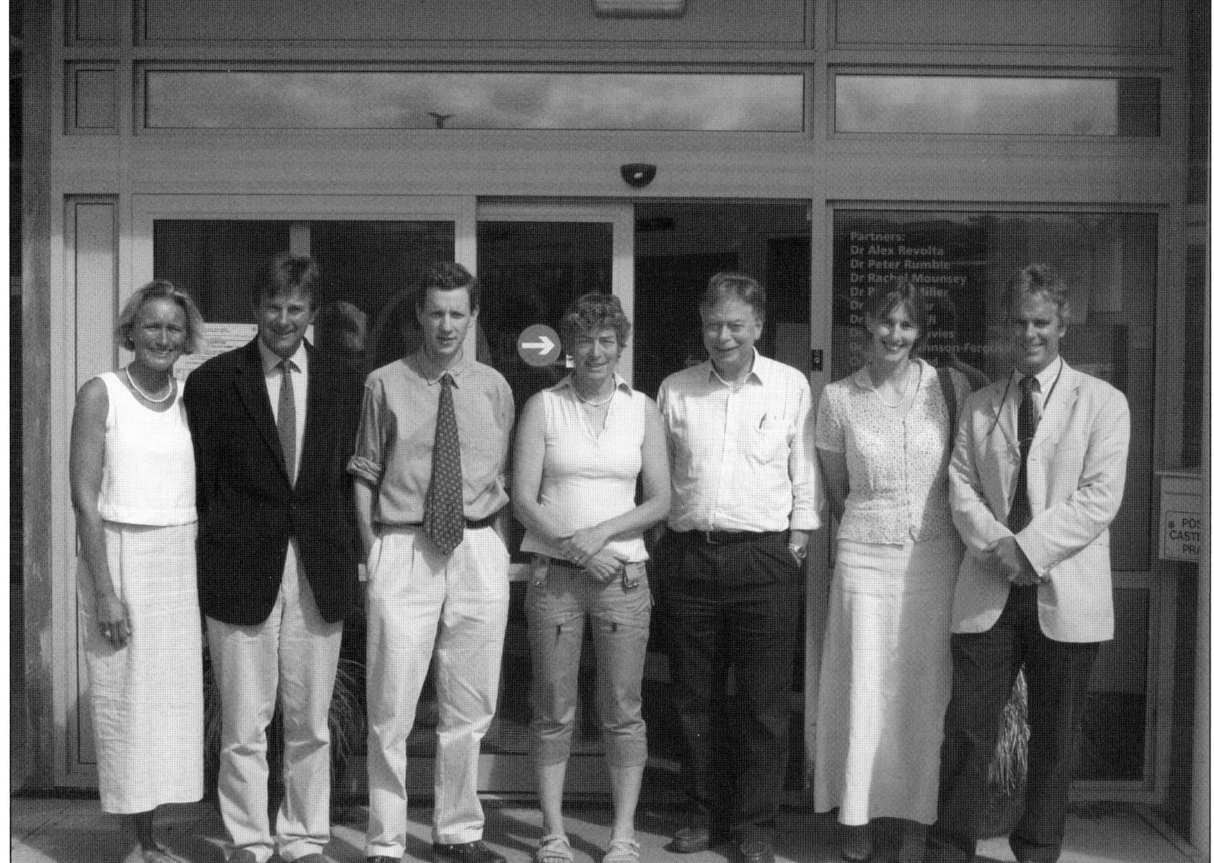

Most of the Castle Place practice outside its new premises next to the hospital. Left to right: *Jane and Patrick Miller, Simon Johnson-Ferguson, Alison Round, Alex Revolta, Rachel Mounsey, Peter Rumble.* JANE MILLER

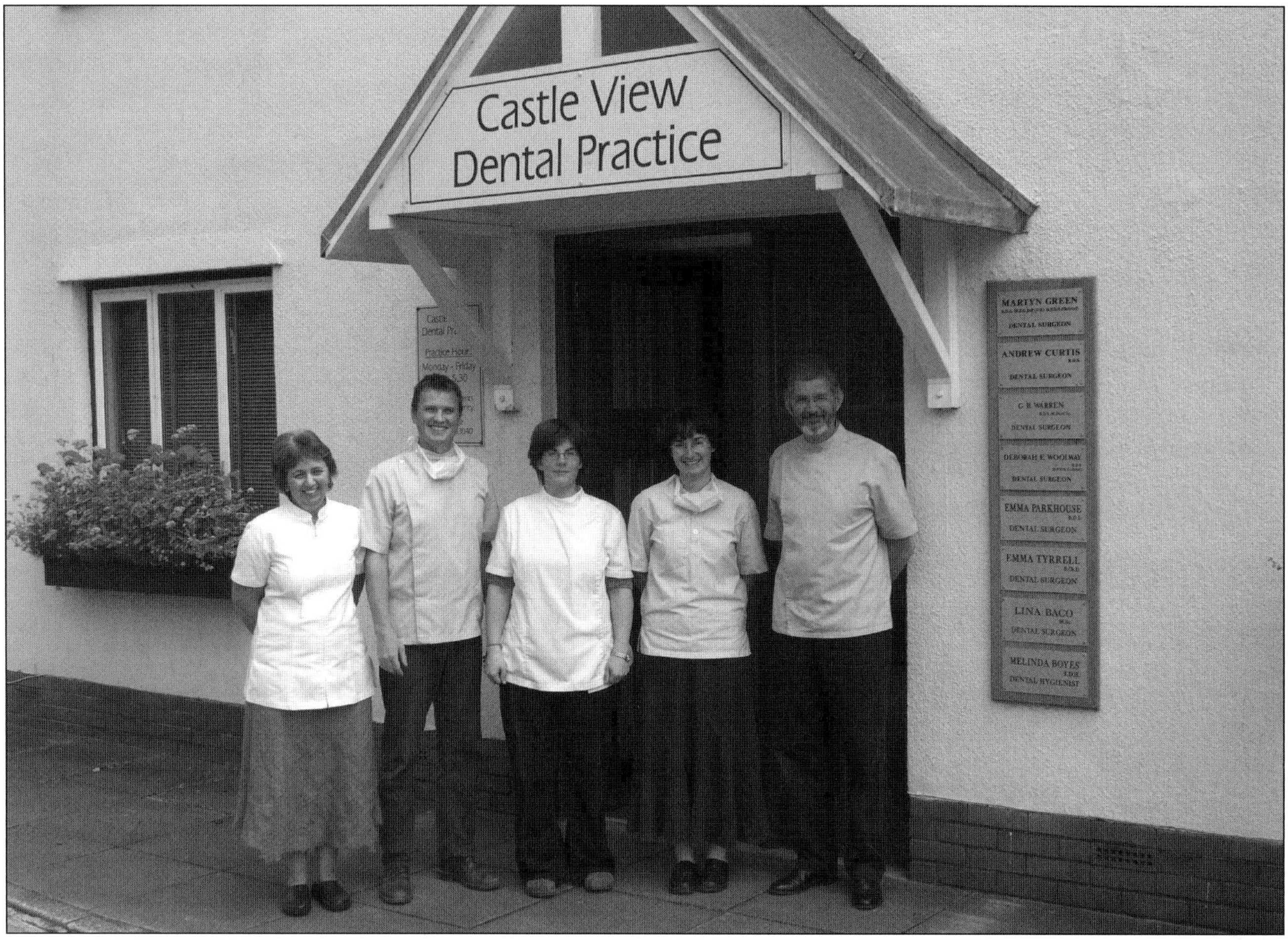

Castle View Dental Practice: Gwyneth Warren, Andrew Curtis, Emma Parkhouse, Debbie Woolway and Martyn Green.
MIKE SHAW

such as Tiverton. One consequence has been the closure of schools like Sunningmead, built in the expectation that more homes meant more children.

Growth has brought new facilities and businesses. The new hospital looks after the ill and the Castle Place doctors have moved to new premises next door, allowing the Castle View Dental Practice to move into their former premises. The new hospital is built on the flood plain and one hopes its designers have coped with that. The new Exe Valley Leisure Centre on Bolham Road caters for the healthy.

Many new and flourishing businesses provide livings. The old factory houses are home to some remarkably high-tech weaving and may well turn out more yards of cloth than than did the old Heathcoat's, but with over 200 employees rather than the 2,000 of earlier years. Of the 'old gang' of industrial businesses Stenners, Lowman Manufacturing

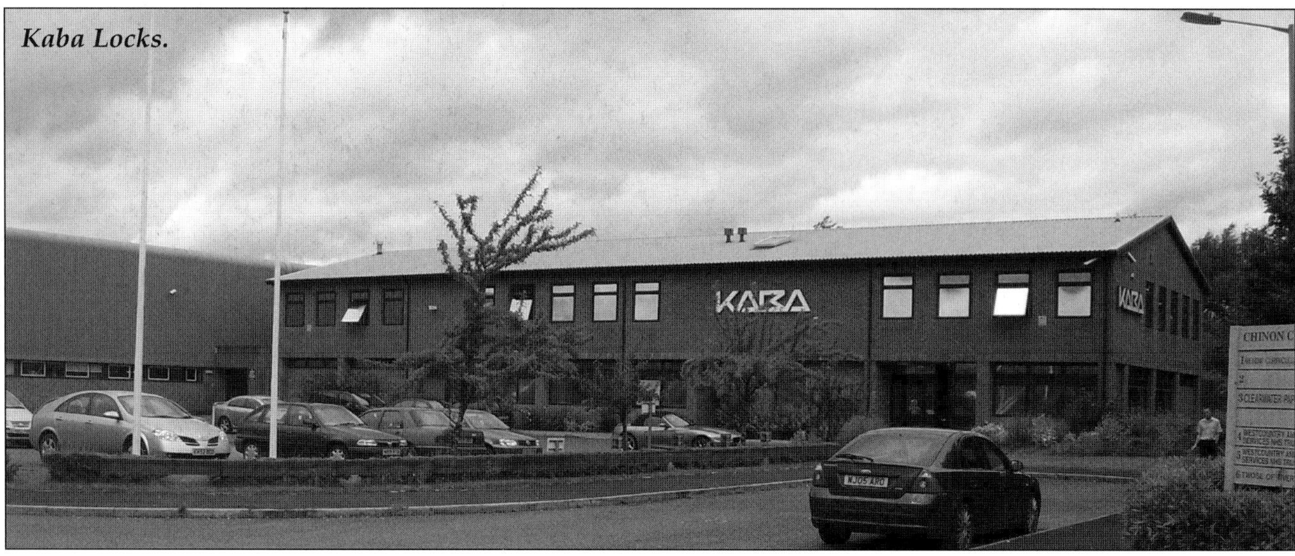

Kaba Locks.

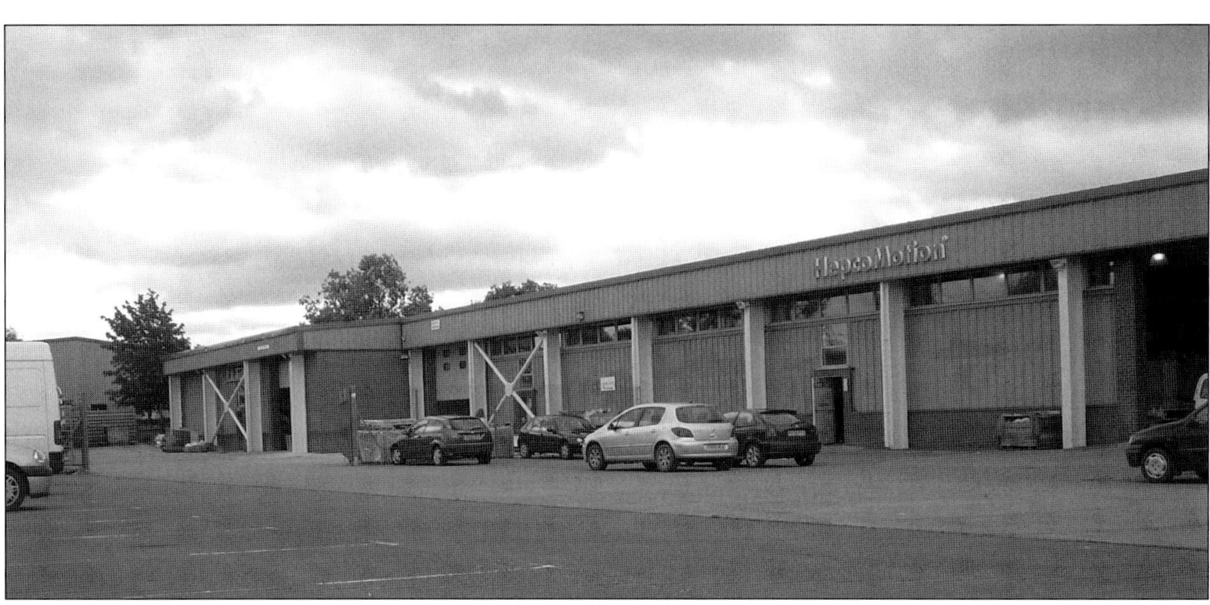

Hepco Motion. ADRIAN NOON

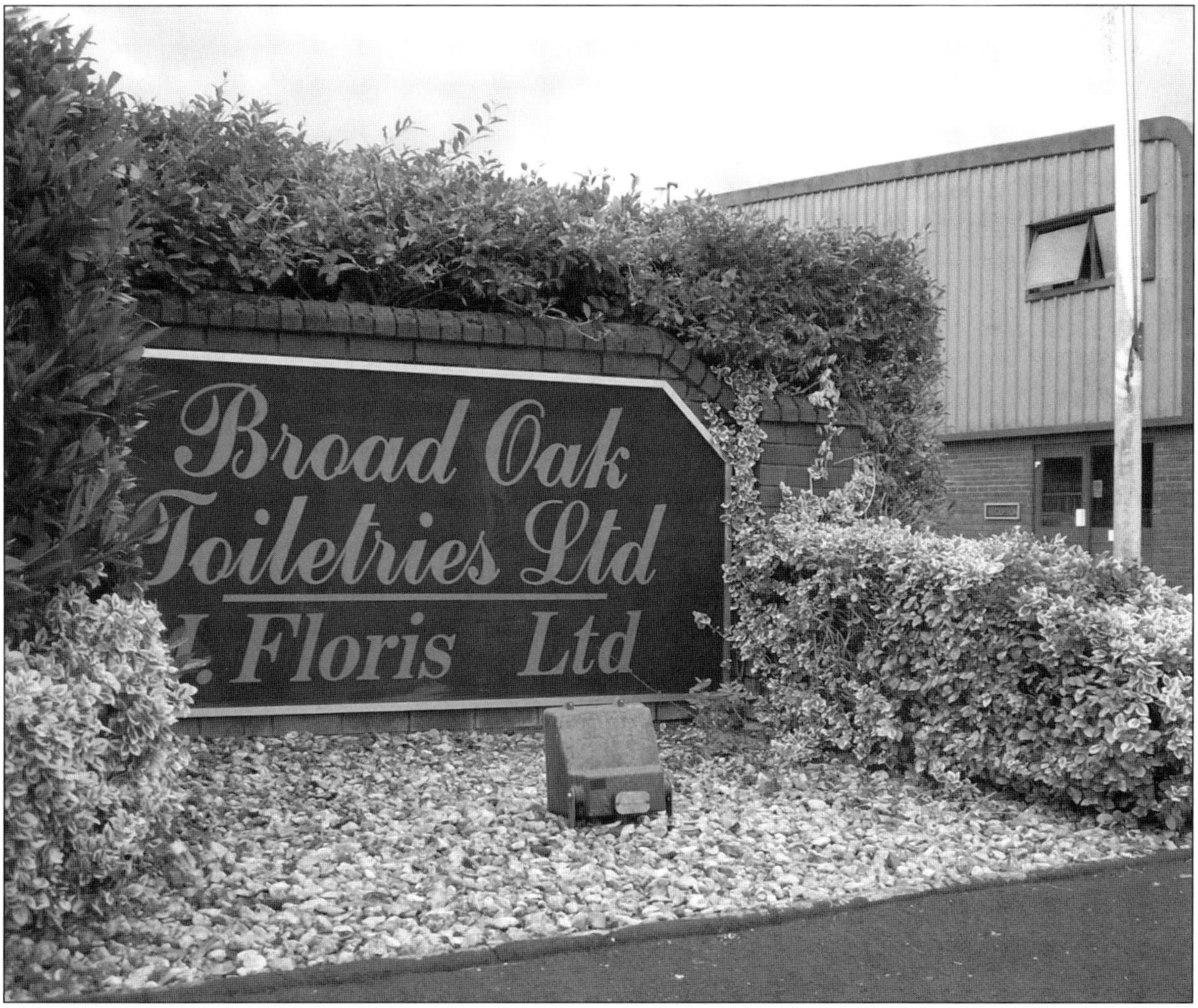

Broad Oak Toiletries Ltd. ADRIAN NOON

and Medland Sanders and Twose (MST) are still very much with us and on the industrial site have been joined by Kaba Locks and Hepco, in their different ways at the forefront of industrial technology. Broad Oak Toiletries came to Tiverton in 1981 and employs more than 200.

A more fragile source of prosperity is the town's role as a sub-regional centre of services and shopping. Older Tivertonians, who can remember the streets in the 1950s, will have noticed enormous changes. There are now very few local or unique shops in the town centre. Tesco and Wm Morrison supermarkets dominate the grocery trade. Banburys survives as a beacon of what Tiverton's shopping once was. There are a handful of niche shops, a great number of charity shops and representatives of national chains such as Boots, W.H. Smith's and Clinton Cards. Banks, building societies and estate agents are everywhere. Shops such as Thorne Brothers, who sold everything for the home, and ironmongers like Webber and Saunders have become Homebase on the industrial estate. Will the period 1850 to 2000 come to be seen as 'the rise, apogee and decline of town-centre retailing' in small towns? That said, the advent of petrol rationing to counter galloping climate change may lead to a renaissance!

The most important hope for Tiverton's prosperity in the twenty-first century must be the performance of its children in its schools. In 2007 a UNICEF report stated that Britain's children get a worse deal than those in any other advanced economy. The overwhelming majority of Tiverton's young teenagers attend the school on Bolham Road, where there is no space to provide them with a locker or a coat peg, so that they have to lug their books and coats around with them. There is no space either for any common-rooms. Although an OFSTED report condemned a few key parts of the school as 'not fit for purpose', teachers there continue to do heroic work (and the latest OFSTED report judged it 'Good').

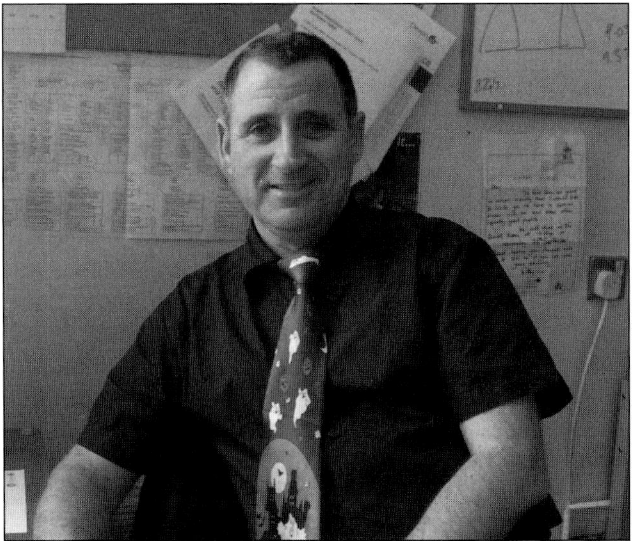

Ray Kerrigan, headmaster of Two Moors Primary School. The author had hoped to include photos of all the heads of the larger primary schools but they proved more bashful or elusive than Mr Kerrigan!

Fortunately the town possesses school facilities that are in most cases capable of being or becoming excellent. All the town's primary schools are in modern buildings on sites that are often generous. St John's RC Primary was once housed terribly, but since 1981 has been located in a modern building. Heathcoat's, Two Moors and Wilcombe are well provided for and Castle is in the old Tiverton Middle School buildings with an extraordinarily generous site for a town centre school. Previous County Councillors have created some problems for Tiverton High School. Not only does Blundell's cream off some of its able pupils, but Uffculme School has some legal ability to select pupils, which Tiverton has not. However, a dynamic new headmaster, Andrew Lovett, and his staff are pushing standards up year by year, and there has been a dramatic turn around. This has been demonstrated yet again by the significant improvement in the 2008 GCSE results, far better than can be set down to national grade inflation. It has recently acquired 'Specialist Art Status' and a modern and well-equipped art block. Tiverton also has the added advantage of East Devon College on its northern doorstep.

It is all there for young Tivertonians to take advantage of and acquire the skills vital for prosperity. In 1815 John Heathcoat brought his great invention to Tiverton because he knew that there was a skilled and reliable workforce here. One hopes that similar situations will be repeated and that the town will remain known for the skill and reliability of its workers and will become through 'skill' a high wage and increasingly prosperous community. Those communities that moan about being in a low wage area may have half a genuine gripe, but the other half of the story is that they have dozily let themselves become a low skills population.

In recent years Tiverton Museum has grown from strength to strength and is one of the 'glories of the town', to borrow a phrase of Defoe's, which he used in the early eighteenth century to describe Old Blundell's. If you have not visited it recently, you may not agree with me, but the museum has become the guardian of the town and district's communal memory. An individual, who has sadly lost his memory, has lost himself, and so it is with communities. A community that has lost its history has lost its soul and become rudderless.

The museum and the Churches care for the town's soul. We are a long way away from those years before the First World War when the Churches could realistically hope that, thanks to one more crusading mission, the whole population would be coming to a church or chapel. However, there are four active Anglican congregations, large Catholic, Baptist, Congregational and Methodist churches as well as a great number of other Christian bodies,

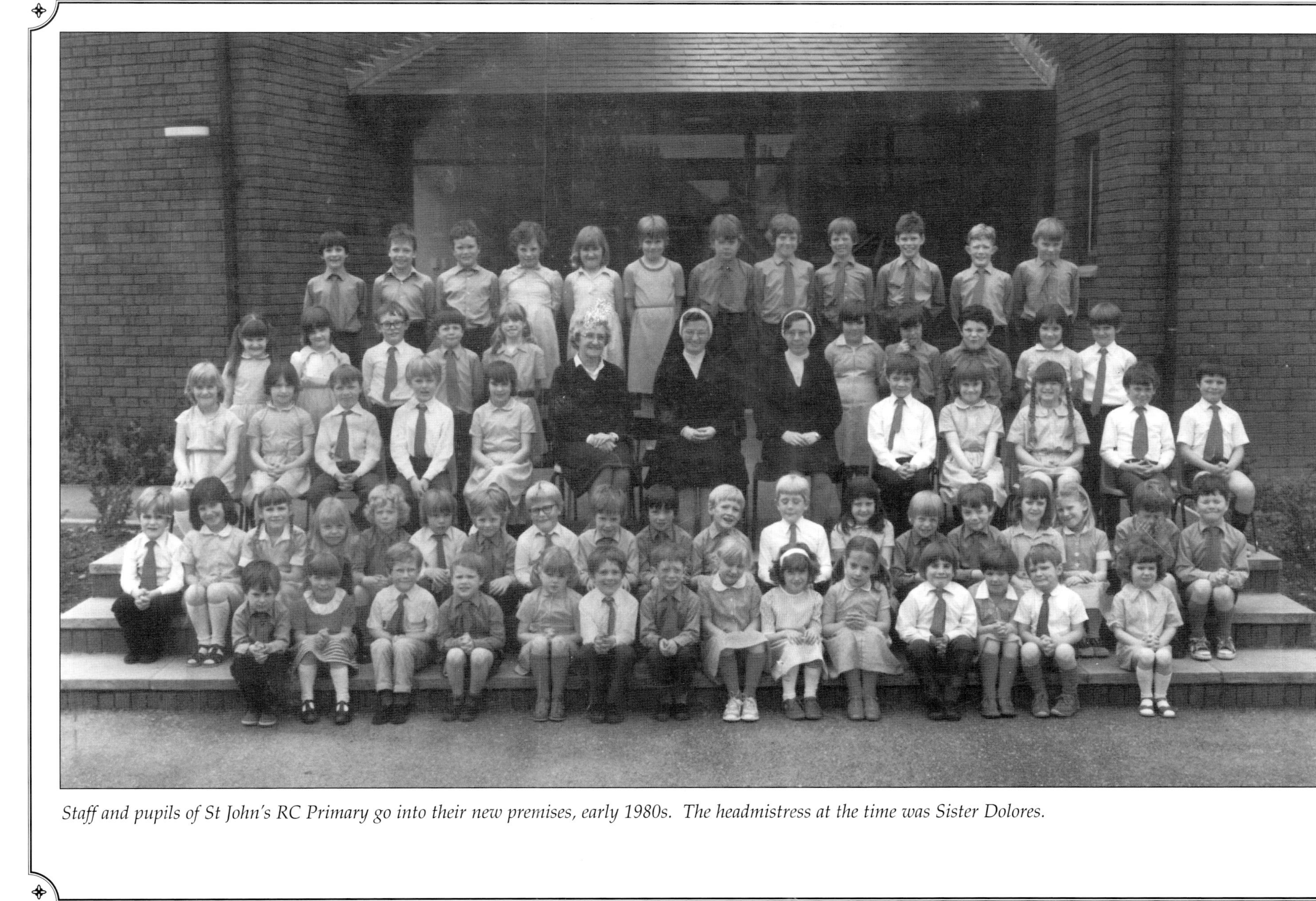

Staff and pupils of St John's RC Primary go into their new premises, early 1980s. The headmistress at the time was Sister Dolores.

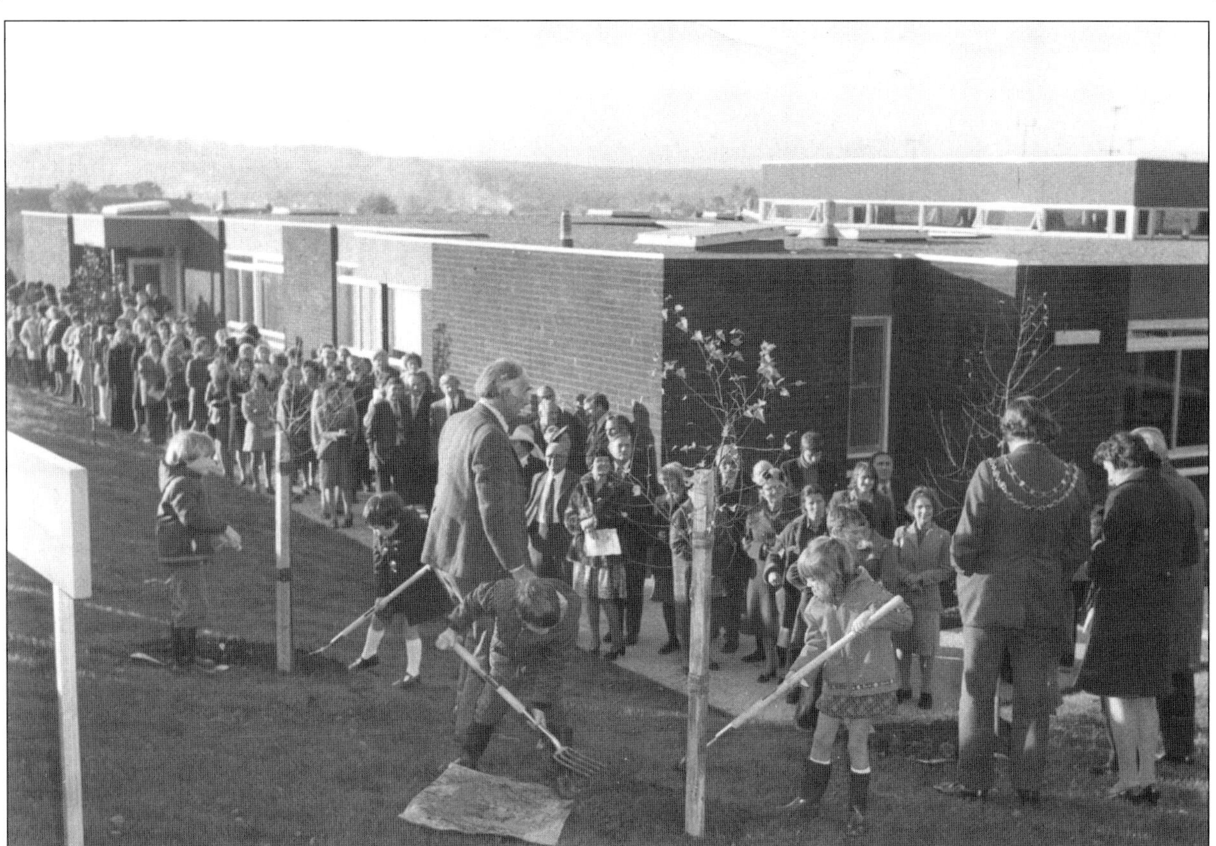

Early days at Sunningmead School. Roy Gynn, who ran the Parks Department oversees tree planting, autumn 1975. Sunningmead was opened to cater for the population growth, but it closed because more houses did not mean more children. MUSEUM COLLECTION

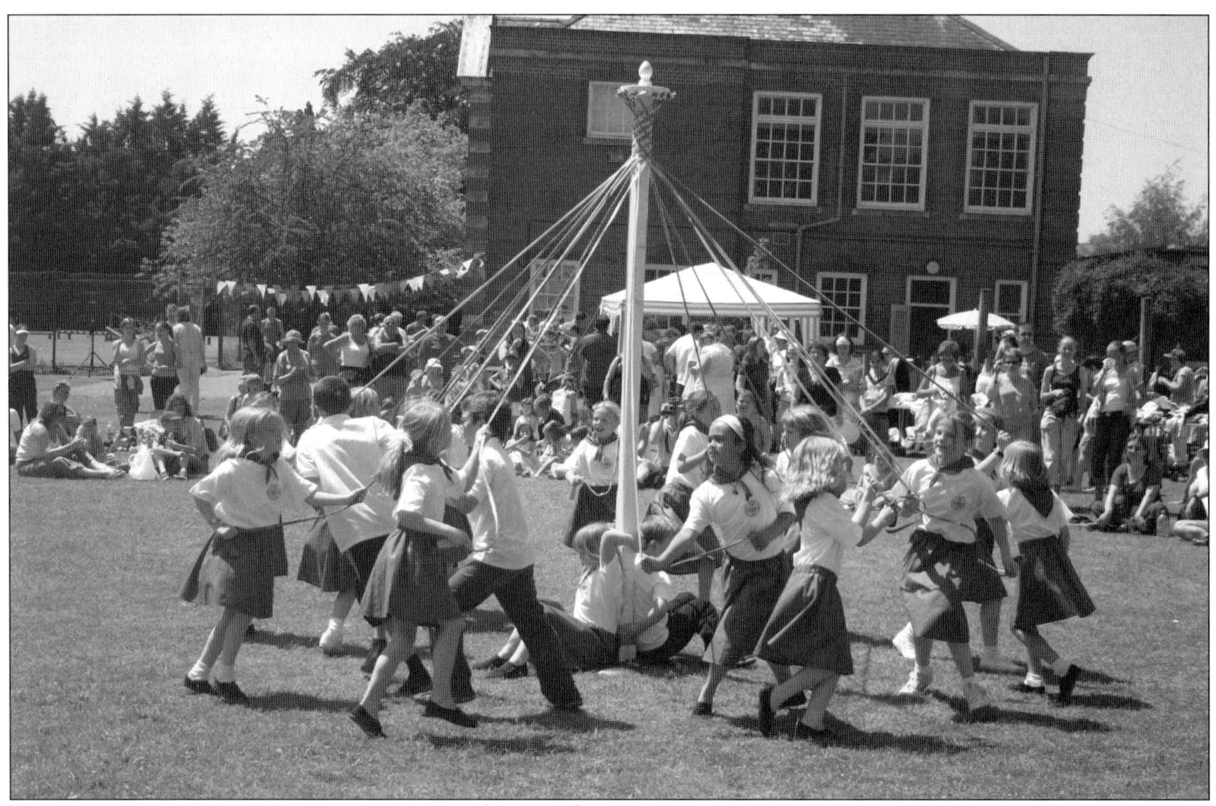

Castle School fête, 2007. *See p83 to see the extraordinary popularity of maypole dancing in Tiverton.*

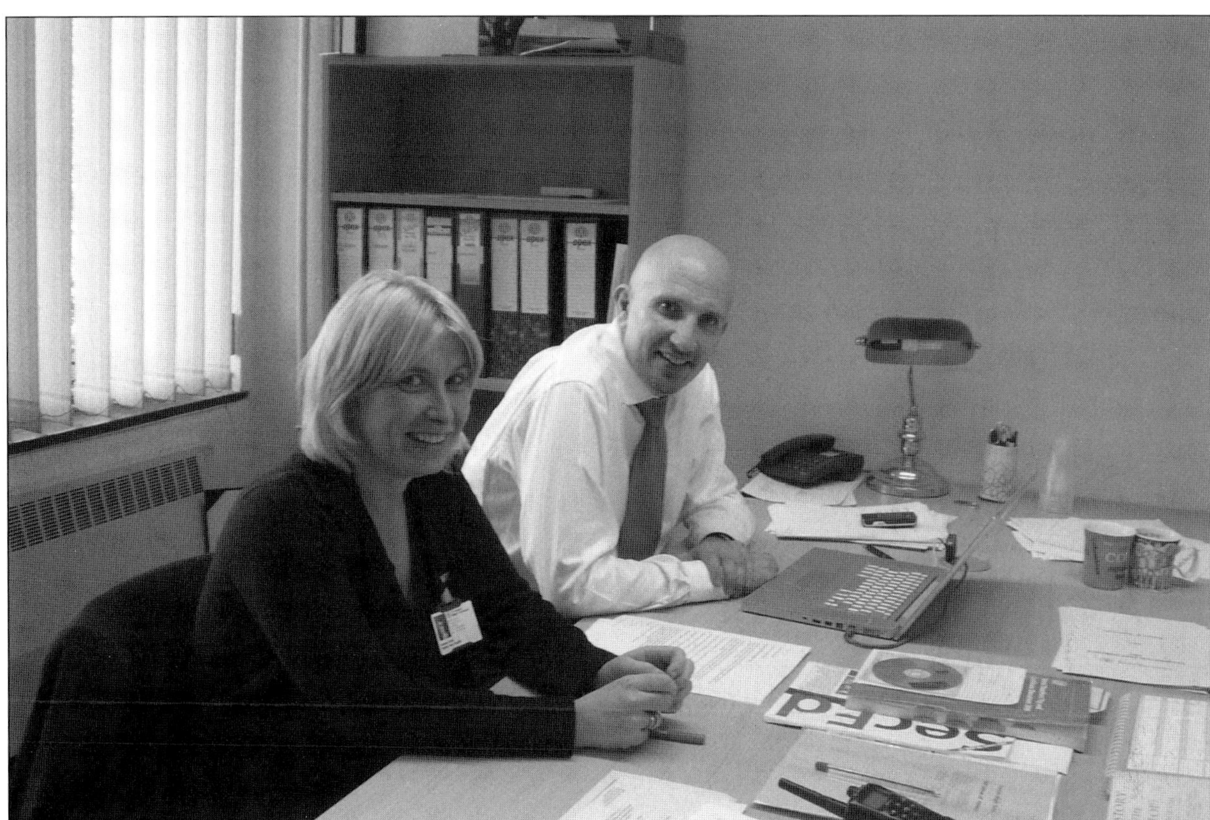

Tiverton High School headmaster Andrew Lovett and deputy Sammy Crook.

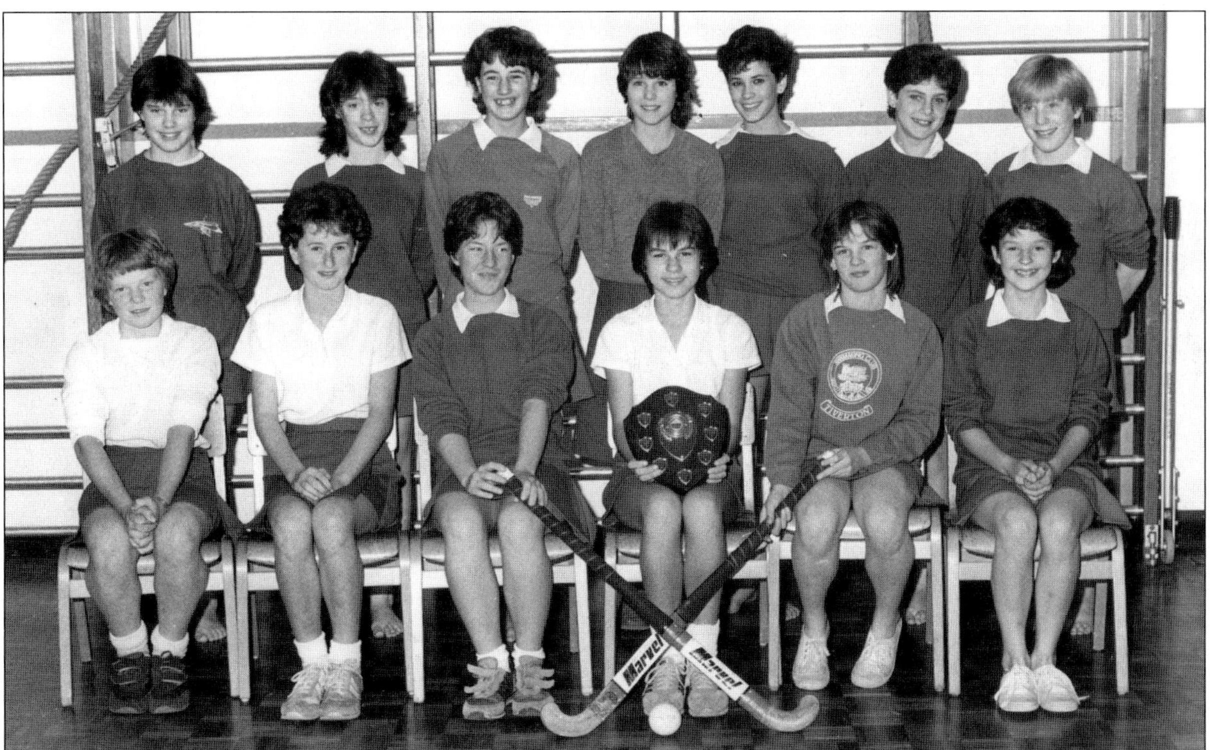

Middle School Hockey Champions, 1984. Left to right, back row: *Sharon Radley, Charlotte Allen, Julie Clarke [sic], Sharon Snell, Maria Hayball, Charlotte Jedbury, Tracey Freemantle;* front row: *Karen Oliver, Julie Rose, Elizabeth Edwards, Gina Maycock, Alison Stirling, Julie Clarke [sic]. Why is this photograph included? Because the school concerned had the wit to name those in its stock of photos. Will Heads please consider posterity and do likewise?* MUSEUM COLLECTION

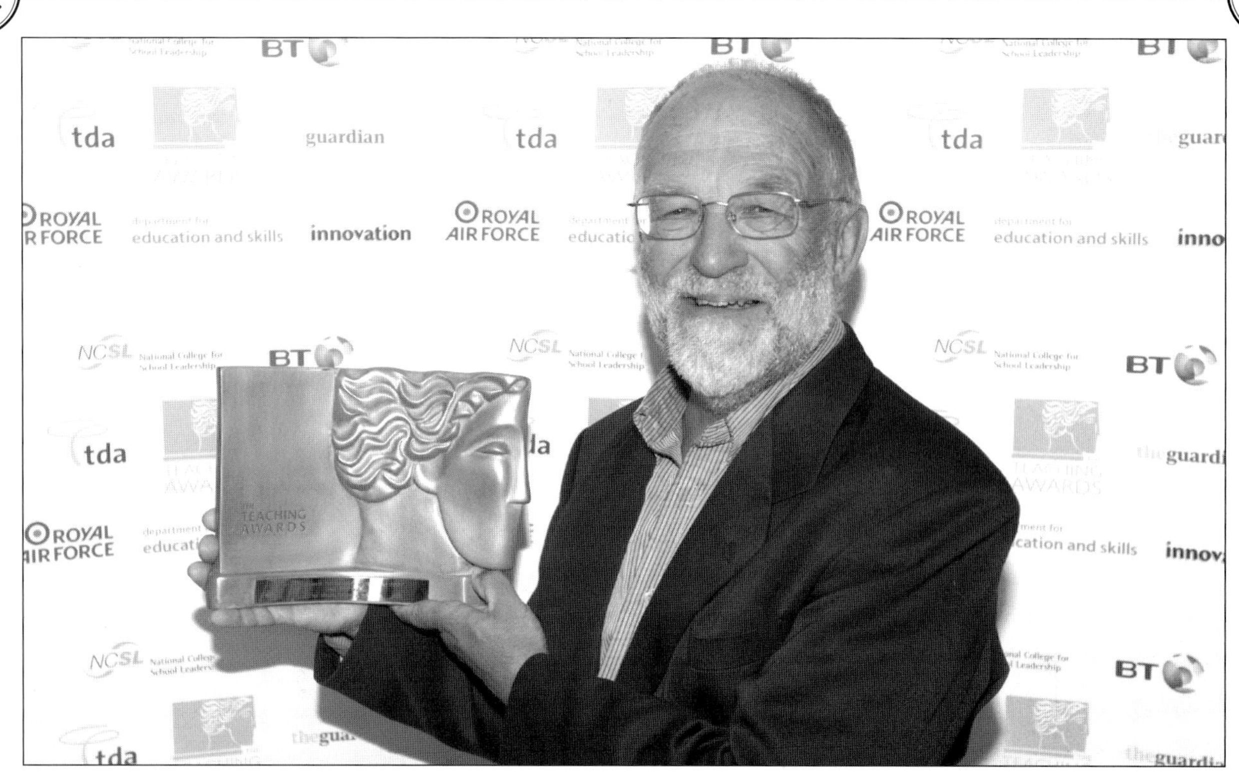

Ivan Godfrey collecting his School Governor of the Year Award, 2007. He has been chairman of Two Moors School from 1998 and before that a governor of Cowleymoor. He taught at Tiverton School between 1981 and 1995. In a previous incarnation he was Head Boy at Blundell's.

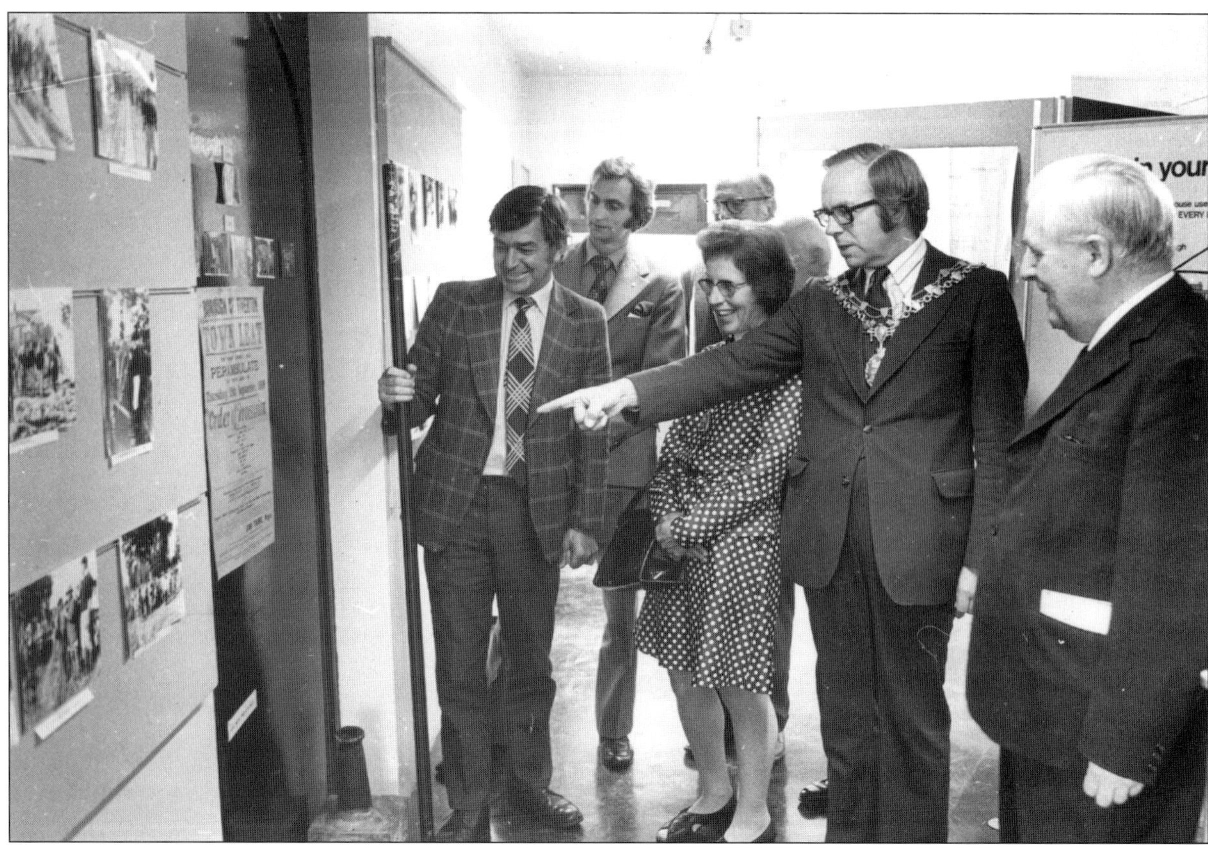

Mayor Suter and Joan visit Tiverton Museum in 1974. Bill Authers and Brian Homer are also in attendance. Brian was Tiverton's youngest twentieth-century Mayor, showing early leadership potential with The Dirty Works gang. He was also a JP and chairman of the bench. MUSEUM COLLECTION

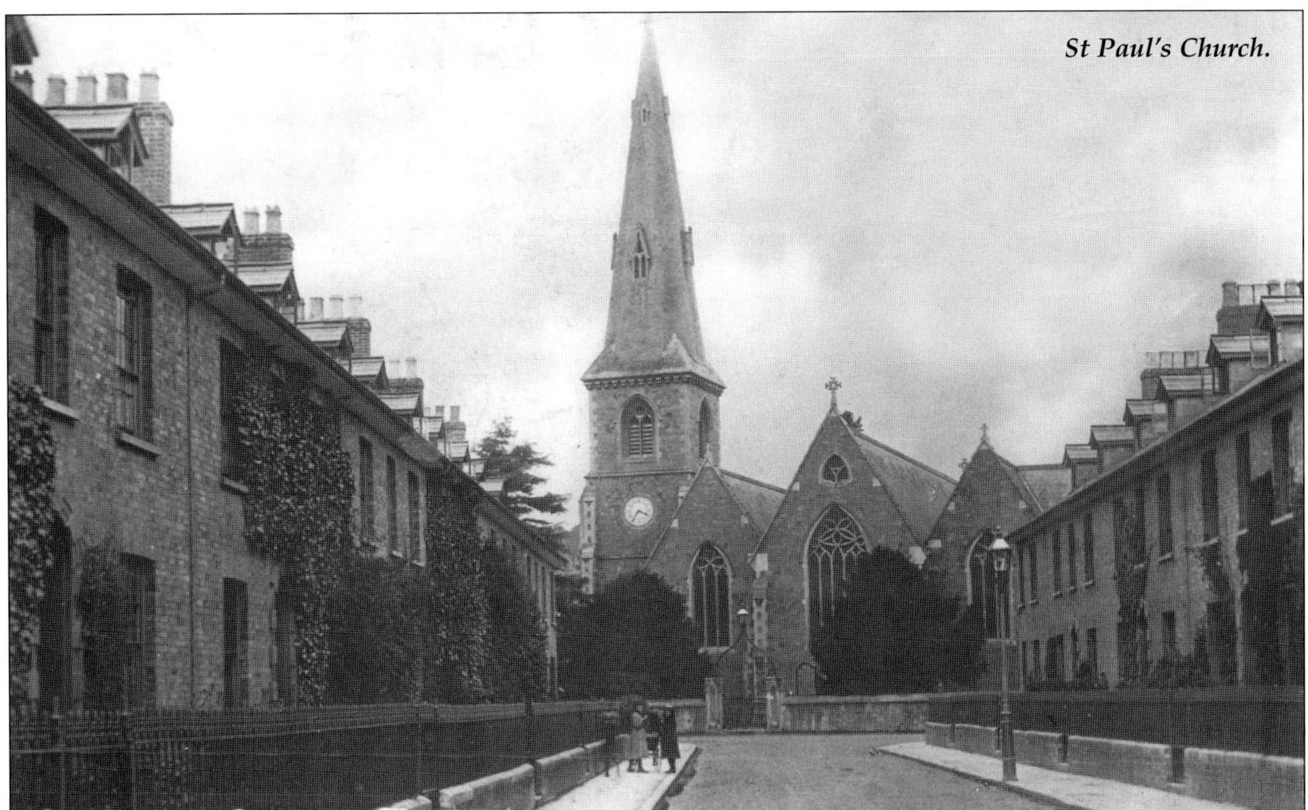

St Paul's Church.

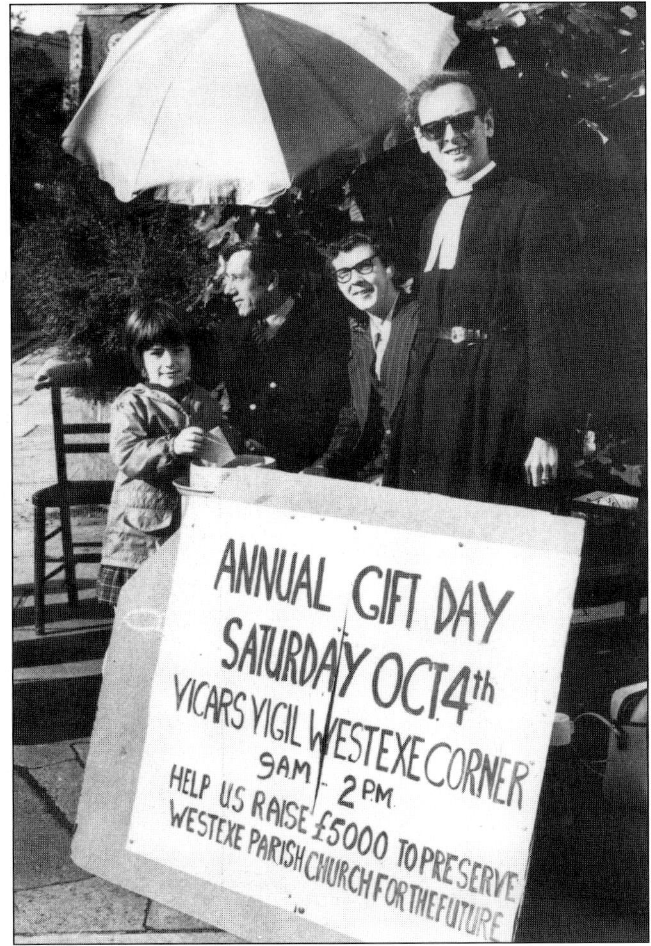

The work to save St Paul's. Norman Annett, headmaster of Wilcombe 1963–88, supports Vicar Stanley Holbrook-Jones.
MUSEUM COLLECTION

which include the Salvation Army, the Christian Spiritualist Church and the King Street Chapel. All these churches are home grown. A newcomer to the town is the Cherith Christian Fellowship, whose web entries suggest American neoconservative origins, but whose real origin, I am informed, comes from a house church established in Tidcombe for some years.

Tiverton is now home to more churches, around 14, than pubs, nine. In the 1970s there was a strong ecumenical movement in Tiverton, but the churches seem to be going their own ways and even the Anglican four do not seem to co-operate much. In the 'old days' pubs and churches ran sports teams, whereas now all the major sports teams in the town seem to run bars on their own premises.

Whether more Tivertonians play or watch sport at weekends than go to church would be an interesting piece of research. Until about 1875 'sport' meant 'field sports', and once Sir John Amory took them up, Tiverton was well served by Fox Hounds, Stag Hounds and Harriers. After 1900 'sport' meant ball games. Cricket was the first to emerge and was flourishing in the 1860s, when the *Blundellian Magazine* tells us that a Blundell's X1 played two matches against 22 Tiverton Tradesmen. This would have been on the Elmore or Athletic Ground, now Amory Park, which was the home of Tiverton town cricket until the mid-1970s, since when all Tiverton cricket has been confined to Heathcoat Cricket Club at Knightshayes. Although the club makes great efforts to train and encourage young players, it is so far from the housing estates that the young without parental

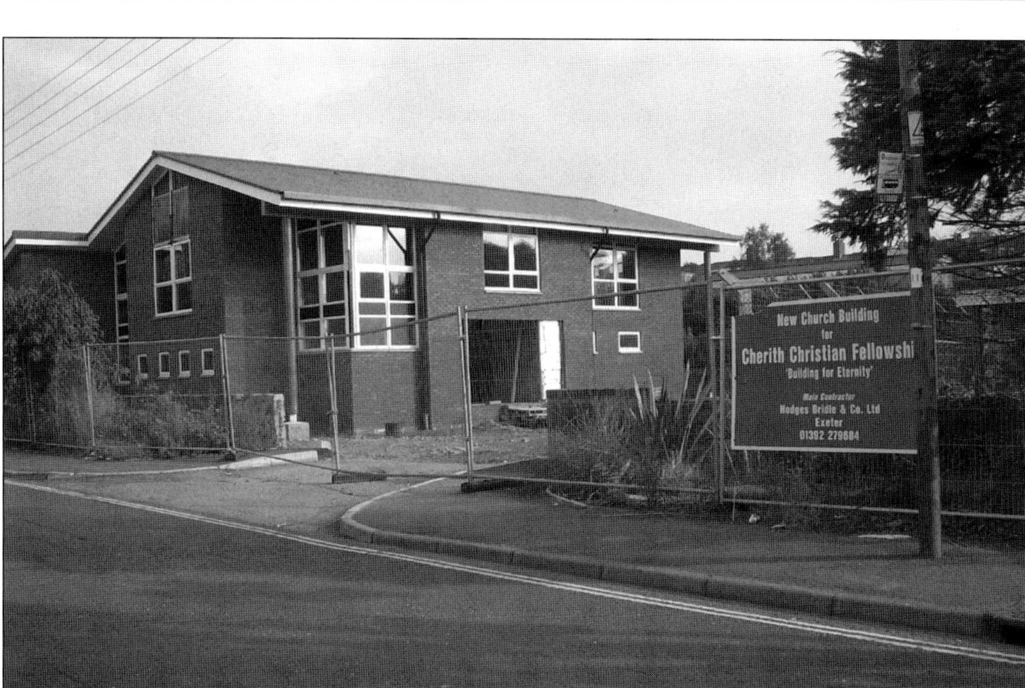

The Cherith Christian Fellowship, being built on Blundell Road. There are now more churches than pubs in the town.

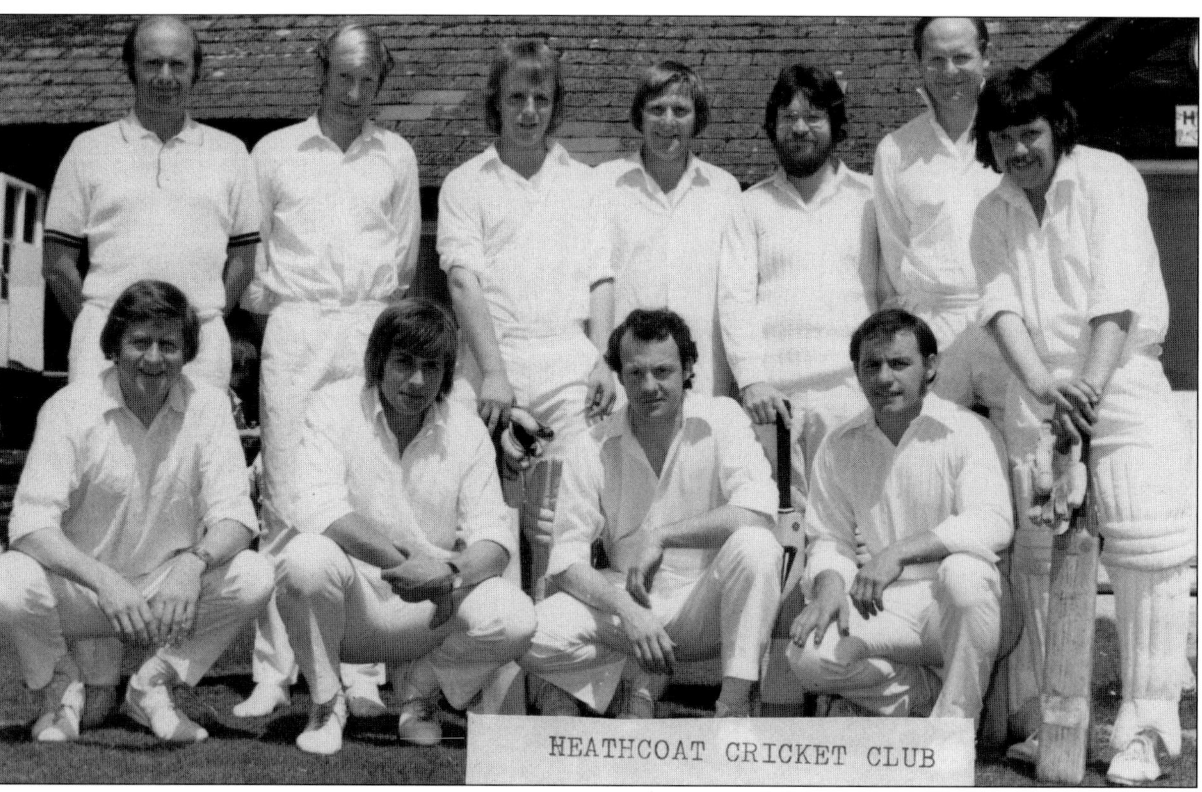

Heathcoat Cricket Club, late 1970s. Left to right, back row: *Mike Hurley, Dougie Woodward, Robert Head, Trevor Davey, Steve Newcombe, Mike Bull (Chief Executive MDDC 1991–2001), Roy Church;* front row: *Paul Ough, David Frankpitt, ?, Derek Taylor.* MUSEUM COLLECTION

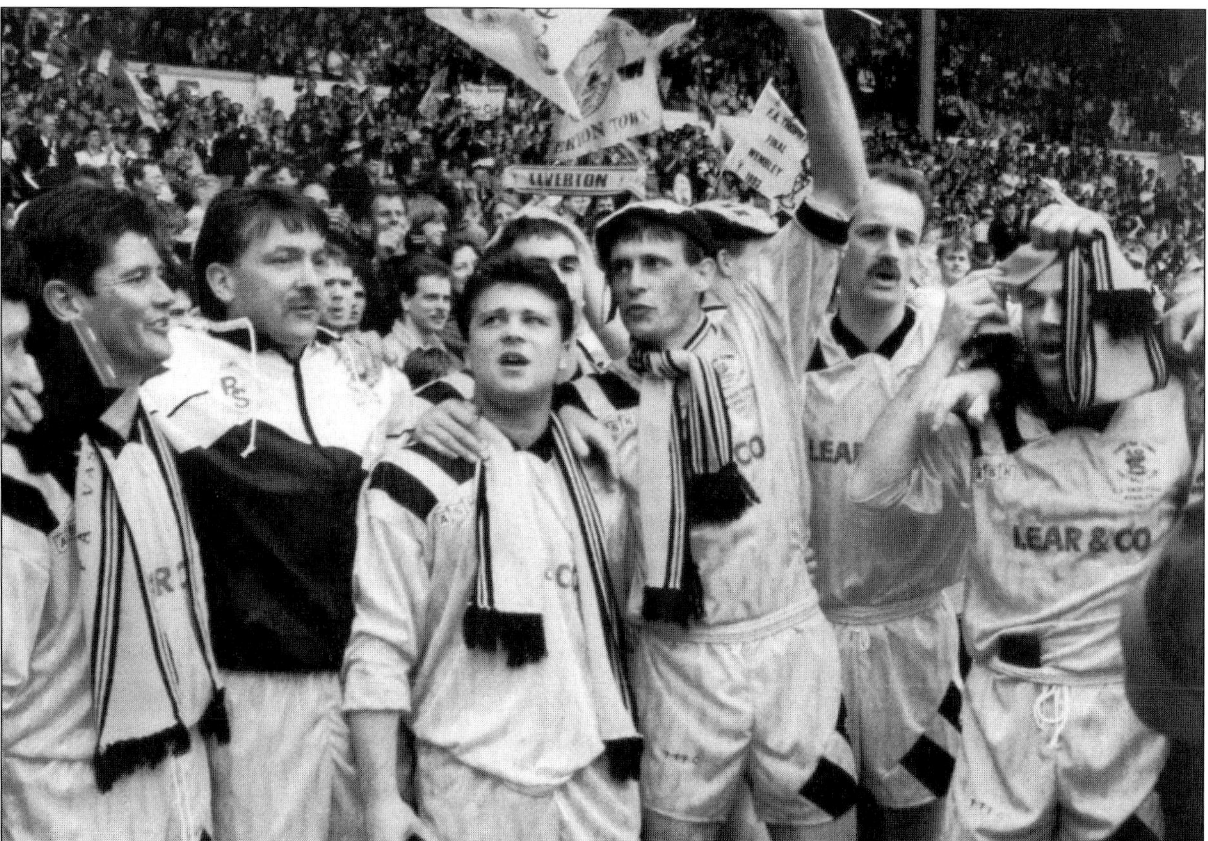

The team that lost to Bridlington in 1993. Martyn Rogers is wearing the track-suit top, and Captain Hedley Steele is waving the banner. MUSEUM COLLECTION

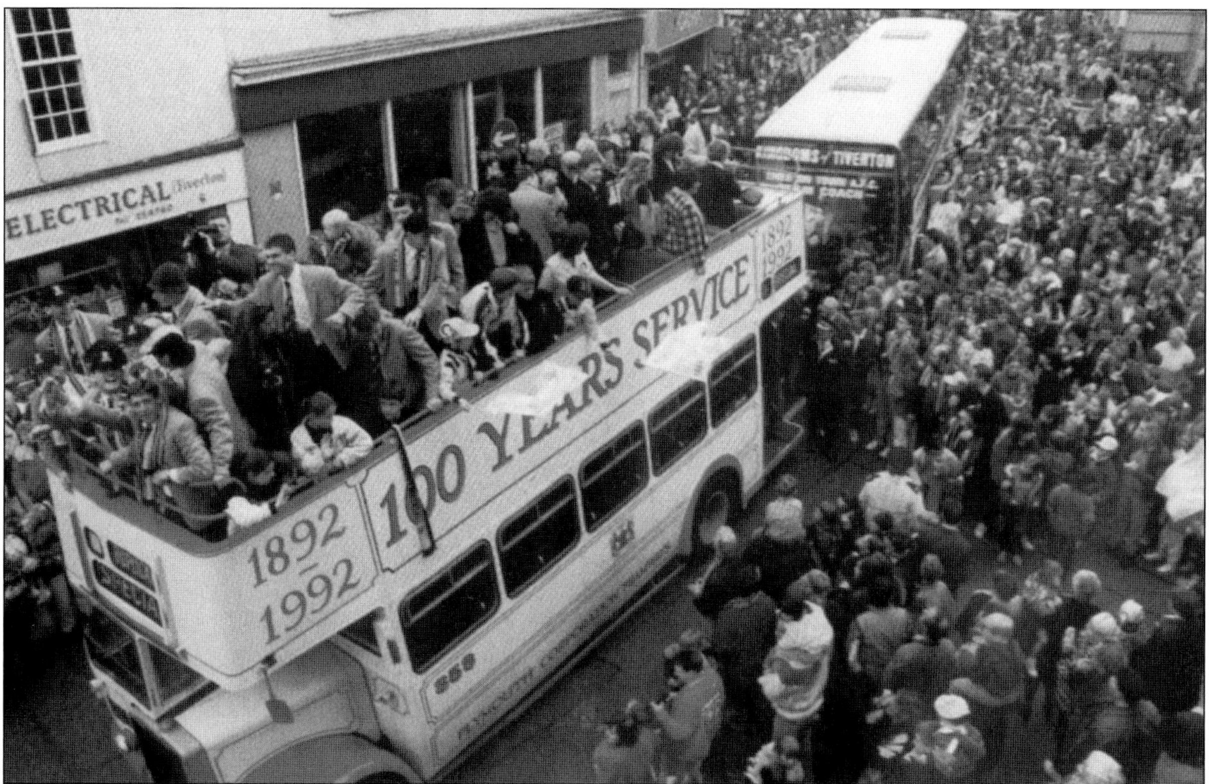

Tiverton Town return through Fore Street after losing 1–0 to Bridlington in 1993. They won their two other Wembley Cup Finals in 1998 and 1999, both 1–0.

transport must find it difficult to get there. (The team that calls itself Tiverton actually plays at Bickleigh.)

Since the coming of widespread motorcar ownership, sports clubs may have a local name, but even amateur teams are often made up of members from afar. Yet surprisingly they engender much local patriotism. Tiverton Association Football Club is a case in point. It was founded in 1913 to play on the Athletic Ground and its leading light was its Secretary, Sid Skinner and the team that played its first match had nine born and bred Tivertonians, one from Uffculme and one from Silverton. Tiverton Association Football Club was then just one of five clubs, Tiverton Green Shields, St Peter's, St George's and Park United being the others. A merger with St Peter's strengthened the club, but the 'new' pitch at the Elms, now under Tesco's car park, was prone to flooding and spectators had to stand on duck-boards. They won the Exeter and District League in 1934, but the players still changed in a Barrington Street pub and the Elms ground was destroyed under a storage dump during the Second World War.

The club restarted in 1946 at Ladysmead, playing north–south not east–west, but with no cover or changing rooms. A stand appeared in 1951, but players still had to change in a pub, now the Cross Keys in Gold Street, until facilities were built at the ground in the early 1960s. During the period when Tom Gillard was secretary, 1957–67, the Club prospered, usually being in the top five of the Exeter and District League. Changing rooms, bar and car park had been built and the pitch turned round. Elmore and Westexe had comparable facilities.

In the 1970s the club joined the Western League Premier Division and the world of professionalism. They were relegated to the First Division in 1981, where they found Elmore, who finished higher than Tiverton between 1982 and 1985. Financial support from Dan McAuley helped get the side back into the Premier Division in 1989, and the appointment of Martyn Rogers as player-manager in 1991 led to greater things, including steady performances in the leagues and three visits to Wembley in 1993, 1998 and 1999. Facilities are regularly improved and local businesses rally to support the team. Although few of the players are 'local', Ladysmead playing host to a home game is where the most obvious manifestations of local spirit can now be found.

Tiverton Rugby Football Club was founded in 1868, though what was played then would be seen now as a curious hybrid of a ball game. Its first team is now in the Western Counties League, though as a Committee member explained 'We go up and down like a yo-yo.' The club runs four senior teams and no less than six junior teams aged between eight and 16. There is also a girls' team and a part-time Youth Development Officer is also employed. The soccer clubs also have a great number of junior sides and one official estimated that over 150 boys have a competitive game of soccer every weekend. The White Eagles Ladies Hockey Club also do their best to encourage girls to take up the sport.

Considering the interest there is in 'sport' and the immense value it can have in giving a sense of belonging, and focus, as well as an interest for young Tivertonians, one hopes that more grass-pitch facilities and decent changing-rooms may be created. (Blundell's with 550 pupils aged 11–18 has 11 rugby or soccer pitches, while Tiverton High School with 1,200 pupils aged 11–16 is home to just two or three. It would be interesting if both establishments were on adjacent sites and co-operating and not at opposite ends of the town.) It would also be interesting if every Town, District and County Councillor, and every school governor were to be invited by the clubs to see and appreciate the enormous contribution the sports clubs are making to the community.

It is impossible in a final chapter to do justice to all the organisations and individuals who do their bit for Tiverton. There are many other organisations that make the town tick. It must be hoped that they will continue to do so in the future and that in spite of the pressures of life that there will be a steady flow of those able and willing to devote energy and talent to the public good. Let me be priggish to the end and paraphrase John F. Kennedy: 'Ask not what Tiverton can do for you, but what you can do for Tiverton.'

Subscribers

Age Concern Tiverton Cullompton and District
Roy Alway, Tiverton, Devon
Norman Annett
Michael and Joan Ashton, Tiverton
Danny Ayshford, Tiverton, Devon
Heather and Andrew Barlow, Stagg Mill, Devon
Janet Barry (née Gregory), Timsbury, Bath, formerly Sampford Peverell
Norman and Beryl Bathurst
Michael L. Beer, Weston-Super-Mare
Godfrey and Mary Bell, Stoodleigh
Barbara J. Blackford, Tiverton, Devon
Gorton House, Blundell's School, Tiverton
Leslie Boyce, Tiverton, Devon
Gill Bridson
John Brigden, Tiverton, Devon
Mrs Joyce Bryant, Tiverton, Devon
Simon, Michele, Mollie and Evie Budden, Tiverton, Devon
Bill Budden, Adelaide, South Australia
Mr and Mrs M.I.R. Bull
Christine Bulley, Tiverton, Devon
Peter and Dianne Burridge, Barnstaple, Devon
Jackie Chalmers, Tiverton
N.E. Chamberlain-Hill, Tiverton
John and Barbara Chatfield, Tiverton
Christopher Chave, Tiverton, Devon
Merv Chidgey, Tiverton, Devon
WG. CDR. and Mrs D.J. Chivers, Tiverton
D. Clarke, Tiverton
Simon S. Cole, Tiverton, Devon
Dora M. Cripps, Tiverton, Devon
Andrew Curtis, Tiverton
Ian Curtis, Tiverton
Mrs Norma Davis (née Rapo), Cornwall
Sandra J. Drew, Chettiscombe, Tiverton
The Family of Bill and Irene Dunsford
Sarah East, Tilehurst, Reading
Tony Edwards, Tiverton
Mrs Mary Ellis
Margaret Kay Firth,
Mr Robin Fouracre, Tiverton, Devon
Mary S. French (née Cosway), Tiverton
Darren and Lisa Garnsworthy
Dr Mark J. Giles, Maida Vale, London
Peter W. Giles Esq, Bickleigh, Tiverton, Devon
Eric J. Gillett, Tiverton, Devon
Roy and Sylvia Goffin, Tiverton, Devon
Martin Gordon and family, celebrating being part of Tiverton life for 25 years, October 2008
The Grieve Family, Tiverton, Devon
David Halestrap
Daniel and Catherine Hancock, Tiverton, Devon
Richard Harding, Tiverton
Ivan and Bett Harper, Tiverton, Devon
Jim and Lesley Harris, Tiverton, Devon
Debbie Hayball, Tiverton, Devon
Derek Heard, Tiverton
Jackie Herniman, Tiverton
Mrs Beatrice Hillyer, Tiverton
B.J. Homer, Tiverton, Devon
Trevor Hughes, Tiverton
Mrs Judith Hunt, Tiverton
Mike Hurley, Tiverton
P.D.V Taylor and G.E. Isted, Tiverton
Maurice and Denise James, Tiverton
Kimmins Family, Tiverton born
Mr E.W. Kirby, Tiverton, Devon
Mrs Elizabeth Kitchen, Tiverton

Brian E. Knowles, Bridgwater, Somerset
Patrick I. Knowles, Tiverton, Devon
Roger and Sue Lambert
Betty Langworthy (née Salter), Cardiff formerly Sampford Peverell
Jonathan and Susan Lawson, Tiverton, Devon
Fred and Ann Leach, Bampton
Mr and Mrs G. Lee, Tiverton
Mrs D. Lee (née Granville), Cheltenham, Glous
Roslyn and Hugh MacBride, Bolham
Vic and Anita Maynard, Sampford Peverell
Bill Maynard, Tiverton
Peter B. Monahan
Mr Steve and Mrs Caroline Monk, Tiverton, Devon
Ben Morgan, Tiverton, Devon
Zak Morgan, Tiverton, Devon
Marika Morgan, Tiverton, Devon
Miss Mary Morrell, Tiverton
Sally Mundy
Mick Norman, Sydney, Australia, (formerly of Tiverton)
Rod (deceased) and Jenny Norman, Tiverton, Devon
Mrs Jenny Parsons, Tiverton
Jean Phillips, Thorverton, Devon
David J. Phillips, Tiverton, Devon
Freda Pilton, Tiverton, Devon
Irene J. Pincombe, Tiverton
Stanley J. Punchard
Robert Rabjohns, Hollymount, Via Taralda, Australia
Mr Stevan Rapo, Tiverton, Devon
Chris Redwood, Tiverton, Devon
G. Richardson, Tiverton, Devon
Derick E. Roach, Tiverton, Devon
Mrs M.D. Rooks, Tiverton, Devon
Sheila Salter, Bristol, formerly Sampford Peverell
Mike Sampson, Tiverton, Devon
Mike and Ange Sanders, Tiverton, Devon
Sheila Scofield, Bampton, Devon
David and Theresa Smale, Tiverton
Ron and Val Sprague, Auckland, New Zealand, (formerly of Tiverton)
Pat and Paul Stagg, Collipriest, Tiverton
Frances Stoneman, Tiverton, Devon
Ian Stoyle, Thorverton
Aisling Taylor, 14 Coleridge Road, Tiverton
The Flaws Family, Tiverton
The Howe Family, Tiverton, Devon
John Vanderwolfe, Town Clerk
Mrs J. Wale, Tiverton
Steve Ward, Tiverton, Devon
Harry Warner, Payhembury, Devon
Shirley Webber, Tiverton
Roy Weston, Tiverton
Mark and Dianne Whitrow, Tiverton, Devon
Derick J. Williams, Tiverton, Devon
Graham and Hazelann Willson
Elizabeth Wilson (née Mills), Tiverton
Mrs Alison Woollaston, Wiveliscombe, Somerset
Jenny and Barry Yendall, Tiverton, Devon

Further Titles

For information regarding up-to-date availability, please check our website at www.halsgrove.com

The Book of Addiscombe • Canning and Clyde Road Residents Association and Friends
The Book of Addiscombe, Vol. II • Canning and Clyde Road Residents Association and Friends
The Book of Ashburton • Stuart Hands and Pete Webb
The Book of Axminster with Kilmington • Les Berry and Gerald Gosling
The Book of Axmouth & the Undercliff • Ted Gosling and Mike Clement
The Book of Bakewell • Trevor Brighton
The Book of Banff • Banff Community Group
The Book of Bampton • Caroline Seward
The Book of Barnstaple • Avril Stone
The Book of Barnstaple, Vol. II • Avril Stone
The Book of Beaminster • Beaminster Museum
The Book of The Bedwyns • Bedwyn History Society
The Book of Bere Regis • Rodney Legg and John Pitfield
The Book of Bergh Apton • Geoffrey I. Kelly
The Book of Bickington • Stuart Hands
The Book of Bideford • Peter Christie and Alison Grant
Blandford Forum: A Millennium Portrait • Blandford Forum Town Council
The Book of Bitterne • Bitterne Local Historical Society
The Book of Blofield • Barbara Pilch
The Book of Boscastle • Rod and Anne Knight
The Book of Bourton-on-the-Hill, Batsford and Sezincote • Allen Firth
The Book of Bramford • Bramford Local History Group
The Book of Breage & Germoe • Stephen Polglase
The Book of Bridestowe • D. Richard Cann
The Book of Bridgwater • Roger Evans
The Book of Bridport • Rodney Legg
The Book of Brixham • Frank Pearce
The Book of Brundall • Barbara Ayers and Group
The Book of Buckfastleigh • Sandra Coleman
The Book of Buckland Monachorum & Yelverton • Pauline Hamilton-Leggett
The Book of Budleigh Salterton • D. Richard Cann
The Book of Carharrack • Carharrack Old Cornwall Society
The Book of Carshalton • Stella Wilks and Gordon Rookledge
The Book of Carhampton • Hilary Binding
The Parish Book of Cerne Abbas • Vivian and Patricia Vale
The Book of Chagford • Iain Rice
The Book of Chapel-en-le-Frith • Mike Smith
The Book of Chittlehamholt with Warkleigh & Satterleigh • Richard Lethbridge
The Book of Chittlehampton • Various
The Book of Codford • Romy Wyeth
The Book of Colney Heath • Bryan Lilley
The Book of Constantine • Moore and Trethowan
The Book of Cornwood and Lutton • Compiled by the People of the Parish
The Book of Crediton • John Heal
The Book of Creech St Michael • June Small
The Book of Crowcombe, Bicknoller and Sampford Brett • Maurice and Joyce Chidgey
The Book of Crudwell • Tony Pain
The Book of Cullompton • Compiled by the People of the Parish
The Second Book of Cullompton • Compiled by the People of the Parish
The Book of Dawlish • Frank Pearce
The Book of Dulverton, Brushford, Bury & Exebridge • Dulverton and District Civic Society
The Book of Dunster • Hilary Binding
The Book of Easton • Easton Village History Project
The Book of Edale • Gordon Miller
The Ellacombe Book • Sydney R. Langmead
The Book of Elmsett • Elmsett Local History Group
The Book of Exmouth • W.H. Pascoe
The Book of Fareham • Lesley Burton and Brian Musselwhite
The Book of Gerrans & Portscatho • Chris Pollard
The Book of Grampound with Creed • Bane and Oliver
The Book of Gosport • Lesley Burton and Brian Musselwhite
The Book of Haughley • Howard Stephens
The Book of Hayle • Harry Pascoe
The Book of Hayling Island & Langstone • Peter Rogers
The Book of Helston • Jenkin with Carter
The Book of Hempnall • Maureen Cubitt
The Book of Hemyock • Clist and Dracott
The Book of Herne Hill • Patricia Jenkyns

The Book of Hethersett • Hethersett Society Research Group
The Book of High Bickington • Avril Stone
The Book of Homersfield • Ken Palmer
The Book of Honiton • Gerald Gosling
The Book of Ilsington • Dick Wills
The Book of Kessingland • Maureen and Eric Long
The Book of Kingskerswell • Carsewella Local History Group
The Book of Lamerton • Ann Cole and Friends
Lanner, A Cornish Mining Parish • Sharron Schwartz and Roger Parker
The Book of Leigh & Bransford • Malcolm Scott
The Second Book of Leigh & Bransford • Malcolm Scott
The Book of Litcham with Lexham & Mileham • Litcham Historical and Amenity Society
The Book of Llangain • Haydn Williams
The Book of Loddiswell • Loddiswell Parish History Group
The Book of Looe • Mark Camp
The New Book of Lostwithiel • Barbara Fraser
The Book of Lulworth • Rodney Legg
The Book of Lustleigh • Joe Crowdy
The Book of Lydford • Compiled by Barbara Weeks
The Book of Lyme Regis • Rodney Legg
The Book of Manaton • Compiled by the People of the Parish
The Book of Markyate • Markyate Local History Society
The Book of Mawnan • Mawnan Local History Group
The Book of Meavy • Pauline Hemery
The Book of Mere • Dr David Longbourne
The Book of Minehead with Alcombe • Binding and Stevens
The Book of Monks Orchard and Eden Park • Ian Muir and Pat Manning
The Book of Morchard Bishop • Jeff Kingaby
Mount Batten – The Flying Boats of Plymouth • Gerald Wasley
The Book of Mulbarton • Jill and David Wright
The Book of Mylor • Mylor Local History Group
The Book of Narborough • Narborough Local History Society
The Book of Newdigate • John Callcut
The Book of Newtown • Keir Foss
The Book of Nidderdale • Nidderdale Museum Society
The Book of Northlew with Ashbury • Northlew History Group
The Book of North Newton • J.C. and K.C. Robins
The Book of North Tawton • Baker, Hoare and Shields
The Book of Notting Hill • Melvin Wilkinson
The Book of Nynehead • Nynehead & District History Society
The Book of Okehampton • Roy and Ursula Radford
The Book of Ottery St Mary • Gerald Gosling and Peter Harris
The Book of Paignton • Frank Pearce
The Book of Penge, Anerley & Crystal Palace • Peter Abbott
The Book of Peter Tavy with Cudlipptown • Peter Tavy Heritage Group
The Book of Pimperne • Jean Coull
The Book of Plymtree • Tony Eames
The Book of Poole • Rodney Legg
The Book of Porchfield & Locks Green • Keir Foss
The Book of Porlock • Dennis Corner
The Book of Portland • Rodney Legg
Postbridge – The Heart of Dartmoor • Reg Bellamy
The Book of Priddy • Albert Thompson
The Book of Princetown • Dr Gardner-Thorpe
The Book of Probus • Alan Kent and Danny Merrifield
The Book of Rattery • By the People of the Parish
The Book of Roadwater, Leighland and Treborough • Clare and Glyn Court
The Book of St Audries • Duncan Stafford
The Book of St Austell • Peter Hancock
The Book of St Day • Joseph Mills and Paul Annear
The Book of St Dennis and Goss Moor • Kenneth Rickard
The Book of St Ervan • Moira Tangye
The Book of St Levan • St Levan Local History Group
The Book of St Mawes • Chris Pollard
The Book of Sampford Courtenay with Honeychurch • Stephanie Pouya
The Book of Sculthorpe • Gary Windeler
The Book of Seaton • Ted Gosling
The Book of Sennen • Alison Weeks and Valerie Humphrys
The Book of Shaugh Parish • Don Balkwill
The Book of Sidmouth • Ted Gosling and Sheila Luxton
The Book of Silverton • Silverton Local History Society
The Book of South Molton • Jonathan Edmunds
The Book of South Stoke with Midford • Edited by Robert Parfitt
South Tawton & South Zeal with Sticklepath • Roy and Ursula Radford
The Book of Sparkwell with Hemerdon & Lee Mill • Pam James
The Book of Spetisbury • Ann Taylor
The Book of Staverton • Pete Lavis
The Book of Stinsford • Kearsey & Cosgrove
The Book of Stithians • Stithians Parish History Group
The Book of Stogumber, Monksilver, Nettlecombe & Elworthy • Maurice and Joyce Chidgey
The Book of South Brent • Greg Wall
The Second Book of South Brent • Greg Wall

The Book of Studland • Rodney Legg
The Book of Swanage • Rodney Legg
The Book of Tavistock • Gerry Woodcock
The Book of Thatcham • Peter Allen
The Book of Thorley • Sylvia McDonald and Bill Hardy
The Book of Tiverton • Charles Noon
The Book of Torbay • Frank Pearce
The Book of Truro • Christine Parnell
The Book of Uplyme • Gerald Gosling and Jack Thomas
The Book of Veryan & Portloe • Diana Smith and Christine Parnell
The Book of Watchet • Compiled by David Banks
The Book of Watchet and Williton Revisited • Maurice and Joyce Chidgey and Ben Norman
The Book of Wendling, Longham and Beeston with Bittering • Stephen Olley
The Book of West Coker • Shorey, Dodge & Dodge
The Book of West Huntspill • By the People of the Parish
The Book of Weston-super-Mare • Sharon Poole
The Book of Whippingham • Sarah Burdett
The Book of Whitchurch • Gerry Woodcock
Widecombe-in-the-Moor • Stephen Woods
Widecombe – Uncle Tom Cobley & All • Stephen Woods
The Book of Willand • James Morrison and Willand History Group
The Book of Williton • Michael Williams
The Book of Wilton • Chris Rousell
The Book of Wincanton • Rodney Legg
The Book of Winscombe • Margaret Tucker
The Book of Witheridge • Peter and Freda Tout and John Usmar
The Book of Withycombe • Chris Boyles
Woodbury: The Twentieth Century Revisited • Roger Stokes
The Book of Woolmer Green • Compiled by the People of the Parish
The Book of Yetminster • Shelagh Hill